9th Edition

MAINE
REAL ESTATE
PRINCIPLES & PRACTICES

ELAINE RICHER

PROFESSIONAL EDUCATION SERVICES, INC.

Professional Edcation Services, INC.

**Maine Real Estate: Principles &
Practices, Ninth Edition**

Elaine Richer

   Art Director: Linda Helcher

   Cover Desinger: KeDesign

   Cover Images: Photodisc /©Getty Images

   Photographers Choice/©Getty Images

   David Papzian/©Corbis

For product information and technology assistance, contact us at**Profesional Education Services, INC, 207-856-1712**

For permission to use material from this text or product,

submit all requests online at info@ProfessionalEducationServices.net

Library of Congress Control Number:

2007928780

ISBN-13: 978-0-324-56062-6

ISBN-10: 0-324-56062-1

Published By:
Professional Education Services, INC
396 Cumberland St
Westbrook, ME, 04092

Printed in the United States of America

BRIEF CONTENTS

CONTENTS

8   LAND USE CONTROLS 134

9   REAL ESTATE FINANCING 148

ILLUSTRATIONS

PREFACE

This book provides beginning students with the principles and practices fundamental to a career in real estate. The subject matter and study materials are presented with the assumption that readers have no previous background in this subject. The overall goal of this book is to prepare each student with the appropriate material, guidance, and practice to enable him or her to become a successful real estate practitioner after passing the state licensing examination.

In covering the material, we have made every effort to present step-by-step explanations and give guidance regarding the most effective use of this material. Chapters begin with a list of Important Terminology, with each term boldfaced at first use within the chapter and defined. In addition, the text's Glossary also defines all key terms for easy reference. Chapters conclude with Important Points, which summarize a chapter's key ideas in a succinct list format, facilitating student review. Chapters also include chapter-end Review Questions to allow students to self-test and apply what they have learned. Finally, a Practice Test completes the text.

The book's practical study features will aid students in understanding and retaining relevant information. More important, the text will help them prepare for a successful career in real estate.

ACKNOWLEDGMENTS

I would like to thank the following reviewer, who read this text in earlier versions and made suggestions toward its improvement: Arthur Gary of the Arthur Gary School of Real Estate.

Elaine Richer

MAINE REAL ESTATE

PRINCIPLES & PRACTICES
Ninth Edition

CHAPTER 1

IMPORTANT TERMINOLOGY

chattel
closing
economic obsolescence
economic supply
estates and interests in land
fixtures
free market
highest and best use
immobility
indestructibility
listing
modification by improvement
nonhomogeneity

personal property
purchase and sale contracts
real estate
real property
REALTOR®
REALTOR ASSOCIATE®
scarcity
situs
specific performance
supply and demand
trade fixtures
Uniform Commercial Code (UCC)

INTRODUCTION TO REAL ESTATE PRINCIPLES

IN THIS CHAPTER

This chapter is a brief overview of real estate and the real estate business. It provides a definition of real property, personal property, and related terms and discusses the factors affecting real estate and the real estate business. Each of the topics introduced here will be discussed in more detail in subsequent chapters.

CHARACTERISTICS OF REAL PROPERTY

Real property consists of land and everything that is permanently attached to the land. Real property also includes all ownership rights in that property. (These ownership rights are referred to as **estates and interests in land**, and these terms will be discussed in Chapter 3.) For all practical purposes, the term real property is synonymous to and is used interchangeably with the term **real estate**.

Ownership in land includes not only the surface of the earth but also the area below the surface to the center of the earth and the area above the surface, theoretically to the highest heavens. These three aspects of ownership in land are separable. For example, the owner of the land may retain the ownership of the surface and the air space above but sell or lease the mineral rights below the surface. The owner may also sell or lease the air rights above the surface.

As mentioned above, real estate includes not only land but everything that is permanently attached to land. All structures on the land, as well as any other improvements, such as fences, swimming pools, flag poles, and things growing in the soil that grow naturally without cultivation and are perennials are all included in the definition of real estate. Therefore, the property owner, when conveying the title to his or her property, conveys all aspects of real estate, unless there is a prior agreement to exempt some portion of the real estate from the conveyance.

The only category of property defined in law other than real property is **personal property**. Therefore, by the definition of real property, we are able to determine that personal property is everything that is not land or not permanently attached to land. Personal property is everything that is moveable in nature. Personal property is an entirely different commodity than real property and does not possess the special characteristics of real property. **Fixtures** (personal property permanently attached to real property) can be the cause of many problems due to the misunderstanding of the parties involved. For example, an owner installs an item, such as a chandelier, in the dining room and then wants to remove it upon the sale of the home. There are several tests that courts may apply to resolve this problem, but from a practical sense, it is far more important for the licensee to realize that he is responsible for seeing that such problems never arise by making certain that contracts are clearly understood by all of the parties.

Trade fixtures are items of personal property installed in a building by a business operator who is renting the space. Examples of these fixtures would be shelves for displaying merchandise. Such fixtures, although attached to the property, are presumed to remain the personal property of the rental tenant and can be removed at the end of the lease period. Of course it is always prudent to ensure that the lease contract is clear on the point of such fixtures.

A special situation occurs when the property owner has financed the purchase of an item. The **Uniform Commercial Code (UCC)**, adopted by a majority of states, provides for the lender to retain a security interest in a **chattel** (personal property) until the lender is paid in full. The security interest is available to the lender even though the chattel is installed in real property. The security interest is created by an instrument called a security agreement.

The existence of such an agreement is evidenced on the public record by the filing of a notice called a financing statement. This notice is filed in the office of the Register of Deeds or the UCS State Agency. The filing of the financing statement provides constructive notice to all the world that there exists a security interest in the item that is the subject of the security agreement. As a result, the attached item will not become a fixture and therefore a part of the real property until the security agreement has been satisfied by full payment. Consequently, the lender can remove the article even though it has been attached to real property in the event that the buyer/borrower defaults in payment. Subsequent purchasers of the real estate as well as any subsequent mortgagee are bound by the filing of the financing statement. Therefore, a purchaser of the home, or a mortgagee accepting the property as security for a mortgage, would either have to complete the payments or permit the removal of the item by the lender in the event the property owner did not satisfy the debt.

The licensee will more likely be involved with the UCC when a mobile home (personal property) on a rented lot is purchased rather than with the purchase of real property. Before the mobile home can be sold, the purchaser or the mortgagee would seek proof from the state that the debt had been satisfied or collect funds at closing to pay the debt.

Real property has certain characteristics that set it apart from other marketable commodities. These characteristics are both physical and economic. The physical characteristics define and pertain to the land itself. The economic characteristics define and pertain to the value of and change in value of the land. The physical and economic characteristics are so interrelated that they have a definite effect on each other and are sometimes difficult to separate in a practical sense. We will discuss both of these characteristics and their effect on real property value.

PHYSICAL CHARACTERISTICS OF REAL PROPERTY

Immobility

A physical characteristic of major importance is the **immobility** of land. This is the primary distinguishing feature between land and personal property, which is highly mobile. Land cannot be relocated from one place to another. This is a unique feature of land as a commodity.

The physical characteristic of immobility is a major reason why the location of real estate is so important and is a major factor in affecting land value. The characteristic of immobility also makes the market for land a strictly local market.

1. Immobility
2. Indestructibility
3. Nonhomogeneity (uniqueness)

Figure 1.1
The physical
characteristics
of real estate

It is because of this local aspect of the real estate market that there are thousands of real estate brokerage firms located in communities across the nation. It is necessary for those who have a specific knowledge of the local market in real estate to be available as specialists to serve the buyers and sellers in each community.

Indestructibility

Land is a permanent commodity. Land cannot be destroyed. It may be altered substantially in its topography or other aspects of its appearance, but it still remains. Land values can, of course, change as a result of changing conditions in the area of the location of the land and may suffer from **economic obsolescence**, which results from changes in surrounding areas that adversely affect its value. For example, the construction of an interstate highway can radically affect land values of property located several miles away on a minor highway that loses a tremendous volume of traffic to the newly constructed nearby interstate.

The permanence or **indestructibility** of land makes it very attractive as a long-term investment. However, the investor should always be alert to changing conditions that may affect the value of the investment.

Nonhomogeneity, (Uniqueness)

Nonhomogeneity means that no two parcels are identical either physically or in a legal sense. Land is much different from cars that come off an assembly line. Two cars may be nearly identical and one could be substituted for the other, which is clearly not the case with real estate. Each parcel of real estate has its own location, topography, soil type, zoning, size, shape, and so on.

This uniqueness of each parcel of land gives rise to the concept of **specific performance**. If a seller contracted to sell his real property, the law does not consider money to be a substitute for his duty. Therefore, if a seller intended to breach the contract and pay financial damages instead, the buyer could refuse to accept the money and insist on taking title to the land as the only acceptable performance of the contract.

Suppose you contracted to purchase a home in a particular neighborhood because it was next to friends, family, or schools. If the seller wanted to change her mind and offer you another, better home on the other side of town, you could hold the seller to specific performance of the original contract for the unique advantages of that property to you.

ECONOMIC CHARACTERISTICS OF REAL PROPERTY

Availability

An important economic characteristic of real property is its availability or **scarcity**. It follows the principle of **supply and demand**, which suggests that the greater the supply of any commodity in comparison to demand, the lower the value will be. Land is a commodity that has a fixed supply base. As we know, no additional physical supply of land is being produced to keep pace with the ever-increasing population.

However, the problems created by an ever-increasing demand for the limited supply of land have been substantially eased by the increase in the **economic supply** of land. This increase has come about as a result of the greater utilization of the existing physical supply of land. Farmers are continuing to increase the utilization of land in the agricultural area. Greater and greater crop yields per acre are being achieved as a result of scientific and technological advances. Today, the agricultural industry is producing more cattle per acre and more bushels of crops per acre than it did just a few years ago. Additionally, in urban areas, land is being utilized to a greater and greater extent.

As a result of advances in science and technology, we are able to create high-rise office buildings, apartment complexes, and multilevel shopping centers. Consequently, one acre of land serves many times the number of people who could utilize the land in the absence of these improvements.

Modification by Improvement

Modification by improvement states that the economic value of land is increased by improvements made to and on the land. The appeal of a parcel of land may increase as it is transformed from a vacant plot to a lot with a completed dwelling. This transformation increases the land's value. Improvements are not limited to buildings. They include landscaping, grading, clearing, connection to public utilities, and better drainage, just to name a few. Note that the construction of highways, bridges, water reservoirs, purification plants, and public utilities increases the economic supply of land. The improvement and expansion of our public air and land transportation system also makes a significant contribution in this regard. These accomplishments in the field of construction and transportation have converted land that was previously not accessible and useful in a practical sense into land that may now be utilized. A substantial increase in the economic supply of land has resulted from modification by improvements to the land (not on the land) that have made previously inaccessible and unusable land now usable in a practical sense.

Permanence of Investment

Ownership of land is considered an investment because land is permanent. Because land is indestructible and immobile, owners of land are willing to invest money to improve the land itself or to place improvements on the land, such as building homes, office buildings, and golf courses.

Location (Situs)

Of all the characteristics of land, location (**situs**) has the greatest effect on property value. The physical characteristic of immobility dictates that the location of a parcel of land is permanent. Therefore, if the land is located in an area where there is a high demand for the available land, the land will have a substantially increasing value. Conversely, if the land is inaccessible from a practical standpoint or is located in an area with very little or no demand, the economic value will be depressed.

Although the location of land cannot be changed, the value of the location, and consequently the value of the land, can be increased as the result of improvements in access and improvements by other modification to the land and on the land.

Additionally, the value of the location can change as the result of the preferences of people. In the 1950s there was a great flight from the urban centers to the suburbs.

1. Availability
2. Modification by improvement
3. Permanence of investment
4. Location (situs)

Figure 1.2
The economic
characteristics
of real estate.

In many cases, this resulted in substantial property value reductions in urban areas. This trend has been reversing itself. People are rediscovering the inner cities and rehabilitating older properties and restoring lost value.

GENERAL CONCEPTS OF LAND USE

Physical Factors Affecting Land Use

Physical factors affecting land utilization are both natural and artificial. Natural factors include location, topography, soil conditions, size and shape, subjection to flooding, action of the sun, and the presence or absence of minerals. Artificial factors include streets and highways; surrounding land use patterns; availability of sewage systems, water, and other utility services; proximity to public transportation; and the existence of commercial and social centers in the area. The natural and artificial physical factors must always be taken into consideration in making an analysis as to the utility of land and the various uses to which the land may be adapted.

Economic Factors Affecting Land Use

Economic factors affecting land use include local property tax assessments and tax rates, wage and employment levels in the community, availability of financing and levels of interest rates, directional growth of a community, the quantity of highly competitive uses within the area, the trading area covered from the site location, governmental regulations such as zoning laws, fire regulations, adequacy of city planning, building codes, the effectiveness of crime control, and the concept of highest and best use. All of these economic factors have a definite effect on the uses to which the land can be or should be adapted.

The concept of **highest and best use** is of extreme importance. In employing this concept to determine the highest and best use of land, all of the physical and economic factors are taken into consideration. The highest and best use of land is the use of the land that will provide a residual income to the land that results in the highest present value of the land. Land must be improved by the employment of capital and labor to make it productive.

To illustrate the concept of highest and best use, let's use the example of a piece of land zoned for business. The optimum size of a building to be constructed on the site must be established. The space should not be overadequate or underadequate. The building must not contain more space than can be rented in the market, nor should it fail to provide the space that the market demands. Neither an *overimprovement* nor an *underimprovement* will provide sufficient income to the land. In either of these cases, the income will be absorbed by the cost of constructing, maintaining, and operating the building and providing a return to the investors to the extent that insufficient income is left, after all of these expenses are paid, to be allocated to the land. As a result, the land has not been put to its highest and best possible use.

There is only one highest and best use for a particular parcel of land at any particular time. The loss of residual income to the land resulting from failure to employ the land to its highest and best use will cause the value of the property to diminish. This form of depreciation is a loss in value resulting from economic obsolescence.

THE REAL ESTATE BUSINESS

The real estate business is very extensive in scope and is a complex industry. Usually when people think of the real estate business they only think of real estate brokerage. However, brokerage is just one of several specializations within the real estate business. In fact, within the field of brokerage, there are several specializations, including farm and land brokerage, residential property brokerage, and commercial and investment property brokerage. In addition to brokerage, other specializations in real estate include property management, appraising, financing, construction, property development, real estate education, and government service.

Real estate transactions can be traced to early written records from biblical times. However, those transactions were between seller and buyer without participation of a real estate broker. The business of real estate brokerage is a product of the twentieth century. In 1917, the state of California became the first state in the nation to enact licensing law legislation. Today, all states in the nation require real estate brokers and salespersons to be licensed.

National Association of REALTORS®

The establishment of the National Association of Real Estate Boards in 1908 was a major development in the field of real estate brokerage. During the 1970s, the name was changed to National Association of REALTORS® (NAR). The term **REALTOR®** is a registered mark of the National Association of REALTORS® and identifies members of local and state associations and the national association. (An individual may be a licensed salesperson or broker without being a member of NAR.) Only the active members of these associations may use the term REALTOR® or **REALTOR ASSOCIATE®**.

One of the most important accomplishments of the National Association of REALTORS® was the creation of a code of ethics in 1913. This code has contributed significantly to the professional stature of real estate brokerage. Other significant contributions of the National Association of REALTORS® have been efforts resulting in the creation of licensing laws in all states, the legislative activity on the federal and state levels to safeguard rights of private ownership in real property from erosion by unnecessary and harmful legislation, and the provision of excellent programs of continuing education for members and nonmembers through the REALTORS® National Marketing Institute.

The NAR and other professional organizations have developed special institutes that award designations and certifications in specialized areas of real estate. This function of the NAR and other groups has added to the professional image of the real estate business. Some of the institutes and designations are listed in Figure 1.3.

THE REAL ESTATE MARKET

A **free market** concept illustrates a market in which there is ample time for buyer and seller to effect a mutually beneficial purchase and sale without undue pressure or urgency. The real estate market is an excellent example of this concept. Properties available for sale are given substantial market exposure, particularly on the local level. Properties are available for inspection by prospective buyers and these buyers have opportunity to inspect several such properties prior to making a final selection.

Figure 1.3
Some of the many real estate institutes, societies, and councils, with their related designations.

NATIONAL ASSOCIATION OF REALTORS®

REALTOR® Institute
— Graduate, REALTOR® Institute (GRI)
— Certified International Property Specialist (CIPS)

American Society of Real Estate Counselors (ASREC)
— Counselor of Real Estate (CRE®)

Commercial-Investment Real Estate Institute (CIREI)
— Certified Commercial-Investment Member (CCIM)

Institute of Real Estate Management (IREM)
— Accredited Management Organization® (AMO®)
— Accredited Residential Manager® (ARM®)
— Certified Property Manager® (CPM®)

REALTORS® Land Institute (RLI)
— Accredited Land Consultant (ALC®)

REALTORS® NATIONAL MARKETING INSTITUTE (RNMI®)
— Real Estate Brokerage Council: Certified Real Estate Brokerage Manager (CRB®)
— Residential Sales Council: Certified Residential Specialist (CRS®)

Society of Industrial and Office REALTORS® (SIOR®)
— Professional Real Estate Executive (P.R.E.)

Women's Council of REALTORS® (WCR)
— Leadership Training Graduate (LTG)

Maine Association of REALTORS®

NATIONAL ASSOCIATION OF RESIDENTIAL PROPERTY MANAGERS

Residential Property Managers (RPM)
Master Property Managers (MPM)
Certified Residential Management Company (CRMC)

APPRAISAL INSTITUTE

MAI — Appraisers experienced in commercial and industrial properties
SRA — Appraisers experienced in residential income properties
RM   — Appraisers experienced in single-family dwellings and two-, three-, and four-unit residential properties
SREA — Appraisers experienced in real estate valuation and analysis
SRPA — Appraisers experienced in valuation of commercial, industrial, residential, and other property

The physical characteristics of land create special characteristics of the real estate market that do not exist in other markets. The immobility of real estate causes the market to be local in character, requiring local specialists who are currently familiar with local market conditions, property values, and availability. The nonhomogeneity, or uniqueness, of each parcel of real estate also requires that the market be local in character. Each parcel of real estate is unique primarily because of its particular location.

The physical characteristic of immobility also results in a market that is slow to react to changes in supply and demand. When supply substantially exceeds demand, existing properties may not be withdrawn from a local market area and relocated to an area in which there is a higher demand because of the characteristic of immobility. Conversely, when the demand exceeds supply, new supplies of housing and business properties cannot be constructed quickly. Therefore, after a recession, it always takes many months for the supply to equal or exceed demand in the real estate market.

Factors Affecting Supply and Demand in the Real Estate Market

There are many factors affecting supply and demand in the real estate market, both on the local and national levels. Examples of these factors include interest rates, availability of financing for purchase and construction, population migrations, variations in population trends and family formations, government regulations, local and national economic conditions, and the availability and cost of building sites, construction materials, and labor.

Historical Trends in the Real Estate Market

Just as the economy as a whole is subject to peaks and valleys of activity that have recurred over the years with fairly reasonable regularity, the real estate industry as part of this economy has also been subjected to recurring periods of recession and prosperity. The real estate industry is often the first industry to feel the adverse effects of depressed conditions in the national and local economies. It also takes the real estate industry a longer period of time to climb out of a recession than the economy as a whole because of the inability of the real estate industry to react quickly to radical changes in supply and demand. Another characteristic of the real estate cycle is that the real estate industry usually attains a much higher level of activity in prosperous times than does the economy in general.

THE FUNDAMENTALS OF A REAL ESTATE TRANSACTION

The Real Estate Licensee

The successful real estate licensee is not engaged in applying techniques of the "hard sell." Rather, he or she is a counselor or advisor working diligently to solve the problems of buyers, sellers, and renters of real estate. Everyone who contacts a real estate office has a problem. The problem involves real property—the need to either buy, sell, or rent. The real estate licensee's ability to solve these problems for the benefit of others results in a successful career.

A career in real estate can provide the practitioner with satisfaction from serving the needs of people and with accompanying financial rewards. Success in the real estate business is built upon knowledge, service to others, and ethical conduct in all dealings.

Listings

A listing is a contract wherein a property owner employs a real estate firm to market the property described in the contract within a specified period of time. Listings are the inventory of a real estate office and are the lifeblood of the business. Without listings, a real estate firm is handicapped and is limited to marketing the listings of other real estate offices.

As *agent of the seller*, the listing licensee is empowered to market the listed property. The listing contract does not authorize the licensee to bind the seller in a contract to sell the property. The listing licensee's purpose is to find qualified prospective buyers

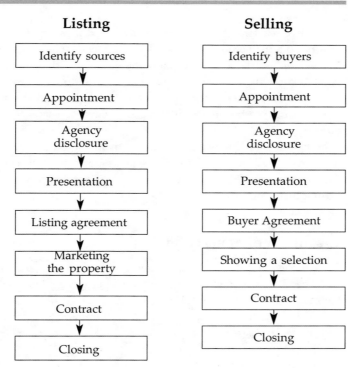

Figure 1.4 Overview of real estate transactions.

for the property and present offers from these buyers to the property owner for acceptance or rejection. The ability to match up qualified buyers with specific properties enables the real estate licensee to create purchase and sale contracts, thereby solving buyers' and sellers' problems.

As agent of the buyer, the buyer agent is empowered to represent the buyer's best interests in locating a property, writing the offer and bringing the transaction to closing. The buyer's agent should do a market analysis on the desired property, provide required disclosures, and give the buyer advice and counsel through the transaction.

Purchase and Sale Agreement

A binding contract to buy and sell real property results from the written acceptance of a valid written offer from the buyer by the seller or the acceptance by the buyer of a new offer or counteroffer made by the seller. When the listing licensee presents the offer to the seller client, the licensee must give his client all information about the transaction. In many instances the selling licensee also may be representing the buyer. As the agent of the buyer, the licensee must give the buyer pertinent information about the transaction prior to or during the preparation of the offer.

Financing

One of the most important aspects of real estate transactions is financing. Most buyers do not have cash funds available to purchase property. Therefore, most real estate transactions cannot be completed without financing. If the property cannot be financed, usually it cannot be sold.

The real estate licensee needs to have a day-to-day working knowledge of the loan programs available from local lending institutions. The licensee must continually keep in touch with these local lenders and develop a cordial working relationship with them. A new licensee should make it a point to personally call upon the local lenders to start a mutually supportive relationship. The lender is interested in working to make the sales transaction possible, but the licensee has to know the lender's guidelines to qualify the transaction. No licensee can ever hope to know all of the details of each program in her area, but she does need to know the fundamental guidelines of each to match these programs to the buyer's needs and to get the financing process started. A licensee's knowledge of financing and the use of modern techniques in this area is essential to successfully concluding the sale of a property.

In tight money markets, that is, where financing is difficult to obtain at favorable rates, the licensee may need to look to the seller as a primary source of financing from the latter's equity in the property. The licensee needs to know when this technique is possible with existing financing.

Closing the Transaction

The completion of the real estate transaction occurs at closing. This is the time when the buyer receives a deed giving title to the property, the seller receives the compensation for the sale of the property, and the real estate licensee receives a well-earned commission. The real estate licensee—along with the attorney for the lending institution, the buyer, and the seller—is a party to the closing and often coordinates the performance of the various activities preliminary to closing.

Other Aspects of the Transaction

In addition to the activities involved in the real estate brokerage business discussed previously, the real estate licensee must be knowledgeable in a variety of other subjects necessary to the satisfactory performance of the licensee's obligations in real estate transactions. These other subjects, which will be discussed in depth in the various chapters of the text, include property ownership and interests, transfer of title to real property, valuation of real estate, land use controls, fair housing law, and federal income tax implications in real estate ownership and sale. It is also very important for the real estate licensee to understand and know the meaning of the various real estate and legal terms involved with real estate transactions. Finally, a basic understanding of the various types of math problems with which the practitioner may be confronted in the activities of real estate brokerage is necessary.

IMPORTANT POINTS

1. The definition of real property includes the surface of the land, all improvements that are attached to it, and things beneath the surface, as well as air space over the land.
2. Personal property is defined in the negative sense of real property, that is, everything that is not real property is considered personal property. Things that are readily moveable, or not attached to the land, are personal property.
3. Real property has the physical characteristics of immobility, permanence, and uniqueness.
4. Real property has unique economic characteristics based on its physical location.
5. The real estate business involves many specialties besides residential brokerage and requires knowledge of many fields, such as financing and other related fields.

6. A real estate market is local in nature and is a fine example of the free market concept.

7. The real estate licensee acts as an advisor or problem solver for the benefit of his client. Because the purchase or sale of a home will involve the most important financial asset of the seller and buyer, it is imperative that the licensee be thoroughly knowledgeable and competent in his duties.

REVIEW QUESTIONS

Answers to these questions are found in the Answer Key section at the back of the book.

1. All of the following are separable ownerships in land except:
   a. surface of the land
   b. area below the surface
   c. nonhomogeneity
   d. air rights

2. The characteristic of land that causes the real estate market to be essentially a local market is the physical characteristic of:
   a. indestructibility
   b. immobility
   c. availability
   d. natural features

3. The concept that no two parcels of land are exactly alike is called:
   a. Immobility
   b. Permanence of investment
   c. Nonhomogeneity
   d. Location

4. An example of personal property would be:
   a. Fence
   b. In-ground swimming pool
   c. Drapes
   d. Dining room chandelier

5. The quality of the location of land and consequently the value of the land can be changed by:
   a. the principle of nonhomogeneity
   b. relocation of the land
   c. changes in the national scope of the real estate business
   d. improvements to the land that result in accessibility not previously available

6. All of the following can affect supply and demand except:
   a. Interest rates
   b. Availability of financing
   c. Demographics
   d. Government regulations

7. Specializations within the real estate business include which of the following?
   a. transportation
   b. farming
   c. accounting
   d. property management

8. Which of the following is a physical factor affecting land use?
   a. Zoning laws
   b. Fire regulations
   c. Availability of utility services
   d. Tax rates

9 The real estate market may be described in all the following ways except:
   a. free market
   b. local market
   c. moveable market
   d. market that is slow to react to changes in supply and demand

10. A real estate firm becomes an employee of a property owner as a result of which of the following?
    a. purchase and sale contract
    b. final settlement
    c. specialized knowledge
    d. listing contract

11. All of the following are real property except:
    a. surface of the earth
    b. area below the surface
    c. readily moveable items
    d. area above the surface

12. Economic characteristics of real property include which of the following?
    a. situs
    b. immobility
    c. indestructibility
    d. nonhomogeneity

13. Which of the following has the greatest effect on real property value?
    a. tax rates
    b. location
    c. availability
    d. indestructibility

14. The real estate market is all of the following except:
    a. Local in Character
    b. An example of the free market system
    c. Quick to react to change
    d. License laws govern the conduct of licensees

15. All of the following are true regarding the National Association of Realtors except:
    a. Works to safeguard rights of private property ownership
    b. Allows all real estate agents to call themselves Realtors
    c. Awards designations and certifications to its members
    d. Created a code of ethics for its members.

IMPORTANT TERMINOLOGY

associate broker
broker
commingle
fraudulent representation
licensed

misrepresentation
police power
Real Estate Commission
sales agent
trust account

LICENSING OF REAL ESTATE BROKERS, ASSOCIATE BROKERS, AND SALES AGENTS

IN THIS CHAPTER

Today, all states require that people engaged in the real estate business be **licensed** by the state. The authority of the state constitution to require licenses falls under the **police power** of the state. This is a power that every state has to enable it to fulfill its obligation to protect the health, safety, welfare, and property of the citizens of the state.

The purpose of license law legislation is to protect the general public. License laws require a licensee to possess the necessary knowledge, skill, and reputation for honesty, fair dealing, and ethical conduct in order to enter the real estate business. License laws also govern the conduct of licensees in their real estate business activities. The following sections define real estate brokerage, real estate broker, associate real estate broker, real estate sales agent.

Real Estate Brokerage (§13001, #2)

"Real Estate Brokerage" means a single instance of offering, attempting to conduct or conducting services on behalf of another for compensation, or with the expectation of receiving compensation, calculated to result in the transfer of an interest in real estate. Real estate brokerage includes, but is not limited to, the following activities conducted in behalf of another:

1. Listing real estate for sale or exchange;
2. Promoting the purchase, sale or exchange of real estate;
3. Procuring of prospects calculated to result in the purchase, sale or exchange of real estate;
4. Advertising or holding oneself out as offering any services described in this subsection;

5. Negotiating the purchase, sale or exchange of real estate;
6. Buying options on real estate or selling real estate options or the real estate under option;
7. Acting as a finder to facilitate and purchase, sale or exchange of real estate; and
8. Buying, selling or exchanging real estate.

[The license law statutes provide for exceptions to the requirement of being licensed in order to legally receive a compensation in a real estate transaction. The following section (§13002) is a list of exceptions:]

Exceptions to Brokerage (§13002)

Real estate brokerage shall not include the following:

1. Transactions by owner or lessor. Transactions conducted by any person who is the owner or lessor of the real estate, or to their regular employees with regard to the employer's real estate, provided that: (a) the real estate transaction services rendered by the employee are performed as an incident to the usual duties performed for the employer; or (b) the real estate transaction services are subject to the provisions of the Maine Condominium Act, Title 33, Chapter 31.
2. Attorney-at-law in the performance of duties as an attorney-at-law. This exception does not apply to attorneys who are regularly engaged in real estate brokerage; and
3. Exception. Any person licensed as an auctioneer under Chapter 5 hired to call bids at an auction, if the person employed does not prepare contracts or otherwise control the actual sale or take custody of any part of the purchase price.

[The Maine license law statute provides for three licensing categories: real estate broker, associate real estate broker, and real estate sales agent.]

Real Estate Broker (§13198)

1. Definition. "Real estate broker" or "**broker**" means any person employed by or on behalf of an agency to perform brokerage and licensed by the commission as a broker.
2. Professional qualifications. The applicant must have been licensed as an associate broker affiliated with a real estate agency for 2 years within the 5 years immediately preceding the date of application submitted to the Commission and completion of a course of study meeting commission established guidelines.
3. Acts Authorized. Each broker license granted entitles the holder to perform all of the acts contemplated under this chapter on behalf of an agency, including being designated by the agency to act for it or as a branch office manager.

Associate Real Estate Broker (§13199)

1. Definition. "Associate real estate broker" or "**associate broker**" means any person employed by or on behalf of an agency to perform real estate brokerage services and licensed by the commission as an associate broker.
2. Professional qualifications. The applicant shall have practiced as a real estate sales agent for 2 years within the 5 years immediately preceding the date of

application, satisfactorily completed a course of study meeting commission-established guidelines. The commission may not issue a license under this section until an individual has completed 2 years as a licensed real estate sales agent.

3. Acts authorized. Each associate broker license granted shall entitle the holder to perform all of the acts contemplated by this chapter, in behalf of an agency, except serving as a designated broker or a branch office manager.

Real Estate Sales Agent (§13200)

1. Definition. "Real estate agent" or "**sales agent**" means any person employed by or on behalf of an agency to perform real estate brokerage services in a training capacity and licensed by the commission as a sales agent.

2. Professional qualifications. Each applicant for a sales agent license shall meet the following qualifications:
   A. The applicant must satisfactorily complete a course of study meeting commission-established guidelines, and
   B. The applicant may appear at such time and place as the director may designate for the purpose of a written sales agent examination.

3. Licensee Term. Sales agent licenses shall be issued for 2 years and may not be renewed. A new sales agent license may not be reissued within 5 years following the date the previous sales agent license was issued.

REAL ESTATE COMMISSION

The responsibility for the supervision and enforcement of the real estate license laws in Maine falls to the state's **Real Estate Commission**. This commission ensures that licensees meet standards that promote public understanding and confidence in the business of real estate brokerage.

The commission consists of four industry members and two public members. Each industry member must be a real estate broker or associate broker for at least five years prior to appointment. The public member, the member's spouse, parents, and children shall have no professional or financial connection with the real estate business, and there cannot be more than one member of the commission from any one county.

Members of the commission are appointed by the governor. Such appointments are subject to review by the joint standing committee of the legislature having jurisdiction over business legislation and to confirmation by the senate. Appointments are for a three-year term.

Director of the Commission

The Director of the Office of Licensing and Regulation, with the advice of the Real Estate Commission and subject to the civil service law, appoints a director of the commission, who is responsible for the management of the commission's affairs, within the guidelines established by the commission.

Complaints to the Commission

The director investigates the actions of any licensee upon receipt of a verified written complaint. A complaint can be made by another licensee or by the general public. Upon completion of the investigation, the director will take one of the following actions:

1. Dismiss the complaint, with the commission's approval.
2. With the consent of the parties and subject to approval of the commission and commission counsel, execute a consent agreement. (The agreement states the violations and the decisions of the director, such as fines, suspension, or the taking of an education course.)
3. Issue a staff petition for hearing before the commission.

If a petition for hearing is filed by the director alleging a violation, the commission shall conduct a hearing. The director may issue subpoenas to compel the attendance of witnesses and the production of documents deemed necessary as evidence. If after the hearing the commission finds that a violation has occurred, it may:

Decisions (§13068)

1. Reprimand the person.
2. Require the person to comply with such terms and conditions as it determines necessary to correct the basis for the violation or prevent further violations by issuing a cease and desist order.
3. Assess the violator a fine of no more than $2,000.00 per violation.
4. Suspend or revoke the license issued.
5. Report its finding and recommendations to the Attorney General or the district attorney.

Other Duties of the Real Estate Commission

Other duties of the Real Estate Commission include the following:

1. Licensing.
2. Establish Fees.
3. Promulgation of rules and regulations.
4. Prescription of curricula and standards for educational programs.
5. Investigations of licensee's conduct.

STANDARDS OF CONDUCT REQUIRED OF LICENSEES

The section of license law statutes requiring every licensee to maintain certain standards of conduct is an important part of license law legislation. These standards of conduct reinforce the obligations of the licensee to her principal—seller or buyer—and the obligations of the licensee to the general public. These standards of conduct are absolutely necessary for the protection of the general public, which is the major purpose of license law legislation. Violations of these statutory requirements by a licensee subjects the licensee to license revocation, suspension, fines, and/or educational requirements.

Typical Prohibitions

The following is a list of typical violations that subject a licensee to license revocation or suspension:

1. Obtaining a license under false or **fraudulent representation**.
2. Having been convicted or entered a plea of no contest upon which a finding of guilty and final judgment has been entered in a court of competent jurisdiction for criminal offenses, such as embezzlement, obtaining money under false pretenses, conspiracy to defraud, forgery, or any offense or offenses that would impact on the ability to conduct business in a trustworthy manner.
3. Making any substantial and willful **misrepresentation**. A misrepresentation occurs when a licensee makes a false statement regarding a material fact—something important to the buyers in their decision to purchase the property. It is misrepresentation for a licensee to indicate knowledge of an important matter in a real estate transaction when in fact the individual has no such knowledge. Example: If a licensee tells a buyer that a house is well insulated when either (a) a licensee does not know whether the house is insulated or not, or (b) knows that it is not properly insulated, he has made a substantial and willful misrepresentation. A misrepresentation also occurs when the licensee is aware of a material defect in a property but does not advise the buyer of such defect.
4. Making any **false promises** of a character likely to influence, persuade, or induce someone to contract. A false promise is simply an untrue promise to a party that something will or will not occur in a real estate transaction. Example: A licensee makes a statement to the buyer that the property under consideration will appreciate 20 percent per year and when the buyer is ready to sell it in three years it will be worth a certain amount of money. It is a false promise if a licensee tells a prospective buyer that something will or will not happen when in

---

License
- Review Maine Real Estate Commission license procedure

Interview
- More than one company
- Independent contractor vs. employee
- Policy and procedures
- Training
- Support

Selection
- Choose an agency that you like
- Choose an agency that meets your needs

Establish Goals and Objectives
- Commitment

First 90 Days
- Orientation: designated broker, office manager, sales manager, support staff
- Develop a business plan
- Training

Figure 2.1

Steps involved in becoming a real estate licensee.

fact the licensee knows that just the opposite is true. It is also a false promise if a licensee promises something when she does not know whether the promise will be kept on the part of the party supposed to perform the promise or when in fact there is no basis for making such a promise.

5. Acting as the agent for the buyer and the seller in a transaction without the knowledge of all parties for whom the licensee acts. It is a violation for a licensee to represent both a buyer and seller in a real estate transaction without informing both parties of the dual representation and obtaining their agreement.

6. Accepting compensation from someone other than the designated broker. A licensee is required to accept compensation in a real estate transaction only from the broker with whom he is affiliated. Also, the licensee may not represent another broker without the knowledge and consent of the broker with whom he is principally associated.

7. Failing to account for and remit funds belonging to others that have come into the licensee's possession. All designated brokers must maintain a **trust account** in the form of either a checking or savings account that may accrue interest. A trust account is opened under the name of the agency, as licensed, and is designated as a real estate trust account. It is used for depositing moneys of clients and customers with whom the agency is dealing, and it is prohibited to **commingle** these funds with the designated broker's personal or business funds. However, a maximum of $500 of company money is allowed to maintain the account. Licensees are required to promptly remit to the agency any earnest money deposits to be placed in the trust account within five business days of acceptance of the offer. All other moneys received shall be deposited within five business days of the trustee's receipt of such moneys.

8. Paying an unlicensed person a commission or valuable consideration for services in a real estate transaction. It is just as much a violation of the license law statute for someone to pay an unlicensed person a compensation for services in a real estate transaction as it is for the unlicensed person to receive the compensation.

9. Performing or attempting to perform any legal service as prohibited by the state statutes concerned with the unauthorized practice of law. A licensee may not prepare legal documents, such as deeds or mortgages, may not give an opinion as to the legal validity of any document or the legal rights of others, and may not perform a title examination and render an opinion as to the quality of the title. In essence, a licensee may not perform any service that must be performed by an attorney-at-law. In all legal matters affecting buyers and sellers, the licensee should recommend that the parties retain the services of a competent attorney.

10. Failing to deliver all necessary documents handled by the licensee to buyers and sellers in a real estate transaction. Licensees are required to present every offer, oral or written, to the seller, as well as any interest in the property that has been communicated to the listing broker. It is the seller's prerogative to accept or reject any offer. Licensees are also required to provide copies of all documents signed by buyer, seller, or both to the buyer and seller. The buyer must receive a copy of the offer and both buyer and seller must receive copies of the executed contract at the time of their signatures. The seller must always be provided with a copy of the listing contract at the time of her signature. Additionally, copies of any other documents—such as options, contract for deed, or contracts of lease—must be provided to the parties.

OTHER LICENSE LAW PROVISIONS

Using the *Maine License Law and Rules Reference Book* and/or this chapter, add the appropriate data to the following outline:

General Licensing Requirements

A. Give reasons for the necessity for license

B. Qualifications for sales agent's license

C. Biennial license fees for:

    1. Broker

    2. Associate real estate broker

    3. Real estate sales agent

D. Displaying of licenses

E. Expiration and renewal of licenses

F. Effect of revocation of a designated broker license or licenses of brokers, associate brokers, and sales agents in the broker's office

G. Transfer of license

H. Branch offices

I. Discharge or termination of employment of brokers, associate brokers, and sales agents

J. Change of location requirements

K. Continuing education requirements for associate brokers and brokers

L. Supervision by designated broker

IMPORTANT POINTS

1. License laws are an exercise of the police power of a state.
2. The purpose of license laws is to protect the public.
3. A real estate sales agent means any person employed by an agency to perform real estate brokerage services in a training capacity.
4. The Real Estate Commission is responsible for the enforcement of license laws.
5. License laws establish standards of conduct for licensees.
6. Real estate commissions are empowered to issue and revoke or suspend licenses.
7. License applicants must be knowledgeable of all the provisions of the license law, commission rules, and other regulations.

REVIEW QUESTIONS

Answers to these questions are found in the Answer Key section at the back of the book.

1. All of the following statements about the license law are correct except:
   a. License laws are an exercise of police power
   b. The purpose of license laws is to protect the public
   c. License laws are to protect licensees from lawsuits
   d. License laws govern the conduct of licensees

2. A licensee is not usually sanctioned for:
   a. Performing a legal service for the client
   b. Making an innocent misrepresentation
   c. Indicating that the property will appreciate in value
   d. Obtaining a license under false representation

3. The listing agent has received a call from another licensee. The licensee indicates that his buyer client wants to make a verbal offer. The listing licensee:
   a. Does not have to present an offer that is less than what the seller wants
   b. May indicate to the other licensee that she only presents written offers
   c. Must present the verbal offer to seller
   d. May reject the offer on behalf of the seller

4. Regarding the real estate trust account, the designated broker:
   a. Has 4 business days to deposit the money in the real estate trust account
   b. Is allowed to have up to $500 of company money in the real estate trust account
   c. The account for earnest money deposits must be a checking account
   d. May place an earnest money deposit in the operating account until the check clears

5. All of the following are true regarding the Maine Real Estate Commission except:
   a. The commission consists of four industry members and two public members
   b. An industry member cannot be a sales agent
   c. Members of the commission are appointed by the governor
   d. Appointments are for a three year term

6. Which of the following most correctly states the purpose of license law legislation?
   a. to provide protection for licensed real estate professionals from competition by unlicensed people
   b. to control the number of people entering the real estate business
   c. to give protection for the general public by requiring the people entering the real estate business to be adequately qualified
   d. to establish a board of arbitration to settle disputes between licensees

7. Upon completion of an investigation of a complaint, the director of the real estate commission will take one of the following actions:
    a. Revoke the license
    b. Reprimand the person
    c. Dismiss the complaint with the commission's approval
    d. Assess the violator a fine of $500

8. In an effort to induce a prospective buyer to enter into a contract to purchase a home, a real estate broker told the buyer that the home was only four years old when it was actually eight years old. The broker knew the actual age of the home. Relying on the broker's statement, the prospect entered into a contract to purchase the property. Given this information, which of the following statement(s) is (are) true?
    a. the broker is in violation of the licensing law
    b. the broker has committed an act of willful misrepresentation
    c. the buyer can be let out of the contract
    d. all of the above

9. A buyer was induced to enter into a contract to purchase a house by the broker's statement that the house was fully insulated. The agent had no knowledge of the house's insulation. Given this information, which is true?
    a. The buyer must complete the contract
    b. The agent is guilty of misrepresentation
    c. The agent is not guilty because he had no knowledge of the insulation
    d. Insulation must be disclosed

10. A seller was so pleased with the manner in which a sales agent handled the listing and sale of her property that she decided to pay an extra commission to go entirely to the sales agent. The agent may accept this special commission provided:
    a. the agent receives it directly from the seller
    b. the agent is an independent contractor
    c. the designated broker shares in the extra commission
    d. the seller pays the extra commission to the designated broker who in turn passes it on to the agent

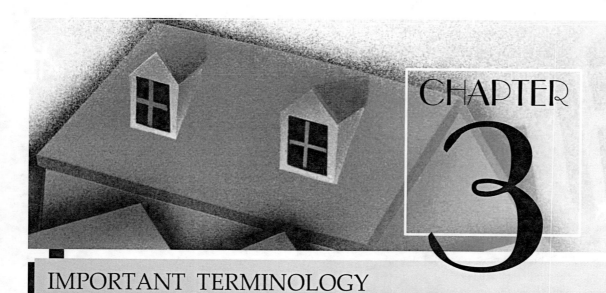

CHAPTER 3

IMPORTANT TERMINOLOGY

affirmative easement
allodial
appurtenance
community property
condominium
condominium association
condominium declaration
conveyance in remainder
cooperative
co-ownership
corporation
curtesy
declarant
dominant tenement
dower
easement
easements in gross
eminent domain
encroachment
encumbrance
escheat
estate
estate at sufferance
estate at will

estate for life
estate for years
estate from year-to-year
estate in remainder
fee simple absolute
fee simple determinable
fee simple subject to a condition subsequent
feudal
freehold
hereditaments
intestate succession
joint tenants
judgment
land
leasehold estates
less than freehold estate
license
lien
life estate
lis pendens
materialman's lien
mechanic's lien
mortgage lien

negative easement
partnership
party wall
periodic tenancy
plat
police power
power of taxation
prescription
pur autre vie
Real Estate Investment Trusts (REITs)
remainderman
reversion
right of alienation
right of survivorship
riparian rights
servient tenement
sole ownership
sole proprietorship
tenancy in common
tenant at sufferance
tenements
testate
trust

PROPERTY OWNERSHIP, INTERESTS, AND RESTRICTIONS

IN THIS CHAPTER

This chapter begins the discussion of the various types of ownership of and interests in real property. Although we will be exploring a variety of legal terms, the real estate licensee is strongly cautioned against the temptation to give legal advice; attorneys are the only ones authorized to practice law. It is, however, our duty as real estate licensee to recognize basic concepts of law as they may affect our clients and prospects and see that our clientele are properly informed of their rights and obligations through appropriate legal counsel.

ESTATES IN REAL PROPERTY

Historical Background

The original system of landownership was the **feudal** system that originated in English law almost a thousand years ago. Under the feudal system, only the king could hold title to real property. The king granted feuds to loyal subjects. These feuds did not provide ownership in land, but simply a right of use and possession of land as long as the holder of the feud provided certain services to the king. The feuds were approximately equivalent to the modern concept of leasehold estates. Under the feuds, outright ownership could never be obtained. Ownership of a feud could continue only as long as the owner provided services to the king.

The feudal system of ownership was transplanted to America when people from England settled and founded the colonies. The King of England or his ambassadors owned and controlled all the land. This system continued until the Revolutionary War. One of the basic reasons for the American Revolution was the colonists' insistence on outright and absolute ownership of land, called **allodial** ownership. Allodial, or private ownership of land, did not begin until 1785, with the passage of the Ordinance of 1785. After passage of the Ordinance, the conveyance of lands from the government to individuals was by patent or land grant. The Ordinance of 1785 also provided the first official survey system, called the government or rectangular survey.

Definition of Estate

An estate in real property is an interest in the property sufficient to give the owner of the estate the right to possession of the property at some point in time. An estate does not necessarily imply an ownership interest in the property. Here, we must distinguish between the right of possession and the right of use. The owner of an estate in land has the right of possession as opposed to a mere right to use the land, as in the case of an easement.

The Latin translation for the word estate is status. This indicates the relationship in which the estate owner stands with reference to rights in the property and establishes the degree, quantity, nature, and extent of interest that a person has in real property. Figure 3.1 lists the various estates and rights that may be held.

Lands, Tenements, and Hereditaments

A concept of the law of real property is that real property consists of lands, tenements, and hereditaments. What then does each of these three things include?

Land is the surface of the earth and also the area below the surface (including minerals) theoretically to the center of the earth itself. The term land also includes the air above the surface of the earth to the highest heavens.

Tenements include all of those things that are included in the definition of land; in addition, tenements include both corporeal and incorporeal rights in land. Corporeal things are tangible—things that can be touched and seen. Incorporeal rights are things that are intangible. Tenements include buildings (corporeal). Tenements also include rights in the property of another, such as an easement (incorporeal).

Hereditaments is a term that includes everything included in the term land and everything included in the term tenements. The term hereditaments includes every interest in real property that is capable of being inherited.

Estates in land are divided into two groups. These are estates of **freehold** and estates of **less than freehold (leasehold estates)**. Each of these two major divisions has various groupings or subheadings within it. The material following provides a description of each of these types of estates.

FREEHOLD ESTATES

Freehold estates have two distinct features. There must be actual ownership of land, and the ownership is for an undetermined period of time. The freehold estates are

Figure 3.1
Estates and rights in real estate property (in descending order of importance).

Freehold Estates	Nonfreehold Estates (Leasehold Estates)	Rights in the Land of Another

I. Fee simple (all inheritable)
  A. Absolute
  B. Conditional
  C. Determinable
II. Life estates
  A. Conventional
  B. Legal
Note: Freehold estates provide title.
	A. Estate for years
	B. Estate from year-to-year (Periodic tenancy)
	C. Estate at will
	D. Estate at sufferance
	Note: Provide possession and control but not title.
		A. Easements
		B. Profits
		Note: Provide a right but not title or possession.

(1) the various fee simple estates and (2) life estates. Fee simple estates are inheritable; life estates are not.

Fee Simple Absolute

The concept of real estate ownership can be readily understood when viewed as a bundle of rights. Under the allodial system, there are rights that the government possesses on real estate ownership, such as police power, eminent domain, the rights of taxation, and escheat. The remaining bundle of rights available for private ownership is called fee simple absolute.

The estate of **fee simple absolute** provides the greatest form of ownership available in real property. This estate may be described as fee simple absolute, fee simple, or ownership in fee. This bundle of rights includes the right to possession of the property; the right of quiet enjoyment of the property; the right to dispose of the property by gift, sale by deed, or by will; and the right to control the use of the property within the limits of the law.

The owner in fee simple absolute may convey a life estate to another either in reversion or in remainder; pledge the property as security for a mortgage debt; convey a leasehold estate to another; grant an easement in the land to another; or give a license to conduct some activity on the property to another. Certain of these rights may be removed from the bundle leaving the other rights intact. For example, if the owner pledges the title as security for a mortgage debt, the balance remaining is a fee simple title subject to the mortgage debt. Also, if the owner conveyed an estate for years or conveyed an easement in the property to another, the remaining rights would be a fee simple subject to a lease or subject to the existence of an easement.

Fee Simple Subject to a Condition Subsequent

The **fee simple subject to a condition subsequent** can continue for an infinite period, as is the case with the fee simple absolute. However, the fee simple subject to a condition subsequent can be defeated and is, therefore, a defeasible title.

The fee simple subject to a condition subsequent is created by the grantor (the one conveying title) specifying in the conveyance of title a use of the property that is prohibited. For example, a grantor conveys property with the condition that it can never be used as a landfill. As long as the property is never used for this purpose, the title will continue indefinitely in the initial grantee or any subsequent grantee. However, at any time in the future if the property is used for a landfill, the original grantor and/or his heirs may reenter the property and take possession or go to court and sue to regain possession. By doing so the title holder's estate is terminated.

Fee Simple Determinable

This is another inheritable freehold estate in the form of a fee simple estate. However, it is a defeasible fee and, therefore, the title can be terminated by the grantor. An example of the **fee simple determinable** is a situation in which a grantor conveyed title to a college and in the conveyance stipulated that the title is good as long as the property is used for scholastic purposes. Title received by the college can be for an infinite period of time. However, if the property is not used for the purpose specified in the conveyance, the title will automatically terminate and revert to the original grantor or the grantor's heirs.

Notice that in the case of a fee simple determinable, the estate in the grantee automatically terminates in the event that the designated use of the property is not continued. This is contrasted with the fee simple subject to a condition subsequent in which the termination is not automatic. In the latter case, the grantor and/or the heirs must either reenter the property or go to court to obtain possession of the property and to terminate the estate in the grantee.

Life Estates

A **life estate** is a freehold estate that is not inheritable. It may be created for the life of the named life tenant or for the life of some other named person. A life estate created for the duration of the life tenant's own life is called an **estate for life**. When the life estate is for the life of another person other than the life tenant, it is called an estate **pur autre vie** (for the life of another).

There are actually two types of life estates. One is an estate in remainder and the other is an estate in reversion. If the conveyance is from grantor to A for life and then to a named person or persons upon the death of A, it is an **estate in remainder** (see Figure 3.2). The person(s) receiving the title upon the death of A (the life tenant) is called a **remainderman** and the conveyance is a **conveyance in remainder**. The remainderman receives a fee simple title. The life tenant has only an estate or ownership for her life. Immediately upon her death or upon the death of some other person named in the conveyance, the title automatically vests in the remainderman. If the conveyance does not specify a person or persons to receive the title upon the death of the life tenant or other specified person, a life estate in **reversion** is created and the title will revert to the grantor or the grantor's heirs upon the death of the life tenant (see Figure 3.3). The grantor has a reversionary interest in the estate.

Many states provide **dower** or **curtesy** rights to a surviving spouse. This is a right that a surviving spouse has to a life estate in the property of the deceased spouse that was owned while they were married. This is an inchoate (future) right of the surviving spouse. If the surviving spouse had not joined in a conveyance of the property, he has a right to a life estate (usually limited to one-third the value) in the property that was owned while they were married. Dower is a wife's right and curtesy is the husband's right (except in Arkansas, Illinois, Kansas, Kentucky, Maryland, Ohio, and Pennsylvania, where the husband's right is also called dower instead of curtesy).

The Maine rules of descent, which are also called the Intestate Succession Laws, have replaced the common law dower and curtesy. **Intestate succession** statutes set forth the manner in which the property of an intestate (one who has died without leaving a valid will) is distributed to heirs. Until July 1984, a spouse's signature was required to release the right of descent if the property transferred. This is no longer required unless

Figure 3.2
Life estate in
remainder.

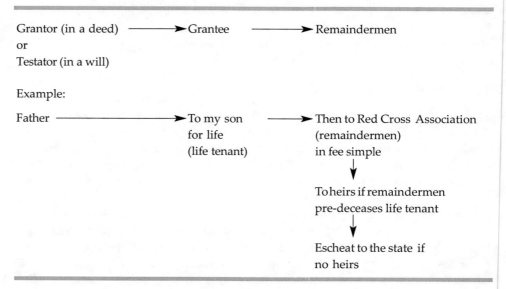

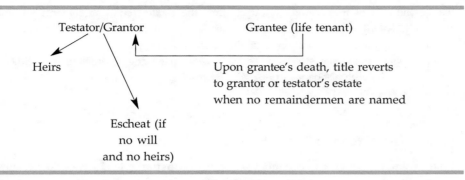

Figure 3.3
Life estate in
reversion.

there is a pending divorce or divorce judgment affecting the interest of the owner in the property.

Rights and Responsibilities of Life Tenants

A life tenant has **the right of alienation**. That is, the life tenant may transfer her title to another person or pledge the title as security for a debt. Of course, the individual cannot give a title for a duration longer than her life or the life of the person named in the creation of a life estate to establish its duration. The life tenant also has the right to the net income produced by the property, if any. The life tenant may legally mortgage the life estate. However, it is unlikely that a lending institution would accept a life estate as security for a mortgage since the estate terminates on the death of the life tenant or some other named person.

A life tenant has certain responsibilities. Basically, the individual must preserve the estate for the benefit of the remainderman or reversionary interest. However, the life tenant has a legal right called the right to estovers. The *right to estovers* provides that a life tenant may cut and use a reasonable amount of timber from the land to repair buildings or to use for fuel. However, the individual may not cut and sell the timber for profit. A violation of the right of estovers is called an act of waste.

A life tenant has an obligation to pay the real property taxes on the property in which she has a life estate. The life tenant also has the duty to pay any assessments levied against the property by a county or municipality for improvements to the property. Assessments are levied against land for improvements made to the land, such as paving of streets and laying of water lines and sewer lines.

The life tenant has a duty to make repairs to the improvements on the land. She cannot permit the property to deteriorate because of lack of repairs and thus cause depreciation to existing improvements.

LEASEHOLD ESTATES

Leasehold estates are less than freehold (less than a lifetime) and are therefore of a limited duration. The leasehold (rental) estates are created by a contract that provides both contractual rights and duties. Leasehold estates provide only possession to the tenant, but not title, which stays with the owner. Leasehold estates create the relationship of landlord and tenant between the parties.

Estate for Years (Fixed Time)

The key feature of estate for years is simply that it exists only for a fixed period of time. The word years is misleading in that the estate does not have to be in effect for a year, but just for any fixed period such as a week or even one day. The important point is that at the end of that stated period of time, the estate (rental agreement) terminates automatically, without any need for either party to give notice to the other. If the lease has any uncertainty about its duration, it cannot be an estate for years.

The laws of many states require the lease to be in writing in order to be valid. If the property is sold with a tenant in possession at the time of sale, the purchaser will have to honor the lease.

Estate from Year-to-Year (Periodic)

Estate from year-to-year is commonly known as a **periodic tenancy**. Its key feature is that it will automatically renew itself at the end of the period unless one party gives notice to the other during a prescribed time at the end of the estate. This notice period may be one to three months, depending upon your state of residence. For example, if the required notice period is one month, and the parties entered the last thirty days of the lease without notifying the other of any change, a new lease would automatically be created for another period at the same terms.

Please note that these first two estates are essentially opposite in terms of what happens at the end of their original lease period; the first terminates, and the second renews itself.

Estate at Will

In the **estate at will**, the duration of the term is completely unknown at the time the estate is created. This is because the estate at will may be terminated by either party at will, by simply giving the other party notice. Statutes often require that the notice of termination be given at least thirty days prior to the date upon which termination is to be effected. Any leasehold interests that are not in writing create only a tenancy at will.

Estate at Sufferance

Estate at sufferance is not truly an estate. The term is simply used to describe someone who was originally in lawful possession of another's property after that person's right to possession has terminated. This could occur upon termination of any of the three previously discussed leasehold estates. The term is used to make a distinction between the tenant at sufferance who was originally in lawful possession of the property and someone who was on the property illegally from the beginning (trespasser). The estate at sufferance will continue until such time that the property owner brings a legal action to evict the person wrongfully holding over or until the one holding over vacates voluntarily. During this period the occupier is called a **tenant at sufferance**.

WAYS IN WHICH TITLE MAY BE HELD

Ownership of real property may be held by one person alone or by many persons, or even nonnatural entities such as partnerships and corporations.

Sole Ownership

When title to property is held by one person, it is called **sole ownership**. It is available to single and married persons. The major advantage of sole ownership is that the owner can make all the decisions regarding the property without having to secure the agreement of co-owners.

Concurrent Ownership

Simultaneous ownership of real property by two or more people is called **co-owner-ship**. The rights of the owners depend upon the type of ownership they have. The types of co-ownership are tenancy in common and joint tenancy.

Tenancy in Common

Tenancy in common is characterized by two or more persons holding title to a property at the same time. Anyone can hold title as a tenant in common. Each title owner holds an undivided interest in the entire property, rather than one specific part of it. There is no right of survivorship, which means that upon the death of a tenant in common, the deceased's share will go to the person's heirs.

A tenant in common may sell his share to anybody without destroying the tenancy relationship. Each tenant in common may also pledge his share of the property in security for a loan that creates an encumbrance against his share only, not the entire property. Tenants in common do not have to have the same amount of interest in the property. For example, one tenant may hold one-half interest, with another two tenants holding one-quarter each.

A tenant in common may bring legal action to have the property partitioned so that each tenant may have a specific portion of the property exclusively. If this can be done fairly with a piece of land, each would receive title to a tract according to his share of interest. If this cannot physically be done to the land, the court may order its sale with appropriate shares of the proceeds distributed to the tenants.

Joint Tenancy

This form of co-ownership requires unity of *time, title, interest, and possession*. **Joint tenants** must have the same interest in the property, receive their title at the same time from the same source, and must have the same degree of undivided ownership and right to possession in the property. For example, if there are three joint tenants, each must own an undivided one-third interest in the property, they must all receive their title from the same source at the same time, and they must continue to hold possession concurrently.

A special characteristic of joint tenancy is the **right of survivorship**. When one joint tenant dies, her share goes automatically to the other surviving joint tenants, instead of passing to the heirs of the deceased. A joint tenant therefore cannot convey ownership by will to another. If a joint tenant sells her share of ownership, the person purchasing this share will not become a joint tenant with the others, but will enter the relationship as a tenant in common. Therefore, the remaining original joint tenants continue as such, with the right of survivorship among themselves. The new purchaser becomes a tenant in common with the original joint tenants and, therefore, does not have the right of survivorship with them.

A court will not recognize a joint tenancy unless the deed of conveyance makes it absolutely clear that the right of survivorship is intended by the parties. To create joint tenancy clear language indicating the intent must be used, such as "to A, D, and C as joint tenants, to their survivor, and to the survivor's heirs and assigns forever."

Community Property

Nine states (Arizona, California, Idaho, Louisiana, Nevada, New Mexico, Texas, Washington, and Wisconsin) are **community property** states. In these states, husband and wife may acquire title to real estate as community property. A husband and wife may hold title to both real and personal property as community property. Title may also be held as husband or wife in severalty as separate property. These concepts of title originated in Spanish law, and all community property states were subject to the influence of Spanish law at the time of their early settlement.

The theory of community property is that husband and wife share equally in the ownership of property purchased by their joint efforts during the community of marriage. The title to such property will vest in husband and wife as community property whether the deed is made only to the husband, only to the wife, or to both husband and wife. Property acquired prior to marriage by either husband or wife is also separate property.

In community property states, separate property is any property acquired by one spouse during marriage by gift or inheritance. Also, any property purchased with the separate funds of the husband or wife becomes the separate property of the purchasing spouse.

Condominiums

Condominium ownership is a form of ownership that is now recognized in all states. All states have statutes that define this type of ownership and set forth the requirements for the creation of a condominium. The first condominium statute enacted in the fifty states was the California Horizontal Property Act. Though the titles of the laws creating condominium ownership vary from state to state, the fundamental principles are reasonably uniform.

A condominium purchaser receives a fee simple title to a unit the same as in any other real estate. The owner can convey title by deed or leave it to an heir by will. In addition to ownership in the unit, the individual also has a co-ownership in the common elements of the condominium along with the other unit owners (see Figure 3.4). Common elements constitute everything except the individual units in which the owners live—the corridors, grounds, parking areas, and recreational facilities, among others. If a common element is restricted for the exclusive use of one or more unit owners it is called a *limited common element* (deck, allocated parking space, etc.). The co-ownership is as tenants in common. Each unit is separately taxed and assessed. The value of the unit plus the value of the allocated interest in the common elements determine the assessment and ultimately the taxes.

The Maine Condominium Act, 33 MRSA Chapter 31, became law on January 1, 1983. The act sets forth the manner in which a condominium is to be created. These include a declaration and bylaws.

The declaration or master deed is prepared and recorded by the developer at the Registry of Deeds. This act of recording creates the condominium as a legal entity. The **condominium declaration** converts a piece of land held under a single deed into a number of individual properties, which are the condominium units. The declaration includes:

1. The name of the condominium and the association
2. A legal description of the property
3. A **plat**, which is a site plan with survey information on the entire condominium
4. A plan, which is a graphic representation of building details
5. A description including location and dimensions of all limited common elements (parts of the common elements that are assigned for the exclusive use of one or more, but fewer than all, the units such as parking areas)
6. A description of the common areas (all physical parts of the condominium except the units, such as the roof)

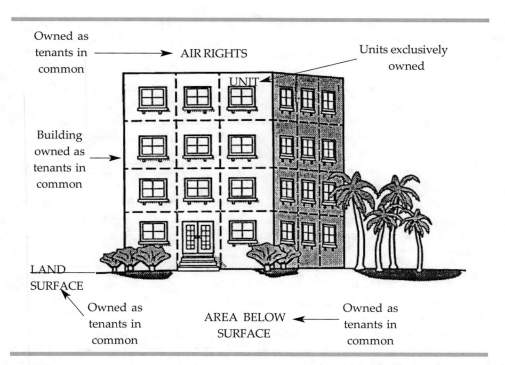

Figure 3.4
Condominium
ownership.

7. A statement describing the allocated percentage interest in the common elements assigned to each unit
8. Restrictions on use, occupancy, and sale of units, such as a policy on pets

The **declarant** (developer) organizes this association and may arrange in the declaration for a specific period of declarant control, which means he may appoint and remove members of the executive board. Declarant control must end 60 days after 75 percent of the units are sold.

The bylaws required for every association must include provisions for the authority, qualifications and election of officers, and the method of amending the bylaws.

Condominium Association

The condominium is governed by a nonprofit corporation whose members are the unit owners of the condominium (usually referred to as the **condominium association**). The powers and responsibilities of the association include adopting and amending bylaws, rules, regulations, and the budget, as well as anything that is necessary to properly operate the association. To efficiently carry out the responsibilities of the association, an executive board of directors is elected. The board conducts the day-to-day activities necessary in the management of a condominium complex.

Consumer protection requirements. The public offering statement for most condominiums sold for the first time must include the following information:

1. Current balance sheet and projected association budget for one year after date of first sale
2. Any expenses that the declarant now is paying that will become common expenses in the future
3. Any special fees that the purchaser will have to pay at closing
4. Any liens, defects, or encumbrances on or affecting title

5. A statement saying that the purchaser may cancel any purchase and sale contract unless he has received a copy of the public offering statement

6. Description of insurance coverage provided for the unit owners

Exceptions to requiring the public offering statement include transfer of a unit by gift, foreclosure, court-ordered sale, or to licensees who intend to sell the units.

In any sales subsequent to the initial sale of a unit, the owner must deliver to the purchaser a resale certificate that includes any restrictions on conveyance or sale of the unit, monthly expenses, anticipated capital expenditures, and a recent balance sheet and expense statement. Along with the certificate, a copy of the declaration and association bylaws, rules, and regulations must be provided to the purchaser.

The creation of a condominium is not limited to residential purposes. Other purposes may be office space, parking space, an industrial park, and so forth. The particular purpose of the condominium must be set forth in the declaration as required by state statute.

A condominium unit can be mortgaged like any other property. Federal Housing Administration (FHA) financing has been available for condominiums since 1961. Also, the Department of Veterans Affairs will guarantee mortgage loans for the purchase of condominiums.

Time sharing is an innovation in condominium ownership. In the time- sharing ownership concept, the owner takes title to an apartment for a period of time. This time period may be one week, two weeks, a month, and so forth, in each calendar year during ownership. The purchaser receives a title to an apartment for the same period of time each calendar year. The owner can sell all of the share or any portion of the time share. The sale is accomplished by a deed of conveyance, as with all real property.

Cooperatives

Ownership in a **cooperative** results from ownership of shares of stock in a corporation that owns a building containing cooperative apartments. The right of stockholders to occupy an apartment is provided by a proprietary lease, usually for a long term. The only real property interest of the stockholders is a leasehold estate providing the right to possession of an apartment. The stockholders, as lessees, pay no rent, but do pay an assessment to cover the cost of maintaining and operating the building, real property taxes, and debt service if there is a mortgage against the building. The owners' rights and obligations are specified in the lease and the stock certificate.

REAL PROPERTY OWNERSHIP BY BUSINESS ORGANIZATIONS

Business organizations can take several different forms. These forms include the sole proprietorship, partnership, corporation, syndicate, joint venture, and real estate investment trust. All of these business organizations can receive, hold, and convey title in the various ways previously discussed.

Sole Proprietorship

A **sole proprietorship** is simply a business owned by one individual. The individual may use her own name as the name of the business or may assume a name for this purpose.

The owner of the sole proprietorship is fully liable for the business debts. If business debts exceed the assets of the business, the personal assets of the owner may be attached by creditors for satisfaction of the business debts.

The sole proprietor can receive, hold, and convey title to real estate either in her own name or in the name of the business.

Partnerships

A **partnership** is a form of business organization in which the business is owned by two or more persons called *partners*. A partnership is created by contract between the partners, as contrasted with a corporation, which is created by the state when it issues the corporate charter. The partners do not have to have the same degree of interest in the partnership. One may own a half interest and two others each a quarter interest, for example. Under the Uniform Partnership Act, which has been adopted by most states, a partnership may hold title to real property in the name of the partnership. Additionally, under the common law, partnerships may hold title to real property in the names of the individual partners.

In *general partnership*, the partners are personally liable for partnership debts exceeding partnership assets. Partners are jointly and severally liable. That is, any individual partner is personally liable for the partnership debts exceeding partnership as sets as well as all the partners being jointly liable.

A *limited partnership* is one consisting of one or more general partners who are jointly and severally liable like partners in a general partnership. In addition to the general partner or partners, there are one or more special, or limited, partners who contribute money to the extent of their ownership in the partnership. The limited partners are not liable for the debts of the partnership beyond the amount of money they have contributed to the partnership and may not participate in the management of the partnership.

The limited partnership organization is frequently used for participation in real estate investments. Typically, a general partner(s) will conceive of the investment opportunity and obtain the money to either construct an improvement or purchase an existing improved property for a number of limited partners. The general partner(s) will do all of the work necessary to create the investment and the limited partners provide the funds. The purpose of the investment may be to provide an income return as well as an eventual capital gain to the investors when the property is sold.

Corporation

A **corporation** is an artificial being, invisible, intangible, and existing only in contemplation of law. A corporation is created by a charter granted to it by its state of incorporation. The corporation's activities are essentially limited to the state within which it is incorporated and may not "do business" in another state without the permission of the secretary of state of such other state. A corporation is called a domestic corporation within the state in which it is incorporated. A corporation doing business in another state is called a *foreign corporation* in that state.

Corporations are divided into two classes according to their objectives and purposes. *Public corporations* are the various governmental corporations, such as cities, towns, counties, school districts, and special bodies for public improvements. *Private corporations* are those corporations not organized to perform governmental functions.

Ownership in a corporation is evidenced by shares of stock. These shares are transferable without having to dissolve the corporation. The stockholders do not have personal liability for the debts of the corporation. Only the corporate assets are subject to the claims of creditors.

To create a corporation, the organizers must file an application for a corporate charter with the secretary of state. The application must contain the names and addresses of the incorporators, the name of the corporation, the object for which it is formed, its duration, location of the principal office, total authorized stock, the names and addresses of the first board of directors, and the terms for which the directors are to serve.

If all is in order, the secretary of state issues a charter to the corporation that contains all of the information on the application and sets forth the powers, privileges, and rights granted to the corporation. The charter must be recorded in the office of the Register of Deeds in the county where the corporate headquarters are located or in such other proper recording office as is prescribed by a particular state.

A corporation has the power to receive, hold, and convey title to real property for all purposes for which the corporation is created. The power to hold, receive, and convey title to real property is normally expressly given in the corporate charter. Corporations are empowered to hold a mortgage on real estate to secure a financial obligation due the corporation and are also empowered to pledge corporate property as security for a mortgage to obtain money to accomplish corporate objectives.

Syndications

A *syndication* is an organization of investors in real estate (or other types of investment). A syndicate normally includes some specialists in real estate such as a developer, a broker, and property manager. A syndicate may exist in the form of a general or limited partnership or as a corporation. Syndications are typically used in cases of multiple continuing projects that require the investment of substantial sums of money.

Joint Venture

A *joint venture* is an organization consisting of two or more parties for the purpose of investing in real estate or any other type of investment. The joint venture may be in the form of a corporation or partnership, or the parties may hold title as joint tenants or as tenants in common. Joint ventures are usually used where the investment is in only one project and the amount of investment is not too substantial.

Trusts

A **trust** is an arrangement in which title to real or personal property is transferred by its owner (trustor) to a trustee. The trustee holds title and manages the property for the benefit of one or more beneficiaries. The trust agreement explains exactly what the trustee is empowered to do on behalf of the beneficiaries. A trust is a fiduciary relationship between the trustee and the beneficiaries of the trust.

A *land trust* is created by transferring the title to a trustee who holds the title for the benefit of others called *beneficiaries*. The power of the trustee is limited to the power granted by the beneficiary when the trust is created. The instrument creating a land trust may be a will or a deed in trust. The trustee may be an individual or a corporation in the form of a trust company. The trust beneficiary may retain control and possession of the property and instruct the trustee to deal with the property for the benefit of the beneficiary.

Real Estate Investment Trusts (REITs) were created in 1967 as a result of changes in the Internal Revenue Code that became effective in September of that year. Qualified real estate investment trusts are given special tax treatment so that they do not pay any federal income tax on trust profits that are distributed to shareholders. However, to qualify, the REIT must distribute each year at least 90 percent of its ordinarily taxable income to the trust beneficiaries. Congress has provided this special tax treatment to qualified REITs to enable small investors to participate in large real estate investments that provide expert management and to help make funds available for financing large real estate developments.

PROPERTY RIGHTS

Air Rights

Ownership of land includes ownership of and the rights to the area above the surface of the earth. The right of ownership of the air space enables the landowner to use that space to construct improvements and to lease or sell the air space to others.

However, the right of ownership and control in the air space is limited by zoning ordinances and federal laws providing for the use of the air space by aircraft. Zoning ordinances often restrict the height of improvements constructed on the land, and federal laws permit the use of the air space by air traffic flying at an altitude above a minimum height specified by the government.

Mineral Rights

A mineral right is the right of the property owner to take minerals from the earth. The owner may conduct mining operations or drilling operations personally or may sell or lease these rights to others on a royalty basis. A mineral lease is one that permits the use of land for mineral exploration and mining operations. The lease may be for a term or for a period as long as the land is productive. A mineral royalty is income received from leases of mineral land.

Riparian Rights

The rights of an owner of property bordering a body of water are known as **riparian rights**. Generally, property adjacent to a river or watercourse affords the landowner the right to access to and use of the water (for example, entry to the water with a boat pier and drawing water for personal use). Actual ownership of the water is a complex issue; it depends on a number of factors as well as location.

GOVERNMENT RESTRICTIONS ON REAL PROPERTY

Although an individual in the United States has maximum rights to the land she owns, these ownership rights are subject to four important powers of federal and local governments. The purpose of these powers is to protect the general welfare of the community over the individual's right to ownership. The four powers are power of eminent domain, police power, power of taxation, and power of escheat.

Power of Eminent Domain

The power of eminent domain is the power to take private property for public use. Governments exercise this power themselves and also delegate it to public utility companies. The taking of property under the power of eminent domain is called *condemnation*.

There are two limitations on the power of eminent domain: (1) the property condemned must be for the use and benefit of the general public, and (2) the property owner must be paid the fair market value of the property lost through condemnation. The property owner has the right to appeal to the courts if she is not satisfied with the compensation offered by the condemning authority.

Police Power

Police power is the power that government has to enable it to fulfill its responsibility to provide for the health, safety, and welfare of the public. Examples of the exercise of the police power affecting property use are zoning ordinances, subdivision ordinances, building codes, and environmental protection laws. Property owners affected by the exercise of the police power are not compensated for the restrictions on their use of property resulting from the exercise of this power. Its underlying premises are that any restrictions imposed must reasonably provide for the health, safety, and welfare of the public.

Power of Taxation

The government's **power of taxation** is well known to everyone. Taxes are imposed upon real property on an ad valorem basis, or according to value. Every city or town has an official with the title tax assessor who is responsible for establishing the value of property within the city or town. This value is then taxed on the basis of an assessment or assessed value. The assessment resulting in tax value may be 100 percent of estimated market value or a substantially lower percentage.

A tax rate, either in dollars or mills, is applied to the assessed value to determine the amount of property tax. The rate must be sufficient to provide the amount of revenue required from property taxes to accomplish the budgetary requirements of the local government unit. Real property taxes are by far the largest source of income for local governments.

Power of Escheat

If a property owner dies and leaves a valid will (**testate**), the individual's property is distributed to heirs as specified in the will. However, if an owner dies without having left a valid will, the deceased's property is distributed to heirs in accordance with state statutory provisions. These statutes are usually called "statutes of intestate succession" and specify how property will be distributed based on the relationship of heirs to the deceased.

In the event there is no one qualified to receive title to property left by the deceased, the property then **escheats** to the state. In other words, if there is no one legally eligible as designated by statute to receive title to the property, the state takes title.

ENCUMBRANCES

An **encumbrance** is anything that diminishes the bundle of rights of real property. Therefore, charges, claims, restrictions, or infringements on a property reduce its overall value in some manner. In this chapter we will discuss encroachments, easements, and liens. Chapter 8 will discuss other land use controls, such as zoning laws and deed restrictions.

Encroachments

An **encroachment** is a trespass on the land of another as a result of an intrusion or invasion by some structure or other object such as a wall, fence, overhanging balcony, or driveway. The encroaching owner may obtain title to the area of the land upon which the encroachment exists by adverse possession (discussed in Chapter 12) or may obtain an easement by prescription in the case of the encroaching driveway if the owner of the land subject to the encroachment does not take appropriate legal action. The owner may sue for damages (a judgment by the court requiring the encroacher to compensate the owner for the encroachment) or may petition the court for a decree ordering the encroachment to be removed.

Easements

An **easement** is a nonpossessory interest in land owned by another. Someone who owns an easement right does not own or possess the land where the easement lies. The easement owner merely owns the right to use or have access to the land. Easements can exist for a great variety of legal uses, such as right-of-way for ingress and egress; a party wall; the right to take water from the land of another; the right to use a watercourse flowing through the land of another; the right of receiving air, light, or heat from over the land of another; the right to obtain water from a well or spring on the land of another; or a right-of-way for the purpose of putting utility lines under and above the surface of the land.

The land that is benefited by the easement is described as the **dominant tenement**. The land encumbered by the easement (the land in which the easement exists) is described as the **servient tenement**. The two property owners are called the *dominant owner* and the *servient owner*. An appurtenant easement can only be used for the benefit of the dominant tenement and may not be used for the benefit of any other land, including land acquired by the dominant owner after the creation of the easement.

Party Walls

A **party wall** is a wall used by two structures as the sidewall of each structure (see Figure 3.5). A party wall is usually constructed so that the property line runs longitudinally down the center of the wall. In this case half of the wall is on each property and the adjoining property owners on whose land the wall is located have an undivided ownership interest in the property as tenants in common. However, if the wall is built entirely within the property of one adjoining owner who will have complete ownership in the wall, the owner may convey a right to use the wall to the adjoining

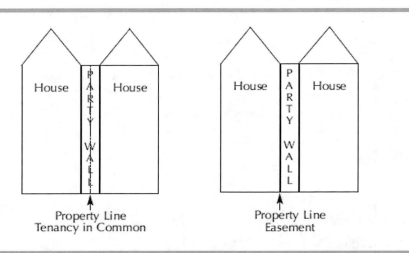

Figure 3.5
Party wall.

property owner in the form of an easement. The adjoining owner can then use the wall as the side wall for a structure built on his property. Because the lands are adjoining, an appurtenant easement is created.

Appurtenant Easement

An **appurtenance** is something that has been added to something else and, as a result, becomes an inherent part of that to which it has been added. In real property law, an appurtenance is the right that one property owner has in the property of another as a result of the property owner's ownership in a particular parcel of real estate. For example, if a purchaser receives a title to a tract of land and included in this title is an easement in the form of a right-of-way across the adjoining land of another, this easement is an appurtenance to that title (see Figure 3.6). Whenever the titleholder conveys that title to another, the conveyance includes the easement since the easement is appurtenant to the title. Since an easement appurtenant moves with a title, it is said to "run with the land."

Easements in Gross

Unlike appurtenant easements, **easements in gross** are not dependent upon ownership of an adjoining property. Typically, the owner of an easement in gross does not own property in the area of the property in which the easement exists.

The most common use of easements in gross is in the form of commercial easements. Commercial easements are prevalent throughout the United States and are typically held by utility companies for the purpose of installing power lines, telephone lines, and gas lines either above the surface of the earth, on the earth itself, or in the ground below the surface. Railroad rights-of-way are another prominent example of commercial easement.

Commercial easements in gross are assignable, can be conveyed, and are inheritable. Personal easements in gross (easements in gross held by an individual) are not assignable, cannot be conveyed, and are not inheritable. Personal easements in gross are practically nonexistent today.

Affirmative and Negative Easements

An **affirmative easement** is one that requires the servient property to permit an activity on the servient estate by the dominant owner (for example, the right to cross over the servient estate for access to a public way). A **negative easement** is one that prohibits the owner

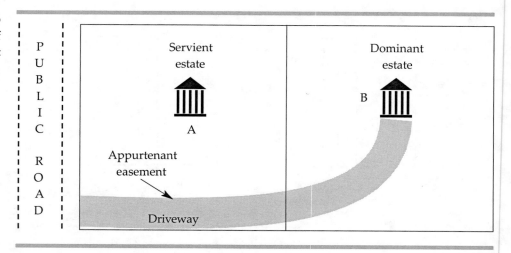

Figure 3.6
An example of an appurtenant easement.

of the servient land from doing something, otherwise lawful, upon the owner's land because it will affect the dominant land (see Figure 3.7). An example would be an easement prohibiting the servient owner from erecting a structure on the land that would interfere with the availability of air and light to the dominant property.

Creation of Easements

Easements may be created by the use of express words, by actions of a person, or by the operation of law (see Figure 3.8).

Express Easements

An owner selling her land can expressly grant an easement to a buyer by using the appropriate language in the deed. In Figure 3.6, if A sold the land to B, A could grant the easement to B to cross A's land. If the situation were the other way around, where B sold the land to A, B would reserve the easement for himself.

The party walls illustrated in Figure 3.5 could be a second example of express easements. A party wall is used by two adjoining neighbors to support the sidewall of each

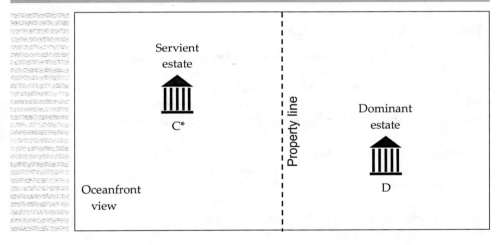

*Servient tenant C is not allowed to erect fence or landscape in such a way that tenant D's view of ocean will be blocked.

Figure 3.7
An example of a negative easement appurtenant.

1. Express (words are used to spell out the agreement)
   a. Grant or reserve
   b. Dedication
   c. Party walls
2. Implied (actions of the parties)
   a. Necessity
   b. Reference to a map
3. Operation of Law (court order)
   a. Condemnation
   b. Prescription

Figure 3.8
The ways easements arise.

unit. If the property line ran down the middle of the wall, each party would have a cross easement in the other, or even a tenancy in common. However, if the wall were entirely within the property of one party, the other would have an easement in the use of the wall.

Easements may be created by dedication, where a portion of a property is set aside for use by the public. For example, a developer may dedicate a portion of land for use by the public, such as roadways or recreation parks in a residential subdivision.

Implied Easements

In certain cases, the actions of a party will create an easement when these actions demonstrate an intent to create an easement.

An easement by necessity is implied if a seller conveys title to a buyer who would be landlocked without access to a road. In Figure 3.6, if A sold the property to B and did not grant A the easement shown, B would have the right to claim such an easement by reason of the necessity to get to the public road. The owner of the servient estate would be entitled to compensation for this easement, even though it was required by law.

An easement by dedication may be implied as well as express. If the developer described above had not expressly granted the roadways in the new subdivision, but had described the property by reference to a map showing the existence of such streets, the easement would be implied. This dedication is implied to the general public as well as to the purchasers in the subdivision.

Easements by Operation of Law

An easement may be obtained by **prescription**, that is, using another's land for a prescribed period of time. The use must be open and well known to others, continued and uninterrupted for the period of time required by laws of the state. The user must prove in court action that she has satisfied all the requirements for the intended use. A prescriptive easement may not be marketable if the land is sold before the required time of use has been met.

Easement can also be created by condemnation under the power of eminent domain of the government. This power enables the government to take private land for the benefit of the general public. In all cases, the property owner must be compensated for differences in value before and after the action by the government. Usually, condemnations for rights-of-way for various public uses are easements and not for acquisition of title.

Termination of Easements

Easements may be terminated as follows:

1. By the release of the easement by the dominant owner to the servient owner
2. By combining the dominant and servient lands into one tract of land
3. By abandonment of the easement by the dominant owner
4. When the purpose for which an easement was created ceases to exist
5. By the expiration of a specified period of time for which the easement was created

Liens

A **lien** is a claim or charge against the property of another. If this claim (lien) is not satisfied in the prescribed time, the lienholder may execute the lien by the process of foreclosure in which the property is sold. Proceeds of the foreclosure sale are applied to the liens in the order of priority of the liens.

Liens fall into two groups: (1) claims against a specific property, such as a mortgage, and (2) claims in general against a person and his property, such as the results of a lawsuit.

Specific Liens

Mortgage Liens

A **mortgage lien** pledges a specific property, such as a home, in security for a debt. If the borrower does not pay the debt as promised (defaults), the lender can foreclose the mortgage by having the property sold at public auction and applying the proceeds of the sale to the debt.

Mechanic's and Materialman's Liens

A mechanic is a person who provides labor to a specific property, such as a carpenter. A materialman is a person or company that provides the materials for construction. If these persons are not paid according to the terms of their contracts, they may file a lien against the property to which they provided work or materials (a **mechanic's lien** or a **materialman's lien**). Priority of these liens is discussed at the end of the chapter.

Real Property Tax and Assessment Liens

The taxes levied by a local government constitute a specific lien against the real estate. State laws provide that real property tax liens have priority over all other liens.

Property is taxed on an ad valorem basis, that is, according to value. The assessment of property for tax purposes involves establishing the value of each parcel of land to be taxed within the taxing unit. An official with the title of tax assessor is responsible for the valuation of property for tax purposes. Property values must be reasonably uniform to provide for equal taxation of property owners. In most states real property is assessed at its full market value, or a 100 percent assessment.

An assessment is a levy against a property for payment of a share of the cost of improvements made to areas adjoining the property. Examples of these are paving of streets, installation of sewer or water lines, and construction of sidewalks. The assessment will constitute a specific lien against the property until paid.

1. Specific Liens: Claims against a particular property
   a. Mortgage
   b. Mechanic's
   c. Materialman's
   d. Real property tax
   e. Vendor's and vendee's
   f. Lis pendens
2. General Liens: Claims against all assets of person
   a. Judgment
   b. Income tax
   c. Estate and inheritance tax liens

Figure 3.9
Classification of liens.

Vendor's and Vendee's Liens

A vendor's (seller's) lien comes into existence upon the sale of real property and conveyance of title to the buyer when the seller does not receive the full purchase price at the time of conveyance. The seller is given a specific lien against the property for the amount of the balance of the purchase price due. If the lien is not satisfied by the purchaser, the seller can foreclose to obtain the money to satisfy the lien.

A vendee's (buyer's) lien is created in the case of default by the seller under a contract of sale for real property. In such case, a buyer has a lien against the property in the amount of money the individual had paid toward the purchase price. The vendee's lien can be enforced by foreclosure.

Lis Pendens

Lis pendens is a notice that a lawsuit is pending (awaiting trial) and that a resulting judgment may create a lien against the property of the defendant. The recording of the lis pendens provides constructive notice of the forthcoming legal action and the potential lien. As a result, a lien resulting from the lawsuit will attach to the property even though the title was transferred to someone else if the transfer occurred after the notice of lis pendens was placed on the public record in the county where the property is located.

General Liens

Judgment Liens

A **judgment** is a court decree establishing that one person is indebted to another and the amount of that indebtedness. A judgment constitutes a general lien against all of the real and personal property that the judgment debtor owns in the county in which the judgment is recorded. The lien takes effect from the time the judgment is recorded. A judgment creditor may record a judgment in any other county in the state and it will constitute a general lien against all the property of the judgment debtor in that county. The judgment will also create a lien against any property that the judgment debtor acquires subsequent to the judgment during the existence of the judgment.

A general lien will not apply to real property owned by husband and wife by the entireties, as joint tenants, or as community property, if the judgment is against only one of them. For the lien to attach to property in such cases, the judgment must be obtained against both husband and wife on a debt they both incurred.

A judgment lien remains in effect for a period of time specified by state statute unless the judgment is paid. Judgment may be renewed and kept in force for an additional period if the creditor brings another action on the original judgment before the original period has elapsed.

Judgment liens have a priority relationship based on the time of recording. The creditor who records a lien before another creditor records a lien against the same judgment debtor will have a prior claim. The judgment debtor's obligation to the creditor having priority must be satisfied before creditors with a lower priority.

Judgment liens are enforced by an order called an execution. This is an order that is signed by the clerk of court that instructs the sheriff to sell the property of the judgment debtor and apply the proceeds of the sale to the satisfaction of the judgment.

Income Tax Liens

The Internal Revenue Service of the United States government and a state's Department of Revenue may create a general lien against all the property of the taxpayer for taxes due and unpaid. This lien is created by filing a certificate of lien against the landowner in the county in which the taxpayer's land is located.

Estate and Inheritance Tax Liens

Most states impose a tax upon the inheritance of real property (as well as personal property). In Maine, this is called an estate tax. The tax is a lien on the property to be inherited until the tax is paid. To satisfy the tax bill, the estate can sell sufficient property.

The federal government imposes a tax on the estate of deceased persons. This tax is called the federal estate tax. This tax creates a lien that attaches to all of the property—both real and personal—in the estate and continues until the tax is paid. The inheritance tax is paid by the heirs inheriting the estate. The federal estate tax is levied against the estate and is paid from the assets of the estate.

Priority of Liens

For most liens, their priority in relationship to other liens is based on the time (day and hour) they were recorded with the proper court officer or, in the case of mortgages, with a Register of Deeds. However, certain liens have special priority by statute, as is the case with mechanics' and materialmen's liens in some states. The highest priority of all liens is given to liens for real property taxes in most states, including Maine.

LICENSE

In real property law a **license** is defined as permission to do a particular act or series of acts on land of another without possessing any estate or interest in the land. A license is a personal privilege and may be revoked by the licensor at any time unless the licensee has compensated the licensor for giving the license, in which case the licensor must permit the activity to continue for the agreed time period.

A license is not assignable and is not inheritable. A license is personal property and not real property. Therefore, the agreement may be oral; it does not have to be written. Examples of activities that may be permitted by licenses are the privilege to hunt or fish on the land of another; the rental of space for camping, parking, or selling merchandise; or admission to a concert, movie, or sporting event. From these examples it can be seen that a license is not only a personal privilege, but also a temporary privilege.

IMPORTANT POINTS

1. The allodial system of real property ownership used in the United States provides for private ownership of real estate.
2. Private ownership of property is, however, subject to the four powers of government: eminent domain, police power, taxation, and escheat.
3. Estates in land are divided into two groups: freehold and estates of less than freehold (leasehold).
4. The freehold estates include fee simple estates, which are inheritable, and life estates, which are not inheritable.
5. The greatest form of ownership in real property is fee simple absolute.
6. Life estates may be in reversion or in remainder.

7. The duration of a life estate may be measured by the life tenant or by the life of another (pur autre vie).

8. Conventional life estates are those created by someone's intentional act. Legal life estates are created by operation of law.

9. A life tenant has the right of alienation, the right of encumbrance, and the right of possession and enjoyment of the property and of deriving certain income from it.

10. A life tenant is obligated to preserve and maintain the property for the benefit of the future interest.

11. When title is held concurrently by two or more persons or organizations it is called co-ownership (also, concurrent ownership). The forms of co-ownership are tenancy in common, joint tenancy, community property, and certain aspects of condominiums and cooperatives.

12. Joint tenancy includes the right of survivorship and requires the unities of time, title, interest, and possession.

13. The owner of a condominium unit holds title to the unit either in severalty or as co-owners with another as well as title to the common areas as tenant in common with the other unit owners.

14. The creation of a condominium requires the recording of a declaration (also called a master deed), articles of association, and bylaws.

15. Ownership in a cooperative results from stock ownership in a corporation that owns a building containing cooperative apartments. Stockholders occupy apartments under a lease.

16. Business organizations may receive, hold, and convey title to real property.

17. The less than freehold estates are also called leasehold estates and are estates of limited duration, providing possession and control, but not title (as in the case of freehold estates).

18. The leasehold estates are estate for years, estate from year-to-year (periodic tenancy), estate at will, and estate at sufferance.

19. An encumbrance is a claim, lien, charge, or liability attached to and binding upon real property. Examples are encroachments, liens, restrictive covenants, easements, inchoate dower, deed restrictions, and government control of land use.

REVIEW QUESTIONS

Answers to these questions are found in the Answer Key section at the back of the book.

1. Personal property attached to real property is prevented from becoming real property by which of the following?
    a. ownership
    b. an appurtenance
    c. security interest and financing statement
    d. mineral rights

2. If the government acquires privately owned real estate through condemnation it is exercising its powers of:
    a. A negative easement
    b. Escheat
    c. Eminent domain
    d. Judgment

3. One property owner held an enforceable right to prevent a second property owner from erecting a structure that would interfere with the passage of light and air to the property of the owner holding the enforceable right. This right is in the form of which of the following?
   a. implied easement
   b. easement by necessity
   c. easement by prescription
   d. negative easement

4. Easements may be created in all of the following ways except:
   a. condemnation
   b. dedication
   c. prescription
   d. assessment

5. Easements may be terminated in all of the following ways except:
   a. When the purpose for the easement ceases to exist
   b. When the dominant and servient tenements are combined into one tract of land
   c. By the expiration of a specified period of time for which the easement was created
   d. When the property is sold

6. A property owner gives another person permission to fish in a lake on the property. The permission is a temporary privilege and exists in the form of which of the following?
   a. license
   b. easement
   c. lease
   d. appurtenance

7. The creation of an easement by condemnation results from the exercise of which of the following?
   a. prescription
   b. eminent domain
   c. dedication
   d. implication

8. Which of the following is defined as a claim or charge against the property of another?
   a. Easement
   b. Deed restriction
   c. Lien
   d. Encumbrance

9. A widow inherits an estate by will, granting her the right of use and possession of a parcel of land for the rest of her life with the provision that the estate will go to her children in fee simple upon her death; she has received:
   a. A devisable freehold estate
   b. A leasehold estate
   c. A life estate in remainder
   d. A fee simple determinable

10. The highest and best form of estate in real property is which of the following?
    a. easement appurtenant
    b. defeasible fee
    c. life estate in reversion
    d. fee simple absolute

11. A life estate created for the life of another is called:
    a. conventional life estate
    b. estate pur autre vie
    c. legal life estate
    d. community property

12. After the termination of a lease, the tenant continued in possession of the property without permission of the property owner. The tenant's status is:
    a. tenant at will
    b. lessee
    c. trespasser
    d. tenant at sufferance

13. In the condominium form of ownership:
    a. The owner receives title for the same time period each year
    b. The real property interest is a leasehold estate
    c. The owner receives a fee simple title for a unit
    d. Ownership is evidenced by shares of stock

14. Which of the following is characteristic of leasehold estates?
    a. They are estates of unlimited duration
    b. The holder of a leasehold estate has title to the property
    c. The estates must be agreed to in writing
    d. The estates provide only possession (occupancy) to the tenant

15. Which of the following types of ownership requires unity of interest, title, time, and possession?
    a. cooperative
    b. tenancy in common
    c. joint tenancy
    d. community property

16. None of the following includes the right of survivorship except:
    a. tenancy in common
    b. joint tenancy
    c. life estate
    d. community property

17. The purchaser of a condominium unit receives title to the land whereon the condominium is situated as a:
    a. tenant by entirety
    b. tenant in common
    c. joint tenant
    d. tenant at sufferance

18. In this estate, the duration of the term is known at the time the estate is created:
    a. Estate at will
    b. Estate at sufferance
    c. Estate for years
    d. Estate from year to year

19. Tenants in common:
    a. Must receive title at the same time
    b. Have the right of survivorship
    c. May convey ownership by will
    d. Must receive the property from the same source

20. Liens, easements, encroachments, and restrictive covenants are all examples of which of the following?
    a. emblements
    b. estovers
    c. estates
    d. encumbrances

CHAPTER 4

IMPORTANT TERMINOLOGY

agency
agent
appointed agency
client
commission
customer
disclosed dual agency
escrow account
fiduciary

misrepresentation
multiple listing service (MLS)
net listing
non-appointed agency
principal
referral fee
single agency
subagency
transaction broker

LAW OF AGENCY

Agency is a relationship in which one party (**agent**) is authorized to act on behalf of another (**principal** or **client**). A vast body of law controls the rights and duties in an agency relationship. To this, Maine license law has added regulations affecting the relationship between licensees, clients, and the public. This chapter will discuss the obligations of a licensee under the law of agency as well as the misconceptions and problems that revolve around the subject of agency today.

CREATION OF AGENCY

In the real estate context, agency is generally created when there is an agreement (written or oral) between the principal, who may be either buyer or seller, and the agent. In Maine, client representation may not be created orally or by implication or be assumed by anyone. If there is no written agency agreement to provide real estate services, the agent is presumed to be acting as a transaction broker and the buyer is a customer. The customer acts in his own behalf without benefit of advice throughout the transaction.

There is a common misconception in regard to agency creation. The myth is that "you work for the person who pays you." Payment of commission does not determine agency, only the agreement between the parties establishes this. The seller may pay the commission, the buyer may pay it, or the fee may be split between the seller and buyer. Since payment of commission does not necessarily determine agency and confusion may arise, agents must be careful to disclose agency relationships. Maine license law requires licensees to disclose the agency relationships that exist to both prospective buyers and sellers where there is a substantive communication regarding a real estate transaction. A licensee is obligated to furnish the parties with a copy of The Real Estate Brokerage Relationships Form (see Figure 4.1) at the first occurrence of either a face-to-face meeting, written communication, or an electronic communication with the prospective buyer or seller. A licensee is not required to provide a copy of the form to a prospective buyer or seller if the real estate consists of less than one or more than four residential dwelling units, or if the licensee has knowledge or may reasonably assume that another licensee has given a copy of the form to a prospective buyer or seller in that transaction.

AGENCY RELATIONSHIPS

Various agency relationships are possible in any real estate transaction. For this reason, it is important to clarify who represents whom. Once a real estate broker enters into a brokerage agreement with the principal, whether buyer or seller, the law of agency applies. This

Figure 4.1   Agency Disclosure Form

Dept. of Professional & Financial Regulation
Office of Professional & Occupational Regulation
MAINE REAL ESTATE COMMISSION
35 State House Station Augusta ME 04333-0035

REAL ESTATE BROKERAGE RELATIONSHIPS FORM

Right Now You Are A Customer

Are you interested in buying or selling residential real estate in Maine? Before you begin working with a real estate licensee it is important for you to understand that Maine Law provides for different levels of brokerage service to buyers and sellers. You should decide whether you want to be represented in a transaction (as a client) or not (as a customer). To assist you in deciding which option is in your best interest, please review the following information about real estate brokerage relationships:

Maine law requires all real estate brokerage companies and their affiliated licensees ("licensee") to perform certain basic duties when dealing with a buyer or seller. You can expect a real estate licensee you deal with to provide the following customer-level services:

√ To disclose all material defects pertaining to the physical condition of the real estate that are known by the licensee;

√ To treat both the buyer and seller honestly and not knowingly give false information;

√ To account for all money and property received from or on behalf of the buyer or seller; and

√ To comply with all state and federal laws related to real estate brokerage activity.

Until you enter into a written brokerage agreement with the licensee for client-level representation you are considered a "customer" and the licensee is not your agent. As a customer, you should not expect the licensee to promote your best interest, or to keep any information you give to the licensee confidential, including your bargaining position.

You May Become A Client

If you want a licensee to represent you, you will need to enter into a written listing agreement or a written buyer representation agreement. These agreements create a client-agent relationship between you and the licensee. As a client you can expect the licensee to provide the following services, in addition to the basic services required of all licensees listed above:

√ To perform the terms of the written agreement with skill and care;

√ To promote your best interests;

  • For seller clients this means the agent will put the seller's interests first and negotiate the best price and terms for the seller;

  • For buyer clients this means the agent will put the buyer's interests first and negotiate for the best prices and terms for the buyer; and

√ To maintain the confidentiality of specific client information, including bargaining information.

COMPANY POLICY ON CLIENT-LEVEL SERVICES — WHAT YOU NEED TO KNOW

The real estate brokerage company's policy on client-level services determines which of the three types of agent-client relationships permitted in Maine may be offered to you. The agent-client relationships permitted in Maine are as follows:

√ The company and all of its affiliated licensees represent you as a client (called "single agency");

√ The company appoints, with your written consent, one or more of the affiliated licensees to represent you as an agent(s) (called "appointed agency");

√ The company may offer limited agent level services as a disclosed dual agent.

WHAT IS A DISCLOSED DUAL AGENT?

In certain situations a licensee may act as an agent for and represent both the buyer and the seller in the same transaction. This is called disclosed dual agency. *Both the buyer and the seller must consent to this type of representation in writing.*

Working with a dual agent is not the same as having your own exclusive agent as a single or appointed agent. For instance, when representing both a buyer and a seller, the dual agent must not disclose to one party any confidential information obtained from the other party.

> ### Remember!
> *Unless you enter into a written agreement for agency representation, you are a customer—not a client.*

THIS IS NOT A CONTRACT

It is important for you to know that this form is not a contract. The licensee's completion of the statement below acknowledges that you have been given the information required by Maine law regarding brokerage relationships so that you may make an informed decision as to the relationship you wish to establish with the licensee/company.

To Be Completed By Licensee

This form was presented on (date)_____

To_____
Name of Buyer(s) or Seller(s)

_____

by_____
Licensee's Name

on behalf of_____
Company/Agency

MREC Form#3 Revised 07/2006
Office Title Changed 09/2011

To check on the license status of the real estate brokerage company or affiliated licensee go to www.maine.gov/professionallicensing. Inactive licensees may not practice real estate brokerage.

means that a fiduciary relationship (position of trust) has been established, and the agent is required to represent her client.

There are several choices available to Maine real estate brokerage companies. They are

- Seller Agency Only
- Buyer Agency Only
- Non-Appointed Agency with Disclosed Dual Agency
- Non-Appointed Agency without Disclosed Dual Agency
- Appointed Agency with Disclosed Dual Agency
- Appointed Agency without Disclosed Dual Agency
- Transaction Brokerage

Single Agency

In a **single agency** relationship, the company and all of its affiliated licensees represent all clients. Seller agency only, buyer agency only, and non-appointed agency without disclosed dual agency are examples of single agency.

Seller Agency

For many years, real estate was practiced in such a manner that agency relationships were only extended to sellers. Today there are some agencies that still have this policy. In a Seller Agency company, all agents in the company represent all seller clients. Any buyers who are interested in the listings of that company will be customers. This company might also include in their policy that the licensees may be transaction brokers when showing other company's listings. In either of these two situations where the buyer is a customer, the licensee has a duty to disclose to the buyer any material defects pertaining to the physical condition of the property.

Buyer Agency

Buyer Agency can exist exclusively where a brokerage **firm** chooses to **only** represent buyers and never sellers, as an exclusive buyer agent. If the buyer has a house to sell, the licensee cannot list the house, but with the permission of the buyer may refer the listing to another company.

Non-Appointed Agency (buyer or seller) without Disclosed Dual Agency

Non-Appointed Agency is a practice in which every affiliated licensee represents every client of the company. A licensee in this company will either represent a buyer or a seller in the same transaction but never both. Because every licensee in the company represents every buyer ad seller client in the company, a conflict may occur when a buyer client wants to buy a seller client's property. The company needs to establish a policy on who is going to be represented by the company when this situation occurs. If the company's policy is to always represent the seller in this situation, the buyer can either become a customer or be referred to another company for representation.

Figure 4.2

Agency Relationships

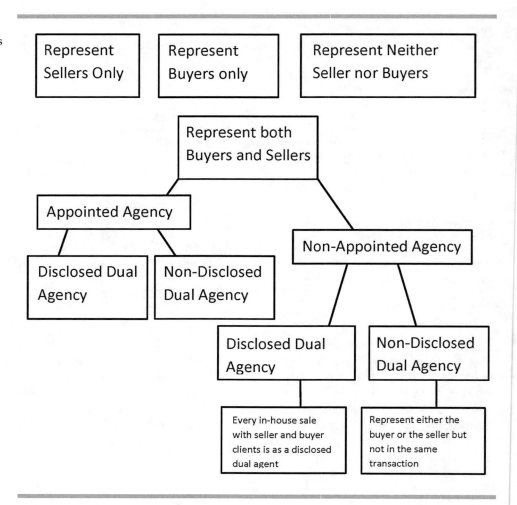

Non-Appointed Agency (buyer and/or seller) with Disclosed Dual Agency

The practice of this company is that every affiliated licensee represents every client of the company. When a non-appointed agency decides to allow the licensees to practice disclosed dual agency, the licensees are not only able to represent either the buyer or the seller in the transaction but can represent both with the informed written consent of both the buyer and seller. A disclosed dual agency exists when either the listing agent is also the buyer agent or a buyer client of the company wants to buy an in-house listing. In the first instance there is only one agent who is the disclosed dual agent and in the second instance there are two agents that are disclosed dual agents. The written consent that both clients are agreeing to indicates that the dual agent may disclose any information to one party that the disclosed dual agent gains from the other party if that information is relevant to the transaction except for the price that either seller or buyer would agree to, the motivation of either party, and the negotiating strategy not disclosed in the purchase and sale agreement.

Appointed Agency

An appointed agent policy means that whenever a licensee has a seller client or a buyer client, the licensee is appointed to that client to represent the client's interests and acts solely for that client to the exclusion of the other licensees in that company. Only the appointed agent has fiduciary duties and responsibilities such as confidentiality and disclosure of material facts to the client. The licensees of this company cannot discuss any client information with other license that may put their clients at a disadvantage in the transaction. Prior to entering into an appointed agency relationship, the licensee must provide a consent form for the writing; otherwise they cannot be represented by the company. An advantage of this policy is that the licensee can sell their buyer client an in-house listing and only represent the buyer client. The seller client in that transaction is also only represented by their respective agent.

Without Disclosed Dual Agency, if the company adopts an appointed agency policy without disclosed dual agency, it is not possible for the licensee to have two clients in the same transaction. Either the buyer client or the seller client would have to be referred. The referral could be to another licensee in the same company.

With Disclosed Dual Agency, if the company adopts an appointed agency policy with disclosed dual agency, the only time disclosed dual agency can occur is if the licensee has both clients in the same transaction. Both the buyer and the seller client must agree to disclosed dual agency in writing. The consent must be given at the time of entering into a written brokerage agreement for an agent-client relationship. The written consent that both clients are agreeing to indicates that the disclosed dual agent may disclose any information to one party that the disclosed dual agent gains from the other party if that information is relevant to the transaction except for the price that either the seller or buyer would agree to, the motivation of either party, and the negotiating strategy not disclosed in the purchase and sale agreement.

Transaction Brokerage

These firms represent neither the buyer nor the seller, but act as facilitators in the transaction. A transaction broker does not give advice or counsel to either party. The licensee may provide a free opinion of value to a seller when the licensee is soliciting the seller to list with the licensee. If an agreement to provide services as a transaction broker is agreed to, the transaction broker may not provide advice to the seller regarding market value from that point on.

If the licensee is working as a transaction broker with a buyer, the licensee should identify what the transaction broker must do and what may not be done. The transaction broker may disclose material defects pertaining to the physical condition of the property, perform ministerial acts as agreed to by the parties. A licensee acting as a transaction broker may not conduct an inspection, investigation or analysis of property for the benefit of a party to a transaction. The license may not verify the accuracy or completeness of statements made by the buyer, seller or third party.

SUBAGENCY

Subagency occurs when a selling licensee shows a property listed with another firm and represents the seller in the transaction. For this to occur, the listing firm or company must allow subagency as part of their agency policy. The buyer does not have representation in this transaction.

There are brokerage firms in Maine that do not allow subagency because they feel that there are legal ramifications inherent in subagency regarding both the seller and the firm. If a cooperating subagent fails to disclose defects or misrepresents the property, the listing firm and seller may be liable for damages to the buyer.

Multiple Listing Services

A **multiple listing service (MLS)** is a system that pools the listed properties of all member companies. This gives a property the widest possible market exposure. Members of the MLS are authorized to show any of the properties in the pool, an arrangement that greatly expands the offerings they can show to prospective buyers.

The pooling of listings is an offer of cooperation and compensation to all MLS members. Agencies that place listings in the MLS have the option of offering subagency, buyer agency, and transaction broker compensation to cooperating agencies. If a cooperating licensee accepts the offer of subagency associated with a listing, he or she works through the listing licensee and is therefore the principal's subagent.

Figure 4.3
Subagency.

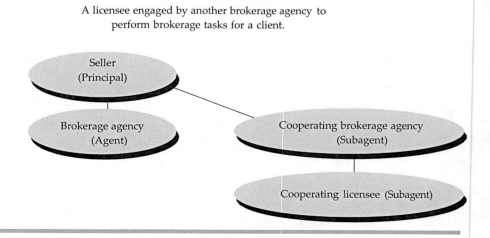

A licensee engaged by another brokerage agency to
perform brokerage tasks for a client.

If the cooperating licensee decides to show property as a buyer agent or as a transaction broker, the licensee needs to check the MLS to see if both cooperation and compensation have been extended to buyer agents or transaction brokers on the properties the client wishes to see. The cooperating licensee may show the property as a buyer agent if she has a client or as a transaction broker if the buyer is a customer.

Before showing a property in the MLS, the cooperating licensee should make his agency status (subagent, buyer agent, transaction agent) clear to the listing licensee, who has a responsibility to inform the seller of this status.

DUTIES AND RESPONSIBILITIES TO PRINCIPAL (CLIENT)

The agency as agent of the principal is in a **fiduciary** relationship. It is a position of trust. The agent of the principal has certain obligations to her as required of every agent by law. The agent's duties and responsibilities are described in the following sections.

Loyalty

The real estate agency must be loyal to the principal and must work diligently to serve the best interests of the principal under the terms of the listing or buyer's broker contract creating the agency. The agent may not work for personal interests or interests of others adversely to the interests of the principal. Real estate agents cannot legally represent any other person that directly affects the principal without disclosing this fact to the principal and obtaining the principal's consent. As stated previously, an agent cannot receive a commission from both without the knowledge and consent of both buyer and seller.

Obedience

It is the duty of the agent to obey all reasonable and legal instructions from the principal. For example, the seller, as principal, may specify that the property only be shown during certain times of the day or avoid days of his religious observance. The buyer being represented might instruct the agent not to disclose the buyer's identity to the parties without the buyer's consent. Of course, the principal cannot instruct the agent to do any illegal acts, such as violating fair housing laws.

Skill, Care, and Diligence

In offering services as a real estate licensee to the public, the licensee is asserting that she possesses the necessary skill and training to perform the employment requirements. In performing duties as an agent, the licensee must exercise the degree of skill and diligence the public is entitled to expect of real estate licensees. If a licensee's principal incurs a financial loss as a result of the licensee's negligence and failure to meet the standards of skill, diligence, and reasonable care the public is entitled to expect from real estate licensees, the agency is liable for any loss incurred by the principal. Additionally, the principal would not be required to pay any compensation to the agency as agreed in the employment contract.

Disclosure of Information

A real estate agent is required to keep the principal fully informed of all important matters. Any information that is material to the transaction for which the agency is employed must be communicated promptly and totally to the principal. As an example, the requirement to disclose information means that the broker must present every offer to the seller (principal). It is the seller's prerogative to decide whether to reject or accept any offer for the purchase of the property. In presenting the offer, the agent should provide the principal with any knowledge of all circumstances surrounding the offer. If the agent serves as a buyer's agent, the agent will indicate to the buyer (the principal) what he feels the market value of the property is and will negotiate to obtain the most favorable terms for the buyer.

Accounting

A designated real estate broker must account for and promptly remit as required all money or property entrusted to the broker for the benefit of others. The broker is required to keep adequate and accurate records of all receipts and expenditures of other people's money so that a complete accounting can be provided. A designated broker must maintain a special account for the deposit of other people's money. This account should be labeled as a "trust account" and the account must be in a financial institution authorized to do business in the state of Maine. It is a violation of the law of agency and the real estate licensing laws for a broker to commingle funds or property that he is holding in trust for others with personal money or property or with the operating account of his business.

Confidentiality

A real estate agent's duty of confidentiality obliges her to keep confidential any information she receives from her client that relates to pricing, motivation, negotiating strategies, or any information that would be of a detriment to the client. An exception to the confidentiality duty would be the disclosure of a material defect on or in the property, such as a defective septic system. A material defect must be revealed to the buyer, but a material fact beyond the boundaries of the property may not be revealed without the permission of the seller.

AGENT'S RESPONSIBILITY TO OTHER THAN THE PRINCIPAL

Even though one of the licensee's obligations to the principal includes the requirement not to disclose certain confidential information to third parties that would be injurious to the principal, the licensee may not misrepresent the property in any way to a third party. The licensee must disclose any material defects of which she has knowledge, or should have had knowledge, regarding the condition of the real estate. Liability may be imposed upon the broker for concealing defects in the property or for failing to disclose the existence of defects of which the broker or licensee has knowledge or should have knowledge.

The basis for the imposition of liability in the case of a **misrepresentation** consists of (1) a false representation of a material defect; (2) the fact that the person making the false representation knew or should have known it to be false; (3) the fact that the misrepresentation was made with an intent to induce the party to act or refrain from acting in reliance upon the misrepresentation; (4) the fact that the party relied upon the misrepresentation in acting or failing to act; and (5) the fact that there was damage to the party who relied upon the misrepresentation in acting or not acting.

A *passive misrepresentation* by a licensee occurs when she conceals a defect in the property from the buyer or makes a false statement to the buyer regarding the existence of a defect. An *unintentional misrepresentation* occurs when the licensee makes a false statement to the buyer about the property and the licensee does not know in fact whether the statement is true or untrue. In either of these situations, the licensee is liable to a customer who suffers a loss as a result of acting or failing to act in reliance upon the misrepresentation. The licensee is not necessarily excused from liability for making a misrepresentation based upon statements made to the licensee by the principal if the licensee, using reasonable care, should have known that the principal's statements were not true. The licensee is required to make a personal diligent investigation before passing on information of any type.

A liability situation may also occur when a misrepresentation is made to the seller by a licensee acting as a buyer's agent. Both the licensee and the buyer may be held responsible for the misrepresentation.

COMMISSION ENTITLEMENT

Types of Commission Arrangements for the Selling Agency

The broker earns a **commission** at whatever point in the transaction he and the owner have agreed upon. In most listing agreements, this point occurs when the broker produces a ready, willing, and able buyer based on the terms set forth by the seller in the agreement. Another arrangement would be that the broker is not entitled to a commission until the transaction is closed. The "ready, willing, and able" agreement affords more protection to the broker because the payment of the commission does not depend on a closed sale.

Percentage of Final Sales Price

The most common type of commission arrangement found in listing contracts is for the commission to be a specified percentage of the final sales price of the property. Notice that this is not a percentage of the listed price (unless the listed price and sold price are identical), but of the price for which the property actually sells.

Flat Fee

Another form of commission is the flat fee. The listing is taken based on a specified payment of money by the seller to the agency at the time the property is listed.

Net Listing

Another type of commission arrangement is the **net listing**. This is a situation in which the seller, when listing the property, specifies an amount of money net that she must receive in the sale. All above the net amount that the seller specifies is designated as the broker's commission in effecting the sale.

The net listing is illegal under Maine law. Even in those states in which it is legal, it is a very poor arrangement of commission schedule. This method can lead to a great deal of dissatisfaction on the part of the seller if the property sells for substantially more than the seller anticipated, thereby resulting in a disproportionate share of the proceeds going to the broker as commission.

Negotiability

The amount or rate of commission to be charged by or paid to a real estate broker is strictly a negotiable matter between the broker and the listed seller. It is illegal for two or more designated brokers to agree to charge certain rates of commission to listing sellers. These activities constitute price fixing and are acts in restraint of trade in violation of the Sherman Antitrust Act.

Competing brokers may not even be a party to a discussion of either commission rates or the boycott of a competitor on the basis of his rates. If a broker or associate is even present in the room where such illegal activities are discussed, this individual might be held to be a party to a price-fixing conspiracy unless the broker or associate takes specific steps to disavow herself from the discussion.

For example, if a broker or salesperson at a meeting of an MLS committee were to say, "I think we ought to charge 10 percent . . . ," other members present at the meetng have a duty to protest that statement, leave the meeting, and report the discussion to the proper authorities to absolve themselves of any complicity to the discussion.

Commissions of Sales Associates

Commissions to be paid to sales associates in a real estate office are established by an agreement between the real estate firm and the associates. This is true whether the associates are licensed as brokers, associate brokers, or sales agents. Under the usual agreement, there are two commissions that may be earned by sales associates. One is a commission for listing the property, and the other is a commission for selling the property. If a licensee sells a property that he has listed, the licensee will receive both the listing and selling commissions. If the agency has a policy to pay a greater commission to its affiliated licensees for an in-house sale versus transactions involving a cooperating real estate brokerage agency, the policy must be disclosed in the written brokerage agreement with a buyer or seller.

Commissions Paid to Cooperating Agencies

When a property is sold as the result of cooperating efforts between two real estate firms, one of which is the listing firm and the other the selling firm, the commission agreed upon in the listing contract is paid to the listing broker on a predetermined basis. The division of the commission to be received by the listing broker should be determined by agreement between the two cooperating broker offices prior to the participation of the selling broker in the transaction. The policy on cooperating and compensating other real estate agencies must be stated in the written brokerage agreement. The policy would indicate who the agency would cooperate with (buyer agent, sub-agent, transaction broker) and if the agency would also compensate the cooperating agency. If the real estate's policy is not to compensate all the real estate brokerage agencies in the same manner, this policy must be included in the statement with a caveat that this policy may limit the participation of other real estate brokerage agencies in the marketplace.

Commission Entitlement to the Buyer's Agent

The buyer's agent can be compensated in a variety of methods. The simplest method would be to share in the commission in the traditional arrangement of listing broker–cooperating broker. The seller is notified and agrees to the commission being split between the listing broker and the buyer's agent. This tends to keep it simple and avoids restructuring of the transaction. An example of restructuring is if the seller paid half the commission and the buyer paid half the commission. This could result in the sale price being lowered by half the commission and a change in value for the sold property. For example:

Traditional Approach		Restructuring Approach	
Sales price:	$100,000	Sales price:	$100,000 (original)
Commission:	7%	If buyer pays commission,	
Listing broker:	– 3,500	house is reduced	
Buyer's broker:	– 3,500	by ¹/₂ commission:	– 3,500
Net to seller:	$ 93,000	New sales price: Minus	$ 96,500
		¹/₂ commission:	– 3,500
		Net to seller:	$ 93,000

Another method of compensation is for the buyer to pay the entire commission to the selling broker; this could be a flat fee, an hourly wage, or a percentage of the price of the house bought.

Referral Fees

Designated brokers will often pay a **referral fee** to other licensed designated brokers outside their respective locality when the other broker refers prospective buyers and sellers. As an example, when you list a property you may find that the seller plans to move out of your market area. Because real estate is a highly local market, you would refer the seller to a broker located in the new market area, and for that referral you would receive a fee at the time of closing. States differ somewhat in regulations regarding referrals across state lines, but all that is usually needed is that both brokers are duly licensed in their respective states. Some states have a provision for a nonresident license so that the broker may actually accompany customers to another state. The more usual situation is that one simply places a referral to a distant point, often with the assistance of a relocation service in the broker's office or franchise affiliation.

IMPORTANT POINTS

1. Agency in Maine is only created by a written agreement between agent and client.
2. Compensation does not determine agency since either seller or buyer may pay the commission.
3. The types of agency relationships are seller agency, buyer agency, and dual agency.
4. A multiple listing service allows its members to place their listings within the service and offer to cooperate with subagents, buyer agents, or transaction brokers.
5. The responsibilities of the agent include loyalty, skill, care, diligence, accountability, and disclosure.
6. A transaction broker represents neither the buyer nor the seller but acts as a facilitator in the transaction.

REVIEW QUESTIONS

Answers to these questions are found in the Answer Key section at the back of the book.

1. An agent's duties to the principal include all of the following except:
   a. loyalty
   b. accountability
   c. obedience
   d. legal advice

2. A licensee presents an offer to the property owner during the listing term for the listed price payable in cash with no contingencies and a 10 percent earnest money deposit. In this situation, which of the following statements is correct?
   a. The property owner is not required to accept the offer
   b. The listing brokerage company is legally entitled to the commission
   c. The property owner must accept the offer
   d. The listing brokerage company is only entitled to a commission if the transaction closes

3. If in a transaction the selling agent is working as a transaction broker, which agent owes loyalty to the buyer?
   a. listing agent
   b. selling agent
   c. both a and b
   d. neither a nor b

4. Maine's Rules and Regulations prohibit which of the following?
   a. dual commission
   b. disclosed dual agency
   c. subagency
   d. net listings

5. A licensee can accept compensation from both the buyer and seller:
   a. only if there is a written listing from both
   b. only if the total amount is equal to the total commission
   c. under no circumstances
   d. only after full disclosure and agreement from both parties

6. When a cooperating broker accepts an MLS offer of subagency, the licensee becomes the fiduciary of the:
   a. listing agency
   b. seller
   c. MLS
   d. buyer

7. The listing broker can discuss with the buyer (customer) all of the following except the:
   a. agency relationship that exists
   b. property disclosure sheet
   c. bankruptcy that the seller is facing
   d. problem with inadequate septic system

8. The selling agent shall obtain the disclosed dual agency written consent:
   a. prior to entering into a written agency agreement
   b. when writing the purchase and sale agreement
   c. prior to the showing of property
   d. at the closing

9. The most common type of commission arrangement found in listing contracts is a:
   a. Percentage of sales price
   b. Flat fee
   c. Net listing
   d. Referral fee

10. The Real Estate Brokerage Relationships form must be given if the real estate consists of:
    a. Land only
    b. 1-4 residential dwelling units
    c. Both 1-4 residential dwelling units and land
    d. Both 1-4 residential dwelling units and commercial units

CHAPTER 5

IMPORTANT TERMINOLOGY

acceptance
accord and satisfaction
assignment
bilateral contract
bond for deed
breach of contract
buyer-agency agreement
carry-over clause
complete performance
conditional sale contract
consideration
consummation
contract
contract for deed
duress
earnest money
exclusive agency listing
exclusive right to sell listing
executed contract
executory contracts
express contract

fraud
implied contract
installment land contract
land contract
liquidated damages
listing contract
mutual agreement
novation
offeree
offeror
open listing
option to purchase
reality of consent
rescission
specific performance
Statute of Frauds
undue influence
unilateral contract
valid contract
voidable contract
void contract

FUNDAMENTALS OF CONTRACT LAW

IN THIS CHAPTER

Contracts play an extremely important part in the real estate business and are involved in the listing of property, the sale or exchange of property, the leasing of property, optioning of property, and property management. Nearly every controversy arising in the real estate business involves the contracts between parties and can be answered by applying basic contract law.

STATUTE OF FRAUDS

An oral contract may be just as valid and enforceable as a written contract. The difficulty with verbal contracts lies in the fact that they lead to misunderstanding of the rights and obligations of the parties, and they may be extremely difficult to prove in a court proceeding if that should become necessary.

Contracts involving the creation or conveyance of an interest in real property must be written to be enforceable. This requirement is created by the **Statute of Frauds**. Derived from an English statute by the same name, this statute requires that real estate contracts be written and contain all the elements essential for contract validity. Oral testimony will not suffice to create obligations under a contract involving transfer of title to real property. A primary purpose of the Statute of Frauds is to prevent fraudulent proof of an oral contract. Oral explanations can support the words of a contract but cannot contradict them.

The statute does not require any particular form of writing. To be sufficient to satisfy the requirements of the statute, the writing may be a short memorandum, a telegram, or a receipt. The contract need not necessarily be in one document. Several documents can be put together to create the contract. However, the best form is to have the entire contract in one writing and signed by the parties.

Examples of real estate contracts falling under the Statute of Frauds are contracts to buy and sell real estate, options, contracts for deed (also called installment contracts, land contracts, and conditional sale contracts), and contracts for the exchange of real estate. Also, lease contracts fall under the Statute of Frauds if the lease term exceeds the statutory time period in a particular state (more than one year in most states).

BASIC CONTRACT TERMS AND CLASSIFICATIONS

A **contract** is an agreement between competent legal parties to do some legal act in exchange for consideration. A contract establishes both the rights as well as the duties, or responsibilities, of the parties. Contracts can be classified as:

1. express versus implied
2. unilateral versus bilateral
3. executory versus executed
4. valid, voidable, or void

Express Contracts

An **express contract** is one in which the parties to the contract have definitely expressed all the terms and conditions as agreed upon between them. An express contract can be either oral or written. However, as we shall see subsequently, certain types of contracts must be in writing to be enforceable.

A real estate listing contract, a buyer agreement, and a real estate sales contract are examples of express contracts. All the terms and conditions of the contractual agreement are set forth in each of these contracts. The contracts are entered into expressly by the parties.

Implied Contracts

An **implied contract** is a contract that is inferred from the conduct and actions of the parties. Implied contracts are enforced when the conduct of the parties clearly illustrates their intention to contract. A court will imply a contract if a benefit has been received by one party at the expense of the other party. A court will require the recipient of the benefit to pay a reasonable compensation to the party rendering the benefit unless the benefit was actually a gift. These contracts arise most often in the agency relationship created by a listing. Under the listing, the seller and the real estate licensee have an express contract. Because the licensee may spend as much time with the buyer customer as with the seller, the buyer may infer that a contract for services exists between the buyer and the licensee. This may occur when the licensee is showing the property or in the negotiation of the offer.

Bilateral and Unilateral Contracts

A **bilateral contract** is one that is based on mutual exchange of promises or acts between the parties at the time the contract is signed. The contract to purchase a home is bilateral because it is based on the mutual promises of the seller to sell and of the buyer to buy.

In contrast, a **unilateral contract** arises when one party makes a promise to the other, and the second party returns an action for the promise. The party making the promise is bound and obligated under the contract. The other party, however, has made no promise and thus is not bound or obligated in any way to perform or act. The typical listing contract is described as unilateral because the seller promises a commission to the agency when the agency finds a buyer. If no buyer is found within the listing period, the homeowner owes no money to the agency.

Executed and Executory Contracts

A contract that has been fully performed by the parties is called an **executed contract**. All contracts that have not been fully performed are **executory contracts**. An example is a purchase and sale agreement prior to closing.

Valid Contracts

A **valid contract** is one that is binding and enforceable. The parties to a valid contract are legally obligated to abide by the terms and conditions of the contract. If a party to a valid contract defaults in the performance of obligations under the contract, the individual is subject to legal action by the other party or parties to the contract. In creating contracts, every effort should be made to ensure that a valid contract is created. When a contract complies with all the requirements of contract law it is a valid contract that is enforceable. The essential requirements or elements of a valid contract are

1. reality of consent
2. offer and acceptance (meeting of the minds)
3. consideration
4. capacity of the parties
5. legality of object

Reality of Consent

To create a valid contract, it must be entered into voluntarily by the parties. The parties must mutually agree to the terms and conditions in the contract. If a person has entered into a written contract, as evidenced by his signature on the contract, the individual is presumed to have assented to the terms and conditions of the contract.

The consent of the parties to enter into a contractual agreement must be a real consent. **Reality of consent** is based on the parties having an accurate knowledge of the facts concerning the terms and conditions of the contract. The failure of contract validity because of the lack of real and mutual consent by the parties results from the presence of mutual mistake, misrepresentation, fraud, undue influence, or duress.

Mutual mistake. A mistake of a material fact may nullify a contract. This does not cover a misunderstanding of the law by one party or the other. However, if an incorrect property description has been used, therefore identifying a property other than the one intended, the contract may be negated.

Misrepresentation. An unintentional *misrepresentation* occurs as a result of an innocent misconception as to the facts on the part of the person making the unintentional misrepresentation. A contracting party who has entered into a contract in reliance upon an unintentional misrepresentation of a material fact (important fact) is legally entitled to rescind the contract. The contract is voidable by any party who relied upon the unintentional misrepresentation as a basis for entering into the contract.

Fraud. **Fraud** is an intentional misrepresentation of a material fact made for the purpose of inducing someone to enter into a contract. If a party enters into a contract because of fraud, the defrauded party can avoid the contract. A false representation is deemed to be fraudulent when (1) a party making the representation knows it to be false or (2) the person making the false representation does not know in fact whether the statement is true or untrue and should have known that the statement is untrue.

If a real estate licensee, as agent of an owner of real property, commits an act of fraud, the injured party may rescind any contract entered into with the seller. Also, the agent is liable to the injured party and the seller for damages incurred.

Duress. The essential element of **duress** is that of fear or threat. One cannot be forced to sign a contract at gunpoint because this defeats the requirement for a voluntary meeting of the minds, or reality of consent. Duress introduced in the negotiation of the contract renders it voidable, thereby allowing the threatened person to escape the contract if she takes a positive action to do so.

Undue influence. **Undue influence** is any improper or wrongful influence by one person over another whereby the will of a person is overpowered so that he is induced to act or prevented from acting of free will. Undue influence occurs when one person takes advantage of another person's lack of mental ability or takes advantage of a special relationship between the parties that enables one party to have an unusual influence over the other party, as in the relationship between legal advisor and client or employer and employee. If a person is induced to enter a contract because undue influence is exerted, the individual may void the contract.

Offer and Acceptance

Each contract must contain an offer and an unconditional **acceptance** of the offer. Another name for offer and acceptance is *meeting of the minds.* The party making an offer is the **offeror** and the party to whom the offer is made is the **offeree**. Since an offer may be withdrawn at any time prior to acceptance, it is very important that any offer be expeditiously presented. The contract is created at the time of communication to the offeror or his/her agent that the offer has been unconditionally accepted in writing.

The offer must be *definite and specific* in its terms. If the offer is vague and indefinite and, therefore, subject to various interpretations, its acceptance will not result in the creation of a valid contract. For example, if an offer is made to a seller to purchase a house in the Executive Heights Subdivision without a specific property description and the seller actually owns three houses in that subdivision, the offer is vague and an acceptance will not result in the creation of a valid contract.

The offer also must not be *illusory* and, therefore, is not binding upon the offeror if accepted. For example, a person cannot offer to buy a seller's home in Pine Tree Estates if his offer is contingent upon his deciding whether he wants to live in Pine Tree Estates. Here the contract is not binding and is therefore illusory, since the offeror has complete control over whether to move to Pine Tree Estates. The acceptance of an illusory offer will not result in the creation of a valid contract.

If a unilateral offer is accepted, and becomes a contract, an action needs to be performed in order for the promise to be fulfilled. If a seller lists his property and agrees to pay a commission, his promise to pay is based on the actions by the listing company that was agreed to in the listing contract. If a bilateral offer is accepted, and becomes a contract, it means that each party exchanges promises to perform an action. In a real estate purchase and sale agreement, the buyer and seller exchange promises to buy and sell. In order for the offer to become a contract, the acceptance of the offer must be communicated to the offeror or her agent. The acceptance of either the bilateral or unilateral offer must be absolutely unconditional. If the acceptance varies in any way from the offer as presented, it will not qualify as an acceptance. Sometimes an offer will specify the manner in which the acceptance of the offer must be communicated to the offeror or his agent.

Offers may be terminated in the following ways:

1. by the expiration of a time limit specified by the offeror prior to written acceptance being communicated to the offeror or his/her agent
2. by the death or insanity of either the offeror or the offeree prior to written acceptance being communicated to the offeror or his/her agent
3. by the revocation of the offer by the offeror prior to written acceptance being communicated to the offeror or his/her agent
4. by the expiration of a "reasonable" period of time after the offer is made and prior to written acceptance communicated to the offeror or his/her agent
5. by the failure of the offeree to comply with the terms of the offer as to the specific manner in which the acceptance must be communicated
6. by the expiration of a power of attorney when either offeror or offeree are acting as attorney-in-fact under a power of attorney
7. by the rejection of the offer. If the offer is rejected, the seller can make a counteroffer, which is actually a new offer wherein the seller becomes the offeror and the prospective purchaser the offeree

8. by communicated acceptance of the signed offer by the offeree

When the offer is accepted in writing, and communicated to the other party or his/her agent, a contract is created.

Consideration

Consideration is the giving of value. Consideration must be present in every contract for the contract to be valid and enforceable. Consideration is anything of value, such as money, or may consist of a promise in return for the performance of a specified act, as is the case in unilateral contracts. Unless there are mutual promises in a bilateral contract, the contract will not be valid. For example, if one party promises to make a gift to another party, the contract will not be enforceable because the one to receive the gift has furnished no consideration. There must be mutuality. Each party to the contract must do something or promise to do something.

Capacity of the Parties

The parties to a contract must have contractual capacity. They must be legally competent to contract. Most people possess contractual capacity; therefore, this subject is discussed by pointing out those who do not: minors and mental incompetents. Minors are those who have not reached the age of majority as established by statutory law in each particular state. In Maine, the age of majority is eighteen. The exception is for married minors, who have limited contractual capacity though they are below the age of eighteen. Married minors have the right to own property and to sell, mortgage, or convey it. They do not have the legal capacity to make binding contracts to purchase property.

If either party to the contract is incompetent, the contract is voidable or dischargeable by the incompetent party and unenforceable against the incompetent. In the case of minors, the contract is voidable at the option of the minor. The minor may hold an adult to a contract but the adult cannot legally hold the minor to the contract. The contract is not legally enforceable against the minor. A minor may fulfill the terms of the contract and, if he does, and does not take steps to terminate the contract after reaching the age of majority, the individual is said to have ratified the contract as an adult and it will be binding. If a party to a contract is intoxicated or under the influence of drugs at the time of entering into the contract so that the person does not understand what is happening, the individual is considered temporarily mentally incompetent to contract and, therefore, the contract will be unenforceable against the person.

Lawful Objective

The contract must be for a legal purpose. A contract for an illegal purpose is void. Examples of illegal contracts include contracts to sell a public office, contracts in restraint of trade, contracts to promote litigation or stifle prosecution, and contracts that restrain freedom to marry.

Voidable Contracts

A **voidable contract** results from failure to meet some legal requirement in negotiating the agreement. One of the parties may elect to void the contract by stating this intention, or she may go ahead and consummate the agreement. For example, if a buyer contracted to purchase a house that was represented to be 2,000 square feet and later found that the actual size was only 1,800 square feet, she could either elect to void the contract or take the house anyway. A contract entered into by a party lacking capacity is voidable by the party lacking the capacity. For example, if the party does not have the mental/emotional capacity to contract, the contract is not enforceable against the party. If the contract was entered into with a minor, the minor may hold the adult to a contract, but the adult cannot legally hold the minor to the contract.

The parties to a voidable contract are not required to discontinue or void the contract. The parties to a voidable contract may fulfill their obligations under the contract and receive their benefits. A voidable contract can be voluntarily performed by the parties. However, at any time prior to complete performance of the contract, the disadvantaged party can elect to discontinue.

Void Contracts

A **void contract** is one that is absolutely unenforceable and has no legal force or effect. If a contract is void, it is void as to all the parties to the contract. If the contract is impossible to complete, it is void; it does not exist. The impossibility to complete can occur if the object of the contract is destroyed by fire, flood, tornado, or other natural or legal causes. If the state condemns the property for a highway, neither party can sue the other for failing to complete the contract. By comparison, a voidable contract is one that can be voided by one or more parties to the contract. A void contract has no legal force or effect from its inception, whereas a voidable contract is not voided until some party to the contract takes action to create this result.

TERMINATION OF CONTRACTS

Contracts may be terminated by

1. agreement of the parties
2. full performance
3. impossibility of performance
4. operation of law

Agreement of the Parties

Executory contracts may be terminated by the **mutual agreement** of all parties to the contract. The release of each party by the other supplies the consideration. The following are forms of agreement.

Accord and Satisfaction

An accord and satisfaction is a new agreement between the parties, often in the form of some compromise, that replaces the original agreement. The situation may arise where the buyer wants to get out of a purchase agreement, that is, default on the contract. A compromise may be reached wherein the seller agrees to accept an amount of earnest money as substitution for full performance of the buyer. The agent should never presume such an agreement unless clear, written intention of the parties is obtained, which would best be done in consultation with their respective attorneys. Maine license law puts a clear burden on the agent to satisfy certain requirements before disbursing money in the trust account.

Novation

A **novation** is the substitution of a new contract for a prior contract or the substitution of a new party for an old party. A new party to the contract agrees to satisfy a former contracting party's obligation to another party in a previous contract. When the novation (new contract) is created, the old contract is discharged.

Full Performance

The usual manner of terminating contracts is by **complete performance.** When all the terms of the contract have been fully performed by all parties, the contract is executed and terminated.

Impossibility of Performance

The general rule is that even though it is impossible for a party to a contract to perform obligations under the contract, the party is still not relieved of liability. The reasoning behind this is that the one who cannot perform should have provided against this possibility by a provision in the contract relieving her from liability.

There are exceptions to the general rule. One exception is in the case of a personal service contract. If a person contracts to render services to another person that cannot be rendered by someone else, the person obligated to render the service is relieved from liability in the event that the individual dies or becomes incapacitated so that he cannot render the service. Another exception to the general rule occurs when the performance of an obligation under a contract becomes illegal as a result of a change in law after the contract was created. As a result, the obligated parties are relieved of responsibility.

Operation of Law

The term *operation of law* describes the manner in which the rights or liabilities or both of parties may be changed by the application of law without the act or cooperation of the parties affected. The following are examples of discharge of contracts by operation of law.

1. Statute of limitations. The time within which a legal action may be brought against a party to a contract by another party to the contract is limited by statute in every state. The statutes are called *statutes of limitations.* If a party to a contract fails to bring a lawsuit against a defaulting party to a contract within the statutory time period, the right of legal remedy is lost to the injured party by operation of law brought about by the expiration of the time period specified in a statute of limitations.
2. Bankruptcy. The filing of a petition in bankruptcy under federal law has the effect of terminating contracts. Bankruptcy law relieves the bankrupt from liability under contracts to which she is a party as of the date of filing the bankruptcy petition with the federal court. The purpose of bankruptcy law is to provide a fresh start to the bankrupt.

ASSIGNMENT OF CONTRACTS

Either party to a contract may transfer or sell the contract rights unless the contract specifically prohibits such a sale or transfer. The **assignment** of the contract, however, does not relieve the *assignor* of the responsibility for performance in the event that the *assignee* fails to perform, unless the assignor has been specifically released by the other contracting party who accepts the assignee in place of the assignor. A typical assignment in real estate happens when a landlord sells rental property to a new owner. Sale of the property does not terminate the lease. The new owner not only owns the real estate but also has been assigned the old owner's rights under the lease to rent.

REMEDIES UPON BREACH OF CONTRACT

The term **breach of contract** may be defined as "failure, without legal excuse, to perform any promise which forms the whole or part of a contract." The effect of the breach of contractual obligations by a party to a contract is to terminate the contract. However, the breach does not terminate the right to legal remedies against the defaulting party by the injured party.

Compensatory Damages

The injured party in a breach of contract is entitled to receive compensation for any financial loss caused by the breach as may be awarded by a court. This is called *compensatory damages*, and is the amount the court is asked to award.

The court determines the amount of compensatory damages that should be sufficient to put the innocent party in the same economic position they would have been in if the contract had been performed as agreed upon by the parties to the contract.

Specific Performance

Another remedy may be that of **specific performance**. Every parcel of land has a unique value that cannot be substituted for by any other commodity. Therefore, if one signals an intention to breach the contract to convey title to real property under a valid written contract, the legal remedy enforced by the courts will probably be to require the **consummation** of the specific contract as agreed. Monetary damages cannot substitute for the unique value of land in a given location. Therefore, the prospective purchaser may insist on title to the property in place of any other remedy.

Rescission

Rescission is a legal remedy of annulling the contract. In essence, a rescission cancels the contract and restores the parties to their original positions prior to the contract. A party may seek to rescind the contract due to a mistake, fraud, or misrepresentation. If a buyer was led to believe that the size of the property was fourteen acres and subsequently learned that the property is only nine acres, he may seek rescission. He would have a refund of all money and there would be no obligation on either buyer or seller to complete the transaction.

Liquidated Money Damages

Contracts include remedies each party has if the other party breaches the contract. These specified remedies are called **liquidated damages**. A common clause is that the buyer forfeits her deposit if she fails to go through with the purchase. The liquidated damages must be reasonable compared with the damage caused by the breach of contract. If the court feels the damages are punitive rather than reasonable, it may not enforce the damages.

LISTING CONTRACTS

The first contract that we encounter in the real estate business is the **listing contract**. A listing contract is a contract whereby the owner of property employs a real estate agency to find a buyer for his property. This contract creates an agency relationship in which the seller is the principal and the broker is the seller's special agent for this particular purpose. If a buyer hires a licensee to obtain property that she may purchase, the licensee is the agent of the buyer who is her principal.

Most states require the listing contract to be in writing because contracts for the conveyance of title must be written; and since listing contracts relate to the sale of real property, they must also be in writing. An exclusive right to sell, an exclusive agency, and a nonexclusive listing agreement must be in writing under Maine law.

Also, it is required that the listing contract be in writing for the broker to be eligible to receive a commission. The broker must prove the existence of an employment contract. A written contract clearly spells out the fact that the broker has actually been hired by the seller and sets forth all the terms and conditions of employment. The requirement for the listing contract to be in writing substantially reduces lawsuits between brokers and property owners concerning matters of the broker's employment.

There are three types of listing contracts in general use. These are the open listing, the exclusive agency listing, and the exclusive right to sell listing. Each gives different rights to the broker and seller. A brief description of each type of listing contract follows.

Open Listing

Under an **open listing**, the seller lists a property with the assistance of one or more agencies. The agency effecting the sale is entitled to the commission. However, if the owner sells the property (not to a prospect generated by a licensee), the owner owes no commission.

This type of listing is not beneficial to the owner or the agency. Usually, an agency cannot afford to spend advertising dollars and sales staff on an open listing. The agency is competing with the owner and with every other agency who has an open listing on the property or who may learn about the availability of the property and obtain an open listing. This type of listing also can lead to disputes over commissions between agencies and can present legal problems for the owner.

All too often, a licensee may rely on an open listing that is simply oral. Although many states do allow such listings, an oral open listing is double trouble. At the very minimum, the licensee should strive to get a written statement of the listing terms and employment authority.

Exclusive Agency Listing

In an **exclusive agency listing**, the property is listed exclusively with one agency. This is the basis for the name "exclusive" listing. If a licensee with that agency effects a sale of the property, she is legally entitled to the commission agreed upon. However, under this type of listing, if the owner sells the property, then the agency earns no commission.

This type of listing is somewhat better than the open listing in that only one agency is involved. However, the agency is still competing with the owner. The agency's advertising programs, including the office's "For Sale" sign on the property, may generate prospects for the owner.

Exclusive Right to Sell Listing

An **exclusive right to sell listing** is the best type of listing contract from both the standpoint of the agency and the seller. Under this listing contract, the property is exclusively listed with only one agency. If the property is sold by anyone during the term of the listing contract, the agency is legally entitled to the commission. The seller is legally obligated to pay the agency's commission if the licensee or the seller or some third party effects a sale of the property during the term of the listing contract.

The exclusive right to sell listing contract benefits the owner because the agency is secure enough in the opportunity to earn a commission that it can afford to spend time and advertising dollars to effect a quick and satisfactory sale of the listed property. Also, with the agreement of the seller, the agency may put the listing in a multiple listing service and thereby provide significantly increased market exposure for the property. Figure 5.1 shows an exclusive right to sell listing contract. In this type of contract, the broker promises to do the following: (1) to attempt to procure a buyer, (2) to take all actions considered appropriate to effect a satisfactory sale of the property, including advertising the property during the listing term, and (3) to provide the owner the benefit of the office staff's knowledge of financing, surveying, and other real estate matters. Additionally, the broker promises to enter the listing in the multiple listing service.

Figure 5.1 is broken down into 11 numbered sections for reference to the following discussion of the contract.

Elements of an Exclusive Right to Sell Contract

1. The property description includes the number and street address, city or town and state, and a reference to the deed.
2. It specifies the listing price of the property.
3. The rate of commission agreed to should be stated either as a percentage of the sales price of the property or a flat fee.
4. The definite term of the listing contract with the inception and expiration dates is clearly stated. The license law specifies that the listing agreement contains an expiration date.
5. The **carry-over clause** provides for the broker's commission in the event of a sale to a prospect who was shown the property during the listing period, but who decided to purchase it after the expiration. The language must include the date upon which all of the broker's rights are terminated, which cannot extend over six months. If the listing agreement expires and the property is listed in good faith with another real estate agency in an exclusive right to sell, the carry-over clause is void.
6. Agency's policy on cooperation and compensation makes the seller aware of the co-brokerage practice of the agency.
7. Fair Housing Clause is often included.
8. Other clauses in the agreement may give permission to the agent to act on behalf of the sellers, such as to place a sign on the property, and to place it in a multiple listing service, and the agency relationships the seller will authorize.
9. A section on other conditions would contain any special conditions specifically asked for by the sellers, or special permission needed by the broker.
10. A copy of the listing contract signed by the sellers (everyone on the deed) should be given to the sellers immediately upon signing. A copy should be retained for the broker's office and a copy should be available for the area multiple listing service if such services are going to be used.
11. Agent's signature implies that the agency has accepted this listing.

BUYER-AGENCY AGREEMENT

The **buyer-agency agreement** is a contract between a prospective home buyer and a real estate company in which the company agrees to locate property for and negotiate in the best interest of the buyer. This contract creates an agency relationship between the buyer and the company. This agreement is required to create a client-agent relationship.

Figure 5.1 Listing agreement.

ABC REALTY
123 PROGRESSION LANE, UPTOWN, MAINE 00000
TEL: 207-555-5555   FAX: 207-555-5556

EXCLUSIVE RIGHT TO SELL AGREEMENT

TO: ABC REALTY of Portland, Maine (hereinafter called "Company"). We, the undersigned, _____
_____(hereinafter called "Seller") hereby retain the
Company to represent me/us in attempting to produce a Buyer for Seller's real estate, located at_____
_____
(hereinafter called "Property") consisting of _____
_____ recorded   at
the_____County Registry of Deeds in Book_____, and Page_____, do hereby give
and grant to Company the EXCLUSIVE RIGHT TO SELL said property at a gross selling price of ($_____)
_____. The EXCLUSIVE RIGHT TO SELL AGREEMENT hereby given
shall begin on_____continue in full force and effect to_____at midnight.
   Seller understands that if a Buyer is produced by Company, Seller or anyone else during said period, which Buyer is ready, willing and able to purchase said Property on the terms of sale herein set forth, or on modified terms acceptable to Seller, Seller shall pay Company directly from closing proceeds a negotiated fee of_____per cent of the aforesaid listing price, or any other price to which Seller may agree. Seller hereby authorizes anyone handling said closing to pay said fee from the closing proceeds.
   Seller further agrees that if within six (6) months after the termination date of the rights herein given, Property is sold, conveyed, transferred or exchanged to any party with whom Broker has held negotiations, or to whom Company provided information, or shown said Property, Company will be deemed to be effective and producing cause of such sale, conveyance, transfer or exchange, and Company shall be entitled to receive the above stated fee upon demand unless an EXCLUSIVE RIGHT TO SELL AGREEMENT, on said Property, has been given to another real estate company. Termination date of this carryover is_____at midnight.
   Company is authorized (1) to accept all earnest money deposits and to place them in a special trust account as provided by law, (2) to place Company 's regular "For Sale" sign upon Property, (3) to otherwise advertise Property for sale including a multiple listing service, (4) to use information for marketing and statistical purposes, (5) to have a key to the building and to install a lockbox and (6) to show Property at reasonable times, (7) to disclose the existence of offers to buyers and other Affiliated Licensees.
   Seller agrees to convey Property by good and sufficient_____deed.
   Seller certifies that Property is not listed with any other real estate company and agrees to refer to Company during term of this agreement all inquires of other brokers or parties interested in Property.
   Occupancy to Property shall be given _____
   Personal property included in the selling price; _____
   Real property excluded from selling price: _____
   It is the policy of the Company to cooperate with, and compensate, buyers agents and transaction brokers. The Company will compensate all buyer agents and transaction brokers the same.
   Affiliated Licensees do not receive a higher commission split for selling in-house listings.
   Seller acknowledges that the Affiliated Licensee has informed Seller of his/her disclosure and certification obligations regarding the presence of lead based paint and lead based paint hazards and a Buyer's right to conduct an inspection or risk assessment of the property to determine the presence of lead based paint or lead based paint hazards.

SPECIAL CONDITIONS; _____

Notice to out of state sellers. You may have 2 1/2 % of the sale price deducted from the sales proceeds as a withholding for Maine income tax due. Consult your attorney, or tax advisor if this is an area of concern for you.

THE COMPANY AND OWNER EACH AGREE THAT THIS PROPERTY WILL BE OFFERED IN COMPLIANCE WITH ALL FEDERAL, STATE AND LOCAL FAIR HOUSING AND CIVIL RIGHTS LAWS.

This is a legally binding document. You are advised to consult an Attorney before signing. This creates an agency/client relationship.

   It is important to the Company that you have read and completely understand this document. By signing this document you are acknowledging you have read it, understand it and sign it willingly, as your free and voluntary act. Signature on this document acknowledges receipt of a copy of this document.

_____   _____   _____
Affiliated Licensee for ABC Realty   Seller   Date

                                                             _____   _____
                                                             Seller   Date
COPYRIGHT © 2015 Professional Education Services, Inc., 396 Cumberland Street, Westbrook, ME 04092

It is required that the buyer-agency agreement be in writing and that it outline the obligation of all parties, the method of broker compensation, and whether the agreement will be an exclusive, exclusive agency, or open agency contract. An exclusive agreement binds the buyer to compensate the agent if the buyer purchases a property within the time period set forth by the contract, regardless of whether the agent showed the property to the buyer. An exclusive agency agreement assures the agent of loyalty relative to other agents, but it allows the buyer to buy on his own without paying compensation to the broker. An open agreement allows the buyer to work with several agents and owe compensation only for services used.

The elements of a Buyer Agreement:

The contract sets forth the names of the buyers and the company they are retaining.

It states the time of commencement and duration of the agency relationship. The duration will depend on the type of property desired, the buyers' specific requirements in a property, and the market conditions.

It outlines the obligations and responsibilities of the agent.

It covers the buyer's responsibilities and explains his role in the transaction.

The contract establishes a retainer fee and payment for services.

Other conditions, such as what properties are covered in the contract.

There may be a section of the contract which contains a fair housing clause.

PURCHASE AND SALE AGREEMENT

Once a real estate licensee has obtained employment authority as evidenced by the executed listing contract, her efforts are directed toward obtaining a buyer for the listed property. The licensee must find a buyer that the property satisfies and who either has the purchase price or is able to obtain the necessary financing. Once such a buyer is located by the licensee, the licensee presents an offer to purchase the property on behalf of the buyer to the listed seller.

Figure 5.3 (pp. 80–82) is the purchase and sale agreement. The offer is created when the purchaser signs the document. The licensee will usually ask for a substantial deposit as **earnest money** with the offer, but this deposit is not required to generate a valid contract. The promise of the buyer to pay the stated amount is sufficient legal consideration to create a contract when accepted by the seller. There are, however, three main purposes for the earnest money: (1) to demonstrate the buyer is sincere (earnest), (2) to demonstrate his financial capability to raise the money called for in the agreement, and (3) to serve as compensation to the seller in the event of default by the buyer.

Elements of a Purchase and Sale Agreement:

The contract has a place for two dates; the date the contract is written by the buyer and the effective date of the contract. If the purchasers are real estate licensees, this should be disclosed. (Example: John Smith, Real Estate Broker.)

The names of the buyers and sellers are stated.

There is a property description which should be accurate and complete enough to identify the property. Buyers and sellers should be aware that fixtures are a part of the property to be conveyed unless otherwise stipulated in the contract. If items of personal property are to be part of the sale, they should be clearly stated. (Example: washer and dryer.)

The contract establishes the purchase price agreed to by the seller and purchaser and the method of full payment.

It explains who will hold the earnest money deposit and the time limit for the seller's decision on whether to accept the buyer's offer. If earnest money is given with the offer, it must be placed in the trust account within five days of the effective date of the contract.

Figure 5.2 Exclusive buyer representation agreement.

ABC REALTY
123 PROGRESSION LANE, UPTOWN, MAINE 00000
TEL: 207-555-5555   FAX: 207-555-5556

EXCLUSIVE RIGHT TO BUY REAL PROPERTY

Retainer agreement: The undersigned buyer clients hereby retain ABC REALTY (hereafter referred to as Company) to represent me/us, for a period commencing_____and terminating at midnight of_____, 20___. Company agrees to search for real property, or properties, of a nature outlined below, and to negotiate terms and conditions for the purchase of such property acceptable to buyers.

Company, during the term of this agreement, will:
1) Diligently seek available real property of a nature suitable to buyers as described below.
2) Assist buyers throughout any transaction(s) in the purchase of real property. Buyers understand that the Company may represent other buyers on the same properties that buyers may have an interest in purchasing.
3) To the best of Company's ability, counsel buyers as to the estimated market value on negotiated properties.
4) Personally present all offers to sellers with seller's permission.
5) Cooperate with, and compensate when appropriate, buyer agents, sellers agents and transaction brokers in locating real property for you under this agreement.

Buyer clients, during the term of this agreement, will:
1) Work exclusively with Company and will be represented by Company in all matters pertaining to the location, negotiation and purchase of real property during the term of this agreement.
2) Furnish Company with all requested personal and financial information necessary to complete this transaction.

Payment of company: If buyer client purchase any real property of a nature described below and located during the term of this agreement, buyer client agree that Company will represent buyers in such purchase and will assure Company, at the closing, a fee as follows:
1) If property is listed with a licensed real estate agency, Company will receive a fee of ($_____) _____
_____or_____% of the sale price.
2) If the property is not listed with a licensed real estate agency, Company will receive a fee of ($_____) _____
_____or_____% of the sale price.
3) Buyer authorizes Company to request payment of professional fee from the seller's listing company or the seller: YES_____NO_____.

Further, the fee will be due and payable if:
1) Prior to the expiration date of this agreement, a property is procured by buyer clients at a purchase price and terms acceptable to buyers, or
2) After the expiration date of this agreement and during the 6 months thereafter (terminating on_____, 20_____) buyer client buys a property he/she was shown, or made aware of, by the Company during the term of the agreement, unless buyers sign an EXCLUSIVE BUYER'S AGREEMENT with another Company after this agreement has been terminated, or
3) During the period of this agreement, buyer client purchases or agrees to purchase a property himself and buyer closes on said property.
   The Company will compensate all buyer agents and transaction brokers the same.
   Affiliated Licensees do not receive a higher commission split for selling in-house listings.
   This creates an agency/client relationship.

Additional terms, conditions or special arrangements:

Type of Property:_____   Price Range: _____

Location:_____   Other Requirements: _____

It is the policy of_____to abide by all local, state and federal fair housing laws and not discriminate against any individual or group of individuals. The licensee may not lawfully disclose the racial, ethnic or religious composition of any neighborhood, community, or building, nor whether persons with disabilities are housed in any home or facility, except that the licensee may identify housing facilities meeting needs of a disable buyer. This is a legally binding document.

    It is important to the Company that you have read and completely understand this document. By signing this document you are acknowledging you have read it, understand it and sign it willingly, as your free and voluntary act. Signature on this document acknowledges receipt of a copy of this document.

_____
Affiliated Licensee for ABC REALTY

_____   _____
Buyer   Date

_____   _____
Buyer   Date

_____
Address

_____

_____
Phone

Figure 5.3 Purchase and sale agreement.

ABC REALTY
123 PROGRESSION LANE, UPTOWN, MAINE 00000
TEL: 207-555-5555   FAX: 207-555-5556
CONTRACT FOR SALE OF REAL ESTATE

_____, 20 _____

1. BUYER(S), SELLER(S) AND PROPERTY DESCRIPTION: Received of _____

whose address is_____(hereinafter

called "Buyer") the sum of ($_____)_____dollars as earnest money deposit

☐ to be delivered with this offer, ☐ to be delivered within_____days of the acceptance of this offer, and _____

_____ shall receive, and hold, the Deposit and act as trustee. Said Deposit shall be

part payment on account of the purchase price of the real estate owned by _____located at

_____in the city/town of _____County of _____

State of Maine, to wit: _____

_____

being all   part of   the property owned by the Seller at said address and described at said County's Registry of Deeds in Book_____

Page_____. If part of, see Section 20 "Other conditions" for an explanation.

2. FIXTURES AND PERSONAL PROPERTY INCLUDED IN THE SALE: Included with the sale are all fixtures (including but not limited to existing storm and screen windows, shades and/or blinds, shutters, curtain rods, electrical fixtures, built-in appliances,) and the following personal property at no additional cost to the buyer:

_____

3. FIXTURES NOT INCLUDED IN THE SALE: The following fixtures are not included in the sale of said property: _____

_____

4. PURCHASE PRICE AND FINANCING: The total purchase price shall be ($_____) _____

_____dollars to be paid as follows: Entire purchase price payable in cash or certified check at the time of closing, subject to Buyer obtaining a/an_____mortgage in the amount of_____% of the purchase price at an interest rate not to exceed_____% amortized over a period of not less than_____years. Buyer to pay origination fee and/or discount points not to exceed_____and Seller to pay_____toward the Buyer's points, closing costs and/or prepaids. Buyer shall apply for said mortgage within_____days of the effective date of contract. Buyer shall provide the Seller, within_____days of the effective date of this agreement, with a mortgage commitment letter from lender showing that the Buyer has secured the loan commitment. If Buyer fails to provide Seller with this mortgage commitment letter within said period, Seller may deliver a notice to the Buyer that this agreement is terminated three days after delivery of such notice, unless Buyer delivers the mortgage commitment letter before the end of the three day period. If this agreement is terminated under the provision of this sub-paragraph, the earnest money shall be returned to the Buyer. Buyer is under a good faith obligation to actively seek, and accept, financing on the above terms, and acknowledges that a breach of the good faith obligation will be a breach of this contract. If necessary, Buyer shall seek financing from more than one source to obtain financing under the terms and conditions set forth in this contract. If Buyer decides to pay cash, instead of finance this transaction, Buyer shall provide Seller with proof of funds to close within the time above for mortgage commitment letter.

5. SALE OF ANOTHER PROPERTY: This contract is subject to the buyer's sale of another property_____yes_____no.

6. LENGTH OF OFFER AND CLOSING DATE: This offer shall be valid until_____(date)_____AM/PM for obtaining Offeree's acceptance; and in the event of Offeree's non-acceptance, the Deposit shall be returned to Buyer. Buyer shall pay the balance of the purchase price and execute all papers necessary for the completion of this purchase on_____, or any other date the Buyer and Seller shall agree to in writing.

_____	_____	_____	_____
Buyer	Date	Seller	Date
_____	_____	_____	_____
Buyer	Date	Seller	Date

Figure 5.3 continued

7. TITLE: A deed showing good and merchantable title shall be delivered to Buyer at time of closing. Should title to the property prove to be unmarketable, Seller, after written notice from Buyer of the defect(s) causing such unmarketability, shall have thirty days (unless otherwise agreed to, in writing, by both parties at the time the defect is discovered) to remedy the defect(s). If defect(s) is/are not corrected so there is marketable title, then Buyer may, at Buyer's option, elect to void said contract and be relieved from all obligations hereunder. If Buyer declares this contract void as a result of this sub-paragraph, Seller agrees that all earnest money shall be returned to the Buyer.

8. DEED: Property shall be conveyed by_____deed and shall be free and clear of all encumbrances except zoning and building restrictions of record, restrictive covenants of record and usual public utilities servicing the property.

9. OCCUPANCY: Occupancy of the property shall be given_____at which time premises shall be in the same condition as at present, excepting only reasonable use and wear. Said premises shall be broom clean, free of all possessions and debris, and in substantially the same condition as at present, accepting reasonable use and wear.

10. RISK OF LOSS OR DAMAGE: The risk of loss or damage to said premises by fire or otherwise until the closing is assumed by the Seller. Seller shall keep the premises insured against fire and other extended casualty risks prior to the closing. If the premises is damaged or destroyed prior to the closing, Buyer may either terminate this agreement and be refunded the earnest money, or close this transaction and accept the premises "as-is" together with an assignment of the insurance proceeds relating thereto.

11. BUYER'S RIGHT TO VIEW PROPERTY BEFORE CLOSING: Buyer shall have the right to view the property within 24 hours prior to closing for the purpose of determining that the premises is in substantially the same condition as on the date of this agreement.

12. PRO-RATIONS: The following items shall be prorated as of date of closing:
    (a) Real Estate taxes for the current municipal year_____Yes_____No,
    (b) Fuel___Yes___No, if yes price will be_____cash price day of closing,
    (c) Rents___Yes___No,
    (d) Condo, association and/or road maintenance fees___Yes___No.
    (e) Other_____.

13. MEDIATION: Any dispute or claim arising out of or relating to this contract or the property addressed in this contract shall be submitted to mediation in accordance with Maine Residential Real Estate Mediation Rules. This clause shall survive the closing of this transaction.

14. HEIRS AND ASSIGNS: All covenants and agreements herein contained shall extend to and be obligatory upon the heirs, executors, administrators, successors and assigns of the respective parties.

15. AGENCY DISCLOSURE; The Buyer(s) and Seller(s) acknowledge that they have been informed that the Selling Licensee is acting as a _____in this transaction and that the Listing Licensee is acting as a _____ in this transaction.

16. INSPECTIONS AND DUE DILIGENCE: Buyer acknowledges receipt of written disclosures about water supply, heating system(s), waste disposal system and hazardous materials. The following inspection(s) will be performed by qualified inspectors chosen, and paid for, by Buyer with results satisfactory to Buyer. If results of any inspection are unsatisfactory to Buyer, Buyer may notify Seller, in writing, within the specified number of days, that the inspections are unsatisfactory and declare the contract void. If the Buyer declares this contract void as a result of an inspection, the Earnest Money shall be returned to the Buyer. If the results of any inspection or other condition specified herein is unsatisfactory to Buyer, and Buyer wishes to pursue remedies other than voiding this Agreement, Buyer must do so to full resolution within the time period set forth below; otherwise the inspection or condition is waived. All written notices of unsatisfactory inspections shall include copies of the inspection reports that reference the unsatisfactory area(s). If Buyer does not notify Seller of an unsatisfactory inspection within the time period set forth below, this contingency is waived by Buyer. In absence of inspection (s) mentioned below, Buyer is relying completely upon Buyer's own opinion as to the property's condition. All time limits in this section are from the effective date of this contract.

Type of Inspection	Yes	No	Results to Seller	Type of inspection	Yes	No	Results to Seller
a. General Building	____	____	within___days	m. Flood maps	____	____	within___days
b. Environmental Scan	____	____	within___days	n. GLAAG	____	____	within___days
c. Sewage Disposal	____	____	within___days	o. Arsenic Treated Wood	____	____	within___days
d. Radon Water Quality	____	____	within___days	p. Pool	____	____	within___days
e. Radon Air Quality	____	____	within___days	q. Insurance Availability	____	____	within___days
f. Water Quality	____	____	within___days	r. Zoning/Shoreland	____	____	within___days
g. Water Quantity	____	____	within___days	s. Code Conformance	____	____	within___days
h. Asbestos	____	____	within___days	t. Mold	____	____	within___days
i. Air Quality	____	____	within___days	u. Heating system(s)	____	____	within___days
j. Lead Paint	____	____	within___days	v. Chimney	____	____	within___days
k. Underground Storage Tanks	____	____	within___days	w. Habitat review	____	____	within___days
l. Pest	____	____	within___days	x. Other	____	____	within___days

_____   _____
Buyer   Date   Seller   Date

_____   _____
Buyer   Date   Seller   Date

Figure 5.3 continued

17. DEFAULT: Should Buyer fails to make any of the payments or any part thereof, including timely payment of earnest money deposits, or to perform any of the covenants on Buyer's part, this Contract shall, at the option of Seller, be terminated and Buyer shall forfeit the Earnest Money Deposit and the trustee is hereby authorized by Buyer to pay over to Seller the deposit. Seller may also employ all available legal remedies. In the event of the Seller's default, the Buyer may employ any and all available legal remedies.

18. NON-RESIDENT WITHHOLDING: Seller is aware that Maine law requires the Buyer to withhold 2 ½% of the sale price, at closing, unless Seller certifies, in writing, that Seller is a resident of Maine at the time of closing, or is otherwise exempt from the state withholding provisions.

19. SHORELAND ZONE: This property ☐ is ☐ is not in a Shoreland Zone.

20. RELEASE OF CONFIDENTIAL INFORMATION: Buyer (s) and Seller (s) hereby give the Company permission to disclose the contents of this document to those people who need access to the information in this document in order to close this transaction. These people include, but are not limited to, attorneys, lenders, appraisers, inspectors, real estate Company's secretaries and managers. Buyer(s) and Seller(s) also authorize the closing agent to provide a closing disclosure to the real estate companies involved in this transaction.

21. LITIGATION: In the event that the Company becomes party to a lawsuit as a result of acting as trustee for the earnest money deposit or any other matter in connection with this contract, the Company shall be entitled to recover all reasonable attorney's and court fees and costs that may be assessed to the Company.

22. FULL AGREEMENT: All representations, statements and agreements entered into by the parties to this agreement are contained herein. This is the full agreement between the parties and it supersedes all previous agreements between the parties whether these agreements were verbal or in writing. All parties to this agreement have had full opportunity to investigate any issues of concern unless contained as a condition in this agreement. The undersigned parties are not relying on statements, or representations, not contained in this agreement.

23. COUNTERPARTS: This agreement may be signed on any number of identical counterparts, such as faxed copies, with the same binding effect as if the signatures were on one instrument. Original, faxed and email signatures are binding.

24. HOME SERVICE CONTRACT: At the closing, the property ☐ will ☐ will not be covered by a Home Warranty Insurance Program to be paid by the ☐ Seller ☐ Buyer at the price of $ _____ .

25. EFFECTIVE DATE: Buyer and Seller hereby give the licensees the right to enter the effective date of this contract on the bottom of this page. The effective date shall be the date upon which the Buyer and Seller have both signed, or initialed as appropriate, this document and the Buyer and Seller or their respective agents, have been notified of the signatures. The first day of all time periods in this document shall be counted as the day following the referenced day. All day shall end at 11:59PM of the specific referenced day.

26. ADDENDA: Refer to Addenda for continuation of Contract._____No_____Yes # s _____

27. OTHER CONDITIONS: This contract shall be subject to the following conditions: _____

_____

_____

_____

_____

A COPY OF THIS CONTRACT IS TO BE RECEIVED BY ALL PARTIES AND BY SIGNATURE, RECEIPT OF A COPY IS HEREBY ACKNOWLEDGED. THIS IS A LEGALLY BINDING DOCUMENT.

Buyer hereby agrees to purchase the Property at the price and upon the terms and conditions set forth herein.

Witness	Date	Buyer

Witness	Date	Buyer

Seller hereby accepts and agrees to deliver the Property at the price and upon terms and conditions above stated and agrees to pay the Listing Company the amount stated in the Brokerage Agreement for professional services rendered, and hereby authorizes the closing agent to pay said fee directly from the closing proceeds. In the event said earnest money deposit is forfeited by Buyer, one-half shall go to said Company, provided however that the Company's portion shall not exceed the full amount of the commission fee specified. If there is no brokerage agreement with the seller, the professional fee shall be paid as agreed in this contract, or as agreed to in writing with the Buyer.

Witness	Date	Seller

Witness	Date	Seller

Offer refused _____   Effective Date (Final Acceptance Date) _____

Page three of three

It sets forth the type of deed to be granted.

The agreement explains that, unless otherwise agreed, occupancy will be given immediately at closing. This is a crucial item to be explained to the seller, who often has the misconception that she is allowed to stay in the house after closing. If there is an agreement to the effect that the seller occupies after closing, rent payment should be discussed and agreement reached in the contract.

There is a section of the agreement which states that the responsible party will be the seller if the property to be conveyed is destroyed or damaged. If the seller cannot replace or repair the property before the closing time, the buyer is not obligated to complete the purchase.

The items to be prorated are identified.

It stipulates that the buyer will have to rely on his own opinion as to the condition of the property, if the buyer fails to indicate on the contract that he wishes to get experts in the fields of radon, asbestos, and so on, to assess the conditions.

One of the most important conditions of the contract is financing. Prior to the writing of the offer, the licensee has qualifying information about the purchaser and is aware of the type of financing, interest rate, and term of the mortgage that a lending institution would approve.

The agreement sets forth the consequences of a breach of contract, including the obligation of both parties to submit to mediation in the case of a dispute.

States that all agreements by the parties must be contained in this contract.

Even though there is an assigning clause in most agreements, the contract may still be assigned without permission from the parties.

Counterparts such as faxed copies are binding.

The agreement contains a definition of the effective date. This date is extremely important because many contingencies in the contract use the effective date as the starting point. For example, this contract is subject to final approval within_____days of the Effective Date.

The terms of the contract are confidential except those parties mentioned.

The agreement allows for a possible extension of the contract in the case that a contingency cannot be met within the time frame of the contract.

BOND FOR DEED

The **bond for deed** agreement for the purchase and sale of real property is also known as **conditional sale contract, installment land contract, contract for deed, or land contract**. The essence of this contract is that the purchaser is contracting to obtain title to the property by paying the purchase price in installments and the seller is agreeing to transfer the title to the purchaser by the delivery of a deed upon payment of the purchase price by the purchaser.

In a bond for deed, the purchaser typically makes a down payment and agrees to pay the dollar balance of the purchase price in specified installments of principal and interest. The seller's obligation under the contract is to deliver a deed and, thereby, convey a marketable title to the purchaser when the purchaser has paid the purchase price. The contract for deed must be in writing to be enforceable, as required by the Statute of Frauds.

This type of contract was originally used to purchase relatively inexpensive pieces of land, but there is no reason why it cannot be used for any type of property. It has major advantages to the buyer in times of tight credit (high interest) markets where the seller can act as a primary lender. Additionally, the buyer may have problems with his credit, such that the commercial lenders may not provide the required financing. In the latter case, the seller may be willing to provide the financing, especially since this form of contract puts the seller in a particularly strong position.

An important caution, however, is that this form of contract must never be used to circumvent loan assumption clauses of the lender.

Caution should be observed in instances where the mortgage contains a due on sale clause. These clauses specify that the entire principal balance due on the mortgage must be paid if a sale of the property is effected. In some situations, the lending institution holding the mortgage may declare the contract for deed to be a sale of property and thereby require the mortgage to be paid off by the seller.

Consultation with legal counsel prior to the creation of the contract for deed is necessary for the protection of all parties. This is especially important if the property is encumbered by a mortgage containing a due on sale clause. In all cases where the property being purchased under a contract for deed is encumbered by a mortgage, the contract must specify that either the seller is to pay off the remaining principal balance due at the time of conveyance of title or provide for the assumption of the mortgage balance at that time by the purchaser.

OPTION TO PURCHASE

An **option to purchase** is a contract wherein a property owner (*optionor*) sells a right to purchase her property to a prospective buyer (*optionee*). The price paid for the option is not escrow money or earnest money or binder, but is money paid for the right to purchase the property at the price specified in the option contract, provided the optionee exercises his right within the time period set forth in the option. Therefore, the option money is paid directly to the property owner and is retained by that individual as agreed in the option contract. Usually a broker does not receive a commission for negotiating an option, but will be paid a commission as agreed in the listing contract if the option is exercised and the property sold.

In Figure 5.4 we see that our optionees are purchasing a right to buy the property under the terms and conditions set forth in the option contract. Once the optionees have paid for the option, they have no further obligation under the contract. They have the right to exercise their option and purchase the property, but they are not required to do so.

However, the option is binding upon the optionor. The optionor is obligated to convey the title to the property if the option is exercised and the purchase price paid as agreed in the contract. Once the option is exercised, it becomes a contract of sale and is therefore binding on both buyer and seller as is the case in any sales contract.

The following is a discussion of each of the numbered sections of the option to purchase illustrated in Figure 5.4.

Figure 5.4 Option to purchase.

---

1   This option to purchase is granted this _____ day of _____, 20_____, by
_____, hereinafter called Seller, _____, hereinafter called
Purchaser. Seller for consideration of $_____paid by Purchaser, grants to Purchaser the exclusive right to purchase
the real property described as follows:

2   _____
_____
_____

3   This option shall be binding upon the Seller from this date until noon, _____, 20_____. The purchase
price for the above described property shall be $_____and is paid as follows:
$_____consideration as stated above and paid Seller for this option.
$_____cash at closing and delivery of deed. $_____by the assumption of a present
mortgage on the property as of_____, to be adjusted to the balance as of the date of closing.
$_____ by a promissory note from Purchaser to Seller secured by a
_____on said property payable as follows:

_____

4   This option shall be exercised by written notice to the Seller and signed by the Purchaser within the time limit set forth
above. Should the Purchaser not exercise this option within the time limit, the consideration for this option in the amount of
$_____will be retained by the Seller.

5   Should the Purchaser exercise this option as provided, final settlement is to be made on or before_____.
Seller to convey a marketable title free from encumbrances except restrictive covenants, recorded easements, zoning regulations,
and ad valorem taxes which are to be prorated as of the closing date. Possession of the property to be given Purchaser on

_____.

Additional Conditions

6

This contract contains the entire agreement between the parties.

7   Purchaser _____   Seller_____

Purchaser _____   Seller_____

Section 1 sets forth the date the option is granted, the names of optionor and optionee described as seller and purchaser, and a recital of the consideration paid for the option.

Section 2 provides a legal description of the optioned property by the government rectangular survey system for property description.

Section 3 contains the time period that the option is binding upon the seller. This section also sets forth the purchase price for the property and the manner in which it is to be paid in the event that the option is exercised.

Section 4 specifies the manner in which the option is to be exercised by the purchaser (optionee). This section also reinforces the optionor's right to retain the option money in the event that the option is not exercised within the time limit.

Section 5 establishes the date of final settlement in the event that the option is exercised and requires the seller to convey a marketable title free from the usual encumbrances. Also, in this section, the purchaser is given possession of the property on the date of final settlement.

Section 6 sets forth any additional or special conditions for this particular transaction, such as guaranteeing that the seller will convey an easement for access to and from the specified public road.

Section 7 contains the execution of the option to purchase by buyer and seller.

Following the option to purchase contract, Figure 5.5 illustrates the exercise of option document for this particular transaction. The option contract and the exercise of option must be in writing as required by the Statute of Frauds.

Figure 5.5 Exercise of option.

_____, 20_____

To_____:

    This is to notify you that pursuant to the option executed by us on the_____day of_____, 20_____, we hereby give notice that we elect to exercise said option to purchase the real property described therein in accordance with the terms and conditions agreed upon.

_____
Optionee

_____
Optionee

IMPORTANT POINTS

1. A contract is an agreement between competent parties, upon legal consideration, to do or abstain from doing some legal act.

2. Bilateral contracts are based on mutual promises. Unilateral contracts are based on a promise by one party and an act by another party.

3. The requirements for contract validity are (1) competent parties, (2) mutual assent, (3) offer and acceptance, (4) consideration, and (5) legality of object.

4. An offer must not be indefinite or illusory.

5. An offer may be revoked by the offeror at any time prior to notification of acceptance.

6. A contract is created by the unconditional acceptance of a valid offer. Acceptance of bilateral offers must be communicated. Communication of the acceptance of unilateral offers results from the performance of an act by the promisee.

7. Mutual assent is defeated and a contract made voidable by (1) misrepresentation, (2) fraud, (3) undue influence, or (4) duress.

8. Contracts are assignable in the absence of a specific prohibition against assignment in the contract.

9. The Statute of Frauds requires that certain contracts be in writing to be enforceable. An important example is the purchase and sale agreement.

10. A listing contract is one in which a property owner employs a broker to find a buyer for her property. The contract creates an agency relationship wherein the seller is the principal and the broker is the special or limited agent of the seller.

11. The types of listing contracts are (1) open, (2) exclusive agency, and (3) exclusive right to sell.

12. If a contracting party defaults in the performance of contractual obligations, then the injured party may sue for damages in a suit for breach of contract. If the contract is for the purchase and sale of real property, then an alternate remedy in the form of a suit for specific performance is available to the injured party.

13. A bond for deed is also called an installment land contract, conditional sale contract, contract for deed, or land contract. It is a contract of sale and a method of financing by the seller for the buyer. Title does not pass until all or some specified part of the purchase price is paid by the buyer.

14. An option to purchase is a contract in which the owner sells a right to purchase his property to a prospective buyer.

15. A buyer-agency agreement is a contract between a prospective buyer and a real estate company calling for the agent to locate property and negotiate in the best interest of the buyer.

REVIEW QUESTIONS

Answers to these questions are found in the Answer Key section at the back of the book.

1. A contract in which mutual promises are exchanged at the time of signing (execution) is termed:
   a. multilateral
   b. unilateral
   c. bilateral
   d. promissory

2. A voidable contract:
   a. Can only be voided by the agreement of both parties to the contract
   b. Is unenforceable and has no legal effect
   c. Many be legally consummated by the parties
   d. Is a contract that is impossible to complete

3. For contracts in general, all of the following are essential elements except:
   a. competent parties
   b. offer and acceptance
   c. legality of object
   d. writing

4. Which of the following is an example of a bilateral contract?
   a. Lease
   b. Listing agreement
   c. Purchase and Sale Agreement
   d. Option

5. Which of the following is the basis of duress?
   a. fear
   b. mistake
   c. indefiniteness
   d. illusion

6. If a buyer withdraws her offer, her action is called:
   a. Rejection
   b. Breach of Contract
   c. Counteroffer
   d. Revocation

7. A contract to sell real property may be terminated by all of the following except:
   a. complete performance
   b. death
   c. mutual agreement
   d. breach of contract

8. Which of the following has the effect of terminating contracts?
   a. consideration
   b. bankruptcy
   c. exercise
   d. assignment

9. A contract in which a property owner employs an agent to market the property creates an agency relationship between which of the following?
   a. buyer and seller
   b. buyer and company
   c. company and seller
   d. agent, seller, and buyer

10. Upon the receipt of a buyer's offer, the seller accepted all of the terms of the offer except the amount of earnest money. This fact was promptly communicated to the offeree by the real estate agent. Which of the folllowing most accurately describes these events?
    a. the communication created a bilateral contract
    b. the seller accepted the buyer's offer
    c. the seller conditionally rejected the buyer's offer
    d. the seller rejected the buyer's offer

11. A buyer who is under contract decides not to buy the property. The earnest money that is forfeited is called:
    a. Compensatory damages
    b. Punitive damages
    c. Liquidated damages
    d. Actual damages

12. In a bond for a deed, all of the following is correct except for:
    a. The purchase price is paid in installments.
    b. Title is delivered upon payment of the purchase price.
    c. Used only in buying land.
    d. The contract must be in writing to be enforceable.

13. During the term of an option, the option is:
    a. Binding on the optionee
    b. Binding on the optionor
    c. Binding on both optionee and optionor
    d. Binding on neither optionee or optionor

14. When a party purchases an option, the optionee is purchasing which of the following?
    a. right
    b. title
    c. land
    d. exercise

15. The clause in a listing contract that protects the broker's commission entitlement beyond the listing term in the event of a sale of the property by the owner to a prospect who was shown the property by the listing firm or its agents is called which of the following?
    a. forfeiture clause
    b. carry-over clause
    c. settlement clause
    d. exclusive right clause

CHAPTER 6

IMPORTANT TERMINOLOGY

anticipation
appraisal
assessed value
book value
capitalization rate
change
competition
competitive market analysis (CMA)
condemnation value
conformity
contribution
cost approach
depreciation
direct sales comparison
economic obsolescence
functional obsolescence
gross rent multipliers (GRMs)

highest and best use
income approach
insurance value
market data approach
market value
mortgage loan value
physical deterioration
quantity survey method
replacement cost
reproduction cost
scarcity
square foot method
substitution
supply and demand
unit-in-place method
value

THE LISTING AND VALUATION PROCESSES

IN THIS CHAPTER

Inventory is the lifeblood of any business, and this is especially true in real estate. Without a well-stocked inventory of listings, a real estate person is at a disadvantage.

Listings create an image of success and reputation for sales ability in the community. The seller wants to deal with an agency with a high success rate, and the buyer wants to deal with an agency with a knowledge of the listing market.

OVERVIEW OF THE LISTING PROCESS

A seller will sometimes initiate a call to a real estate agency to list his property because he was a satisfied customer, referred by a satisfied customer, or is aware of the agency's reputation. Often, a seller will receive a call from a licensee because the seller is trying to sell his house alone or because the licensee is canvassing a certain area. Whatever the initial contact, the agent should set up an appointment to collect data on the property. The quality of the listing presentation, pricing of the home, accurate presentation of the home, and marketing the home effectively will depend on a thorough inspection of the property and a careful notation of the data. Some agents prefer a one-stop listing approach while others prefer a two-appointment approach. Whether it is the former or the latter, the licensee needs to make an effective listing presentation in which she begins to establish rapport with the seller. At the presentation, the licensee should include information about herself, the company, and the benefits of listing with the agency. The employment begins when the seller has agreed to list the house and signs the listing agreement with the agency. A listing agreement is an employment contract creating an agency relationship between the agency and the seller and empowering the licensee to sell the property at a certain price for a fixed period of time.

Once the property is listed, a marketing program aimed at potential buyers for that particular property may begin. This marketing plan should include the following:

1. distributing information to all agency sales people
2. placing a sign on the property
3. placing the property with the multiple listing service
4. advertising the property in any appropriate media

The level or type of marketing exposure that the listing receives can make the difference between a listing that sells and one that does not sell.

Property Data Sheet and Disclosures

When conducting an inspection, the licensee should obtain as much information as possible and record it on a property data sheet so he can accurately represent and market the home. Under Maine law, listing licensees are responsible for obtaining information necessary to make disclosures to buyers and shall make a reasonable effort to ensure that the information is conveyed to selling licensees. Selling licensees are responsible for obtaining the necessary information for making disclosures from the listing licensee and to ensure that the disclosures are made to buyers.

Items contained in the property data sheet that can be obtained through inspection and confirmed by the seller should include

1. property address
2. building style
3. number of rooms, bedrooms, baths
4. age
5. personal property to be included in sale
6. date of occupancy
7. type of hot water system
8. type of heating system
9. type of foundation and size
10. garage or other buildings

Information that is necessary to verify with someone other than the seller includes

1. taxes (municipality)
2. zoning (municipality)
3. lot size (registry of deeds)
4. type and assumability of mortgage (bank)
5. type of ownership (registry of deeds)
6. deed restrictions such as easements (deed)
7. restrictive covenants such as association or condo bylaws (deed)
8. DEP policies regarding sale of property (Department of Environmental Protection)

The Real Estate Commission requires that disclosures on the water supply, heating system, waste disposal system and hazardous materials be in writing and conveyed in writing to prospective buyers prior to or during preparation of an offer. (see Figure 6.1) When the information is not available, that fact shall also be conveyed in writing.

There is a federal rule adopted March 6, 1996 (Section 1019 of the Residential Lead-based Paint Hazard Reduction Act of 1992) requiring disclosure of known lead-based paint and/or lead-based paint hazards by persons selling or leasing housing constructed before the phase-out of residential lead-based paint use in 1978 (see Figure 6.2). Sellers and lessors must provide buyers and lessees with copies of any available records or reports pertaining to the presence of lead-based paint and/or lead-based paint hazards. They must also provide a pamphlet titled "Protect Your Family from Lead in Your Home."

Real estate licensees must ensure that sellers and landlords are aware of their obligations and that they disclose the proper information to buyers and tenants. Sales contracts and leases must include proper disclosure language and proper signatures. (Licensees must retain a copy of the completed disclosure form (Figure 6.1) for three years from the closing date sales and commencement of the leasing period for leases.)

Figure 6.1   Real estate data and disclosure sheet.

ABC REALTY
123 PROGRESSION LANE, UPTOWN, MAINE 00000
TEL: 207-555-5555   FAX: 207-555-5556
PROPERTY DATA SHEET

Property Address: **Price:**

Licensee: **Licensee's Phone Number :**

Seller:

Address:

Seller's phone #:

Tenant's phone #:

Tenant's name:

Showing instructions: Key #:

     Call first, if no answer use key.

     Vacant, use key anytime.

     By appointment only.

     Listing licensee must be present.

     Lockbox combo:

Directions:

Personal property included in sale:

( ) Range   ( ) Refrig   ( ) Wood stove   ( ) Dish washer

( ) Hood   ( ) Fan   ( ) Compactor   ( ) Disposal   ( ) Micro

Real property excluded from sale:

Other:

Rooms	Bedrooms	Baths	Fam room	Fireplace
Garage	Storm win	Driveway surface		Siding

	Base	First	Second	Third
Living Rm				
Dining Rm				
Kitchen				
Bedroom				
Bath				
Fam Room				

Remarks:

	Basement			
Full	Part	Crawl	Slab	Posts
Tax map and lot number			Zone	Flood zone
Book	Page	Lot size	Taxes	Tax year
Out conveyances		Restrictions		Deed
Body of water		Wrt frt	Road frt	Occupancy
220	Fuses/CB	Amps	Surveyed	Hot water
Build age	Roof age	Driveway	Condo dues	Assoc. dues
Insulation Type	Attic	Ext. walls.	Crawl space	Floors

Style	Foundation size	Color	Chimneys: Number: Lined: Yes No Unknown
			Home warranty? Yes No TB BA

To the best of my/our knowledge the above information is correct. All systems and equipment are in working order. I give my/our permission for this document to be released to the public. All blanks have either been filled in or crossed out. It is important to the Company that you have read and completely understand this document. By signing this document you are acknowledging you have read it, understand it and sign it willingly, as your free and voluntary act. Signature on this document acknowledges receipt of a copy of this document.

Seller: **Seller:**   **Date:**

It is important to the Company that you have read and completely understand this document and by signing you are acknowledging you have read it, understand it and sign it willingly, as your free and voluntary act. Signature on this document acknowledges receipt of a copy of this document.

Buyer: **Buyer:**   **Date:**

Page one of two

Figure 6.1 continued

ABC REALTY
123 PROGRESSION LANE, UPTOWN, MAINE 00000
TEL: 207-555-5555   FAX: 207-555-5556
PROPERTY DISCLOSURE SHEET

Property address:

WATER SUPPLY DISCLOSURE: Private: Public:

	Dug	Drilled	Driven point	Spring	Lake	Other
Type						
Location						
Malfunctions						

Date of installation: Date of most recent water test:

Any unsatisfactory water test or water test with notations?

Other information:

HEATING DISCLOSURE

	System/Source #1	System/Source #2	System/Source #3	System/Source #4
Type(s)				
Age of system/source(s)				
Name of company who services				
Date of most recent service call				
Annual consumption (gallons, cords, etc.)				
Malfunctions within the last two years				

Other information:

WASTE DISPOSAL SYSTEM DISCLOSURE

Public or quasi-public? Yes   No   If yes, any system or line malfunctions? Yes   No

Private waste disposal system? Yes   No

Type of system   Type of tank   Size of tank

	Tank		Leachfield
Location			
Malfunctions			
Date installed			

Date of most recent servicing of system   Contractor servicing system

Other information:

HAZARDOUS MATERIALS DISCLOSURE

Are you, the seller, making any representations regarding current or previously existing known hazardous materials in or on your real estate?
Yes   No   If yes, what are the representations?

Does your property now, or has it ever had asbestos in: Heating system   Shingles   Floor tiles   Other

Has there been a radon air test done?   Yes   No   Unknown   If yes to either, what are the results?

Has there been a radon water test done?   Yes   No   Unknown   If yes to either, what are the results?

Does your property contain lead based paint? Yes   No   Unknown

Does your property now, or has it ever contained underground storage tanks? Yes   No   Unknown

If the tanks were removed, when were they removed?   Who removed the tanks?

Is there now, or has there been, mold growing in the basement, attic, walls, etc. of the buildings? Yes   No   Unknown

Other information:

The buyer is encouraged to seek information from professionals regarding any specific issues of concern about hazardous materials.

Are there any structural defects to this property? Yes   No

If yes, please explain.

Is there any current wetness in the basement? Yes   No   Previous wetness in the basement? Yes   No   Unknown

If yes to either, please explain.

Are there any liens, encroachments or restrictions on this property? Yes   No   Unknown

If yes, please explain.

Is your land in Tree Growth? Yes   No   Unknown   Is your land in Open Space? Yes   No   Unknown

To the best of my/our knowledge the above information is correct. All systems and equipment are in working order. I give my/our permission for this sheet to be released to the public. All blanks have either been filled out or crossed out It is important to the Company that you have read and completely understand this document. By signing this document you are acknowledging you have read it, understand it and sign it willingly, as your free and voluntary act. Signature on this document acknowledges receipt of a copy of this document.

Seller: **Seller:**   **Date:**

I have read and been given a copy of this property disclosure sheet.

Buyer: **Buyer:**   **Date:**

Page two of two

Figure 6.2 Lead hazard disclosure form.

United States Environmental Protection Agency	Prevention, Pesticides, and Toxic Substances (7404)	EPA-747-F-96-002 March 1996 (Revised 12/96)

FACT SHEET

EPA and HUD Move to Protect Children from Lead-Based Paint Poisoning; Disclosure of Lead-Based Paint Hazards in Housing

SUMMARY

The Environmental Protection Agency (EPA) and the Department of Housing and Urban Development (HUD) are announcing efforts to ensure that the public receives the information necessary to prevent lead poisoning in homes that may contain lead-based paint hazards. Beginning this fall, most home buyers and renters will receive known information on lead-based paint and lead-based paint hazards during sales and rentals of housing built before 1978. Buyers and renters will receive specific information on lead-based paint in the housing as well as a Federal pamphlet with practical, low-cost tips on identifying and controlling lead-based paint hazards. Sellers, landlords, and their agents will be responsible for providing this information to the buyer or renter before sale or lease.

LEAD-BASED PAINT IN HOUSING

Approximately three-quarters of the nation's housing stock built before 1978 (approximately 64 million dwellings) contains some lead-based paint. When properly maintained and managed, this paint poses little risk. However, 1.7 million children have blood-lead levels above safe limits, mostly due to exposure to lead-based paint hazards.

EFFECTS OF LEAD POISONING

Lead poisoning can cause permanent damage to the brain and many other organs and causes reduced intelligence and behavioral problems. Lead can also cause abnormal fetal development in pregnant women.

BACKGROUND

To protect families from exposure to lead from paint, dust, and soil, Congress passed the Residential Lead-Based Paint Hazard Reduction Act of 1992, also

known as Title X. Section 1018 of this law directed HUD and EPA to require the disclosure of known information on lead-based paint and lead-based paint hazards before the sale or lease of most housing built before 1978.

WHAT IS REQUIRED

Before ratification of a contract for housing sale or lease:

- Sellers and landlords must disclose known lead-based paint and lead-based paint hazards and provide available reports to buyers or renters.

- Sellers and landlords must give buyers and renters the pamphlet, developed by EPA, HUD, and the Consumer Product Safety Commission (CPSC), titled *Protect Your Family from Lead in Your Home.*

- Home buyers will get a 10-day period to conduct a lead-based paint inspection or risk assessment at their own expense. The rule gives the two parties flexibility to negotiate key terms of the evaluation.

- Sales contracts and leasing agreements must include certain notification and disclosure language.

- Sellers, lessors, and real estate agents share responsibility for ensuring compliance.

Figure 6.2 continued

WHAT IS NOT REQUIRED
- This rule does not require any testing or removal of lead-based paint by sellers or landlords.

- This rule does not invalidate leasing and sales contracts.

TYPE OF HOUSING COVERED
Most private housing, public housing, Federally owned housing, and housing receiving Federal assistance are affected by this rule.

TYPE OF HOUSING NOT COVERED
- Housing built after 1977 (Congress chose not to cover post-1977 housing because the CPSC banned the use of lead-based paint for residential use in 1978).

- Zero-bedroom units, such as efficiencies, lofts, and dormitories.

- Leases for less than 100 days, such as vacation houses or short-term rentals.

- Housing for the elderly (unless children live there).

- Housing for the handicapped (unless children live there).

- Rental housing that has been inspected by a certified inspector and found to be free of lead-based paint.

- Foreclosure sales.

EFFECTIVE DATES
- For owners of more than 4 dwelling units, the effective date is September 6, 1996.

- For owners of 4 or fewer dwelling units, the effective date is December 6, 1996.

THOSE AFFECTED
The rule will help inform about 9 million renters and 3 million home buyers each year. The estimated cost associated with learning about the requirements, obtaining the pamphlet and other materials, and conducting disclosure activities is about $6 per transaction.

EFFECT ON STATES AND LOCAL GOVERNMENTS
This rule should not impose additional burdens on states since it is a Federally administered and enforced requirement. Some state laws and regulations require the disclosure of lead hazards in housing. The Federal regulations will act as a complement to existing state requirements.

FOR MORE INFORMATION
- For a copy of *Protect Your Family from Lead in Your Home* (in English or Spanish) , the sample disclosure forms, or the rule, call the National Lead Information Clearinghouse (NLIC) at (800) 424–LEAD, or TDD (800) 526–5456 for the hearing impaired. You may also send your request by fax to (202) 659–1192 or by Internet E-mail to ehc@cais.com. Visit the NLIC on the Internet at http://www.nsc.org/nsc/ehc/ehc.html.

- Bulk copies of the pamphlet are available from the Government Printing Office (GPO) at (202) 512–1800. Refer to the complete title or GPO stock number 055–000–00507–9. The price is $26.00 for a pack of 50 copies. Alternatively, persons may reproduce the pamphlet, for use or distribution, if the text and graphics are reproduced in full. Camera-ready copies of the pamphlet are available from the National Lead Information Clearinghouse.

- For specific questions about lead-based paint and lead-based paint hazards, call the National Lead Information Clearinghouse at (800) 424–LEAD, or TDD (800) 526–5456 for the hearing impaired.

- The EPA pamphlet and rule are available electronically and may be accessed through the Internet. Electronic Access:
  Gopher: gopher.epa.gov:70/11/Offices/PestPreventToxic/Toxic/lead_pm
  WWW: http://www.epa.gov/opptintr/lead/index.html
            http://www.hud.gov
  Dial up: (919) 558–0335
  FTP: ftp.epa.gov (*To login, type "anonymous." Your password is your Internet E-mail address.*)

For more information and to obtain this booklet visit this site:

http://www2.epa.gov/lead/protect-your-family-lead-your-home-real-estate-disclosure

BASIC VALUATION CONCEPTS

This section of the chapter discusses types of value that can be established by appraisals, factors and forces affecting appraisals, and the three approaches used in arriving at the appraised value. Even though real estate licensees are not required to be professional appraisers, they need to have a working knowledge of the approaches to determining value of the property to be listed and sold. Part of the listing process is to determine value for the property. The licensee often will do a competitive market analysis (discussed later in this chapter) or, if the property is unique, suggest to the owner that he have the property appraised by a licensed appraiser.

An **appraisal** is an estimate of value, based on factual data, on a particular property, at a particular time, for a particular purpose. It is an opinion as to the worth of a given property. The opinion must be supported in writing with collected data and logical reasoning. The person making the appraisal must be objective and unbiased, with no undisclosed interest in the property. She must base her opinion wholly upon facts relating to the property, such as age, square footage, location, cost to replace, and so on.

The usual purpose of an appraisal is to estimate the fair market value of a particular property. However, this is not always the case as can be seen by the discussion of assessed value, insurance value, mortgage loan value, condemnation value, and book value.

Value, Price, and Cost Distinguished

The terms *value, price*, and *cost* do not have the same meaning. **Value** results from the anticipation of future benefits resulting from ownership of a particular property. Cost is a measure of expenditures of labor and materials made some time in the past. Therefore, we see that value is based on the future, whereas cost is based on the past.

Price is the amount of money paid for a property. Price may be more than or less than value or cost. However, under normal market conditions, price is generally in line with value because usually the owner will not accept a price substantially less than value nor will a purchaser pay an amount significantly in excess of value. The more knowledgeable buyers and sellers are of property value, the more closely related price and value will be.

Types of Value

Market Value

Market value is defined by the Appraisal Institute as follows: "The highest price in terms of money which a property will bring in a competitive and open market under all conditions requisite to a fair sale, the buyer and seller, each acting prudently, knowledgeably and assuming the price is not affected by undue stimulus."

Implicit in this definition is the consummation of a sale as of a specified date and the passing of title from seller to buyer under conditions whereby

1. buyer and seller are typically motivated
2. both parties are well informed or well advised, and each acting in what the individual considers her own best interest
3. a reasonable time is allowed for exposure in the open market
4. payment is made in cash or its equivalent
5. financing, if any, is on terms generally available in the community at the specified date and typical for the property type in its locale
6. the price represents a normal consideration for the property sold unaffected by special financing amounts or terms, services, fees, costs, or credits incurred in the transaction

Assessed Value

The **assessed value** of real property is the value to which a local tax rate is applied to establish the amount of tax imposed on the property. In some states, the assessed value is equivalent to the market value, but the reevaluation to accomplish this may be done once every several years. In other states, the assessed rate may be set at a lower percentage of the actual market value. The tax rate is usually changed every year. The tax rate may be in units such as dollars per $100 of assessed value or mills, a tenth of a cent. In Maine, when assessed value in a town or city falls below 80 percent of market value, the town or city must have a reevaluation.

Insurance Value

In estimating the value of property as a basis for arriving at the amount of insurance that should be provided to adequately protect the structure against loss by fire or other casualty, the insurance company is concerned with the cost of replacing or re-producing structures in the event of a total loss caused by an insured hazard. This cost is calculated by multiplying a square foot replacement cost by the number of square feet in the structure. Land value is not included in calculating **insurance value**.

Mortgage Loan Value

In making a mortgage loan, the lender is interested in the value of the property pledged as security for the debt. In the event of a foreclosure, the lender must recover the debt from the sale of the property.

Condemnation Value

When real property is condemned under the power of eminent domain, the prop- erty owner is entitled to receive the fair market value of the property to compensate for the loss. In the case of a condemnation of an entire property, this **condemnation value** is not difficult to estimate. However, in the case of a partial condemnation, the problem becomes more complex. In this case the property owner is entitled to be compensated for the difference in the market value of the property before and after condemnation. This amount will typically be an amount greater than the value of the amount of property condemned as a percentage of the entire property value.

Book Value

Book value is an artificial value used for accounting or tax purposes, in connection with establishing a depreciation schedule for a property based on the property's useful life. Often this value has nothing to do with the actual useful life of the prop- erty. In 1980 the tax schedule assumed a property had a useful life of 40 years; in 1981 this became 15 years, and now the useful life is 27.5 years for residential property.

Basic Real Estate Appraisal Characteristics

For a property to have value, it must have certain legal and economic characteristics. The characteristics are: (1) utility, (2) scarcity, (3) transferability, and (4) effective demand.

Utility

For the property to have value it must have the ability to satisfy a need. A property must be useful. It must be possible to use or adapt the property for some legal purpose. If a property cannot be put to some beneficial use to fill a need of some kind, it will not have value.

Scarcity

The degree of **scarcity** is based on the supply of the property in relation to the effective demand for the property. The more abundant the supply of property in comparison to the effective demand for property at any given time, the lower the value. Conversely, the fewer properties available on the market in comparison to the effective demand or bidding for these properties at any given time, the greater the value of the properties will be.

Transferability

This is a legal concept that must be present for a property to have value. It must be possible for the owner to transfer the ownership interests to a prospective buyer. These ownership interests include all of those previously discussed as expressed in the bundle of rights theory.

Effective Demand

Effective demand is a desire or need for property that is coupled with the financial ability to satisfy the need. In times of excessively high interest rates, many people with a strong desire and substantial need for housing are priced out of the mortgage ma ket; therefore, the demand for property is not an effective demand because individuals who want to buy do not have the financial ability to satisfy the demand.

In creating housing or other types of properties, such as office buildings, shopping malls, and hotels, a developer must take into consideration not only the need for these types of property, but also the financial ability of prospective tenants or purchasers to satisfy their need.

Forces and Factors Influencing Value

The forces that affect real property value are (1) physical, (2) economic, (3) social, and (4) governmental.

Physical Forces

The forces in this category are both natural and artificial. Natural forces are such things as topography, soil conditions, mineral resources, size, shape, climate, and location. Artificial factors include utilities, proximity to streets and highways, available public transportation, and access.

Economic Forces

Economic forces are such things as employment levels, income levels, availability of credit, interest rates, price levels, and the amount of real property taxes.

Social Factors

Social factors include rates of marriage, birth, divorce, and death; the rate of population growth or decline; and public attitudes toward such things as education, cultural activities, and recreation.

Government Factors

Governmental factors include regulations such as zoning laws, building codes, fire regulations, city or county planning, and regulations designed to retard growth and development.

Basic Valuation Principles

Many economic principles may affect the value of real property. In establishing an estimate of value, an appraiser considers the following principles.

Supply and Demand

The economic principle of **supply and demand** is applicable to the real estate industry just as it is applicable to other economic activities in the free enterprise system. This principle states that the greater the supply of any commodity in comparison to the demand for that commodity, the lower the value will be. Conversely, the smaller the supply and the greater the demand, the higher the value will be. Therefore, factors influencing the demand and supply of real estate will affect property values either beneficially or adversely.

Anticipation

The principle of **anticipation** provides that property value is based on the anticipation of the future benefits of ownership. This may also be stated as the present value of future income. Therefore, it is the future and not the past that is important in estimating the value of property. Changes in the expected demand for property can result from the creation of various improvements in an area such as schools, shopping centers, freeways, and other beneficial developments in the area. Therefore, it is important for real estate agents to be aware of plans for future development in their local market area. There may be changes that will adversely affect the expected demand for property resulting from such things as changes in surrounding land use patterns having an adverse effect on future demand. Changes causing a demand increase will increase property values, whereas changes causing a reduction in demand will cause depreciation.

Substitution

The principle of **substitution** provides that the highest value of a property has a tendency to be established by the cost of purchasing or constructing another property of equal utility and desirability, provided that the substitution can be made without unusual delay. Therefore, if two properties are on the market, each having the same degree of desirability and utility, and one is priced at $100,000 and the other priced at $95,000, a buyer would substitute the $95,000 property instead of purchasing the $100,000 property. Simply put, the buyer will select the property that gives him the same amenities at the lesser price.

Conformity

Conformity means "like kind" or compatible uses of land within a given area. It results from the homogeneous or compatible uses of land within a given area. Adherence to the principle of conformity will result in maximizing property values. Failure to adhere to the principle will result in disharmonious and incompatible uses of land within the area, with the consequence of depreciating property values. In residential subdivisions, conformity is achieved through the use of restrictive covenants in the deed. In other areas, this is accomplished through zoning laws and subdivision ordinances of the municipalities.

Contribution

The principle of **contribution** states that various elements of a property add value to the entire property. For example, if a typical buyer would pay $5,500 more for a property with a garage than for the same property without a garage, we infer that the element adds a value of $5,500 by itself. This principle is used in the market data approach to the value estimate in making adjustments for differences between the comparable properties and the subject property (the property that is the subject of the appraisal). For example, the subject property may have a fireplace, whereas a comparable does not. In making the appraisal, we must estimate the value increase resulting from the presence of the fireplace in the subject property as compared with the loss in value resulting from the absence of the fireplace in the comparable. The principle of contribution also applies to decisions regarding expenditures to modernize or improve an existing property. For example, will the addition of a garage or carport increase the value of a home sufficiently to cover the cost of constructing the improvement?

This principle also applies to improving an investment property. For example, will the cost of improving the property by installing an elevator in a four-story office building be offset by the increase in rental income resulting from the installation of the elevator? In other words, does the elevator make a sufficient contribution to value in the form of additional property income to offset all the cost associated with creating the improvement?

Competition

The principle of **competition** states that when the net profit generated by a property is excessive, the result will be to create very strong competition. For example, if a growth area contains only one or two properties of a certain type, such as one or two apartment complexes or office buildings, these properties will produce excess profits from rental income. The result will be to attract a number of competitors eager to participate in the profits. Competition will cause a reduction in excess profits as the supply of competing services increases until excess profits are finally eliminated.

Change

The principle of **change** states that change is continually affecting land use and therefore continually changing value. Every property and every area is constantly undergoing change. Nothing remains the same. The only constant is that change will occur. Change may cause an appreciation in value or a decrease in value. Change is constantly occurring in both the physical and economic conditions of property.

Highest and Best Use

The principle of **highest and best use** is defined as "that possible and legal use or employment of land that will preserve its utility and yield a net income flow in the form of rent that forms, when capitalized at the proper rate of interest, the highest present value of the land." There may be a variety of uses to which land may be put at any given time; however, there is only one highest and best use for a particular property at a particular time. The highest and best use of property will be different at different periods of time. For example, the highest and best use for land sometime in the past may have been for agricultural purposes, whereas the highest and best use at the present time may be for a shopping mall, apartment complex, or office building.

The principle of highest and best use may be illustrated by an example of the necessary activities and decisions to create an improvement on land to make the land productive. To accomplish the objective, there must be a coordinator who visualizes the investment opportunities and coordinates and employs capital and labor to create an improvement on land adhering to the principle of highest and best use. The coordinator or coordinators will typically be specialists in one or more fields of real estate, such as a broker, builder, developer, and property manager. For example, let's assume that the coordinators determine that the highest and best use of a particular parcel of land at that time is to construct an apartment complex. The next decision is to determine the number of units to be constructed. Capital and labor are highly mobile, whereas land has the physical characteristic of immobility; therefore, capital and labor have the top priority on the income produced by the improvement. The remaining income goes to the land that receives the residual income.

A coordinator's objective in adhering to the concept of highest and best use is to provide a residual income that, when capitalized at the proper rate of interest, creates the highest present value of the land. To accomplish this objective, care must be taken not to create an overimprovement or an underimprovement. If an overimprovement is created (too many apartment units are constructed), there will not be sufficient residual income for the land after the requirements of the coordinator, capital, and labor are satisfied. In other words, the investment in the improvement will exceed the ability of the improvement to provide sufficient net income to cover the priority demands and still provide a residual income that will result in the highest land value.

The same result will occur if an underimprovement is created (an insufficient number of apartment units being constructed). In this case, the improvement will not produce sufficient income to result in a residual income to create maximum land value.

The creation of either an underimprovement or an overimprovement will result in depreciation of the property in the form of economic obsolescence. Therefore, in adhering to the principle of highest and best use, the coordinator must not only establish the type of use, but also the capacity of the land to support a certain number of rental units to be constructed.

The income that is allocated to the land as residual income under the principle of highest and best use is defined as *economic rent*. This is the rent that the land is capable of producing if the most efficient use is made of the land to the optimum capacity of the land. Rent that is agreed upon in a contract between landlord and tenant is called *contract rent*. The principle of highest and best use also applies to the construction of a single-family residence. For example, if a $225,000 cost is involved in constructing a home in a neighborhood of $175,000 houses, the result will be an overimprovement. Conversely, if a $150,000 house is constructed in an area of homes valued at $225,000 and up, an underimprovement will result. Consequently, the owner will have suffered a loss in value by not applying the land to its highest and best use in this location.

APPROACHES TO VALUE (MARKET, INCOME, COST)

An appraisal is an estimate of property value based on factual data. In estimating property value, an organized and systematic program must be followed (see Figure 6.3). The orderly progression of the appraisal process includes the following steps listed in chronological order:

1. Define the appraisal problem. This includes the determination of the purpose of the appraisal and the type of value to be estimated.

Figure 6.3
Approaches to value
(appraisal methods).

1. Competitive market analysis (**direct sales comparison**)
   Compares subject to similar properties sold
2. The income method
   Applies capitalization formula to the income (rent) produced
3. The cost method
   Theoretically rebuilds the structure anew and adjusts to its
   present condition

2. Obtain a complete and accurate description of the property that is the subject of the appraisal. The appraisal report must contain a legal description of the property to precisely locate and identify the property. The identification must specifically define the limits of the area included in the appraisal.
3. Inspect the surrounding area and the property to be appraised.
4. Determine the specific data required as the basis for the value estimate.
5. Analyze the data and arrive at a value estimate by each of the three appraisal methods: market data, cost, and income.
6. Correlate the results obtained by each of the three methods and thereby arrive at a value estimate.
7. Prepare the appraisal report.

Competitive Market Analysis

Part of the listing process is to recommend to the owner a market price that will be the listed price if agreed upon by the owner. The **competitive market analysis (CMA)** is the primary appraisal approach for estimating the value of single-family, owner occupied dwellings and vacant land. The competitive market analysis is a comparison of the property that is the subject of the appraisal with other properties that offer comparable utility that have sold recently. No two properties are exactly alike; however, there are many that are comparable or similar in desirability and utility. In making the comparisons between the subject property and selected comparables, allowances are made for the differences by following the principle of contribution.

A minimum of three comparables is absolutely necessary. If available, as many as six comparables are appropriate. Comparables should be as similar as possible in all respects to subject property. Comparables may be found in real estate office files of closed sales, in the closed sales data of a multiple listing service, from other appraisers, and from the declaration of value form that can be found in the local tax assessor's office. The more recent the date of sale of the comparable, the more valuable the comparable to the appraisal process. Also of great importance is the degree of similarity of the physical characteristics of the comparable and the location of the comparable.

In making the selection of comparables, certain property characteristics and nonproperty characteristics of each comparable must be specifically identified. Property characteristics include such things as size, type of construction, age, design, special features, and location. Nonproperty characteristics include the date of sale, verified sales price, method of financing used by the purchaser, and the seller's motivation in the sale.

An important point to understand before using the chart is that the data values assigned are the result of careful analysis and records. For example, as in Figure 6.4, a value of $5,500 for a garage is not an arbitrary number pulled from the air, but rather the result of careful paired sales analysis data. To arrive at the proper value of an element, the licensee must constantly abstract or reflect from the marketplace what the average buyer will pay for the element.

1. Home no. 1: 1,500 sq. ft., 3 bedrooms, 2 baths, garage	$ 87,500
2. Home no. 2: Same features, no garage	− 82,000
3. Garage value (to the buyer)	$ 5,500

Figure 6.4
Market data comparison.

All of the data used in making the adjustments between the comparable properties and the subject property must be laid out in an orderly, detailed, and accurate manner, as illustrated in Figure 6.5. The comparison sets forth all of the property and nonproperty characteristics utilized in this particular value estimate.

As can be seen, plus and minus adjustments are made to reconcile the differences and arrive at a value estimate for subject property on the basis of the price for which each comparable was sold. A plus adjustment to a comparable is made when the comparable is deficient in a particular respect when compared to subject property, as illustrated in Figure 6.6. The adjustment indicates that comparable #1 would have sold for $500 more had its lot size been as large as subject property. A minus adjustment to a comparable is made when it contains a specific feature that subject property does not contain. Therefore, if comparable #1 had only the same square feet as subject property, it would have sold for $2,000 less than it did. There is an adjustment of $4,000 to comparable #3 because the purchaser in that sale used a VA-guaranteed loan to purchase the property, whereas subject property may only be sold to a buyer using conventional financing. In identifying this nonproperty characteristic of comparable #3, it was determined that the sale price included $4,000 to cover the discount points paid by the seller to enable the purchaser to obtain that type of financing. Therefore, the adjustment is made because, had the purchaser used conventional financing, the discount points would not have been required and the seller would have been willing to accept a price $4,000 less than the $82,500 for which the property sold.

After all adjustments are made, the net adjustment amount for each comparable is calculated and this result is applied to the price the comparable sold for to arrive at an adjusted price. The adjusted price is an estimate of the price for which the comparable would have sold if all factors had been the same as subject property. The three adjusted prices are correlated to arrive at an indicated market value for subject property. This correlation is arrived at by calculating a weighted average. Comparables with a high degree of similarity are given more weight than comparables with a lesser degree of similarity. In Figure 6.5, comparable #2 is given the greatest weight because it requires the fewest number of adjustments and (though this cannot be determined from the illustration) it is located in the same subdivision and just around the corner from the subject property. Comparable #1, next in order of similarity, is located in the same subdivision as the subject property. However, comparable #1 does not have the same degree of similarity to subject property as comparable #2. Comparable #3 is given the least weight because it is located in a different subdivision and is the least similar to subject property.

Estimated Net to the Seller

A seller's main concern is how much money she will net from the sale of her property.

Every licensee's responsibility is to suggest a market price to the seller and prepare an estimated net sheet of the property for the seller (see Figure 6.7), so that the seller has full knowledge of the financial implications of the sale.

Income Approach

If a property is in the category of apartment complexes, single-family rental houses, office buildings, or any property that produces income, the **income approach**, or appraisal by

Figure 6.5 Competitive Market Analysis.

Date: 12-9-CY	Subject Property	Comparable No. 1	Adjustment	Comparable No. 2	Adjustment	Comparable No. 3	Adjustment
Address	524 Amortization Dr.	602 Amortization Dr.		301 Acceleration Circle		12 Redemption Lane	
Sale Price		$92,000		$85,500		$82,500	
Sale Date		11-10-CY	+ 600	10-20-CY	+ 1,200	6-11-CY	+ 3,300
Financing	Conventional	Conventional	0	Conventional	0	VA	− 4,000
Location	Good	Good	0	Good	0	Fair	+ 1,000
Lot Size	150 × 175 (26,250 sq.ft.)	140 × 170 (23,800)	+ 500	150 × 170 (25,500)	0	125 × 150 (18,750)	+ 1,500
Age	5	6	0	7	0	8	0
Condition	Good	Good	0	Fair	+ 1,000	Fair	+ 1,000
Square Footage	1,800	1,900	− 2,000	1,800	0	1,650	+ 3,000
Total Rooms	6	6	0	6	0	6	0
Bedrooms	3	4	0	3	0	3	0
Bathrooms	2½	3	− 1,000	2½	0	2	+ 1,000
Style	Ranch	Ranch	0	Ranch	0	Ranch	0
Construction	Frame	Brick & Frame	0	Frame	0	Frame	0
Air Conditioning	Central	Central	0	Central	0	None	+ 1,000
Garage	Garage-2 Car	Garage-2 Car	0	Garage-2 Car	0	Carport-1 Car	+ 2,000
Driveway	Paved	Paved	0	Gravel	+ 1,000	Gravel	+ 1,000
TOTAL ADJUSTMENT			− 1,900		+ 3,200		+ 10,800
ADJUSTED PRICE			$90,100		$88,700		$93,300

Comparable No. 1 $90,100 × 35% = $31,535
Comparable No. 2 $88,700 × 40% = $35,480
Comparable No. 3 $93,300 × 25% = $23,325

(Not all three properties are given the same importance. The appraiser has assigned the most weight to No. 2 since he feels it is most similar to the subject; No. 3, with the largest adjustment, is deemed to be least similar and is assigned the least weight.)

Weighted Average = $90,340 rounded to $90,300 indicated value of subject property

In this example, the inferior property has no garage, the subject property has a one-car garage, and the superior property has a two-car garage. The appraiser must adjust for these discrepancies.

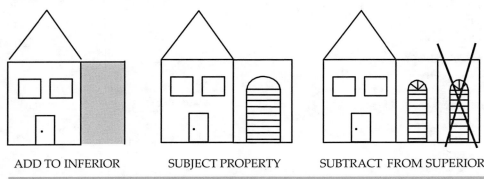

ADD TO INFERIOR   SUBJECT PROPERTY   SUBTRACT FROM SUPERIOR

Figure 6.6
When adjusting comparables to subject property, an appraiser must add to inferior properties and subtract from superior comparables to arrive at an adjusted comparison.

Brokerage commission (_____%)	$ _____
Points (#_____)	_____
Attorney's fees (deed preparation)	_____
Transfer tax	_____
City/town real estate taxes	_____
Discharge of existing mortgage	_____
Existing mortgage balance	_____
Approximate total closing costs	$ _____
Contract sales price	$ _____
Total closing costs	$ _____
Balance due seller at closing	$ _____

Figure 6.7
Estimated net proceeds to seller.

capitalization, would be the primary method used to estimate the present value. The approach is based on the net operating income produced by the property.

The net operating income is determined by subtracting the expenses from the gross income. The net operating income is then divided by the capitalization rate to find the appraised value. This procedure is illustrated in Figure 6.8 and the accompanying analysis. The information provided is used in the analysis, which applies the capitalization formula

$$\text{Value} = \frac{\text{Net Operating Income}}{\text{Cap Rate}}$$

Analysis of Operating Statement

Income

Referring to the sample operating statement in Figure 6.8, the apartment complex has a potential gross income of $1,350,000. This is the income that would be produced if every apartment was rented 100 percent of the time at $450/month for a 12-month period. It is not realistic to expect any rental property to be occupied 100 percent of the time on a continuing basis. Therefore, the potential gross income must be reduced by an allowance for vacancies (5 percent) that will inevitably occur and losses due to some tenants failing to pay their rent or paying with checks that are not collectible (1 percent). In the example, it is anticipated that vacancy and credit losses will amount to 6 percent of gross potential income, or $81,000 per year.

Figure 6.8
Operating statement.

250-unit apartment complex with rent schedule of $450 per month per unit.

Potential gross income: 250 × $450	× 12		$1,350,000
Less vacancy and credit losses (6%)			81,000
Plus other income			25,000
Gross effective income			$1,294,000
Less fixed expenses			
Property insurance		$ 24,500	
Property taxes		95,300	
Licenses and permits		1,200	$ 121,000
Less operating expenses			
Maintenance		$106,000	
Utilities		103,200	
Supplies		16,000	
Advertising		7,500	
Legal & accounting		15,000	
Wages & salaries		90,000	
Property management		64,700	402,400
Replacement reserve		$ 25,000	25,000
Total expenses			$ 548,400
Net operating income			$ 745,600

This apartment complex has other income generated by vending machines and laundromat facilities used by the tenants. This income is projected to be $25,000 per year. With the addition of other income, the gross effective income equals potential gross income minus vacancy and credit losses plus other income. This gross effective income is the amount of money the apartment complex may realistically be expected to generate in a 12-month period.

Expenses

To arrive at net operating income, which is the basis for calculating the value estimate in the income approach, various expenses must be subtracted from gross income. These expenses are divided into fixed expenses, operating expenses, and the expense of replacement reserve.

Fixed expenses. These are the expenses that do not fluctuate with the operating level of the complex. The fixed expenses remain essentially the same whether the occupancy rate is 95 percent or 75 percent and include the following: (1) an expense of $24,500 is incurred in the form of an annual premium for a hazard insurance policy to protect against financial loss caused by fire or other casualty; (2) real property taxes are one of the largest expense items and amount to $95,300; and (3) the $1,200 cost for licenses and permits represents fees paid to local governments as may be required for the operation of vending machines and other income-producing facilities. The fixed expenses total $121,000 and are 9.27 percent of gross effective income.

Operating expenses. Operating expenses in general fluctuate with the operating level or occupancy level of the property. As in the case of this apartment complex, maintenance is a major operating expense amounting to $106,000. This operating expense will vary with the level of operation and is related to a large degree to the age and condition of the property when purchased. Older properties will naturally require a higher level of expenditures for maintenance than newer properties. The maintenance covers not only the cost of repair and maintenance to the structures, but also the maintenance of grounds and parking areas. The cost of utilities for the common areas and the cost of wages and salaries paid to employees follow maintenance costs as the next largest expense.

The property manager's fee of $64,700 is a percentage of the gross effective income. The property management fee in this example is 5 percent of gross effective income. The small expense items of legal and accounting fees, advertising, and supplies round out the operating expenses, which total $402,400, or 31.09 percent of gross effective income. Operating expenses represent the largest group in the three types of expenses.

Replacement reserve. This expense item of $25,000 represents an amount of money that is set aside each year to replace short-lived equipment such as hot water heaters, ranges and ovens, dishwashers, and disposals. Setting aside an amount of money for this purpose each year enables the project to avoid the impact of a substantial expenditure in any given year when a number of short-lived items must be replaced.

Total expenses and net income. The total of the three types of expenses amounts to $548,400, which represents 42.38 percent of gross effective income. It should be noted that debt service (mortgage principal and interest payments) are not included in the list of expenses for appraisal purposes. For this purpose, debt service is considered to be a personal obligation of the property owner. In this way, the appraisal process puts all comparable properties on the same basis by eliminating an item that will vary substantially from one property to another. Outside of the appraisal process, debt service would be deducted from gross effective income to arrive at cash flow. Cash flow is the amount of money the owner will actually receive in a given year prior to the subtraction of the income tax liability for the property. To calculate net taxable income before depreciation, the payment of mortgage interest, but not principal, is deductible. Net operating income is arrived at by subtracting total expenses from gross effective income.

Application of the Capitalization Rate

The final step in estimating property value by the income approach is the application of the capitalization formula (see Figure 6.9). This involves the simple process of dividing net operating income by a **capitalization rate**. The difficulty lies in arriving at the proper capitalization rate.

The appropriate rate is that rate of return investors in comparable properties are achieving on investments in the same locality at the time of the appraisal. The rate of return on any investment includes a consideration of the risk factor. The greater the risk of loss taken by the investor, the higher potential rate of return the investor is entitled to expect.

$$\frac{I}{R \times V}$$

$$\frac{\text{Income}}{\text{Rate} \times \text{Value}}$$

e.g., $\dfrac{\$745,600}{12\%}$ $= V = \$6,213,333$

Figure 6.9
The capitalization (cap rate) formula.

In the application of the capitalization formula to the apartment complex, we have adopted a rate of 12 percent as being the appropriate rate for this investment in this area at this time. By dividing the net operating income of $745,600 by 0.12, a value estimate of $6,213,333 (typically rounded to $6,213,000) is indicated. In other words, if an investor paid this price for the apartment complex and continued to realize a net operating income of $745,600, the investor would realize a return of 12 percent before deductions for debt service and income tax. As discussed in the chapter on income tax implications in real estate, the imposition of federal income tax may be eliminated or substantially reduced as a result of the deduction for depreciation or the new accelerated cost recovery.

The importance of the selection of a proper capitalization rate cannot be overemphasized. Even a slight variation in this rate will result in a substantial change in the value estimate. For example, if a 13 percent rate had been used in the foregoing example, the value estimate would be $5,735,384, which represents a reduction of indicated value of $77,949, or 7.69 percent of the original estimate. The higher the capitalization rate, the lower the value estimate will be and, conversely, the lower the rate, the higher the resulting value estimate. Other examples of the application of the capitalization formula are found in the chapter on real estate mathematics.

Gross Rent Multiplier (GRM)

Gross rent multipliers (GRMs) are not a part of the income approach to the value estimate, but they may be used to estimate the value of property producing rental income. GRM is a factor calculated from comparing sales of income-producing property and the gross rental income of properties for one- to four-unit residential properties (see Figure 6.10). There is a degree of unreliability in the use of this method because calculations are based on gross income rather than net income. If the property has been efficiently managed, the gross income will provide a reliable basis for calculating an estimate of value. However, if expenses are out of line, gross income will not fairly reflect property value.

Gross rent multipliers are calculated by dividing either the monthly or annual gross rent of a property into the price for which it was sold. It does not matter whether gross annual or gross monthly income is used as long as one or the other is used consistently. Figure 6.11 provides examples of calculating gross income multipliers on both a monthly and an annual basis. As can be seen, a much lower multiplier will result from the calculations based on annual income.

Figure 6.10
Application of gross rent multiplier.

A. $\dfrac{\text{Comparable's sales price}}{\text{Rent}} = \text{GRM}$

B. Subject's rent × GRM = Estimate of subject's value

Figure 6.11
Calculating gross rent multipliers.

Comparable	Price	Monthly Gross	GRM	Annual Gross	GRM
No. 1	$6,213,000	$107,833	58	$1,294,000	4.8
No. 2	5,865,000	101,000	58	1,212,000	4.8
No. 3	5,125,000	90,000	57	1,080,000	4.7
No. 4	6,060,000	103,000	59	1,236,000	4.9
No. 5	7,250,000	125,000	58	1,500,000	4.8
No. 6	6,588,000	111,000	<u>59</u>	1,332,000	<u>4.9</u>
Average GRM			58		4.8

In estimating the value of an income property, gross rental incomes may be established for comparable income properties that have sold recently. An average of the gross rent multipliers obtained can be used as a multiplier for the monthly gross or annual income produced by a property under consideration to provide an indication of property value. For example, if the property being considered produced a gross monthly income of $99,000, this would be multiplied by the average gross rent multiplier of 58 as shown in the illustration. This multiplication ($99,000 × 58) provides a value indication of $5,742,000. This indicated value will be as reliable as the gross monthly incomes and prices used in calculating the average gross rent multiplier.

Cost Approach or Approach by Summation

The **cost approach** is used as the primary method for estimating the value of properties that are not single-family dwellings or vacant land, and are not properties that produce rental income. Examples of the type of structures that are appraised by this method include schools, factories occupied by the owning industry, fire stations, hospitals, government office buildings, libraries, and new construction.

Step one in the cost approach is to estimate the cost of reproducing or replacing the structure. There is a definite difference between **replacement cost** and **reproduction cost.** Reproduction cost is the cost of constructing an exact duplicate of the property when new. Replacement cost is based on constructing a building of comparable utility using modern building techniques and materials. If the subject property was constructed many years ago, it will often be impossible to estimate the cost of reproducing that property today. The materials and craftsmanship just may not be available. Therefore, the basis of the cost approach for older structures is replacement cost new. Reproduction cost new may be used for properties that have been constructed recently.

The methods of estimating reproduction or replacement costs include the quantity survey method, unit-in-place method, and the square foot method. Of these methods, the **quantity survey method** is the most accurate, but also the most complex and time-consuming method. This is the method that most builders use in calculating a cost estimate for a construction job. It involves the detailed determination of the exact quantity of each type of material to be used in the construction, and the necessary material and labor costs applicable to each unit. The final estimate includes a profit to the builder.

In the **unit-in-place method**, the cost of each component part of the structure is calculated including material, labor, and overhead costs, plus a profit to the builder.

The cost by the **square foot method** is calculated by multiplying the number of square feet in the structure being appraised by the cost per square foot to construct the building using the current cost per square foot. The estimated cost figures employed in any of these three methods are available through construction cost services that publish construction cost estimates for various types of structures and structural components.

Step two in the value estimate by the cost approach is to deduct from the estimated cost of replacing or reproducing the property with new construction any observed depreciation existing and resulting from any of the three forms of depreciation. The deduction of the dollar amount of depreciation will provide the depreciated value of the structure as it presently exists. Next, the depreciated value of any other site improvements is added to the value of the structure to provide an estimate of the total depreciated value of all improvements.

Step three in the cost approach is to estimate the value of the site as though it were vacant. The site value is estimated by the market data approach, which employs the use of comparable parcels of land to arrive at the value estimate. The site is compared to comparable parcels of land that have sold recently as a basis for the land value. The estimate of the land value by the market data approach is added to the estimate of the total depreciated value of the improvements to provide a value estimate for the total property by the cost approach.

The various steps and calculations employed in the cost approach are illustrated by the example of the cost approach calculations in Figure 6.12.

Depreciation

In using the cost approach, the appraiser must determine if there is any **depreciation.** Depreciation is defined as a loss in value from any cause. The loss in value is estimated by the difference between the present cost of constructing a new building of equal utility and design, and the market value of the depreciated property. Depreciation results from the following three causes: (1) **physical deterioration**, (2) **functional obsolescence**, and (3) **economic obsolescence.**

Each of these three types of depreciation is caused by forces having an adverse affect on the structure. The following are examples of these forces classified by the type of depreciation that results from the action of these forces:

Physical Deterioration
1. Unrepaired damage to the structure caused by fire, explosion, vandalism, windstorm, or other action of the elements, and damage caused by termites or other woodboring insects.
2. Wear and tear resulting from normal use of the property when adequate maintenance measures are not taken to keep the property in good condition.

Functional Obsolescence
1. Inadequacy or overadequacy of such things as wiring and plumbing, heating and cooling system, and insufficient or over sufficient number of bathrooms, closets, and other facilities.
2. Equipment that is out of date and not in keeping with current style and utility.
3. Faulty design resulting in inefficient use of floor space, poor location of various types of rooms in relation to other types, such as location of bathrooms in relation to bedrooms and such things as ceilings being too high or too low.

Figure 6.12
Cost approach calculations.

Replacement or reproduction cost:		
21,000 square feet @ $52.50 sq. ft.		$1,102,500
Less structure depreciation:		
Physical deterioration	$33,075	
Functional obsolescence	44,100	
Economic obsolescence	-0-	77,175
Depreciated value of structure Depreciated		$1,025,325
value of other improvements:		
Retaining walls	$10,000	
Paved drive and parking	15,000	
Exterior lighting	2,000	
Fencing	1,500	28,500
Depreciated value of all improvements:		$1,053,825
Land value by market data approach		253,000
Total property value		$1,306,825
Rounded to		$1,307,000

Economic Obsolescence

1. Changes in surrounding land use patterns resulting in increased vehicular traffic, air pollution, noise pollution, inharmonious land uses, and other hazards and nuisances adversely affecting the quality of the area.
2. Failure to adhere to the principle of highest and best use and thereby creating an overimprovement or underimprovement on the land, such as building a $150,000 house in a $300,000 neighborhood or a $300,000 house in a $150,000 neighborhood, or constructing an insufficient or excess number of rental units.
3. Changes in zoning and building regulations that adversely affect the use of property.
4. A reduction in demand for property in the area caused by local economic factors, changes in growth patterns, population shifts, or other economic factors adversely affecting property value.

Depreciation in the form of physical deterioration and functional obsolescence results from forces at work within the property. These two forms of depreciation may be curable or incurable. It may be physically possible and economically practical to correct the causes of physical deterioration and functional obsolescence, or it may not be possible or economically practical to effect the necessary changes. In cases where it is not physically possible or economically practical to cure the depreciation, typically the structure will be torn down and replaced by a new structure.

Economic obsolescence is caused by forces outside the property. Economic obsolescence is never curable by the property owner. The owner has no control over the properties owned by others, and therefore is not able to take necessary corrective measures.

Correlation and Appraisal Report

In making an appraisal, a professional appraiser will use the relevant approach to the value estimate as the primary appraisal method. Which method is most relevant depends on the type of property that is the subject of appraisal. For example, in estimating the value of a single-family, owner-occupied dwelling, the most relevant method is the **market data approach**. In addition, the qualified appraiser will also estimate the value of the property by each of the other two methods. In the case of the single-family dwelling, the appraiser would treat the property as though it were rental property and estimate the value using the income approach. Lastly, the appraiser would arrive at a value estimate by the cost approach. As a practical matter, the results obtained by these three methods will not be identical. There must be a correlation or reconciliation of the three different results to provide the most reliable estimate of value.

In the correlation of the reconciliation process, three factors are taken into consideration:

1. the relevancy of each of the three methods to the subject property
2. the reliability of the data on which each estimate is based
3. the strong points and weak points of each method

After these considerations, the greatest weight should be given to the estimate resulting from the use of the most appropriate or relevant method for the type of property that is the subject of the appraisal. For example, if the property is an office building, the most relevant approach, and the one to receive the greatest weight, would be the income approach. Even though the results obtained by the different approaches will not be exactly the same, they should be reasonably close. Therefore, each approach used provides a check on the other two. If the result by one particular method is considerably out of line with the others, this indicates some calculation error or some error in the data used as a basis.

The final step in the appraisal process is the preparation of the appraisal report. The report contains the appraiser's opinion of value based on the observation of the results obtained by the three methods and the appraiser's reasons for adopting the final estimate of value. The appraisal report may be either in narrative form or may be a form report. The narrative report provides all the factual data about the property and the elements of judgment used by the appraiser in arriving at the estimate of value. When a standard form is used to report the various property data used and the appraisal method employed, it is called a form report. A form report does not contain narrative information, but simply sets forth various facts and figures used in the appraisal process and the correlation of the final estimate of market value.

MAINE REAL ESTATE RULES AND REGULATIONS RELATING TO LISTINGS

Ch. 114–13177 Brokerage Agreements

A brokerage agreement between a real estate agency and a client must be in writing and at a minimum include the following:

The signature to be charged
The terms and conditions of the brokerage services to be provided
The method or amount of compensation to be paid
The date upon which the agreement will expire and
A statement that the agreement creates an agency-client relationship

A brokerage agreement may not be enforced against any client who in good faith subsequently engages the services of another real estate brokerage agency following the expiration date of the first brokerage agreement. Any brokerage agreement provision extending a real estate brokerage agency's right to a fee following expiration of the brokerage agreement may not extend that right beyond 6 months.

Ch. 410, Sect. 1 Advertising

Advertising must be done in the real estate brokerage agency's trade name as licensed with the commission and the trade name must be prominently displayed. A real estate brokerage agency or its affiliated licensees shall not advertise any real estate for sale without first obtaining the written permission of the owner or the owner's authorized representative. Advertising must be free from deception and shall not misrepresent the condition of the real estate, terms of the sale or purchase, real estate brokerage agency policies, or real estate brokerage services.

Ch. 410, Sect. 3 List Price/Market Value

A. A licensee shall make a careful and thorough analysis and interpretation of all factors affecting the value of real estate before rendering an opinion of value in connection with listing for sale that real estate.

B. A licensee shall disclose to his client any substantial discrepancy between the listed price and market value of which he is aware, or acting in a reasonable manner should have been aware.

Ch. 410, Sect. 3 Market Value

A transaction broker may not provide advice to either party regarding market value, but may provide comparable market data to a buyer or seller for the buyer or seller to deter-

-mine market value or list price. Providing comparable market data is performing a ministerial act.

A licensee who represents a buyer or seller client shall advise the client of any factors or conditions actually known by the licensee, or if acting in a reasonable manner, should have been known by the licensee, that my materially impact the client's interest as it pertains to the market value of real estate.

Ch. 410, Sect. 4 Net Listing Prohibited

A net listing shall be prohibited. A net listing is a type of listing in which the agency receives, as commission, all excess money over and above the minimum sale price set by the seller.

Ch. 410, Sect. 5 Duty to Furnish Real Estate Brokerage-Related Documents

A licensee shall furnish copies of brokerage agreements, offers, counteroffers and all types of contracts to all parties at the time of their signatures. Upon obtaining a written acceptance of an offer or counteroffer to purchase real estate, a licensee shall, within a reasonable time, deliver true, legible copies of the purchase and sale contract, signed by the seller and buyer, to both seller and buyer.

Ch. 410, Sect. 5 Disclosure of Real Estate Brokerage Agency Compensation Policy

Written brokerage agreements must include a statement disclosing the real estate brokerage agency's policy on cooperating with and compensation other real estate brokerage agencies in the sale or purchase of real estate. If the real estate brokerage agency's policy is not to compensate all other real estate brokerage agencies in the same manner, this policy must be included in the statement and include a notice to the buyer or seller that this policy may limit the participation of other real estate brokerage agencies in the marketplace.

Ch. 410, Sect. 10 Solicitation of Written Brokerage Agreements

A licensee shall not solicit a written brokerage agreement from a seller or buyer if the licensee knows, or acting in a reasonable manner should have known, that the buyer or seller has contracted with another real estate brokerage agency for the same real estate brokerage services on an exclusive basis. This section does not preclude a real estate brokerage agency from entering into a written brokerage agreement with a seller or buyer, when the initial contact is initiated by the seller or buyer, provided that the written brokerage agreement does not become effective until the expiration or release of the previous written brokerage agreement.

IMPORTANT POINTS

1. The listing inventory is the life blood of the real estate company.

2. For a property to have value, it must possess the characteristics of utility, scarcity, and transferability, and there must be effective demand.

3. Value, price, and cost are not the same.

4. The various types of value include market value, assessed value, insurance value, mortgage loan value, and condemnation value.

5. The basic valuation principles are highest and best use, substitution, supply and demand, conformity, anticipation, contribution, competition, and change.

6. Depreciation is the loss in value from any cause. In structures (land does not depreciate), the causes of depreciation are
   (1) physical deterioration,
   (2) functional obsolescence, and
   (3) economic obsolescence.

7. An appraisal is an estimate (not a determination) of value based on factual data.

8. The market data, or comparison approach, to the value estimate is the most relevant appraisal method for estimating the value of single-family, owner-occupied dwellings and vacant land.

9. The income approach, or appraisal by capitalization, is the most appropriate appraisal method for estimating the value of property that produces rental income.

10. The cost approach, or appraisal by summation, is the primary appraisal method for estimating the value of property that does not fall into the other categories.

11. A gross rent multiplier may be appropriate for estimating the value of rental property.

12. An appraisal report provides a value estimate based on a correlation of the estimates obtained by all three approaches.

REVIEW QUESTIONS

Answers to these questions are found in the Answer Key section at the back of the book.

1. Listings can be secured through:
   a. repeat business from satisfied customers
   b. centers of influence
   c. advertising for listings
   d. all of the above

2. Sellers who want to list their property for sale may be attracted to list with you because of:
   a. an image of success
   b. your professional ability
   c. your reputation for integrity
   d. all of the above

3. A real estate listing contract is:
   a. a list of all property for purposes of taxation
   b. the employment of an agency, by the owner to sell
   c. a list of all property owned by one person
   d. the total of the broker's listings

4. Items which would be essential to know when listing a property would include:
   a. real estate taxes
   b. zoning
   c. property in a flood area
   d. all of the above
   e. a and b only

5. What would be the best source of information as to the taxes on a piece of property?
   a. Registry of Deeds
   b. owner
   c. assessor's office
   d. tax bill

6. In deciding on a price for a prospective listing, which information would you rely on most heavily?
   a. comparable homes now on the market
   b. comparable homes recently sold
   c. comparables of expired listings
   d. what the seller needs to buy another house

7. All of the following characteristics must be present for a property to have value except:
   a. utility
   b. obsolescence
   c. transferability
   d. effective demand

8. Value is closely related to which of the following?
   a. price
   b. anticipation of future benefits
   c. supply
   d. all of the above

9. Inadequacy of wiring is an example of which of the following?
   a. anticipation
   b. economic obsolescence
   c. competition
   d. functional obsolescence

10. Which of the following causes of depreciation are not curable by the property owner?
    a. economic obsolescence
    b. functional obsolescence
    c. competitive obsolescence
    d. physical deterioration

11. The principle followed in making adjustments to comparables in an appraisal by the market data approach is which of the following?
   a. competition
   b. change
   c. contribution
   d. conformity

12. An appraisal is which of the following?
   a. estimate of value
   b. appropriation of value
   c. correlation of value
   d. determination of value

13. The primary appraisal method for estimating the value of vacant land is which of the following?
   a. cost approach
   b. market data approach
   c. income approach
   d. appraisal by capitalization

14. If the annual net income used in the appraisal by capitalization is $480,000, and the capitalization rate is 11 percent, which of the following will be the estimate of property value?
   a. $2,290,000
   b. $2,990,000
   c. $4,363,636
   d. $5,280,000

15. If a property produced a gross income of $103,000, and the GRM was 7.5, which of the following would be the indication of value?
   a. $137,333
   b. $772,500
   c. $927,000
   d. $1,373,333

CHAPTER 7

IMPORTANT TERMINOLOGY

actual eviction
assignment
constructive eviction
escalated lease
estate for years
eviction
freehold estate
graduated lease
gross lease
ground lease
index lease
landlord
lease
leasehold estate

lessee
lessor
net lease
percentage lease
periodic tenancy
reappraisal lease
right of first refusal clause
sandwich lease
subletting
tenancy at sufferance
tenancy at will
tenant
Tenant Security Deposit Act

LANDLORD– TENANT LAWS

IN THIS CHAPTER

It is important for a real estate licensee who lists and sells multiunit buildings or who acts as a rental agent to understand the rental relationship and the Maine statutes that establish the duties and rights of both landlord and tenant.

RELATIONSHIP BETWEEN LANDLORD AND TENANT

Definition of Parties

A **leasehold estate** arises when an owner of land transfers possession of that land to another for a period of time and terms. A **lease** is a contract between the owner of the property and the tenant that creates a relationship of landlord and tenant. The **landlord** is the owner of the property, who gives the lease, and is therefore also known as the **lessor**. The one who receives the lease is the **lessee**, or **tenant.**

The landlord retains title to the property, but has handed over possession to the tenant for a period of time. During this time, the tenant (lessee) possesses a leasehold estate and the landlord (lessor) possesses a reversion estate that enables her to retake possession at the end of the lease period. Therefore, it can be seen that in the creation of a lease, both **freehold** and nonfreehold estates would exist at the same time.

Estates and Contracts

A lease is both an estate in land and a contract. An estate in land may vary widely in both the quantity and quality of interest in real property. The landlord maintains the highest quantity of interest by holding title to the land. His bundle of rights is diminished, however, by giving the tenant the right of possession of the property, essentially, to the landlord's exclusion. The second concept, that of contract law, establishes both the rights and the duties of the parties as outlined in the lease. For a valid lease to exist, it must meet the usual requirements of a contract.

The parties to the lease contract must be legally competent to contract as is required for the creation of a valid contract. For validity the lease must contain a recital of consideration as is required for validity of any type of contract. The consideration is the conveying of the leasehold estate to the lessee by the lessor and the agreement on the part of the lessee to pay the specified rent to the lessor. As with other contracts, the lease must be for a legal purpose. If the lease is created for the purpose of permitting the lessee to use the property in a manner that is illegal, the lease will not be valid.

In essence, the lease contract must meet all requirements for validity for contracts in general and in addition must meet certain special requirements as previously discussed.

Landlord's Rights and Duties

The landlord who retains the title to the property during the lease term has the right of possession upon termination of the tenancy. The landlord's major duty is to provide fit premises (in residential property), that is, fit for human habitation within the unit she is renting. The landlord must comply with building codes, maintain and repair common areas, and repair utilities such as heat, plumbing, electrical, and appliances provided. Generally, she must do whatever is needed to make and keep the unit habitable. The landlord owes a duty to the tenants and their invitees to maintain common areas in a safe condition. This duty does not extend to trespassers or others who come for their own purpose. A landlord may not terminate utilities such as water, electricity, or heat unless repairs are in progress.

Tenant's Rights and Duties

The tenant has an exclusive right of possession and control of the property during the lease term. The tenant's primary duties are to pay the rent when due, maintain the individual living unit, keep the unit safe, and be responsible for any destruction, defacement, or damage. If the unit rented becomes unfit for human habitation due to landlord's negligence, the tenant can rescind the lease or file a complaint against the landlord in either district or superior court. The landlord under any circumstances may not seize the tenant's furniture, cut off his electricity, or use padlocks on the unit.

The tenant is obligated to return the property at the end of the lease in good condition and is not entitled to make alterations in the property without the consent of the landlord. In the absence of a specific prohibition against an assignment of the lease or subleasing the premises, the tenant is entitled to assign (or sublet) the lease to another.

Tenant Security Deposit Act

Landlords are allowed to require a security deposit from their tenants to cover unpaid rent or damage to the premises. Landlords in Maine must follow Maine's **Tenant Security Deposit Act** unless the building has five or fewer apartments, one of which is occupied by the owner.

The security deposit must be held in an escrow account and not commingled with the assets of the landlord. There is no requirement to pay interest on security deposits except for some types of federally subsidized housing.

The maximum amount that may be collected for security deposit may not exceed the equivalent of two months' rent. If there is a written rental agreement, the landlord must return the deposit to the tenant not more than thirty days from the date of the termination of the lease. If there is no written lease, it must be returned within 21 days of the termination of the tenancy.

Permitted uses of the deposit generally are limited to (1) damage to the unit; (2) nonfulfillment of the rental period; (3) unpaid bills; (4) court costs of eviction; and (5) costs of rerental if the tenant breaches the lease. If the landlord retains any portion of the security deposit, she must provide the tenant with a written statement itemizing the reasons for the retention; otherwise, the landlord is liable for double the amount withheld.

LEASEHOLD OR NONFREEHOLD ESTATES

These estates are less than freehold (less than a lifetime) and are, therefore, of a limited duration. These estates may be called tenancies, estates, or leaseholds and are more fully described next.

Estate for Years (Fixed Time)

The key feature of **estate for years** is simply that it exists only for a fixed period of time. The word *years* is misleading in that the estate does not have to be in effect for a year but just for any fixed period such as a week or even one day. The important point is that at the end of that stated period of time, the estate (rental agreement) terminates automatically, without any need for either party to give notice to the other. If the lease has any uncertainty about its duration, it cannot be an estate for years.

The lease must be in writing (as all leases in Maine) because a verbal lease will create a tenancy at will. If the lease is to run for a term of more than two years, it must be recorded in the Registry of Deeds.

Estate from Period-to-Period

Estate from period-to-period is commonly known as a **periodic tenancy** and can only be created if it is in writing. Its key feature is that it will automatically continue for successive periods unless one party gives proper notice to the other during a prescribed time. If the period is less than a year, a notice equal to the length of the period (not less than 30 days) is required; a tenancy of a year or more requires a 6 month notice. For example, if the required notice period is 6 months and parties entered the last 6 months of the lease without notifying the other of any change, a new lease would automatically be created for another period at the same terms.

These first two estates are essentially opposite in terms of what happens at the end of their original lease period; the first terminates, and the second renews itself.

Tenancy at Will

Tenancies at will may be created by an express or implied agreement. In Maine, a verbal lease creates only a tenancy at will.

In the estate at will, the duration of the term is completely unknown at the time the estate is created. This is because the estate at will may be terminated by either party at will, by simply giving the other party notice. For example, an owner of a property in Portland might allow some college students to occupy his home while he spends a portion of the winter in Florida. Both profit in that the owner has his home looked after in his absence and the students have a place to stay for an indefinite period of time. However, either party may terminate the arrangement by simply providing notice to the other. The period of notice must be 30 days and in writing, with the day of termination stated in the notice. If a 30 day notice is not given, it will not terminate the tenancy. If the rent is paid up beyond the 30-day period, the notice shall be made to expire on the rent day (the next due date for rent). The purpose for the notice is to allow ample time for the landlord to rent the unit again or to allow the tenant a reasonable time to find other accommodations.

The 30-day notice could be reduced to 7 days if: (1) substantial damage to the premises has been caused without repair, (2) a nuisance or a violation of the law exists, (3) the tenant has caused the unit to be unfit for habitation, or (4) the tenant is 7 or more days in arrears in rent.

If the tenant who is in arrears pays the full amount of rent due before the expiration of the 7 days, the notice shall become void.

A tenancy at will will also terminate upon the death of either party. A sale of the premises will also automatically terminate this type of tenancy.

Tenancy at Sufferance

Tenancy at sufferance is not truly an estate. The term is simply used to describe someone who was originally in lawful possession of another's property after that tenant's right to possession has terminated. This could occur upon termination of any of the three previously discussed leasehold estates. The term is used to make a distinction between the tenant at sufferance who was originally in lawful possession of the property and someone who was on the property illegally from the beginning (trespasser). The estate at sufferance will continue until such time that the property owner brings a legal action to evict the person wrongfully holding over or until the one holding over vacates voluntarily. During this period, the occupier is called a tenant at sufferance.

ESSENTIAL ELEMENTS OF A LEASE

A lease, as previously stated, is a conveyance of an interest in land (that is, an estate) and is therefore a contract. There are essential elements that are standard to all leases, and there are some provisions that can be added for protection of landlord or tenant. For example, a purchase and sales agreement is usually assignable unless otherwise specified, whereas it is a common practice to prohibit both subletting or assignment of leases in everyday practice without approval of the landlord.

The following are common elements of all leases.

Purpose

The purpose of the lease, first and foremost, is to convey (grant) a nonfreehold estate in return for valuable consideration. The properly drafted lease agreement, as with any other contract, establishes both the rights and the duties of each party.

Parties to the Lease

The names of all parties (lessors and lessees) to the lease must be included. If the property is owned by a married couple, both must execute (sign) the agreement since it is a contract conveying an estate for a period less than their own estate. All parties who will be considered tenants (lessees), obligated to pay rent, and bound by the terms of the contract must sign or be mentioned in the lease.

Property Description

Each lease must provide an accurate description of the leased premises. In leasing residential property, the street address, city, and state are sufficient for identification of the leased premises. In the case of a commercial lease, or a lease for mining or forestry operations, a more detailed description, such as a survey, would be necessary to define the scope of the premises being rented so that the tenants are aware of what space they may or may not use.

Term

The specific term of the lease, including a beginning and ending date, is a critical element in defining the estate. From the beginning date, the lease may run for a fixed period (estate for years), or an initial period with defined rights of renewal (periodic estate).

Rent and Deposits

The lease should indicate the amount of the rent and specify when and where it is due. If there is a penalty clause for late payments or forfeiture, that must be included, as well as the amount of security deposit requested by the landlord within the confines of the law. Any agreement by the tenant to participate in the payment of real property taxes, property insurance, utilities, maintenance, and so on, should be so noted.

Other Provisions

In addition to the previous essential elements for all leases, a number of other important issues should be addressed. In the absence of clear definition, the basic law of leasehold estates may provide other than what the grantor intended.

Assignment, Subletting, and Right of First Refusal

In the absence of a specific prohibition against an **assignment** of the lease or subleasing the premises, the lessee is entitled to assign the lease to another or sublet to another. An assignment transfers the lessee's entire interest in the lease without providing for any reversion of interest to the lessee. For example, if the lessee has a remaining term of 10 years in a lease and transfers the right to possession of the entire remaining 10-year term to another, an assignment is created. However, if the lessee transfers only 6 years of the remaining 10-year term to another, this is a sublease, or subletting, of the premises.

Subletting has the effect of creating a new lease wherein the original lessee becomes a lessor and the subtenant the lessee. This new lease is called a **sandwich lease**. The new leasehold interest is sandwiched in between the original lessor and the sublessee.

The lease may contain a **right of first refusal clause**. This provides the lessee with the opportunity to purchase the property at a price and terms determined by an offer received on the property by a third party. The lessor promises to give the lessee in this situation a first chance to purchase the property after informing him of the offer and the terms of that offer.

Use of the Leased Premises

The lessor may restrict the use of the leased premises by insertion of a clause to that effect in the lease. If the lease does not state a specified purpose, the tenant may use the premises for any lawful purpose.

Right of Entry

The landlord may not enter the leased premises without the consent of the tenant. The lease may point out under what circumstances the landlord may enter the property. Maine law states that a tenant cannot withhold consent for the landlord to enter if it is for the purposes of making repairs or exhibiting it to prospective buyers if a reasonable notice is given (24 hours).

Sample Lease

A sample lease that illustrates the provisions common to most leases is shown in Figure 7.1.

Figure 7.1 Agreement lease.

A

THIS LEASE made as of the_____day of_____20_____, by and between_____(hereinafter called "Landlord"), and _____of_____(hereinafter called "Tenant"), witnesseth that:

The Landlord leases to Tenant and the Tenant leases from the Landlord the premises known as Apartment Number_____, _____Pine Point, Scarborough, Maine, consisting of_____rooms for a term of_____months from _____20_____to_____20_____under the following terms and conditions:

B

1. Rent: The Tenants promise to pay rent in the amount of $_____per month, payable in advance on the _____day of each month, without demand, commencing on_____20_____at_____.

2. Security Deposit: Tenant shall deposit $_____with Landlord at the signing of this lease, which deposit may, at Landlord's sole option, be used to cure any default hereunder by Tenant, including costs for damage to the leased premises, missing items or cleaning of the leased premises. Landlord agrees to refund to Tenant the security deposit less any sums expended by Landlord in accordance with this lease.

C

3. Premises: Tenant shall maintain the premises, including the grounds, in a clean and orderly manner and shall deliver up the premises at the expiration or termination of this lease in good order and tenantable condition reasonable wear and tear expected.

4. Furnishings and Equipment: There is included in this lease all furniture, furnishings and equipment contained in the leased premises including, but not limited to, (a) a cooking range, (b) refrigerator, (c)_____and the same, together with all plumbing and electrical systems, shall be maintained by the Tenant in good clean order and repair, at Tenant's expense, and Tenant shall replace any damaged or broken furniture, furnishings, or equipment, reasonable wear and tear excepted, with that of like kind and quality.

D

5. Parking: Tenant shall have the right to park_____registered motor vehicle in the parking lot. If Tenant desires to park more than_____motor vehicle in said lot, special arrangements must be made, in writing, with Landlord. Landlord reserves the right to designate a specific parking place for Tenant's motor vehicle. Tenant agrees not to clean or repair said motor vehicle in said parking lot except as Landlord may authorize, not to store or park trailers, boats or snowmobiles thereon.

E

6. Alterations: Tenant agrees not to make any alterations, including making any holes in the walls or woodwork, or to paint the leased premises without first obtaining the express written permission of Landlord.

7. Utilities:_____shall pay all charges for heat and electricity as they come due. Tenant shall pay all charges for telephone services as they come due.

F

8. Use of Premises: Tenant agrees to use the leased premises only as a private residence. Tenant agrees not to do or permit any act or thing on the leased premises, or its grounds, that shall be unlawful or create a nuisance or shall interfere with the rights, comforts or conveniences of other tenants. Tenant specifically agrees not to make any noise, or to play loud music, audible in the other apartments after 11:00 p.m. Tenant further agrees not to use any electric or other type of auxiliary heater in the leased premises without the express written permission of Landlord, not to use the leased premises for any purposes which shall vitiate any insurance against fire thereon, or shall be deemed extra-hazardous by Landlord's insurance carriers. No water beds shall be used.

9. Occupants and Guests: Tenant and any of Tenant's children listed below shall be the sole occupants of the leased premises. No guest shall remain in the leased premises for more than four (4) days without first obtaining the express written permission of Landlord.

G

10. Assignment: Tenant shall not assign this lease or sublet the leased premises.

H

11. Pets: Tenant shall not keep or harbor any pets or animals on the leased premises.

I

12. Restrictions: No external television or radio antennas and no clothes lines shall be installed outside the leased premises, nor shall signs or other devices be hung from the exterior thereof. Tenant shall not use nails, tacks, staples or other similar devices for hanging articles from the interior walls. No damaging articles are to be placed on the walls, ceilings or floors of the leased premises. The toilets and sinks shall not be used for any purposes other than those for which they were constructed nor shall rubbish, rags or other improper articles be thrown into the same. No grease shall be poured into any sink. Damage to the building, furniture, furnishings and equipment caused by misuse of the same shall be borne by Tenant; such damage shall be cause for immediate termination of this lease.

13. Repairs: All repairs to the leased premises, furniture, furnishings and equipment shall be made or carried out by Landlord.

J

14. Tenant's Property: All Tenant's property on the leased premises shall be at Tenant's own risk; and Landlord shall not in any way be responsible therefor. Any personal property not removed by Tenant within seven days following the termination of the lease shall be deemed abandoned. Tenant shall not store any property on the porches of the leased premises or in any common area of the buildings and grounds of the_____.

(continued)

Figure 7.1 continued

15. Indemnification: The Tenant agrees that it will indemnify and hold harmless the Landlord from any loss, damage, claim, demand, suits, judgments or liabilities which the Landlord may incur and any costs or expenses to which the Landlord may be put, arising from any injury or death to persons or property, or any claim on account thereof resulting from the Tenant's use of the premises or the Tenant's failure to remove snow and ice. The Tenant further agrees to carry a suitable tenant's insurance policy including liability coverage for the premises.

16. Inspection: Landlord or its agents may enter to examine the leased premises at all reasonable times, and to make repairs and perform such maintenance as it deems necessary, or to show the leased premises to prospective purchasers or tenants.

17. Breach: If the Tenant shall fail to pay the rent when it is due, damage the leased premises, or the furniture, furnishings, or equipment contained therein, or shall fail to keep or perform any of the covenants contained herein, the Landlord may immediately declare a forfeiture, re-enter the premises, expel the Tenant (by force if necessary) sue for rent or resort to any other legal remedy. Tenant agrees to reimburse Landlord for any expenses occasioned by such breach, including but not limited to, reasonable attorneys' fees and other collection costs.

18. Termination: Upon the expiration or other termination of this lease, the Tenant agrees to deliver up the premises in good clean and tenantable condition, reasonable wear and tear expected. Tenant shall deliver all keys to Landlord and shall not be entitled to a refund of the security deposit until and unless all such keys are returned to Landlord.

IN WITNESS WHEREOF, the parties hereto have caused the lease to be executed the day and year first written above.

WITNESS   LANDLORD

_____   _____

                                          TENANTS

_____   _____

_____   _____

       Children of Tenant   Age

_____   _____

Section A. Basic Information. The first section indicates (1) the date the lease was signed, (2) the parties, landlord, and tenant, (3) the premises to be leased, and (4) the term of the lease from beginning to end.

Section B. The payment of the rent including the amount, the due date, and where the rent will be paid is established. The amount of the security deposit is indicated and, under Maine law, cannot exceed two months' rent. The lease outlines the reasons why the landlord may withhold the security deposit or any part thereof.

Section C. Clauses 3 and 4 spell out how the unit will be maintained during the term and the conditions of the unit upon delivery.

Section D. Parking is often limited as to the number of cars that can be parked on the premises and many leases will usually indicate the designated areas to park.

Section E. Any alterations need to receive written permission before proceeding. Section F.

There is an acknowledgment that the leased unit will be used for a residence only and outline what will be (or not be) permitted on the premises. A lease should list all tenants who plan to occupy the unit and contain a provision to handle a new tenant to the premises.

Section G. Unless otherwise stated, a lease, like any other contract, can be assigned. Most residential leases contain a clause that does not allow assignments or subletting unless the landlord agrees. The landlord will usually check references before any assignment is made.

Section H. Pets are not usually allowed in leased units due to the damage that can be incurred, as well as increased cleaning costs.

Section I. Landlords may detail any restrictions to the use of premises and indicate that if there is damage to the unit, who will be responsible for doing the repairs.

Section J. Clauses 14 and 15 deal with liability relating to the tenant's property and any injury resulting from tenant's negligence.

Section K. This clause allows the landlord to enter the premises for the purposes of repair, maintenance, and showing the premises.

Section L. In the event there is a breach of contract, this clause indicates the course of action that will be taken by the landlord, including any legal expenses.

Section M. This clause defines what needs to be done by the tenant upon term nation of the contract in order to recover the security deposit.

Section N. In order to be valid, the lease must be signed by both landlord and tenant. All parties who will occupy the unit are to be listed.

CLASSIFICATIONS OF LEASES

Gross and Net Leases

There are two primary classes of leases, based on the arrangement of paying the expenses of the rental property. A **gross lease** provides for the owner (lessor) to pay expenses. A **net lease** means that the tenant (lessee) pays some or all of the expenses such as taxes, assessments, maintenance, insurance, and utilities. Some use terms such as *net net*, or even *triple net*, depending upon how many property expenses the tenant pays.

Percentage Lease

Many commercial leases are **percentage leases**. The rent in a percentage lease includes a fairly low fixed amount of rent per month plus an additional monthly rent, which is a percentage of the lessee's gross sales. The majority of commercial leases are percentage leases in cases where the lessee is using the property to conduct a retail business. This is especially true of shopping malls. The percentage lease provides the lessor with a guaranteed monthly rental plus the opportunity to participate in the sales volume of the lessee on a percentage basis.

Graduated Lease

A **graduated lease** is one in which the rental amount changes from period to period over the lease term. The change in rental amount is specified in the lease contract. For example, a lease may be at $1000 per month for the first year, $1100 per month the second year, and $1200 per month the third year.

Index Lease

An **index lease** is one in which the rental amount is changed in proportion to changes in the Consumer Price Index (CPI) published by the United States Department of Labor, or other similar index. The lease will specify a percentage change in relation to the number of points the CPI changes annually.

Reappraisal Lease

A **reappraisal lease** is one in which changes in rental amount are based on changes in property value as demonstrated by periodic reappraisals of the property. Such appraisals may occur at three- or five-year intervals in the case of a long-term lease. The rent changes a specified percentage of the previous year's rent as spelled out in the contract.

Ground Lease

This is a lease of unimproved land. The **ground lease** normally contains a provision that a building will be constructed on the land by the lessee. The lease should always contain a provision as to the disposition of the improvements on the land constructed by the lessee at the end of the lease term. In the absence of a provision as to the disposition of the improvements at the end of the lease term, the improvements will automatically belong to the lessor as owner of the land. The ground lease is a long-term lease because the lessee must have sufficient time to recoup any costs and earn a profit during the term of the lease.

Escalated Lease

An **escalated lease** provides for rental changes in proportion to the changes in the lessor's costs of ownership and operation of the property. As changes occur in the lessor's obligations for real property taxes and operating expenses, the lease will change in specified proportions.

EVICTION

Eviction is a procedure for removing a tenant from the premises by due process of law.

Actual Eviction

When a tenant has breached a condition of the lease, such as through nonpayment of rent or bringing animals into a "no pets" apartment, the landlord may begin a process called **actual eviction** to remove the tenant from the premises unless she complies with the terms of the lease agreement.

Constructive Eviction

Constructive eviction results when the landlord renders the premises so unfit for habitation that the tenant must actually abandon the premises. If the lessor fails to maintain the property through personal fault or negligence, the lessee is entitled to sue for damages, but the tenant must first actually abandon the premises.

Eviction of a Tenant at Will

The majority of eviction proceedings involve tenants at will. There does not need to be a cause for the eviction. The steps involved include the following:

1. The tenancy may be terminated by giving a written 30 notice. The 30 day notice must expire on or after the date through which the rent has been paid. It must include the address of the premises and the effective date of the termination.
2. The notice could be either hand delivered to the tenant or sent by certified mail, return receipt requested, and marked restricted delivery for proof that the tenant received it.

3. If the tenant has not complied with the notice, an action of forcible entry and detainer may be started by the sheriff serving a summons and complaint. This gives the tenant 7 days after he has been served to prepare for a hearing.

4. If the hearing results in favor of the landlord, the tenant will have 10 days to appeal to superior court. If after the 10 days no appeal has been made, a writ of possession is issued and the sheriff proceeds to evict the tenant.

Under this scenario, the eviction process can take a minimum of 60 days. As noted earlier in the chapter, the eviction notice can be 7 days rather than 30 days, and the whole eviction process will take a minimum of 30 days from start to finish. The 7-day notice must state the reason for the notice.

Eviction of a Tenant Under a Written Lease

Often leases are written to terminate automatically if certain conditions of the lease are ignored (for example, assignment of a lease that specifically states no assignment) or not fulfilled (for example, nonpayment of rent). The effective date of the termination will be governed by the terms of the lease itself. If it is immediate upon breach of contract, then the effective termination date can be the same date the notice is delivered. The lease might indicate a specified number of days for termination of the lease after breach of contract. The remainder of the proceeding follows the eviction process as previously outlined under the heading "Tenant at Will."

Generally the landlord–tenant statutes do not cover hotel and motel owners. The determining factor of whether it is covered does not depend on the occupant being permanent or transient, but in control. If the occupant retains exclusive control, the relationship of landlord and tenant will arise. If the owner provides services to the "guest," such as regular change of linen or supplying maid service, then in all likelihood, the owner is exempt from the landlord–tenant laws.

Abandonment

If the unit is abandoned and property remains on the premises, the property will be considered abandoned and must be stored in a safe, dry secure location. A notice must be send to the tenant at the tenant's last known address. The notice must contain an itemized list of the items abandoned and a statement that the property will be disposed of after 14 days if the tenant has not responded.

If the tenant makes an oral or written claim for the property within 7 days after the date the notice is sent, the landlord may not condition the release of the property to the tenant upon the tenant's payment of any rental arrearages, damages and costs of storage as long as the tenant makes arrangements to retrieve the property by the 14th day after the notice is sent.

If the tenant fails to retrieve the property by the 14th day, the landlord may employ one or more of the following remedies

- Condition the release of the property upon the tenant's payment or all rental arrearages, damages and costs of storage.
- Sell any property for a reasonable fair market price and apply all proceeds to back rent, damages, and costs of storage and sale. All remaining balances forwarded to the Secretary of State or
- Dispose of any property that has no reasonable fair market value.

Mobile Home Parks

Landlord–tenant laws apply to people who own their own mobile homes and are renting a lot in the mobile home park

Security deposits are handled differently in a mobile home park. When the deposit is returned, it must include a pervailing annual interest rate added to the deposit. No portion of the security deposit can be retained to pay for normal wear and tear and, if retained, the park owner shall provide to the tenant a written statement itemizing the reasons for the retention within 21 days after the termination of tenancy.

For nonpayment of rent, the tenancy may be terminated by 30 days' notice in writing; otherwise, the park owner needs to give 45 days' notice in writing to the tenant. If the park owner has made at least three witnessed good-faith efforts on 3 separate days to serve the tenant and has been unsuccessful, the notice must be mailed by first class mail to the last known address and a copy of the notice left at the tenant's space in the park. The eviction process is the same as previously outlined in this chapter.

IMPORTANT POINTS

1. A landlord is the lessor who retains a freehold estate (ownership) at the same time conveying a nonfreehold estate (possession) to the tenant.

2. A rental interest involves both the concepts of contracts and estates.

3. The landlord is required to maintain "fit premises" by maintaining the common areas, plumbing, and heating and cooling systems.

4. The Tenant Security Deposit Act requires landlords to account for tenants' funds by depositing the funds in a separate account. Maximum limits for the amount of funds that may be held are equal to 2 months' rent. Funds must be accounted for and returned within 30 days of the termination of the lease, or if there is no lease, it must be returned within 21 days of tenant moving out of the apartment.

5. The landlord is prohibited from physically barring the tenant from the unit as well as seizing the tenant's personal property.

6. A tenant cannot withhold rent, but can seek court action for a refund or be excused from the lease if the landlord breaches his or her duty.

7. There are four primary types of leases: (1) an estate for years is for a fixed period of time; (2) an estate from period-to-period automatically renews itself in the absence of notice by either party within a prescribed period; (3) a tenancy at will is for an indefinite or undetermined period of time and is not in writing; and (4) a tenancy at sufferance arises when a tenant is still in possession of the premises after her legal rental period has expired.

8. The two primary classifications of leases are a gross lease where the owner pays any of the expenses of the property, and a net lease in which the tenant pays all of the expenses.

9. Types of leases based on the payment arrangement include percentage, graduated, indexed, reappraisal, and escalated. A ground lease is for the rental of the land alone, which may be improved by the tenant.

10. Termination of leases may occur by (1) breach of condition, (2) expiration of the rental term, (3) mutual agreement, and (4) condemnation of the property.

11. Actual eviction (ejectment) occurs when the lessee fails to adhere to conditions of the lease. Constructive eviction results from action or inaction of the lessor that renders the premises uninhabitable.

12. Lease contracts that extend for two years or more are required to be recorded in order to be enforceable.

REVIEW QUESTIONS

Answers to these questions are found in the Answer Key section at the back of the book.

1. All of the following are characteristics of leasehold estates except:
   a. they are all estates of unlimited duration
   b. the lessor retains title to the property
   c. the lessee has possession and control of the property
   d. the lessor may enter the property with proper notice

2. All of the following statements regarding an estate for years are correct except:
   a. the duration of the estate must be definite
   b. the duration of the estate must be at least one year
   c. the estate automatically terminates without notice
   d. the contract creating an estate for years must be in writing for validity

3. Which is an estate that automatically renews itself for consecutive periods?
   a. estate at will
   b. life estate
   c. estate from year-to-year
   d. estate for years

4. All are true of estates for years, estate for year-to-year, estates at will except they:
   a. are leasehold estates
   b. create a legal relationship between the parties of landlord and tenant
   c. give no title to the property
   d. encumber title of the owner

5. All of the following are typical provisions that may be found in lease contracts creating an estate for years except:
   a. provision for a term of indefinite duration
   b. right of first refusal
   c. right to make alterations
   d. option to renew

6. A transaction in which a property owner sells the property and leases it from the purchaser is described as which of the following?
   a. option to renew
   b. sale and leaseback
   c. ground lease
   d. sublease

7. The type of lease that is commonly used in shopping malls is:
   a. net lease
   b. index lease
   c. graduated lease
   d. percentage lease

8. An estate which is to continue for a fixed or definite time is called:
   a. an estate for years
   b. a tenancy at will
   c. a periodic estate
   d. a freehold estate

9. A verbal lease will result in which of the following?
   a. tenant for years
   b. tenant at sufferance
   c. tenancy at will
   d. periodic tenant

10. With a tenant at will, how many days does a landlord have to return a security deposit once a tenant turns the apartment over to the landlord?
    a. 21 days
    b. 7 days
    c. 30 days
    d. 60 days

CHAPTER 8

IMPORTANT TERMINOLOGY

building codes
certificate of occupancy
cluster zoning
coastal wetlands law
comprehensive plan
conditions
covenant
declaration of restrictions
deed restrictions
enabling acts
Environmental Policy Act of 1969
Environmental Protection Agency (EPA)
freshwater wetlands law
injunction
Interstate Land Sales Full Disclosure Act
nonconforming use

planned unit developments (PUDs)
planning board
private land use control
public land use control
restrictive covenants
reversion of title
run with the land
setbacks
shoreland zoning
spot zoning
subdivision
subdivision ordinances
variance
wetlands
zoning map
zoning ordinance

LAND USE CONTROLS

IN THIS CHAPTER

The understanding of land use controls is very important to the real estate agent. Almost every property will be subject to some form of control, whether it is the zoning ordinance of a city, the general restrictions of a subdivision plan, the unique deed restrictions of one parcel of land, or the impact of state and/or federal legislation. Any of these may have a major impact on the owner's rights.

Real estate agents are obligated to be knowledgeable of existing public and private land use controls within their market area and must keep abreast of changes in the requirements as they occur. This knowledge is necessary so that real estate agents can fulfill their obligations to their clients and customers. Lack of knowledge in these areas may subject real estate agents to civil liability to injured parties and possible criminal liability under certain federal laws.

HISTORICAL DEVELOPMENT OF LAND USE CONTROLS

Private control of land use was the forerunner of **public land use controls**. In 1848, the courts first recognized and enforced restrictive covenants regulating land use in residential subdivisions. However, it was not until 1926 when the United States Supreme Court upheld the validity of zoning ordinances that public land use controls became legally reliable. Prior to these two important legal events, there was no way by which a developer or governmental unit could regulate land use, even though the need for such controls was readily apparent.

The increase in population density dictates the necessity for land use controls. The abuses of a few property owners in the use of their land can have a substantial adverse effect on the rights of other property owners and cause depreciation of their property.

PRIVATE LAND USE CONTROLS

Individual owners have the right to place private controls on their own real estate. These restrictions take the form of individual deed restrictions or subdivision restrictive covenants that affect the entire subdivision. (See Figure 8.1.)

Individual Deed Restrictions

Individual **deed restrictions** exist in the form of covenants or in the form of conditions. A **covenant** may exist in a deed to benefit property that is sold or to benefit a property that is retained in the case of a sale of adjoining property. For example, an owner selling an adjoining

Figure 8.1
Private land
use controls.

1. Individual deed restrictions
2. Restrictive covenants
   (Declaration of restrictions)

property provides in the deed that a structure may not be erected in a certain area of the property sold to protect the view from the property retained or to prevent the loss of reception of light and air to the property retained. These restrictions are covenants that **"run with the land,"** meaning that they move with the title in any subsequent conveyance. Covenants may be enforced by a suit for damages or by injunction. Restrictions that provide for a **reversion of title** if they are violated are called **conditions**. If a condition is violated, ownership reverts to the grantor.

Restrictive Covenants

Restrictive covenants are restrictions placed on the use of land by the developer of a residential subdivision. The purpose of these covenants is to preserve and protect the quality of land in subdivisions and to maximize land values by requiring the homogeneous use of land by purchasers of property in the subdivision. The covenants are promises on the part of the purchasers of property in the subdivision to limit their use of their property by complying with the requirements of the restrictive covenants and, therefore, are negative easements. The deed conveying title to property in the subdivision will contain a reference to a recorded plat of the subdivision and a refer-ence to the recording of the restrictive covenants; or, the restrictions may be recited in each deed of conveyance. Restrictions must be consistent, reasonable, and beneficial to all property owners alike.

If the subdivision is in a zoned area, the restrictive covenants will have priority over the zoning ordinance to the extent that the covenants are more restrictive than the zoning requirements. For example, if the zoning permits multifamily dwellings and the restrictive covenants limit land use to single-family dwellings, the restrictive covenants will be enforced. However, if restrictive covenants are contrary to public law and public policy, they will not be enforced. For example, a restrictive covenant requiring discrimination on the basis of race, color, religion, sex, or national origin is invalid. Also, restrictive covenants are not valid unless they are recorded on the public record in the county where the land is located.

Figure 8.2
Restrictions applied
to land retained.

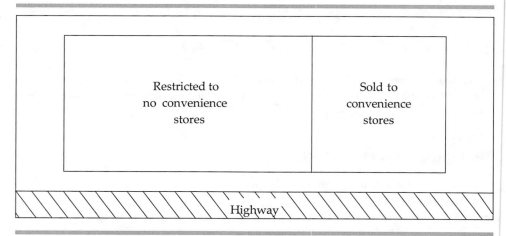

Restrictive covenants are land use limitations that provide a general plan for development of a subdivision. Prior to the start of development, the developer will establish a list of rules each lot purchaser will be required to adhere to in the use of the property. These rules controlling the use of land are then recorded in an instrument called **declaration of restrictions**. The declaration is recorded simultaneously with the plat and will include a reference to the plat. Typical restrictive covenants include the following:

1. Only single-family dwellings may be constructed in the subdivision.
2. Dwellings must contain a specified minimum number of square feet of living area.
3. Only one single-family dwelling may be constructed on a lot.
4. No lot may be subdivided.
5. Dwellings must be of a harmonious architectural style. To ensure this, a site plan and plans and specifications for the structure must be submitted to and approved by a committee before the start of construction. Sometimes a height restriction on the building is also included.
6. Structures must be set back a specified distance from the front property line and a specified distance from interior property lines.
7. Temporary structures may not be placed on any lot.
8. Covenants may be enforced by any one property owner or several property owners of land within the subdivision by taking appropriate court actions.
9. A specified time period for which the covenants will remain in effect. Also, there may be specified automatic renewal periods that may be changed by a vote of the property owners.

It is important for real estate agents to be aware of the existence of restrictive covenants in subdivisions where they are selling property. The agent should provide prospective buyers with a copy of the covenants, which may be obtained from the developer if he is still on the site, or from the Registry of Deeds in the county in which the property is located. In preparing offers to purchase in the subdivision, the real estate agent should include a provision that the offeror acknowledges the receipt of a copy of the restrictive covenants.

Termination of Covenants

Restrictive covenants may be terminated in the following ways:

1. Expiration of the time period for which the covenants were created.
2. Unanimous vote of the property owners to terminate the restrictions, unless the restrictions provide for termination by vote of a smaller number of landowners.
3. Changes in the character of the subdivision that make it unsatisfactory for the type of use specified by the restrictions to continue. For example, as a result of the failure of property owners in a subdivision restricted to single-family residential use to enforce the restrictions, the area gradually changes to commercial use. Consequently, the subdivision is no longer suitable for limitation to residential use.
4. The right to enforce particular restrictions may be lost by abandonment, which occurs when the property owners have violated their restrictions and many of them have participated in the violations. As a result, a court may rule that there has been an abandonment of the original general plan by the property owners and, therefore, the court will not enforce the restrictions.

5. Failure to enforce restrictions on a timely basis. An owner or owners cannot sit idly by and watch someone complete a structure in a subdivision in violation of the restrictive covenants and then attempt to enforce the restriction by court action. The court will not apply the restriction against the violator. Therefore, the restriction is terminated by the failure of action on a timely basis by the property owners to enforce restrictive covenants.

Enforcement of Covenants

Private land use controls are enforced by public law. This is accomplished by the action of a court known as an injunction. An injunction will prevent a use contrary to the restrictions of record, or order the removal of any such uses that have been implemented. In a practical sense, the individuals who bear the primary responsibility for seeing the restrictions are enforced are the other owners of property in the affected area. Failure of these neighbors to enforce the restrictions on a timely basis might lead to the eventual loss of the right to enforce the restrictions at all.

Enforcement of the covenants is not limited to the original purchasers of property in the subdivision. Subsequent purchasers must abide by and may enforce the restrictive covenants until such time as the covenants may be terminated as previously discussed. That is, the restrictions "run with the land."

PUBLIC LAND USE CONTROLS

Private land use controls are definitely limited in scope. Only a specific area can be subject to private use controls in the form of restrictive covenants. The owners of property in subdivisions in which restrictive covenants exist have absolutely no control over surrounding land uses. Therefore, a subdivision may be adversely affected by an uncontrolled use of an adjoining property outside the subdivision. As a result, people became aware of the need for planning and land use controls for large areas. This is provided by zoning ordinances, the first of which was enacted in 1916.

The legality of zoning laws was upheld by the United States Supreme Court in 1926. The early zoning ordinances were concerned primarily with height regulations and front, side, and rear yard requirements to ensure that the population had adequate air and light. Zoning regulations later emphasized the separation of residential neighborhoods from nonresidential uses, such as commercial and industrial.

Planning and Zoning

The purpose of planning is to provide for the orderly growth of a community that will result in the greatest social and economic benefits to the people in the community. State legisla tures over the years have passed **enabling acts** that provide the legal basis for cities and counties to develop long-range plans for growth. Planning and zoning are based on the police power of government to enable it to fulfill its responsibility for the protection of the health, safety, and welfare of the people.

Zoning starts with city or county planning. The zoning laws implement and enforce the plan. Violations of zoning laws can be corrected by a court injunction requiring the violation to be discontinued, even to the extent of ordering an unlawful structure to be demolished.

Maine law requires that a comprehensive plan is necessary for any zoning ordinance to be adopted. Prepared by the planning board, a **comprehensive plan** is a compilation of policy standards, goals, maps, and pertinent data relative to the past, present, and future trends of the municipality with respect to its population, land use, and public facilities.

The first step taken in developing this plan is to determine what the city contains by making a survey of the community's physical and economic assets. With this information as a basis, a master plan for orderly growth can be created. As a result of the plan, the various uses to which property may be put in specific areas is designated.

A **zoning ordinance** consists of two parts: (1) the **zoning map**, which divides the community into various designated districts and (2) text of the ordinance, which sets forth the type of use permitted under each zoning classification and specific requirements for compliance. The extent of authority for zoning ordinances is prescribed by the enabling acts passed by the state legislatures. These acts specify the types of uses subject to regulation and limit the geographical area subject to the ordinances to the boundaries of the government unit enacting the zoning laws. For example, city zoning ordinances may not apply into the county beyond the city limits. However, it is not unusual for a county government to authorize the extension of city zoning for some specified distance into the county and, in some cases, cities have been empowered by the state to specifically extend zoning beyond the city limits.

There are several zoning classifications established by local ordinances: (1) residential, which can be subdivided into single family and various levels of multifamily dwellings, (2) commercial, (3) light manufacturing, (4) heavy industrial, (5) shoreland preservation, (6) resource protection, and (7) multiple use or **cluster zoning**. The latter category provides for **planned unit developments (PUDs),** which create a neighborhood of cluster housing and supporting business establishments.

In addition to simply specifying a type of permitted use or special exceptions within a zone, zoning laws also define certain standards and requirements that must be met for each permitted type of use. These requirements will include such things as minimum **setbacks** from the front property line to the building line, as well as setbacks from the interior property lines, lot size on which a structure may be placed, height restrictions to prevent the interference with the reception of sunlight and air to other properties, regulations against building in flood plains, and requirements for off-street parking.

Development of a zoning ordinance begins with the creation of a **planning board**, which inventories the land within the city/town and assembles a draft zoning document. This plan is presented to the city/town council for review. After a public hearing and final approval of the planning board and town council, it goes into effect. The use standards will vary according to the district, but usually contain the following:

1. Permitted use. These uses are permitted as a matter of right.
2. Special exceptions. Uses that require a special permit approved by the planning board. Approval is on a case-to-case basis.
3. Prohibited uses. These would be uses not allowed under any circumstances.
4. Minimum lot size. These would be minimal requirements for building a structure on the lot.
5. Minimum setback requirements. The structure on the lot has to be a minimum number of feet from the front, side, and back boundaries of the lot.

Nonconforming Use

A **nonconforming use** occurs when the use of property in a zoned area is different from that specified by the zoning code for that area. When zoning is first imposed on an area or when property is rezoned, the zoning authority cannot require the property owners to discontinue a use that does not now conform to the zoning ordinance. The nonconforming use must be permitted because it would be unconstitutional to require the property owners to terminate the nonconforming use. Therefore, in these cases, the property owner is permitted to continue a nonconforming use, and thus, a lawful nonconforming use. Otherwise, a nonconforming use is unlawful. However, the nonconforming user is subject to certain requirements that exist to gradually eliminate the nonconforming use. Examples of these requirements are as follows:

1. If the property owner abandons the nonconforming use, the owner cannot resume that type of use at a later date, but may only use the property in a manner that conforms to the zoning ordinance.
2. The property owner may not make structural changes to the property to expand the nonconforming use or change the use to a different nonconforming use. The owner is only permitted to make normal necessary repairs to the structure.
3. The nonconforming use cannot be changed from one type of nonconforming use to another type of nonconforming use.
4. If a nonconforming structure is destroyed by fire or other casualty, it cannot be replaced by another nonconforming structure.
5. Some ordinances provide for a long-term amortization period during which the nonconforming owner is permitted to continue the nonconforming use. At the end of this long-term period, the owner would have to change the use to conform with the zoning ordinance, rebuilding the structure if necessary.

Variance

A **variance** is a permitted deviation from specific requirements of the zoning ordinance. For example, if an owner's lot is slightly smaller than the requirements of the zoning ordinance as to the minimum lot size upon which a structure may be built, the owner may be granted a variance by petitioning the appropriate authorities.

Variances are permitted where the deviation is not substantial and where strict compliance would impose an undue hardship on the property owner. The hardship must be applicable to one property only and be a peculiar or special hardship for that property under the zoning law. The special hardship does not exist where all of the property owners in the zoned area have the same difficulty.

Spot Zoning

Spot zoning occurs when a certain property within a zoned area is rezoned to permit a use that is different from the zoning requirements for that zoned area. If the rezoning of a particular property is simply for the benefit of the property owner and has the effect of increasing the land value, the spot zoning is illegal and invalid; however, when spot zoning is used for the benefit of the community and not for the benefit of a particular property owner (or owners), the spot zoning is not illegal and is valid. Legal spot zoning may typically occur in urban development areas to permit shopping areas for the benefit of the community in locations where these uses existed previously.

Implementation and Enforcement

Zoning ordinances are implemented and enforced usually by the code enforcement officer (building inspector) and the Zoning Board of Appeals. On a day-to-day basis, the code enforcement officer enforces the ordinance, inspecting code violations and reviewing applications for building permits. If the application is not in conformance with the ordinance, the permit will be denied or sent to the Zoning Board of Appeals to grant a special exception or variance. (This is granted in Maine only when there is "undue hardship.")

Subdivision Law

As of September 1971, the state of Maine defined a **subdivision** as a parcel of land divided into 3 or more lots during a 5-year period. Lots of 40 or more acres generally are not counted as lots unless they are in a shoreland area. To be legal, the subdivision must be approved by its municipality, and it must be recorded. The track of land must be contiguous and in the same ownership. Exceptions to the law include divisions of the land accomplished by device; condemnation; order of court; gift to a person related by blood, marriage, or adoption; or transfer of the land to owners of abutting properties unless the intent of the transfer is to avoid the objectives of the law.

Effective July 1990, a subdivision now includes the division placement or construction of a structure on a parcel resulting in 3 or more units within a 5-year period. Since modifications and changes have been made to the original law, a licensee should not give advice or interpretation regarding the regulation, but should refer interested parties to someone of authority. In June 2001, the exemption for lots created by gift to a person related to the donor by blood, marriage, or adoption was narrrowed. In order to qualify for this exemption, the land has to have been held by the donor for a continuous period of five years prior to the gift; and exempt gifts will now only be those made to a spouse, parent, grandparent, brother, sister, child, or grandchild related by blood, marriage, or adoption. A gift, however, will now be defined as being for consideration not in excess of one-half the assessed value of the real estate, implying that gifts can now involve some consideration being paid. The exemption for land conveyed to owners of abutting land has also been modified. There is now a requirement that a conveyance to an owner of abutting land must be a conveyance of land that does not create a separate lot. In addition, if the land conveyed is transferred within five years without all of the abutting land it was merged with, then the original conveyance will be treated as creating a lot for purposes of the subdivision law. There has been an exemption in the subdivision law commonly referred to as the "homestead exemption." If two lots are conveyed out by a grantor who retains the remaining land and has used it as a single-family residence for five years prior to the second conveyance, a subdivision has not been created. The change in June 2001 simply clarifies that the retained land must have been used as the divider's principal residence and the five-year period must be immediately preceding the division.

Subdivision Regulation

The state subdivision law is administered by local planning boards that review applications for subdivisions. The purpose of subdivision regulations is to protect purchasers of property within the subdivisions and to protect the taxpayers in the city or county from the imposition of significantly increased tax burdens resulting from the demands for services generated by a new subdivision.

Subdivision ordinances typically address the following requirements: (Some towns also have a Roads, Ways, and Street Acceptance Ordinance.)

1. Streets must be of a specified width, be curbed, have storm drains, and not exceed certain maximum grade specifications.
2. Lots may not be smaller than a specified minimum size.
3. Dwellings in certain areas must be for single-family occupancy only. Specific areas may be set aside for multifamily dwellings.
4. Utilities, including water, sewer, electric, and telephone, must be available to each lot.
5. All houses must be placed on lots to meet specified minimum standards for setbacks from the front property line as well as from interior property lines.

6. There must be adequate area drainage to provide for satisfactory runoff of rainfall to avoid damage to any properties.

Building Codes

Building codes provide another form of control of land use for the protection of the public. These codes regulate such things as materials used in construction, electrical wiring, fire and safety standards, and sanitary equipment facilities.

The codes require that a permit must be obtained from the appropriate local government authority before the construction or renovation of a commercial building or residential property may be started. While construction is in progress, frequent inspections are performed by local government inspectors to make certain that the code requirements are being met.

After a satisfactory final inspection has been made, a **certificate of occupancy** will be issued. This permits the occupation of the structure by tenants or the owner. Many cities today require that a certificate of occupancy, based upon a satisfactory inspection of the property, be issued prior to occupancy by a new owner or tenant of any structure even though it is not new construction and/or has not been renovated. Inspection is required, to reveal any deficiencies in the structure requiring correction, before the city will issue a certificate of occupancy for the protection of the new purchaser or tenant.

Interstate Land Sales Full Disclosure Act

The **Interstate Land Sales Full Disclosure Act**, a federal regulation of the interstate (across state lines) sale of unimproved lots, became effective in 1969 and was made more restrictive by an amendment in 1980. The act is administered by the secretary of Housing and Urban Development (HUD) through the office of Interstate Land Sales registration.

The purpose of the act is to prevent fraudulent marketing schemes that may occur when land is sold by misleading sales practices on a sight unseen basis. The act requires that a developer file a Statement of Record with HUD before offering unimproved lots in interstate commerce by telephone or through the mails. The Statement of Record requires disclosure of information about the property specified by HUD.

The developer is also required to provide each purchaser or lessee of property with a printed property report, which discloses specific information about the land before a purchase contract or lease is signed by the purchaser or lessee. The property report contains specific information about the land for the protection of the purchaser or lessee. Required information includes such things as the type of title a buyer will receive, number of homes currently occupied, availability of recreation facilities, distance to nearby communities, utility services and charges, and soil or other foundation problems in construction. If the purchaser or lessee is not supplied with a copy of the property report prior to signing a purchase contract or lease, the purchaser may avoid the contract.

The act provides for several exemptions, the most important of which are the following:

1. Subdivisions in which the lots are of five acres or more.
2. Subdivisions that consist of less than 25 lots.
3. Lots that are offered for sale exclusively to building contractors.
4. Lots on which a building exists or where there is a contract that obligates the lot seller to construct a building within two years.

If a developer offers only part of the total tract owned, and thereby limits the subdivision to less than 25 lots to acquire an exemption, the developer may not then sell additional lots within the tract. HUD considers these additional lots to be part of a "common plan" for development and marketing, thereby eliminating the opportunity for several exemptions for the developer as a result of a piecemeal development of a large tract in sections of fewer than 25 lots at a time.

The act provides severe penalties for violation by a developer or a real estate agent participating in marketing the property. The developer and/or the real estate agent can be sued for damages by a purchaser or lessee and is potentially subject to a criminal penalty by fine of up to $5,000 or imprisonment for up to five years or both. Therefore, it is extremely important for real estate agents to ascertain that a developer has complied with the law or is exempt prior to acting as an agent for the developer in marketing the property.

Environmental Protection Legislation

The national **Environmental Policy Act of 1969** *requires filing an environmental impact statement with the* **Environmental Protection Agency (EPA)** *prior to changing or initiating a land use or development*, to ensure that the use will not adversely affect the environment. Typical subject areas regulated by the Act include air, noise, and water pollution, as well as chemical and solid waste disposal.

Since 1969, several amendments and companion legislation have been passed to more clearly define the EPA's role in land use. The Resource Conservation and Recovery Act (RCRA), passed in 1976, defined hazardous substances. Then, in 1980, Congress passed the Comprehensive Environmental Response, Compensation and Liability Act (CERCLA) to provide solutions to the environmental problems created over the years by uncontrolled disposal of wastes. Under CERCLA, a program was created to identify sites containing hazardous substances, ensure that those sites were cleaned up by the parties responsible or by the government, and establish a procedure to seek reimbursement for clean-up from the party responsible for placing the hazardous substance.

In 1986, CERCLA was amended by the Superfund Amendments and Reauthorization Act (SARA). The amendments imposed stringent clean-up standards and expanded the definition of persons liable for the costs of clean-up. Under CERCLA and SARA, every land owner is potentially affected. More recent environmental issues include protection of habitats for wildlife, wetlands, shorelines, and endangered species, as well as issues such as lead-based paint, radon, formaldehyde, and asbestos.

Maine has enacted several statutes in order to protect its environment. Many of these statutes impact upon the practice and sale of real estate.

1. **Mandatory shoreland zoning**. In 1971 the Maine legislature enacted the Shoreland Zoning Act to protect water quality, limit erosion, conserve wildlife and preserve the natural beauty of Maine's shoreland areas. Since 1971, the law has been expanded and new guidelines adopted to provide municipalities with shoreland zoning standards to enact, administer and enforce local ordinances.

   The law requires municipalities to identify all shoreland areas and then establish specific districts within those areas such as commercial fisheries and resource protection districts. The shoreland zones include land within:
   - 250 ft. of the high-water line of any pond over 10 acres, any river that drains at least 25 square miles, and all tidal waters and salt water marshes;
   - 250 feet of a freshwater wetland over 10 acre; and
   - 75 feet of certain streams

Under the law, there are some allowances for limited improvements to properties that do not conform to the statue. Nonconforming structures that existed on January 1, 1989 and are sited too close to the water may be expanded by less than 30% during the remainder of its lifetime. The 30% is based on both the floor area and the volume of the structure, and only applies to the part of the building that is within the required setback. A municipality may adopt an alternative to the 30% expansion rule, but no expansions can occur within 25 ft. of the normal high-water line. The expansion would be limited in square footage and height depending on the distance from the normal high-water line.

Minimum shore frontage and overall lot size standards vary depending on whether the property is residential or commercial and if it is tidal waters or inland waters.

	Tidal Waters	Inland Waters
Residential Lot Size	30,000 sq. ft.	40,000 sq. ft.
Residential Lot Frontage	150 ft. shore frontage	200 ft. shore frontage

2. **Minimum lot size law.** This law requires that lots supporting a subsurface waste disposal system be at least 20,000 sq. ft. If the lot abuts a water body, it must have a minimum of 100 feet of frontage. Subsurface waste disposal systems include holding ponds, septic tanks, and drainage fields, as well as any other system that disposes of wastes or waste waters on or beneath the surface of the earth. Most communities are moving to increase the amount of frontage and the square footage of lots, especially with both a private water supply and a septic system. Licensees need to be aware of the ever-changing rules and requirements of the state and the specific community in which the property is located.

3. **Conversion of seasonal dwellings.** In 1977 the Maine legislature enacted a law requiring that before a seasonal residence could be converted to a principal dwelling or year-round use, the owner must obtain a conversion permit from the local plumbing inspector. To be granted a permit, the owner must prove that his subsurface disposal system meets the standards of the state plumbing code, or that a new or replacement system can be installed in the event the current system malfunctions.

4. **Transfers of shoreland property.** If a property is located within a shoreland area and has a subsurface waste water disposal system and is to be sold, the owner must provide the buyer at the closing with a sworn statement certifying that the system has been properly functioning for the last 180 days prior to the sale.

5. **Coastal wetlands law.** This prohibits dredging, filling, and erecting permanent structures in a coastal wetland without a permit from the Department of Environmental Protection. **Wetlands** are all lands, including submerged lands, that flow by the tide at any time except maximum storm activity.

6. **Freshwater wetlands law.** This prohibits dredging, filling, and erecting a permanent structure in an area that is defined as 10 or more contiguous acres that are characterized predominately by wetland soils and vegetation.

7. **Site location development law.** The construction of structures with a ground area in excess of three acres must have approval from the Board of Environmental Protection.

8. **The Natural Resources Protection Act.** The purpose of NRPA is to set environmental standards to limit changes to ponds, rivers, streams, tidal waters, coastal dunes, wetlands, and significant wildlife habitat. The actions that impact these resources may require permits from the state. The activities would include filling, dredging, bulldozing; or removing or displacing

soil in a water body or wetland within 75 feet of a water body and certain wetlands. Constructing, repairing or altering a permanent structure in, on or over a water body, wetland or within 75 feet of a water body and certain wetlands would also require a permit.

9. **Farmland Adjacency Act.** An act to put abutting landowners and potential buyers on notice as to the agricultural Chemicals that a registered farm is using. If the farmland was registered prior to July 1, 2012 the law prohibits the abutter from building a residence, drilling a well or building a playground within 100 feet of the farm's lot line. If the registration is after July 1, 2012 it prohibits the abutter from having a water supply within 50 feet of the farm's lot line

10. **Coastal Shoreland Zone Act.** This act has the same 180 day statement that is required in Shoreland zoning but adds that the buyer is required to have the subsurface waste disposal system inspected by a state of Maine certified Inspector prior to the purchase. There are exceptions to the rule such as impossibility due to weather conditions. If the inspector finds that the system has malfunctioned, the system must be repaired or replaced within one year of closing.

11. **Real Estate Tree Growth.** The intent of this law is to protect and preserve the forest land. The area must be at least 10 acres and the owner must have a registered forester evaluate the forest at lease every 10 years. The land in tree growth is taxed at a much lower rate. There are major penalties for removing from tree growth or not following the forest plan established by the forester.

Enforcement of Public Land Use Laws

Like private land use restrictions, public land use laws also can be enforced by a court injunction requiring the violation to be discontinued, such as a violation of a zoning law, or corrected by extreme measures, such as by demolishing an unlawful structure.

On a local level, a code enforcement officer and/or a plumbing inspector would review complaints of violations and oversee local land use ordinances such as zoning and building codes.

On the state level, due to the unprecedented growth of the 1980s, the Maine State Legislature responded with major land use laws. It established a Land Use Regulation Commission within the Department of Conservation to implement these laws within unorganized townships. (Standards, rules, and ordersissued by the Maine Land Use Commission have the force and effect of law.) In compliance with the laws, cities and towns are empowered and directed to develop comprehensive plans and land use ordinances. Any person who violates any provision of the land use laws is subject to a civil penalty payable to the state of not more than $10,000 for each day of violation. In addition, permits and approvals may be revoked or suspended and the court may order restoration of any area affected by the action.

On the federal level, the U.S. Army Corps of Engineers regulates activities in navigable waters such as the Kennebec River to Moosehead Lake; tributaries to navigable waters; intermittent streams; wetlands; and other waters where the use or d struction of these waters could affect interstate or foreign commerce. The Corps issues different types of permits to authorize construction and fill activities. The permits could require detailed project descriptions and drawings as well as site visits, coordination with other agencies, and data analysis. The Army Corps of Engineers is authorized under the Rivers and Harbors Act of 1899, Coastal Zone Management Act of 1972, and the Clean Water Act of 1977. Failure to receive the required permits could result in fines of up to $25,000 per day and/or imprisonment.

IMPORTANT POINTS

1. Private land use controls are in the form of deed restrictions and restrictive covenants.

2. Restrictive covenants must be reasonable and must be equally beneficial to all property owners.

3. Restrictive covenants are recorded on the public record in an instrument called a Declaration of Restrictions. They are not legally effective and enforceable unless recorded.

4. Restrictive covenants are enforced by court injunction upon a petition by the property owners on a timely basis.

5. The purpose of planning is to provide for the orderly growth of a community that will result in the greatest social and economic benefits to the people.

6. The plan for development is enforced by zoning ordinances. Planning and zoning are an exercise of police power.

7. The types of zones include residential, commercial, planned unit developments (PUDs), industrial, agricultural, shoreland, and resource protection.

8. In addition to specifying permitted uses, zoning ordinances define standards and requirements that must be met for each type of use.

9. A nonconforming use is one that is different than the type of use permitted in a particular zone. The nonconforming use may be lawful or unlawful.

10. A variance is a permitted deviation from specific requirements of a zoning ordinance because a special hardship would be imposed on a property owner by strict enforcement.

11. Spot zoning occurs when a certain property within a zoned area is rezoned to permit a use that is different from the zoning requirements for that area. Spot zoning may be valid or invalid.

12. Subdivision ordinances regulate the development of residential subdivisions to protect property purchasers as well as to protect area taxpayers from increased tax burdens to provide essential services to the subdivisions.

13. Building codes require that certain standards of construction be met. The codes are primarily concerned with electrical systems, fire and safety standards, and sanitary systems and equipment.

14. The Interstate Land Sales Full Disclosure Act regulates the sale of unimproved lots in interstate commerce to prevent fraudulent schemes that may occur when land is sold on a sight unseen basis.

15. Environmental protection laws are a form of land use control to protect the public against abuses of the environment.

16. Maine has enacted several statutes in order to protect its environment, which include mandatory shoreland zoning, minimum lot size, conversion of seasonal dwellings, transfers of shoreland property, and the Coastal Wetlands Law.

REVIEW QUESTIONS

Answers to these questions are found in the Answer Key section at the back of the book.

1. All municipalities must zone within _____ feet of shore or be covered be covered by a state imposed ordinance.
   a. 100 ft.
   b. 250 ft.
   c. 500 ft.
   d. 1,000 ft

2. Deed restrictions that run with the land are which of the following?
   a. conditions
   b. variances
   c. declarations
   d. covenants

3. The instrument used for recording restrictive covenants is called:
   a. plat
   b. master deed
   c. covenant
   d. declaration of restrictions

4. Restrictive covenants may be terminated in all of the following ways except:
   a. expiration
   b. transfer of title
   c. failure to enforce on a timely basis
   d. abandonment

5. Restrictive covenants are enforced by which of the following?
   a. zoning
   b. injunction
   c. police power
   d. condemnation

6. The rezoning of a zoned area made a use by one property owner to be not in compliance with the type of use required by the new zoning ordinance. If the owner continues this use, it is called which of the following?
   a. variance
   b. lawful nonconforming use
   c. spot zoning
   d. unlawful nonconforming use

7. A permitted deviation from the standards of a zoning ordinance is called:
   a. variance
   b. nonconforming use
   c. spot zoning
   d. unlawful nonconforming use

8. Rezoning of a particular property for the benefit of the community is called:
   a. variance
   b. nonconforming use
   c. spot zoning
   d. unlawful nonconforming use

9. Building codes require which of the following?
   a. property report
   b. PUDs
   c. certificate of occupancy
   d. statement of record

10. Exemptions to the Interstate Land Sales Full Disclosure Act include all of the following except:
    a. subdivisions of fewer than 100 lots
    b. lots offered only to building contractors
    c. lots on which there is a building
    d. subdivisions in which the lots are five acres or more

CHAPTER 9

IMPORTANT TERMINOLOGY

acceleration clause
acknowledgment
alienation clause
annual percentage rate (APR)
closing disclosure
default provision
defeasance clause
deficiency judgment
Equal Credit Opportunity Act (ECOA)
equity of redemption
Federal Home Loan Mortgage Corporation
   (FHLMC) (Freddie Mac)
Federal National Mortgage Association (FNMA)
   (Fannie Mae)
foreclosure
Government National Mortgage Association
   (GNMA) (Ginnie Mae)
interest
loan estimate
lien theory

Maine State Housing Authority (MSHA)
mortgage
mortgage broker
mortgage company
mortgage deed
mortgagee
mortgage note
mortgagor
prepayment penalty
principal
Real Estate Settlement Procedures Act (RESPA)
recordation
Regulation Z
secondary mortgage market
title theory
Truth-in-Lending Simplification and Reform Act
   (TILSRA)

REAL ESTATE FINANCING

IN THIS CHAPTER

In this chapter we will discuss financing instruments, such as mortgage notes and deeds, and the various sources of real estate funds. Federal government regulation of lending institutions such as Regulation Z and RESPA will also be covered.

MORTGAGE INSTRUMENTS

When real estate is pledged as collateral for a loan, it is necessary for the lender, in order to protect his interests, to create documents that establish his claim against the property. These documents are the mortgage note and the mortgage deed, and they contain all the agreements between the borrower (mortgagor) and the lender (mortgagee).

Mortgage Note

In making a mortgage loan, the lender requires the borrower to sign a **mortgage note**, or *promissory note* (see Figure 9.1). The note is a financing instrument that acknowledges that a debt exists and states the conditions for repayment. The note contains a promise that the borrower will be personally liable for paying the amount of money set forth in the note and specifies the manner in which the debt is to be paid. Payment is typically in monthly installments of a stated amount, commencing on a certain date with a part of each payment applied first to payment of **interest** (the money paid for using someone else's money) and the remainder applied to the **reduction** of principal (the amount of money borrowed). The note will also state the interest rate, the payment due dates, and the amount of each payment.

Mortgage Deed

The personal promise of the borrower to pay the debt is not security enough for the large amount of money involved in the mortgage loan. Indeed, it is most unlikely that an average person could guarantee such a debt out of personal funds alone. Therefore the lender requires the additional security of the property itself to serve as collateral for the loan. Pledging the property as security for the loan is accomplished through the **mortgage deed**.

There are two primary lending practices, known as theories of financing. Each type of theory has special considerations on who will hold title and how foreclosure proceedings would take place if they were to become necessary. In a **title theory** state, the borrower does not actually keep title to the property during the loan term. The lender holds title to the property as security only until all loan payments have been made. The lender delivers the deed back to the borrower only after the loan obligation has been

Figure 9.1
A sample note.

PROMISSORY NOTE

_____, 20_____

_____[City]_____[State]

_____[Property Address]

1. **Borrower's promise to pay**
    In return for a loan I have received, I promise to pay U.S. $_____[principal] plus interest to the order of the Lender. The Lender is_____.
    I understand that the Lender may transfer this note.

2. **Interest**
    Interest will be charged on unpaid principal until the full amount of principal has been paid. I will pay interest at the yearly rate of_____%.

3. **Payments**
    A. **Time and place of payments**
        I will pay principal and interest by making payments every month on the_____day of each month beginning on_____, 20___and continuing until said principal and interest have been paid.
    B. **Amount of monthly payments**
        My monthly payments will be in the amount of $_____(U.S.).

4. **Borrower's right to repay**
    I may prepay this note in whole or in part at anytime without penalty.

5. **Borrower's failure to pay as required**
    A. **Late charge for overdue payment**
        If the Note Holder has not received the full amount of monthly payment by the end of _____calendar days after the date is due, I will pay a late charge of $_____to the Note Holder.
    B. **Default**

        If I do not pay the full amount of each monthly payment on the date it is due, I will be in default. If I am in default, the Note Holder may require me to pay immediately the full amount of the principal that has not been paid plus accrued interest.

6. **Uniform secured note**

    This note is secured by a mortgage deed dated the same date as the note and protects the Note Holder from possible losses that might result if I do not keep the promises I make in this note. That security instrument describes how and under what conditions I may be required to make immediate payment in full of all amounts I owe under this note.

    Witness the Hand(s) and Seal(s) of the undersigned

    _____

                                                        Borrower

    _____

                                                        Borrower

---

satisfied. In a **lien theory** state, the borrower holds the deed to the property during the mortgage term and the property acts as security for the underlying loan. The document that places the lien on the property is called the mortgage. Maine is a lien theory state.

Requirements for Validity of a Mortgage Deed

1. The mortgage must be in _writing_ as required by the Statute of Frauds because the mortgage pledges or conveys title to real property to secure the payment of the note.
2. There must be a _valid debt_ to be secured by the mortgage. The existence of the valid debt is evidenced by the note.

3. The mortgagor must have a *valid interest* in the property pledged or conveyed to secure the debt in the mortgage.

4. There must be a legally acceptable *description* of the property.

5. The mortgage will contain a **defeasance clause** that defeats the lien and conveyance of title when the mortgage debt is fully satisfied.

6. The mortgage must be delivered to and *accepted* by the mortgagee (lender). It states that the title will be given to the borrower after all terms are met.

Mortgage Clauses and Covenants

The following are examples of the various clauses and covenants that may be included in a mortgage.

1. The mortgage, which will be dated, contains the names of mortgagor and mortgagee.

2. *Acceleration clause.* This clause will enable the lender to declare the entire balance due and payable if the borrower is in default or for other reasons stated in the deed.

3. *Prepayment clause.* This clause may either give the lender the right to charge the borrower a penalty for paying off a loan early, or allow the borrower to pay off the loan at any time prior to the expiration of the full mortgage term without incurring a financial penalty for the early payoff.

4. The mortgage will require the borrower to pay all real property taxes and assessments on a timely basis, keep the buildings in a proper state of repair and preservation, protect the buildings against loss by fire or other casualty by an insurance policy written in an amount that is at least 80 percent of the value of the structures, and names the lender as the mortgagee interest.

5. *Defeasance clause.* The mortgage will contain a defeasance clause that provides for the borrower's right to defeat and remove the lien by paying the indebtedness in full.

6. *Default provision.* The mortgage includes a **default provision**, or a right of foreclosure to the lender, in the event that the borrower fails to make payments as scheduled or fails to fulfill other obligations as set forth in the mortgage.

7. *Redemption clause.* This clause gives the right to the mortgagor to update any deficiencies in the mortgage until foreclosure proceedings begin. This is commonly called the equity of redemption.

8. In the mortgage form, there will always be a covenant specifying that the mortgagor has a good and marketable title to the property pledged to secure the payment of the note.

9. *Alienation clause.* The mortgage may contain an **alienation,** or "due on sale," clause. This clause entitles the lender to declare the principal balance immediately due and payable if the borrower sells the property during the mortgage term. This clause makes the mortgage unassumable without the lender's permission. Permission to assume the mortgage at an interest rate prevailing at the time of assumption is often permitted if the new owner meets the lender's requirements.

10. The mortgage will provide for **acknowledgment** by the borrower to make the document eligible for recording on the public record for the protection of the lender.

Rights of Lender

1. The lender has the right to take *possession* of the property if and when the borrower defaults in mortgage payments.
2. The lender has the right to foreclose on the property in the event that the borrower defaults in the payments. The property may be sold at a foreclosure sale and the proceeds of the sale, after certain other items are paid, applied to the satisfaction of the mortgage debt.
3. The lender has the right to *assign* the mortgage. This right enables the lender to sell the mortgage, if she so desires, and thereby frees up the money invested. The right of assignment provides liquidity to mortgages since the lender can sell the mortgage at any time and obtain the money invested rather than waiting for payment of the loan over an extended period of time.

Rights of Borrower

1. The borrower has the right to possession of the property during the mortgage term as long as the borrower is not in default.
2. The defeasance clause gives the borrower the right to redeem the title and have the mortgage lien released at any time prior to default by paying the debt in full. This is often referred to as no **prepayment penalty.**
3. The borrower has the right of **equity of redemption**. This is the borrower's right, after default, to redeem the title pledge or conveyed to secure a mortgage debt up to the time of a foreclosure sale by paying the debt, interest, and costs.

Recordation

Recordation gives order to the system of land ownership and transfer. Recorded documents affecting real estate can be found in public records at the Registry of Deeds in the county where the property is located. Mortgage deeds should always be recorded. This protects those with any present or future interest in the property by providing constructive notice to the general public of ownership and any other interest in the property. To be recorded, a deed must be notarized.

Releases/Discharges

Recording a release of a mortgage deed is just as important as recording the original documents. Failure to do so may cloud the title to the property.

FORECLOSURE OF MORTGAGES

If the borrower (mortgagor) does not make his payments or fulfill other mortgage requirements, the borrower is in default on the loan. The ultimate power of the lender is to foreclose. Foreclosure is the liquidation of title to the real property pledged in order to recover funds to pay off the mortgage debt. The Maine statute had provided five methods of foreclosing a mortgage, and in 1975 the Maine legislature added a new method: judicial sale.

Foreclosure by Judicial Sale

If the court finds the mortgagor in default, a judgment of foreclosure and sale is issued. If the mortgagor does not pay the amount due during a 90-day redemption period, the mortgagee places a notice of a public sale of the property in a newspaper of general circulation once a week for 3 successive weeks. The mortgagee must sell the property to the highest bidder at the public sale. It requires about four months to complete by judicial sale and, therefore, is a favored method of foreclosure.

In the following methods, which are a form of strict foreclosure, the mortgagor has one full year in which to redeem his property, once foreclosure has started.

Foreclosure by Possession

If the mortgagee wishes to obtain possession of the property for the purpose of foreclosure, she would proceed thus:

1. *By writ of possession.* This is separate legal action in which the mortgagee alleges default. If the court agrees, it will determine the amount due the mortgagee and allow possession if the mortgagor fails to pay the amount due plus interest within two months. An abstract of the writ stating time must be recorded within 30 days after possession.
2. *By consent.*   The mortgagee may obtain possession by consent of the mortgagor in writing. The consent endorsed with the mortgagee's affidavit and time of entry must be recorded in the Registry of Deeds 30 days after entry to the property.
3. *By peaceful entry.* The mortgagee may enter openly and peaceably if not opposed. Two witnesses must be present at the time of possession. A certificate to this fact must be signed by these witnesses and recorded within 30 days of entry to the property.

Foreclosure Without Possession

1. *By public notice.* The mortgagee gives notice of default and foreclosure by publishing this information in a newspaper 3 weeks successively. A copy of the printed notice of foreclosure is recorded in the Registry of Deeds within 30 days after the last publication of notice.
2. *By service of notice.* At the request of the mortgagee, the sheriff will serve notice of foreclosure on the mortgagor. The notice and the sheriff's return (information stating the time and manner in which he delivered the copy of the notice to the mortgagee) must be recorded in the Registry of Deeds within 30 days after service is made.

Under both of these last two types, the mortgagee does not obtain possession until a year from the date of the first publication or service of notice unless the mortgagor redeems.

Equity of Redemption

In either foreclosure by possession or without possession, the mortgagor may redeem the mortgaged property at any time within the one-year period by paying the amount of debt plus interest and cost of foreclosure and by performing all conditions set in the mortgage.

Distribution of Sale Proceeds

The proceeds of the mortgage foreclosure sale are distributed in the following order of priority:

1. All *expenses of the sale* are paid. These include court costs, trustee's fee, advertising fees, legal fees, accounting fees, and so on.
2. Next, any real property *tax liens* and *assessment liens* against the property are paid.
3. If there are no other lienholders with liens having priority over the lien of the mortgage, the *lender* is paid.
4. Any other creditors holding *liens* against the property are paid.
5. Any remaining money after items 1 through 4 have been satisfied is paid to the *borrower*.

Deficiency Judgments

The borrower in a mortgage loan is *personally liable* for the payment of the note. Therefore, in the event that the proceeds of a foreclosure sale are not sufficient to satisfy the balance due the lender, the lender can sue for a **deficiency judgment** on the note. A deficiency judgment is a court order stating that the borrower still owes the lender money.

SOURCES OF PRIMARY MARKET FINANCE

Savings and Loan Associations

The primary purposes for which *savings and loan associations* exist are to encourage thrift and to provide financing for residential properties. These organizations make loans for the construction of housing, for the purchase of existing housing, and to effect improvements in existing housing. Many now have the ability to provide personal property loans, such as for autos.

Because savings and loan associations have traditionally served local communities, their mortgage lending policies have been less stringent. These policies helped fuel the S&L crisis of the late 1980s, leading Congress to enact the Financial Institutions Reform, Recovery, and Enforcement Act in 1989. FIRREA provides structure for S&Ls in several ways. It provides for stricter lending policies, and it created the Office of Thrift Supervision (OTC) to audit and oversee the industry. It established that the FDIC will now manage the insurance funds for savings and loans as well as for commercial banks. Another important provision of FIRREA is the creation of the Resolution Trust Corporation (RTC). The RTC was established to fairly and quickly liquidate the holdings of failed savings and loans.

Mutual Savings Banks

Mutual savings banks are very similar to savings and loan associations, as their main objectives are to encourage thrift and to provide financing for housing. These organizations exist primarily in the northeast portion of the United States and are chartered and regulated by the states in which they are located.

Mutual savings banks play a prominent role in the financing of housing in the states where they are located. Also in recent years, mutual savings banks have been granted the ability to broaden the base and type of loans. These institutions currently differ from other depositor institutions primarily in form of ownership: they are depositor owned.

Commercial Banks

There are both federally and state chartered commercial banks. In either case, these banks are sources of mortgage money for construction, purchase of existing housing, and making home improvements. The loan policies of commercial banks are usually more conservative than other types of lending institutions.

Mortgage Companies and Mortgage Brokers

Mortgage companies operate primarily as intermediaries between borrowers and lenders, acting as loan correspondents for the construction of housing and purchase of existing housing.

There is a definite difference between a mortgage company and a mortgage broker. A **mortgage company** originates mortgage loans. A **mortgage broker** brings a lender and borrower together for a fee paid by the lending institution just as a real estate broker brings a buyer and seller of real property together for a fee.

Credit Unions

Credit unions may be an excellent source of mortgage money for their members. Usually, credit unions offer mortgage loans to their membership at an interest rate below the commercial rate at any given time. To be financially able to make long-term mortgage loans, the credit union must be of substantial size. The Federal Employees Credit Union, a state employees credit union, or the credit union of a major industry are examples of large credit unions.

Individual Investors

There are individuals in every area who invest in mortgages. These investors are usually an excellent source for second mortgage loans.

The seller of real property is definitely not to be overlooked as an individual investor. The seller may finance the sale of her property by taking a first mortgage, taking a second mortgage, or financing through means of a contract for deed. In times of extremely high interest rates a sale often cannot be made without the seller providing a substantial part of the financing for the buyer.

THE SECONDARY MORTGAGE MARKET

The primary mortgage market consists of lending institutions that make loans directly to borrowers. By contrast, the **secondary mortgage market** is the purchase and sale of mortgages that have been created in the primary mortgage market. One of the requirements for mortgage validity is that it be assignable. As a result, the lender holding the mortgage may assign or sell the rights in the mortgage to another. In this way, the lender may free up the money invested in the mortgage without waiting for the debt to be repaid by the borrower over the long mortgage term.

The sale of the mortgage by the lender does not in any way affect the borrower's rights or obligations. The lending institution typically continues to service the loan for the purchaser of the mortgage. Therefore, the mortgagor continues to make the necessary mortgage payments to the same lending institution that made the mortgage loan. Occasionally, the purchaser of the mortgage will prefer to service the mortgage itself. In these cases the original lender simply notifies the mortgagor to make payments to a different lender at a different address.

The benefit of the secondary mortgage market to lending institutions and in turn to the borrowing public is to provide liquidity to mortgages. The mortgage can be converted to cash (a liquid asset) by the lending institution selling the mortgage in the secondary market. The sale of the mortgage by the lender is especially beneficial in cases of low-yield mortgages. The lender may get the money out of these mortgages to reinvest in new mortgage loans at current higher yields. This provides stability in the supply of money for making mortgage loans. Therefore, the secondary mortgage market benefits the borrowing public by enabling lending institutions to make money available for loans to qualified applicants.

Mortgage liquidity available in the secondary market reduces the impact of disintermediation on lending institutions. Disintermediation is the loss of funds available to lending institutions for making mortgage loans and is caused by the withdrawal of funds from these institutions by depositors for investment in higher-yield securities in the times of unusually high interest rates. Without the secondary mortgage market, disintermediation would result in the "drying up" of funds available to lenders to the extent that these loans would be practically unavailable.

Secondary Market Activities

Not all lending institutions participate in the secondary mortgage market, but instead limit their mortgage loans to their own assets. For lenders in Maine that do participate in this secondary market, two types of markets are available: (1) the purchase and sale of mortgages between lending institutions and (2) the sale of mortgages by lending institutions to organizations that provide a market for this purpose.

Activities Between Lending Institutions

A major activity of the secondary mortgage market is the purchase and sale of mortgages by and between lending institutions. In this way the market facilitates the movement of capital from those institutions having available funds to invest to lenders in short supply of money for this purpose. For example, at any given time, the demand for mortgage loans may be very low in a particular locality. As a result, institutions with funds available for making loans in those areas are unable to invest these funds in the local market by making primary mortgage loans. Consequently, the funds of these institutions that should be invested in mortgages and earning interest are lying idle. At this same time, in another part of the country, there may be a very high demand for mortgage loans. A lender in such an area may be in short supply of available funds to lend to qualified loan applicants. The problems of both of these lending institutions can be solved by the sale of existing mortgages on hand by the institution whose funds are in short supply to a lender in another area having a surplus of available funds and faced with a very low demand for mortgage loans. As a result, the lender with otherwise idle funds has them invested in mortgages earning interest as they should be, and the lender in short supply of money has freed up capital invested in mortgages to meet the high demand for new mortgage loans in that area.

Sales of Mortgages to Organizations

There are four organizations that actively participate in the purchase of mortgages from financial institutions: the Federal National Mortgage Association (FNMA), the Government National Mortgage Association (GNMA), the Federal Home Loan Mortgage Corporation (FHLMC), and the Maine State Housing Authority (MSHA).

Federal National Mortgage Association (FNMA)

The **Federal National Mortgage Association (FNMA)** is usually referred to by its nickname **Fannie Mae**. It is the oldest secondary mortgage institution and is the single largest holder of home mortgages. Fannie Mae was created in 1938 as a corporation completely owned by the federal government to provide a secondary market for residential mortgages. By 1968 it had evolved into a privately owned corporation. It is a profit-making organization with its stock listed on the New York Stock Exchange.

As a government-owned corporation, Fannie Mae was limited to purchasing FHA-insured mortgages and VA-guaranteed mortgages. As a privately owned corporation, it may now also purchase conventional mortgages, which are now a major portion of its business.

Fannie Mae buys mortgages on a regular basis. Mortgage companies are major sellers of mortgages to Fannie Mae. Additionally, savings and loan associations, mutual savings banks, commercial banks, and life insurance companies also sell mortgages to Fannie Mae. Fannie Mae sells interest-bearing securities (bonds, notes, and debentures) to investors. These securities are backed by specific pools of mortgages purchased and held by Fannie Mae.

Government National Mortgage Association (GNMA)

The popular name for the **Government National Mortgage Association (GNMA)** is **Ginnie Mae**. It was established in 1968 when Fannie Mae was fully converted to a private corporation. Ginnie Mae is an agency of the Department of Housing and Urban Development (HUD).

Included in the various activities of Ginnie Mae is the purchase of mortgages to make capital available to lending institutions. As a government agency, Ginnie Mae is limited to the purchase of VA or FHA mortgages.

Ginnie Mae guarantees the Ginnie Mae Pass-Through, which is a mortgage- backed security providing participation in a pool of FHA-insured or VA-guaranteed mortgages. The pass-throughs are originated by lending institutions, primarily mortgage bankers. Ginnie Mae guarantees these securities and thereby makes them secure investments for purchasers. The yield on each pass-through issue is guaranteed by the full faith and credit of the United States government, the pass-throughs are secured by the FHA- and VA-guaranteed loans, and there is also a guarantee by the lending institution originating the pass-through.

The Federal Home Loan Mortgage Corporation (FHLMC)

Like the other organizations, the **Federal Home Loan Mortgage Corporation (FHLMC)** also has a nickname—**Freddie Mac**. Like the other two, Freddie Mac exists to increase the availability of mortgage credit and provide greater liquidity for saving associations. These objectives are achieved by the purchase of mortgages by Freddie Mac.

Freddie Mac was created by an act of Congress in 1970. A major reason for the creation of Freddie Mac was to establish a reliable market for the sale of conventional mortgages. Fannie Mae purchased a very small amount of conventional mortgages, and Ginnie Mae may not purchase conventional mortgages. Therefore, prior to the creation of Freddie Mac, lending institutions holding conventional mortgages were fairly well limited to the purchase and sale of these mortgages between each other.

Freddie Mac sells mortgage-participation certificates (PCs) and guaranteed-mortgage certificates (GMCs). These are securities that represent an undivided interest in specific pools of mortgages. The payment of principal and interest is guaranteed to the purchaser of PCs or GMCs by Freddie Mac.

Freddie Mac was part of and was wholly owned by the Federal Home Loan Bank system. In 1989 FHLMC became a private corporation, and it now competes with FNMA. It is no longer limited to buying S&L association mortgages.

MaineHousing (Maine Housing Authority)

The **Maine State Housing Authority (MSHA)** was established in 1969 for the purpose of providing housing to low and moderate income Maine families. It meets this purpose through the sale of tax exempt bonds to investors who are willing to buy the bonds at a relatively low interest rate because they are tax exempt. Thus it borrows money at a lower than market interest rate and then loans that money at a slightly higher rate to qualified Maine homebuyers in the form of mortgages.

The MaineHousing Program is a low to middle income, first-time homebuyer program. The definition of a first time buyer is one that has not owned a primary home in the past three years at the time of application.

There are income limitations and also maximum purchase price limits by county with this program..

Buyers can finance property with a conventional, VA, FHA, or RD (Rural Development) loan, with the down payment conforming to the program selected. For example, using the VA program, the down payment would be 0 percent.

The program offers both 0 point and 2 point rate options. The zero point option is the most popular because the borrower needs less cash for closing. With the 2 point rate option, the points can be paid by either the homebuyer or the seller.

Other Aspects of the Market

Primary lenders wishing to sell mortgages to Fannie Mae or Freddie Mac must use uniform loan documents meeting criteria established by FNMA and FHLMC. For example, these organizations will not purchase mortgages containing a prepayment penalty. This requirement is particularly advantageous to individual borrowers when they are required to pay off their mortgage as a condition of a contract of sale. In some cases prepayment penalties can be extremely high and, therefore, pose a real hardship to sellers.

GOVERNMENT REGULATIONS ON MORTGAGE LENDING

Truth-in-Lending Simplification and Reform Act (TILSRA)

The Truth-in-Lending Law is a part of the Federal Consumer Credit Protection Act, which became effective July 1, 1969. It was subsequently amended to be known as the **Truth-in-Lending Simplification and Reform Act (TILSRA)** of 1980. The Truth-in-Lending Act empowered the Federal Reserve Board to implement the regulations in the act. TILSRA now requires four chief disclosures, that is, annual percentage rate, finance charge, amount financed, and total of payments. The Federal Reserve Board implemented these regulations by establishing **Regulation Z.**

Regulation Z does not regulate interest rates but instead provides specific consumer protections in mortgage loans for residential real estate. All real estate loans for personal, family, household, or agricultural purposes are covered by Regulation Z. The regulation does not apply to commercial loans. Regulation Z also standardizes the procedures involved in residential loan transactions. Regulation Z requires that the borrower be made fully informed of all aspects of the loan transaction (see Figure 9.2). In addition, the regulation applies to the advertisement of credit terms available for residential real estate. The specific requirements of Regulation Z are discussed in the following paragraphs.

Disclosure

At the time of loan application or within 3 business days thereafter, the lender must provide the borrower with a Loan Estimate which since October 3, 2015 must include disclosures required under the Truth in Lending Act. The disclosure must set forth the true, or effective, annual interest rate on a loan. This rate is called the **annual percentage rate (APR).** This rate is usually higher than the interest as expressed in the mortgage because certain fees and discount points charged by the lender are subtracted from the loan amount, and this results in increasing the true rate of interest. This is because the borrower, as a result of the subtraction, has received a smaller loan amount and is paying interest on a larger amount; therefore, the effect is to increase the interest rate being paid.

In addition to stating the true or effective annual interest rate on the loan, the disclosure statement must specify the finance charges, which include loan fees, interest, and discount points.

If the borrower is refinancing an existing mortgage loan or obtaining a new mortgage loan and is pledging a principal residence already owned as security for such loan, the disclosure statement must provide for a right of rescission for the loan transaction. The right to rescind, or cancel, requires that the loan must be exercised by the borrower prior to midnight of the third business day following the date that the transaction was closed. The three-day right of rescission does not apply where the loan is to finance the purchase of a home or the construction of a dwelling to be used as a principal residence. The right of rescission is waived when the refinance is transacted with the original lender for the existing balance and the new loan term does not exceed the original loan's term.

Advertising

Regulation Z also applies to any advertising of credit terms available for the purchase of a home. The only specific item that may be stated in the advertisement without making a full disclosure in the advertisement is the annual percentage rate, spelled out

Figure 9.2
Loan Estimate
sample page.

Additional Information About This Loan

LENDER	**MORTGAGE BROKER**
NMLS/___ LICENSE ID	NMLS/___ LICENSE ID
LOAN OFFICER	**LOAN OFFICER**
NMLS/___ LICENSE ID	NMLS/___ LICENSE ID
EMAIL	**EMAIL**
PHONE	**PHONE**

Comparisons	Use these measures to compare this loan with other loans.
In 5 Years	Total you will have paid in principal, interest, mortgage insurance, and loan costs. Principal you will have paid off.
Annual Percentage Rate (APR)	Your costs over the loan term expressed as a rate. This is not your interest rate.
Total Interest Percentage (TIP)	The total amount of interest that you will pay over the loan term as a percentage of your loan amount.

Other Considerations

Appraisal	We may order an appraisal to determine the property's value and charge you for this appraisal. We will promptly give you a copy of any appraisal, even if your loan does not close. You can pay for an additional appraisal for your own use at your own cost.
Assumption	If you sell or transfer this property to another person, we ☐ will allow, under certain conditions, this person to assume this loan on the original terms. ☐ will not allow assumption of this loan on the original terms.
Homeowner's Insurance	This loan requires homeowner's insurance on the property, which you may obtain from a company of your choice that we find acceptable.
Late Payment	If your payment is more than ___ days late, we will charge a late fee of _____
Loan Acceptance	You do not have to accept this loan because you have received this form or signed a loan application.
Refinance	Refinancing this loan will depend on your future financial situation, the property value, and market conditions. You may not be able to refinance this loan.
Servicing	We intend ☐ to service your loan. If so, you will make your payments to us. ☐ to transfer servicing of your loan.

LOAN ESTIMATE   PAGE 3 OF 3 · LOAN ID #

in full, that is, not abbreviated as APR. If any other credit terms are included in the advertisement, a full disclosure must be provided. If an ad contains one or more of the following:

1. The amount of down payment as a percentage or dollar figure or a state-ment that there is no required down payment
2. The amount of any installment as a percentage or dollar amount
3. The number of installments
4. The period or term of repayment
5. The dollar amount of the finance charge or a statement that there is no finance charge

then the ad must also contain:

1. The cash price
2. The cash down payment or a statement that there is no required down payment
3. The number and due dates of the payments
4. The amount of the finance charge expressed as "annual percentage rate"

Statements of a general nature regarding the financing may be made without a full disclosure being required. Such statements as "good financing available," "FHA fi- nancing available," or "loan assumption available" are satisfactory for this purpose. Real estate agents must take special care not to violate the advertising requirements of Regulation Z. The Truth-in-Lending Act is regulated on the state level by the Bureau of Consumer Credit Protection and on the national level by the Federal Trade Commission.

Penalties

The violator of Regulation Z is subject to criminal liability and punishment by a fine of up to $5,000, imprisonment for up to one year, or both. In the event the borrower has suffered a financial loss as the result of the violation, the borrower may sue the vi- olator under civil law in federal court for damages.

Equal Credit Opportunity Act (ECOA)

The **Equal Credit Opportunity Act (ECOA)** was enacted by Congress in 1975. The purpose of ECOA is to prevent discrimination in the loan process on the part of lending institutions. The act requires financial institutions engaged in making loans to do so on an equal basis to all creditworthy customers without regard to discriminatory factors. The Equal Credit Opportunity Act is implemented by Regulation B of the Federal Reserve Board.

Requirements of ECOA

This act makes it unlawful for any creditor to discriminate against any loan applicant in any aspect of a credit transaction as follows:

1. On the basis of race, color, religion, sex, national origin, marital status, or age (unless the applicant is a minor and, therefore, does not have the ca-pacity to contract).
2. Because part of the applicant's income is derived from a public assistance program.

3. Because the applicant has in good faith exercised any right under the Federal Consumer Credit Protection Act of which the Truth-in-Lending Law (Regulation Z) is a part.

Real Estate Settlement Procedures Act (RESPA)

The **Real Estate Settlement Procedures Act (RESPA)** was enacted by Congress in 1974. It regulates lending activities of lending institutions in making mortgage loans for housing.

Purpose of the Act

RESPA was enacted by Congress for the following purposes:

1. To effect specific changes in the settlement process resulting in more effective advance disclosure of settlement costs to home buyers and sellers.
2. To protect borrowers from unnecessarily expensive settlement charges resulting from abusive practices.
3. To ensure that borrowers are provided with greater and more timely information on the nature and cost of the settlement process.
4. To eliminate referral fees or kickbacks that increase the cost of settlement services. In this regard, lenders are only permitted to charge for services that are actually provided to home buyers and sellers and in an amount that the service actually costs the lender.

RESPA Requirements

The following are required by the act:

1. A *good faith estimate.* Within three working days of receiving a completed loan application, the lender is required to provide the borrower with a good faith estimate of the costs likely to be incurred at settlement.
2. *Homebuyer's Guide to Settlement Costs.* At the time of loan application, the lender must provide the borrower with a booklet entitled "A Homebuyer's Guide to Settlement Costs." The guide includes the following information:

   - An explanation of what affordability means.

   - Description of credit and how it affects the loan

   - An explanation of mortgages choices available to the buyer

   - Contrasting the tradeoff between points and interest rates

   - An explanation of the closing costs

3. *HUD Form No. 1.* In making residential mortgage loans, lenders are required to use a standard settlement form that is designed to clearly itemize all charges to be paid by both borrower and seller as part of the final settlement. The form has become known as **HUD Form No. 1** (see Chapter 13, Figure 13.9). This form must be made available for inspection by the borrower at or before final settlement.

IMPORTANT POINTS

1. The purpose of a mortgage is to secure the payment of a promissory note.
2. The two legal theories regarding a mortgage are the lien theory and the title theory. Maine is a lien theory state.
3. The requirements for mortgage validity are (1) writing, (2) competent parties, (3) valid debt, (4) valid interest, (5) description, (6) defeasance clause, (7) execution by borrower, (8) delivery to and acceptance by lender.
4. The lender's rights are (1) possession upon default, (2) foreclosure, and (3) right to assign the mortgage.
5. The borrower's rights are (1) possession prior to default, (2) defeat lien by paying debt in full prior to default, and (3) equity of redemption.
6. The two types of foreclosure are judicial and non-judicial. Foreclosure sale proceeds are distributed in a special order of priority. If the sale proceeds available to the lender are insufficient to satisfy the debt, then the lender may sue for a deficiency judgment.
7. Federal laws that regulate lending institutions in making consumer loans include Regulation Z, RESPA, and ECOA.
8. The primary mortgage market is the activity of lending institutions making loans directly to individual borrowers. The secondary market is the activity of lending institutions selling and buying existing mortgages. The secondary market consists of the purchase and sale of mortgages between lenders and the sale of mortgages by lenders to Fannie Mae (FNMA), Ginnie Mae (GNMA), Freddie Mac (FHLMC), and the Maine Housing Authority. The market provides liquidity to mortgages, thereby reducing the effect of disintermediation for the benefit of lending institutions and borrowers as well.

REVIEW QUESTIONS

Answers to these questions are found in the Answer Key section at the back of the book.

1. All of the following statements are applicable to promissory notes except:
   a. must be written
   b. the borrower is personally liable for payment
   c. provides evidence of a valid debt
   d. provides security for the loan

2. One of the purposes of RESPA is to:
   a. Prevent discrimination in the loan process
   b. Regulate interest rates
   c. Eliminate kickbacks that increase cost of settlement
   d. Enables the lender to foreclose in the event of default

3. The clause that makes a mortgage unassumable is which of the following?
   a. defeasance
   b. alienation
   c. mortgaging
   d. prepayment

4. Which of the following gives the borrower the right to pay the debt in full and remove the mortgage lien at any time prior to default?
   a. defeasance
   b. prepayment
   c. equity of redemption
   d. foreclosure

5. A deed in lieu of foreclosure conveys a title to which of the following?
   a. lender
   b. borrower
   c. trustee
   d. mortgagor

6. Which of the following is paid first from the proceeds of a foreclosure sale?
   a. mortgage debt
   b. real property taxes
   c. mortgagee's equity
   d. sale expenses

7. A deficiency judgment may be available to the:
   a. mortgagee
   b. mortgagor
   c. trustee
   d. trustor

8. Which secondary market is limited to the purchase of FHA and VA mortgages?
   a. FNMA
   b. FHLMC
   c. GNMA
   d. MaineHousing

9. Which secondary market has a stipulation of not owning a primary home within the last 3 years?
   a. Freddie Mac
   b. MaineHousing
   c. Fannie Mae
   d. Ginnie Mae

10. The primary market that is owned by stockholders and makes loans secured by real property is:
    a. Real Estate Investment Trusts
    b. Life Insurance Companies
    c. Credit Unions
    d. Mortgage Brokers

CHAPTER 10

IMPORTANT TERMINOLOGY

adjustable rate mortgage (ARM)
amortizing mortgage
balloon mortgage
Certificate of Reasonable Value (CRV)
conventional mortgage loans
discount points
FHA-insured loan

junior mortgage
mortgage assumption
open-end mortgage
private mortgage insurance (PMI)
term mortgage
up-front MIP (UFMIP)
VA-guaranteed loan

REAL ESTATE FINANCING PRACTICES

IN THIS CHAPTER

In this chapter we will discuss several aspects of financing real estate transactions, such as the various types of loans and the requirements of those loans. Knowledge of these financing methods is of great importance to real estate agents. Except in the unusual case of a cash sale, the knowledge or lack of knowledge of the ways in which a sale may be financed will make the difference between a successful or unsuccessful career in real estate.

TYPES OF SALES TRANSACTIONS

Cash Sales

Although cash sales are the exception in real estate, they are perhaps the simplest real estate transactions to process. They can be as simple as the seller providing a deed and the buyer providing the cash. Unfortunately, the simplicity of these cash transactions may cause an inexperienced real estate licensee to make costly mistakes. No mortgage company or bank is involved in the transaction to demand an appraisal, a survey, a structural inspection, payment of taxes, a title search, or recording of the deed. A real estate licensee, in her fiduciary duty to the client, should always recommend experts, such as attorneys, accountants, and building inspectors, to deal with the specific issues in the transaction.

New Financing

Most real estate transactions require new financing. Lending institutions constantly analyze the risks in making real estate loans, and these risks often lead to tightening the requirements for new financing. One of the risks is delinquency by the borrower that may result in the need to foreclose, and if the loan amount is greater than the liquidation value of the property, this would result in a loss to the lender. Real estate licensees should have a general knowledge of lending requirements such as third-party contributions, closing costs regulations, down payment requirements, and the different programs that the lending institutions have to offer. These are essential to a successful real estate transaction involving new financing.

Mortgage Assumption

Although most conventional loans are not assumable, some are, including some FHA-insured and VA-guaranteed loans. When a purchaser assumes the seller's existing mortgage, the purchaser assumes liability for the mortgage and personal liability for the payment of the note. Therefore, if the purchaser defaults in the mortgage payments, the purchaser is subject to lose property as a result of a foreclosure sale and is also subject to a deficiency judgment obtained by the lender.

In the case of a **mortgage assumption**, the seller whose mortgage was assumed remains liable on the mortgage and the payment of the note unless specifically released from liability by the lender. Therefore, if the purchaser defaults and the proceeds of a foreclosure sale are insufficient to pay off the mortgage, the seller whose mortgage was assumed is subject to a deficiency judgment by the lender. In the case of a mortgage assumption, if there is a default, the lender can foreclose against the current titleholder and sue the original borrower or anyone who has assumed the mortgage for a deficiency judgment if the proceeds of the foreclosure sale do not satisfy the mortgage debt.

Taking "Subject To" a Mortgage

If property is sold and title conveyed subject to the lien of an existing mortgage, but that lien is not actually "assumed," the lender can foreclose against the property in the event of a default in mortgage payments. However, in *taking title subject to a mortgage,* the purchaser does *not* become liable for the payment of the note. Therefore, the lender cannot sue the purchaser for a deficiency judgment, but may only obtain a deficiency judgment against the seller, who remained personally liable for the payment of the debt as evidenced by the note. Most residential mortgage agreements prohibit transfer of title without an approved assumption.

METHODS OF FINANCING— MORTGAGE LOANS

In this part of the chapter we will discuss the various ways in which the purchase of real property may be financed by the buyer in obtaining a mortgage loan from a lending institution.

There are various types of mortgage loans that may be obtained from lending institutions. We will discuss the following: (1) **conventional mortgage loans** are mortgage loans in which there is no participation by an agency of the federal government and (2) **Federal Housing Administration (FHA)**, **Department of Veterans Administration (VA)**, and **Rural Development Loans (RD)** are those in which the federal government participates either by insuring the loan to protect the lender (FHA-insured loans) or by guaranteeing that the loan will be repaid (VA and RD-guaranteed mortgage loans).

Conventional Loans

A conventional loan may be either a regular conventional loan or an *insured* conventional loan. In the regular conventional loan, the borrower's equity in the property is such that it provides sufficient security to the lender in making the loan and, therefore, insurance to protect the lender in case of the borrower's default is not required. In these cases, the borrower is obtaining a loan that does not exceed 75 to 80 percent of the property value and, therefore, has an equity of 20 or 25 percent. The regular conventional loan is less difficult to obtain than insured conventional loans or FHA and VA loans.

Insured conventional loans are conventional loans in which the borrower has a down payment of less than 20 percent and is therefore borrowing more than 80 percent of the property value. Typically the borrower has a down payment of 5 to 10 percent and therefore borrows 90 to 95 percent of the property value. The repayment of the top 20 to 25 percent of the loan to the lender must be insured in the event that the borrower defaults. The insurance is called **private mortgage insurance (PMI),** and the policies are issued by private insurance companies. The PMI company underwrites the loan, evaluating the credit and property value risks in the same way that the lender does. Should a default occur, the lender can foreclose and sell the property to liquidate the debt and then be reimbursed by the PMI company for any remaining amount up to policy value. The company also has the option of buying the property from the lender for the balance due and then being responsible for foreclosing.

The premium for the insurance is paid by the borrower and is typically 1 percent of the amount of the loan for the first year. The monthly PMI is point 5 percent of the mortgage amount divided by twelve months. PMI is cancelled when the loan to value is 78 percent. The value is a combination of loan paydown, improvements, and appreciation. No value would be given to appreciation unless the improvements and/or paydown increased the value.

To qualify a buyer conventionally, the bank applies a formula such as requiring that the total monthly home payments do not exceed a percentage such as 33 percent of the buyer's monthly gross income. Also, the total of all long-term debts does not exceed a certain percentage, such as 38 percent of the buyer's monthly gross income. If the buyer qualifies for the home and has the necessary money for closing costs and down payment, the bank will consider the loan. The buyer's credit and job stability will also be factors in the approval of this loan (see Figure 10.1).

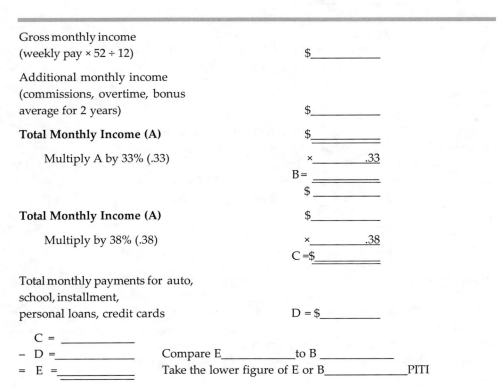

Figure 10.1
Conventional loan qualification worksheet.

Gross monthly income
(weekly pay × 52 ÷ 12) $_____

Additional monthly income
(commissions, overtime, bonus
average for 2 years) $_____

Total Monthly Income (A) $_____

    Multiply A by 33% (.33)   ×_____.33

                         B = _____

                         $_____

Total Monthly Income (A) $_____

    Multiply by 38% (.38)   ×_____.38

                       C = $_____

Total monthly payments for auto,
school, installment,
personal loans, credit cards   D = $_____

    C = _____
  − D = _____   Compare E_____ to B _____
  = E = _____   Take the lower figure of E or B_____ PITI

This figure is the monthly mortgage payment you should use for qualifying the customer. This payment includes principal and interest, taxes, insurance, and PMI (if applicable). Automated underwriting could allow much higher ratios due to buyer profile.

FHA-Insured Loans

Part of the mission of the Federal Housing Administration (FHA), created during the depression of the 1930s, was to make home ownership available to more people, to improve housing construction standards, and to provide a more effective and stable method of financing homes. It succeeded in this mission and provided leadership to standardize procedures for qualifying buyers, appraising property, and evaluating construction. FHA is an agency of the U.S. Department of Housing and Urban Development (HUD).

FHA does not make mortgage loans, but insures mortgage loans to protect lenders. This insurance protection enables lenders to provide financing when there is a very high loan-to-value ratio. This means that the loan amount is very high in comparison to the property value, thereby requiring only a small down payment to be made by the borrower. The amount of insurance protection to the lender is usually sufficient to protect the lender from a financial loss in the event of a foreclosure sale.

Advantages and Disadvantages of FHA

Advantages of the FHA program include

- low down payment requirement
- entire down payment can be gifted by a relative
- seller or other third party can participate in paying the buyer's closing costs
- loans are assumable (since 1986 the new purchaser needs to qualify)
- down payment as low as 3.5% of sales price

Disadvantage of the FHA program

- a mortgage insurance premium is required up front and an annual renewal premium paid monthly is charged. This monthly premium may be for the life of the loan depending on the down payment.

Many of the FHA programs available in the past are no longer available or are no longer widely used. The program still in existence is the FHA 203(b) loan, which allows an owner–occupant to purchase a one-to-four-family dwelling with an FHA-insured loan. The FHA 245 graduated payment mortgage, the FHA 203(b), FHA 243(c) condominium loan, and the 203(k) rehabilitation loan are also available when circumstances warrant.

203(b) FHA Regular Loan Program

This is the original and still the basic FHA program. This program provides for insuring loans for the purchase or construction of one-to-four-family dwellings. FHA does not set a maximum sales price, only a maximum loan amount. A buyer may purchase a home for more than the FHA maximum loan amount (it differs from county to county), but she will have to pay anything above the maximum loan amount in cash. The maximum loan amount is based on the combination of FHA-appraised price or sales price,

How Can FHA Help Me Buy A Home?

How can FHA help me buy a home?

FHA insured mortgages offer many benefits and protections that only come with FHA:

Easier to Qualify: Because FHA insures your mortgage, lenders may be more willing to give you loan terms that make it easier for you to qualify.

Less than Perfect Credit: You don't have to have a perfect credit score to get an FHA mortgage. In fact, even if you have had credit problems, such as a bankruptcy, it's easier for you to qualify for an FHA loan than a conventional loan.

Low Down Payment: FHA loans have a low 3.5% downpayment and that money can come from a family member, employer or charitable organization as a gift. Other loan programs don't allow this.

Costs Less: FHA loans have competitive interest rates because the Federal government insures the loans. Always compare an FHA loan with other loan types.

Helps You Keep Your Home: The FHA has been around since 1934 and will continue to be here to protect you. Should you encounter hard times after buying your home, FHA has many options to help you keep you in your home and avoid foreclosure.

FHA does not provide direct financing nor does it set the interest rates on the mortgages it insures. For the best interest rate and terms on a mortgage, you should compare mortgages from several different lenders. In order to initiate the loan application process, please contact an FHA approved lender.

An FHA insured mortgage may be used to purchase or refinance a new or existing 1-4 family home, a condominium unit or a manufactured housing unit (provided the manufactured housing unit is on a permanent foundation).

HUD's internet site can provide additional information on FHA mortgages by going to: http://portal.hud.gov/hudportal/HUD?src=/topics/buying_a_home

You can also find an FHA approved lender in your area by going to: http://www.hud.gov/ll/code/llslcrit.html

You may also wish to contact a HUD approved housing counseling agency in your area for unbiased counseling on your particular situation.
You can find a list of these agencies at
http://www.hud.gov/offices/hsg/sfh/hcc/hcs.cfm
or call HUD's interactive voice system at 1-800-569-4287.

There are also many local and State government programs available that use HUD and/or non-HUD funds to provide grants for the downpayment or to help pay closing costs.

REFERENCE
http://portal.hud.gov/hudportal/HUD?src=/buying/loans

DISCLAIMER
All policy information contained in this knowledge base article is based upon the referenced HUD policy document. Any lending or insuring decisions should adhere to the specific information contained in that underlying policy document.

whichever is lower, plus those buyer's closing costs that FHA will allow to be financed. A minimum investment of 3.5 percent is required.

The combination of the FHA appraised value and the buyer's closing costs is called the acquisition cost on which the loan amounts are based.

These loans are available for dwellings that are more than one year old or, if less than one year old, were built to FHA specifications and under FHA supervision. New construction requires inspections throughout construction.

FHA 234(c) Condominium Loan

The FHA 234(c) loan is similar to the FHA 203(b) except that it insures loans for the individual condominium units. The condominium complex must meet FHA requirements for construction, number of units, owner occupancy, and homeowner association structure.

FHA 203(k) Rehabilitation Program

With this loan, a buyer can secure a long-term fixed-rate mortgage on a one- to four-family dwelling to finance both the acquisition and the rehabilitation of the property. The mortgage amount is based on the value of the property with the completed improvements. The rehabilitation portion of the loan is placed in an escrow account and disbursed as the work is completed.

Contract Requirement

In the event that a sales contract contingent upon the buyer's obtaining any FHA-insured loan is created prior to an FHA appraisal and commitment to insure is made, the contract must contain the following wording as required by the FHA:

> It is expressly agreed, that notwithstanding any other provisions of this contract, the purchaser shall not be obligated to complete the purchase of the property described herein or to incur any penalty by forfeiture of earnest money deposit or otherwise unless the seller has delivered to the purchaser a written statement issued by the Federal Housing Commissioner setting forth the appraised value of the property (exclusive of closing costs) of not less than $_____, which statement seller hereby agrees to deliver to the purchaser promptly after such appraised value statement is made available to the seller. The purchaser shall, however, have the privilege and option of proceeding with the consummation of this contract without regard to the amount of the appraised valuation made by the Federal Housing Commissioner. The appraised valuation is arrived at to determine the maximum mortgage the Department will insure. HUD does not warrant the value or the condition of the property. The purchaser should satisfy himself/herself that the price and the condition of the property are acceptable.

Many lenders also use a special form to be signed by the seller for this same purpose.

FHA Mortgage Insurance Premium

The FHA program was intended to be a self-supporting entity. To this end, an insurance premium was added to the loan. There have been many revisions to the mortgage insurance premium calculation over the last several years to keep pace with the cost of the FHA program. There is a one-time premium of 1.75 percent of the base loan amount and it is designated as an **up-front MIP (UFMIP).** This premium may be paid in cash at closing or added to the mortgage balance. An additional annual MIP of 1.85 percent calculated on the unpaid principal balance is escrowed monthly and paid annually to HUD. The length of time this annual MIP must be paid depends upon the loan-to-value ratio.

FHA Loan Qualification

Under the qualifying guidelines for FHA loans, the monthly housing expenses composed of principal, interest, taxes, homeowner's insurance, MIP paid monthly, and homeowners' association dues or assessments, if any, should not exceed 31 percent of gross income. These expenses, plus any recurring monthly debts, cannot exceed 43 percent of effective gross income. See Figure 10.2 for an FHA loan qualification example. Eighty-five percent of rental income can be used if the borrower is buying a 2–4 unit property.

Figure 10.2
FHA qualifying worksheet.

Gross Monthly Income

Borrower's base pay, monthly $ _____
   (gross weekly × 52 ÷ 12)

Coborrower's base pay, monthly $ _____

Other earnings (overtime, child
   support, bonus, etc.) $ _____

TOTAL MONTHLY EFFECTIVE GROSS INCOME $ _____ (A)

Total Monthly Debts

Revolving charge accounts
   (monthly minimum payment) $ _____

Installment accounts (auto, personal $ _____
   student loans, etc. with more than 10
   remaining payments)

TOTAL MONTHLY PAYMENTS $_____(B)

RATIOS

Gross monthly income (A) × 31%* =_____(C) Housing ratio

   $ Gross monthly income (A) × 43%_____(D) Housing & debt ratio

(D) $ (B) = _____ (E) Compare (E) to (C). Use the lowest figure of (E) or
                                   (C) for the monthly mortgage payment (PITI).

LOWER OF (E) OR (C) =   _____   PITI

                PITI :   _____

           – TAXES :   _____

     – MIP – INS./DUES :   _____

             = P & I :   _____

*Allows for higher ratios in some cases.

Department of Veteran Affairs Guaranteed Loan Program

Under the VA loan program, an eligible veteran can receive up to a 100 percent no down payment mortgage.

While the FHA is an insured loan program, the VA is a guaranteed loan program. The guaranty is actually a partial guaranty against loss for the lender, covering 25 to 50 percent of the loan amount, depending on the size of the loan. The lender remains liable for the excess of the loss over the guaranteed amount.

The maximum amount the U.S. Department of Veterans Affairs will allow on a home loan for a qualified VA-eligible borrower is called entitlement. The amount of entitlement is found on the VA Certificate of Eligibility, which notes any portion of the entitlement that has been used by the veteran already. The VA provides this backing to the lender, to encourage lenders to make loans to veterans. If a borrower has full entitlement, then the amount the VA will guarantee a lender would be 25% of the loan amount, up to $104,250 in most U.S. counties. The amount may be higher in counties with higher conforming loan limits such as in some areas of California and Massachusetts. . Each VA-eligible borrower starts with basic entitlement of $36,000 for a VA-backed mortgage of up to $144,000. For a veteran's home loan over $144,000, additional entitlement, up to $68,250, is available. When basic and additional entitlements are used together, a qualified military borrower may have enough federal backing to get a VA backed mortgage of up to $417,000. In high-cost counties, it's the additional entitlement number that goes up. Additional entitlement is calculated by subtracting $144,000 from the VA loan limit and multiplying by 25%. For example:($800,000 - $144,000) X 25% = $164,000.

The veteran must certify in writing at the time he obtains the loan that the property being purchased with the loan proceeds will be occupied by the owner. If the property is a multifamily dwelling (maximum of four units), the veteran must occupy one of the apartments, and have property management experience.

Entitlement does not qualify a military member for a VA loan, and having full entitlement does not mean you will qualify for a loan of up to $417,000. Entitlement only tells the lender how much the government is willing to guarantee for that person in the event they qualify for the loan. The veteran will still have to prove to be a satisfactory risk by the combined income and credit qualifying standards of the VA and the VA-approved lender.

Eligibility

Most members of the military, veterans, reservists and **National Guard** members may be eligible to apply for a VA loan if he/she meets one or more of the following conditions:

- Served 90 consecutive days of active service during wartime, **OR**
- Served 181 days of active service during peacetime, **OR**
- Has more than 6 years of service in the National Guard or Reserves, **OR**
- Is the spouse of a service member who has died in the line of duty or as a result of a service-related disability.

Restoration of Eligibility

When a veteran is discharged from the service, he receives a Certificate of Eligibility. This certificate states the maximum guarantee in effect at the time the veteran is discharged. In the event that a veteran has used the full eligibility in obtaining a VA loan, he may have that eligibility fully restored in one of two following ways:

1. The loan is paid in full and the veteran has disposed of the property; or
2. The veteran purchaser from the original veteran borrower assumes the VA loan and has as much remaining eligibility as the original veteran used to obtain the loan and also satisfies the VA requirements for income, credit, and occupancy. The assuming veteran must meet the same requirements as an original VA loan applicant.

These are only two ways in which the veteran borrower's eligibility can be restored. A mere release of liability by the lender and the VA does not in itself restore eligibility. Anyone can assume a VA loan. However, only an assumption by a qualified veteran will restore the selling veteran's eligibility. In the event that a veteran has used part of her eligibility and sold the property to a nonqualifying veteran or nonveteran who assumed the loan, the veteran may still have eligibility remaining.

Contract Contingency

In the event that a contract of sale subject to the buyer obtaining a VA-guaranteed loan is created prior to an appraisal and commitment by the VA, the contract must contain the following statement as required by the Department of Veteran Affairs:

It is expressly agreed that, notwithstanding any other provisions of this contract, the purchaser shall not incur any penalty by forfeiture of earnest money or otherwise or be obligated to complete the purchase of the property described herein, if the contract purchase price or cost exceeds the reasonable value of the property established by the Veterans Administration. The purchaser shall, however, have the privilege and option of proceeding with the consummation of this contract without regard to the amount of the reasonable value established by the Veterans Administration.

Qualifying for VA Loans

The VA loan analysis form (see Figure 10.3) is used to organize information on income, long-term debts (ten months or longer), and the expenses of owning a home. Whether a veteran will be qualified to purchase the home will depend on whether the balance is equal to or exceeds the minimum family support requirements. The total obligation to income ratio may not exceed 41 percent without justification as determined by the VA. In mid-1986, the VA announced new qualification standards for loan applications after October 1, 1986. The new standards require the borrower to qualify under both a net family support standard and a gross monthly income ratio. A gross monthly ratio of 41 percent can be used if residual for family support is 120 percent of requirements.

Other qualifications include two years of satisfactory credit history and two years of satisfactory employment. If the property is a multiunit, 75 percent of the rental income may count if the buyer has a lease or a statement from a tenant verifying the payment. Also, landlord experience is required as well as six months' principal, interest, taxes, and insurance (PITI) in the account after closing.

Figure 10.3
Family support standards in the northeast.

A. MONTHLY EXPENSES

1. Principal & interest at_____% for_____years $_____
2. Real estate taxes $_____
3. Estimated homeowners insurance $_____
4. Maintenance $_____
5. Utilities (includes heat, elec., water) $_____
6. Federal income tax (see tax chart) $_____
7. State income tax (if applicable, see tax charts) $_____
8. Social security (7.65% × gross monthly income) $_____
9. Child-care or job-related expenses $_____
10. Long-term debt (6 months or more to repay) $_____
11. Alimony and/or child support payments $_____
12.   **TOTAL MONTHLY EXPENSES** $_____

B. MONTHLY INCOME

13. Gross taxable income $_____
14. Non-taxable income $_____
15.   **TOTAL MONTHLY INCOME** $_____
16. LESS total monthly expenses (line 12) $_____
17.   **BALANCE AVAILABLE FOR FAMILY SUPPORT** $_____

Family Support Requirements	Family Support Requirements
(Loan amounts to $79,999)	(Loan amounts $80,000 & above)
1. $390 4. $888	1. $450 4. $1025
2. $654 5. $921	2. $755 5. $1062
3. $788	3. $909

OVER 5—ADD $80 FOR EACH ADDITIONAL MEMBER.
BALANCE AVAILABLE FOR FAMILY SUPPORT MUST EQUAL OR EXCEED THE
MINIMUM FAMILY SUPPORT REQUIREMENTS.

C. RATIO CALCULATION

18. Total obligations (lines 1+2+3+10+11) $_____
19. Total gross monthly income (line 15) $_____
20. Total obligations/gross income $_____

TOTAL OBLIGATION/INCOME RATIO MAY NOT EXCEED 41% WITHOUT JUSTIFICATION
AS DETERMINED BY VA.

Rural Development Loans

There are two types of Rural Development Loans: the Direct Loan program which is available only through Rural Development offices and the Guarantee Loan program which is available through participating lenders. The properties financed for both loans cannot be designed for income producing activities and must be in a rural area that is considered eligible by the USDA. The lot value cannot exceed 30% of the appraised value of the property and cannot be large enough to be subdivided.

Rural Development 502 Direct Loan Program

This program assists low and very low income applicants to purchase, build, repair or renovate home.in eligible rural areas by providing payment assistance to increase an applicant's repayment ability. Payment assistance is a type of subsidy that reduces the mortgage payment for a short time. Borrowers are required to repay all or a portion of the payment subsidy received over the life of the loan when the title to the property transfers or the borrower is no longer living in the dwelling. The amount of assistance is determined by the adjusted family income. Applicants interested in obtaining a direct loan must have an adjusted income that is at or below the applicable low-income limit for the area where they wish to buy a house. The income eligibility guidelines can be found on the USDA website. Applicants must also be unable to obtain a loan from other resources on terms and conditions that can reasonably be expected to meet.

The loan is typically a 33 year fixed interest rate loan based on current market rates and when modified by payment assistance the rate can be as low as 1%. No down payment is typically required but if the applicant's assets are higher than the asset limits, they may be required to use a portion of those assets. Applicants are required to complete an approved homeowner education course prior to closing.

Applications for this program are accepted through the local RD office. The offices are located in Scarborough, Lewiston, Bangor and Presque Isle. Processing times vary depending on funding availability and program demand in the area in which an applicant is interested in buying and completeness of the application package.

Rural Development 502 Guaranteed Loan Program

This program provides loan guarantees to approved lenders to assist rural Maine families in obtaining affordable housing. This is 100% loan to value financing but unlike the Direct program there is a guarantee fee of 2.75% that can be paid at closing or financed (102.75%) and a .5% annual fee paid monthly over the life of the loan.

On properties financed with this program, the lender must provide documentation that the lot cost is typical for lots in the area and cannot be subdivided. The applicant must have an adjusted annual family income that does not exceed the moderate income limit for household size and county where the home is located. Income limits are available at Rural Development offices, approved lenders and on the USDA website.

MAINE HOUSING FIRST HOME PROGRAM

The First Home loan program offers below-market or competitive interest rates on 30-year fixed rate mortgages to first time homebuyers (have never owned a home or not owned a home in the last 3 years). Other qualifications for the program include meeting income and purchase price limits as well as an acceptable credit score.

There is little or no down payment when a MaineHousing mortgage is combined with a government guaranty (FHA/RD/ VA) or with United Guaranty private mortgage insurance.

The loan program has some unique features such as $3,500 in down-payment and closing cost assistance (Advantage program) and up to $35,000 in additional loan financing for house improvements (Purchase Plus Improvement Program). Attending a Home Buyer Education course is a requirement if the borrower used the Advantage program. There is also a program called Maine HOPE which is payment protection for a borrower who becomes unemployed. If the borrower qualifies, Maine Hope may be able to help by making four mortgage payments including taxes and homeowner's insurance. The amount paid becomes a junior mortgage with no interest due when the mortgage is paid off.

ALTERNATIVE METHODS OF FINANCING

Open-End Mortgage

An **open-end mortgage** is one that may be *refinanced without rewriting* the mortgage and thereby incurring closing costs. The original mortgage provides the security for additional funds advanced to the borrower.

Participation Mortgage

The term *participation mortgage* is used to describe a mortgage in which *two or more* lenders participate in making the loan. The participation agreement between the lenders may provide that each participating lender owns a pro rata share of the mortgage and each will receive her share of mortgage payment of principal and interest as it is made.

Construction Loan

This is a form of *short-term financing* used to obtain the funds to create improvements on land. The applicant for a construction loan submits the plans and specifications for the structure to be built. The lender will make the construction loan based on the value resulting from an appraisal of the property and the construction plans and specifications. The loan contract will specify that disbursements will be made as specified stages of the construction are completed. Upon completion, the lender makes a final inspection and closes out the construction loan, which is then converted to permanent, long-term financing.

Purchase Money Mortgage

This is a mortgage given by a buyer to the seller to cover part of the purchase price. Here the seller becomes the mortgagee and the buyer the mortgagor. The seller has conveyed title to the buyer who immediately reconveys or pledges it as security for the balance of the purchase price.

Bridge Loan

This is short-term financing for borrowers who want to close on their new purchase prior to the sale of their current home. The lender writes one loan that requires interest-only payments. The new loan pays off the mortgage(s) on the current home as well as funds the purchase of the property. When the current home eventually sells, the borrower must refinance the new property.

Junior Mortgage

The term **junior mortgage** describes any mortgage that is *subordinate* (lower in priority) to another mortgage. It may be a second mortgage, third mortgage, and so on. Each of these is subordinate to the prior mortgage on the same property.

In the event of a foreclosure sale, the holder of a third mortgage is not entitled to any of the sale proceeds until the second mortgage is fully satisfied, and so on down the line of priorities. The priority is established by the time (date and hour) that the mortgage is recorded on the public record in the county where the property is located.

Package Mortgage

Usually real estate mortgage loans are secured by real property. If the cost of appli- ances, furniture, or any equipment are included in the financing, the mortgage is referred to as a package mortgage.

Blanket Mortgage

A mortgage that covers and is secured by more than one property is called a blanket mortgage. If a mortgage covered a house lot and two other lots and the owner wished to sell one of the lots, it would be necessary to have the property released from the blanket mortgage. The original mortgage agreement would specify the procedure to release the lot with a partial release clause.

METHODS OF MORTGAGE PAYMENT

Amortizing Mortgage

The Federal Housing Administration (FHA) was created by the National Housing Act of 1934 for the purpose of insuring mortgage loans to protect lending institutions in the event of borrower default. The FHA will only insure amortizing mortgages. As a result of this and as a result of the hardship that may be created for borrowers under the term mortgage, the typical home mortgage loan in use today is the **amortizing mortgage**.

Amortization provides for the paying of a debt by installment payments. A portion of each installment payment is applied first to the payment of interest and the remainder to the reduction of principal. See Figure 10.4 for an example of an abbreviated amortization table. The interest is charged only on the declining balance.

The rate of interest is an annual percentage rate as specified by the note and mortgage. The interest rate is calculated by multiplying the annual percentage rate by the unpaid principal balance and dividing the result by 12 (months) to determine the amount of interest due and payable for any monthly installment.

Amortization Table (monthly payments per $1000)

Figure 10.4
Amortization Table.

Annual Interest Rate	1	3	5	10	15	20	25
3.00	84.69	29.08	17.97	9.65	6.90	5.54	4.74
3.25	84.80	29.19	18.08	9.77	7.02	5.67	4.87
3.50	84.92	29.30	18.19	9.88	7.14	5.79	5.00
3.75	85.03	29.41	18.30	10.00	7.26	5.92	5.13
4.00	85.14	29.51	18.41	10.11	7.39	6.05	5.27
4.25	85.25	29.62	18.52	10.23	7.51	6.18	5.40
4.50	85.36	29.73	18.63	10.35	7.63	6.31	5.54
4.75	85.48	29.84	18.74	10.47	7.76	6.44	5.68
5.00	85.59	29.95	18.85	10.59	7.89	6.58	5.82
5.25	85.70	30.06	18.97	10.71	8.01	6.71	5.96
5.50	85.81	30.17	19.08	10.83	8.14	6.85	6.11
5.75	85.93	30.28	19.19	10.95	8.27	6.99	6.26
6.00	86.04	30.39	19.30	11.07	8.40	7.13	6.40
6.25	86.14	30.50	19.41	11.19	8.53	7.26	6.55
6.50	86.26	30.61	19.53	11.32	8.67	7.55	6.85
6.75	86.37	30.72	19.64	11.43	8.80	7.55	6.85
7.00	86.59	30.84	19.76	11.56	8.94	7.70	7.01

Years to fully amortize loan

After deducting the interest, the remainder of the payment is used to reduce the principal balance. Therefore, the amount of interest paid with each installment reduces because the interest rate is applied against a smaller and smaller amount of principal. In this way, the loan is amortized so that the final payment in a fully amortizing mortgage will pay any remaining interest and principal (see Figures 10.5 through 10.8).

Adjustable Rate Mortgage (ARM)

To say that the 1980s was a decade of turbulent development in the real estate financing market is certainly an understatement. In the late 1970s, no sage would have predicted that interest rates would soar from 9 to 18 percent or better. In a like fashion, who would have predicted in 1982 the 5 percent rates seen in 2013. Nevertheless, such was to be history. Given these circumstances, it is possible to understand the motivation of lending institutions to shift the burden of unpredictability from themselves to the mortgagor. We can therefore appreciate the development of the **adjustable rate mortgage (ARM)** from the lendors standpoint.

Figure 10.5
An amortized loan.

Example: Assume a home purchase price of $87,500 with a conventional mortgage of 80% of the sale price at a rate of 8.5% for 30 years.

1. Amount of the loan = $87,500 × 80% = $70,000
2. Divide $70,000 by 1,000 = $70 (thousands)
3. The factor for 30 years is 7.69.
   This is the payment per month per thousand dollars of the loan.
4. Multiply $70 × 7.69 = $538.30. This is the monthly payment of principal and interest to amortize a loan of $70,000 at 8.5% for 30 years.

Figure 10.6
Interest paid per month.

Example: Use the data in Figure 10.5 to calculate how much of the payment (P & I) went to the interest portion (I).

1. Interest (I) at any point is the principal (P) times the rate (R) times the period of time (T) you had the money, or:

   $I = P \times R \times T$

2. In the example,
   I = $70,000 × 8.5% × $1/12$ of a year, or

   $I = \dfrac{\$70,000 \times 0.085}{12} = 495.83$

3. Therefore, of the total payment of $538.30, in the first month, $495.83 went only to interest.

Figure 10.7
Loan balance after a payment.

What is the loan balance after a payment?

1. Calculate the amount that went to principal (P), e.g., $ 42.47
2. Subtract this amount from the previous balance, e.g., $70,000.00

3. The remainder is the new balance on the loan, e.g., $70,000.00
                                                                           -     42.47
                                                                           $69,957.53

How much interest is paid over the life of the loan?

1. Calculate the monthly payment, e.g., $538.30
2. Calculate the total number of months to be paid, e.g., 30 years is 12 months ×
   30 = 360 payments
3. Multiply the monthly payment times the total number of months to be paid to calculate
   the total of the payments, e.g., $538.30 × 360 payments = $193,788 total payback
4. Subtract the amount of the loan borrowed from the total of the payback to calculate the amount that went to interest, e.g.,

$193,788.00
– 70,000.00
$123,788.00   total interest paid

Figure 10.8
Total interest paid over the life of the loan.

The ARM entered as one solution to the problem of the uncertainty of future financial rates. In the ARM, the parties agree to base mortgage rates on the fluctuations of a
standard index. Common indices include the cost of funds for savings and loan
institutions, the national average mortgage rate, or the more popular one-year rate for
the government's sale of Treasury bills.

An ARM will designate an index and then add a margin (measure of profit) above this
index. For example, if the T-bill index was 5 and the lender's margin was 2.50, the ARM
would call for an interest rate of 7.5 percent. (Margins are sometimes expressed as a basis
point, each basis point being 1/100 of 1 percent, or 250 basis points in the previous
example.)

The ARM has definite advantages for the buyer, especially the short-term owner
who may expect to sell his home in the near future, such as through a transfer of employment. However, the long-term owner may fear the possibility of an ever-increasing
mortgage rate. Such an apprehension should be moderated by the understanding that not
only do economic cycles rise and fall, but that in the case of inflation, the value of the
property would rise as well.

A significant concern would be an ARM that is structured with the possibility of
negative amortization. In this case, the index rises while the payment is fixed, causing the
payments to fall below the amount called for by the index. Such shortfall is added back to the
principal, causing the principal to grow larger after the payment (negative amortization). In
some ARMs, this event will be expected if the payment contract rate falls below the internal
accrual rate by 1/2 percent.

Many ARMs are structured with caps that limit both the annual adjustment and the
total adjustment during the lifetime of the loan and prohibit negative amortization. For
example, on one ARM, annual increases could be limited to 1 or 2 percent interest and
the lifetime cap might be no higher than 5 or 6 percent.

There are intermediate ARMs that are fixed for periods of time (i.e., 3, 5, 7, 10
years) and then adjust either annually or on some other adjustment schedule.

Graduated Payment Mortgage (GPM)

In the graduated payment mortgage (GPM) the monthly payments are lower in the
early years of the mortgage term and gradually increase at specified intervals until the
payment amount is sufficient to amortize the loan over the remaining term. The
monthly payments are kept down in the early years by not requiring the borrower to pay
all of the interest, which is added back to the principal.

Buydown Loan

In a buydown plan the lender may agree to reduce the rate for some years in return for some compensation. In an original version of the plan, common interest rates were 9 percent, which the buyer could pay for the full 30 years, or "buydown" the rate for the compensation of a number of discount points. In this version, buyers could pay up to 8 points (each point costs 1 percent of the loan), which reduced the interest rate by $1/4$ percent to reduce their fixed rate loan to 7 percent for the full 30 years. If the loan amount was $50,000, the cost to the buyer would be: 8% × $50,000 = $4,000.

Other versions of the buydown concept, known as temporary buydowns, may cover only the early years of the loan. For example, a 3:2:1 buydown plan would reduce the interest rate 3 percent for the first year, 2 percent for the second, and 1 percent for the third year by having the seller pay points up front on behalf of the borrower. Certain sellers, such as builders, might be interested in paying the required discount points, as a seller concession, to make the home more affordable in the first years and thus help the buyer get started.

Term Mortgage

A term mortgage requires the borrower to *pay interest only* for a specified term. At the end of the term, the borrower is required to pay the principal. This is the type of mortgage that was generally in use at the time of the depression of the 1930s. Many borrowers were unable to pay the principal when it came due and lenders had become unable to refinance the principal for the borrower as had usually been the case in more prosperous times. As a result, many homeowners lost their property through foreclosure.

Balloon Mortgage

The **balloon mortgage** provides for installment payments that are not sufficient in amount to pay off the principal and interest over the term of the mortgage loan. Therefore, there must be a final payment called a balloon payment that is *substantially larger* than any previous payment in order to satisfy the remaining principal and interest. If this so-called balloon payment is to be a substantial amount, the note will usually provide for refinancing by the lender to provide the funds to the borrower in the event that he or she cannot otherwise make the payment.

Shared Appreciation Mortgages (SAMs)

In the *shared appreciation mortgage (SAM)* the lender shares in the appreciation of property value and in turn provides a lower rate of interest to the borrower. Typically, for a one-third share in value increase, the lender will make the loan at a rate one-third less than the going rate for a fixed-term conventional loan at the time the loan is created.

The increase in value in which the lender shares is demonstrated by the price for which the property is sold by the borrower as compared to the price paid for the property. However, federal regulations require that if the property is not sold within 10 years, there must be an appraisal of the property and the lending institution must receive its one-third of the value increase as shown by the appraisal. This could result in a substantial hardship for the borrower who does not sell within the 10-year term. This borrower may have to refinance in order to obtain the money to pay the lender the one-third share of value increase.

QUALIFYING REQUIREMENTS
FOR MORTGAGE LOANS

In deciding whether to make any type of mortgage loan, a lending institution must consider two aspects: (1) the value of the property proposed to be pledged as security for the payment of the note and (2) the income, assets, and credit history of the loan applicant.

Property Appraisal

To estimate the value of the property, the lender retains the services of an appraiser who performs an appraisal based on certain criteria specified by the lender. The appraisal is performed to estimate the value of the property. The lender's concern regarding the value is the amount of money that may be obtained in a foreclosure sale.

Income, Assets, and Credit History of the Loan Applicant

In evaluating the loan applicant, the lending institution requires the applicant to have an effective income sufficient to enable the borrower to make the loan payments and continue to meet other recurring financial obligations. The effective income may be a combination of an applicant's and coapplicant's income (husband and wife, for example). The applicant must also have a satisfactory credit history.

The applicant is required to furnish credit information covering the two-year period immediately preceding the date of the application. If the applicant's credit history is unsatisfactory, then the application will be denied regardless of the amount and quality of the applicant's income in relation to the loan payments.

The applicant's assets are also taken into consideration by the lending institution. If the applicant's income is borderline in relation to the mortgage payment required, but the individual has sufficient good-quality assets, the existence of these assets may make the difference between approval and disapproval of the loan application.

There are non-conforming loans available that have higher down payments and/or interest rates for those situations that do not meet traditional guidelines.

DISCOUNT POINTS CHARGED
ON MORTGAGE LOANS

In making mortgage loans, lending institutions may charge the buyer **discount points**. One point is equal to 1 percent of the loan amount. The lender's purpose in charging these discount points is to increase the yield to the lender by increasing the effective interest rate in an amount exceeding a maximum rate that may be charged under certain conditions. Discount points represent interest paid in advance and are paid at the time of closing.

Points bridge the gap between interest rates, allowing the lender the ability to make the loan at a lower interest rate. While the value of points can vary depending on the financial market, 1 point generally buys the interest rate by $1/4$ percent.

IMPORTANT POINTS

1. A buyer assuming a seller's mortgage assumes liability on both the mortgage and the note. The seller remains liable on the note unless specifically released by a mortgage clause or by the lender. A buyer taking title subject to an existing mortgage has no liability on the note.
2. A fully amortizing mortgage requires payments of principal and interest that will satisfy the debt completely over the mortgage term.
3. Various types of mortgages include balloon, open-end, graduated payment, adjustable or variable rate, shared appreciation (SAM), participation, blanket, construction, purchase money, and junior.
4. The major sources of residential financing are savings and loan associations, mutual savings banks, commercial banks, and mortgage companies.
5. The methods of financing are insured and uninsured conventional mortgage loans, FHA-insured loans, VA-guaranteed loans, and the various types of seller financing.
6. Conventional loans are not required to be insured if the loan amount does not exceed 80 percent of the property value. Most conventional insured loans are 90 percent and 95 percent loans. The insurance is called private mortgage insurance (PMI). The premium is paid by the borrower.
7. FHA and VA loans are made by qualified lending institutions.
8. The FHA programs include 203(b), 245, 203(b) (2), and 203(k). The FHA insurance is called mortgage insurance premium (MIP) and protects the lender from a financial loss in the event of a foreclosure. The premium is paid by the borrower. The loan amount is a percentage of the acquisition cost as established by the FHA.
9. VA loans are guaranteed loans. VA loans are 100 percent of the property value established by a VA appraisal and stated in the Certificate of Reasonable Value (CRV), which is issued by the VA.
10. FHA and VA loans require escrow accounts, are assumable, and do not impose a prepayment penalty. The down payment can be borrowed if secured by collateral.

REVIEW QUESTIONS

Answers to these questions are found in the Answer Key section at the back of the book.

1. The type of mortgage requiring the borrower to pay only interest during the mortgage term is a(n):
   a. balloon mortgage
   b. open-end mortgage
   c. term mortgage
   d. closed mortgage

2. The amount of interest paid in an amortizing mortgage for a month in which the principal balance is $73,000 and the rate is 12 percent is which of the following?
   a. $876
   b. $730
   c. $600
   d. $1,369

3. A mortgage that is not on a fully amortizing basis and, therefore, requires a larger final payment is called a(n):
   a. graduated mortgage
   b. balloon mortgage
   c. open-end mortgage
   d. flexible mortgage

4. Which of the following statements regarding adjustable rate mortgages is (are) correct?
   I. The interest rate changes according to changes in a selected index.
   II. Adjustable rate mortgages do not contain a prepayment penalty.
   a. I only
   b. II only
   c. Both I and II
   d. Neither I nor II

5. The type of mortgage in which the lender reduces the interest rate for a part of the profit realized when the property is sold is a:
   a. Participation mortgage
   b. price level adjusted mortgage
   c. wraparound mortgage
   d. shared appreciation mortgage

6. A mortgage in which two or more parcels of land are pledged is called a(n):
   a. blanket mortgage
   b. package mortgage
   c. all-inclusive mortgage
   d. wraparound mortgage

7. A mortgage that is subordinate to another is called a:
   a. leasehold mortgage
   b. blanket mortgage
   c. junior mortgage
   d. participation mortgage

8. The priority of mortgages in relation to each other is based on which of the following?
   a. time of execution
   b. time of recording
   c. time of delivery
   d. time of acknowledgment

9. A mortgage given by a buyer to a seller to secure payment of part of the purchase price is which of the following?
   a. purchase money mortgage
   b. earnest money mortgage
   c. participation mortgage
   d. graduated payment mortgage

10. Insurance for the protection of lending institutions making conventional loans is called:
    a. mutual mortgage insurance
    b. conventional mortgage insurance
    c. institutional insurance
    d. private mortgage insurance

11. The FHA programs are for which of the following purposes?
    a. making housing loans
    b. guaranteeing housing loans
    c. purchasing housing loans
    d. insuring housing loans

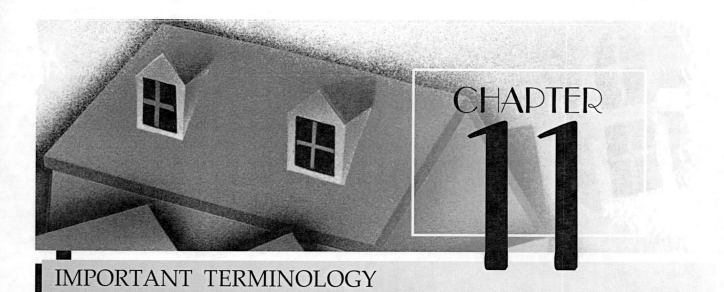

IMPORTANT TERMINOLOGY

counteroffer
debt ratio
housing ratio

PITI
qualify a buyer

SELLING: PRACTICES AND PROCEDURES

IN THIS CHAPTER

Prior to buyer agency being practiced in Maine, licensees developed selling prospects through their listings. They advertised, held open houses, and placed their listings in the MLS. Another source of buyers came from the sphere of influence (past clients, friends, relatives, and service providers).

Today, these sources still remain but there may be a difference in the relationship. In the past the buyer was always the customer and today the licensee is encouraged to represent the buyer as a buyer agent. Prior clients are now a valuable source for new clients.

INTERVIEWING THE BUYERS

At the initial interview, before any discussion of a substantive real estate nature occurs, the licensee must present MREC Brokerage Relationships Form #3 to the buyer. The form is a disclosure of the agency relationships that occur in the marketplace. Before the buyer is asked to read the form, the licensee should explain the difference between client and customer and whether their company has a policy of appointed, single or disclosed agency. After the form is read, the licensee should ask if there are any questions.

The interview is the time that the buyer and the licensee will decide what their relationship will be as they proceed through the transaction. The choices, seller agent, buyer agent, disclosed dual agent or transaction broker, depend on what the agency office policy is and whose listing is involved. The buyer should be educated on these choices and what is involved in buying a home before making a relationship decision. The licensee should also determine, through a series of questions, the motivation, urgency, needs, expectations and previous home buying experience of the buyer.

The interview may also be the first step in establishing rapport between the licensee and the buyer. Conducting this interview involves diplomacy, tact, and empathy on the part of the licensee.

QUALIFYING DATA

Prior to showing property the licensee should inquire as to whether the buyer has been pre-approved for a loan and what are the terms of the pre-approval. The pre-approval letter should contain information on the interest rate, term of the loan, the PITI (Principal, Interest, Taxes and Insurance) and the loan amount. The loan officer who qualified the buyer and recommended a specific loan program based that qualification on the following:

    1. Gross monthly income (An annual income of $48,000 would generate a
        $4000 gross monthly income.)

Figure 11.1
Home buying
process.

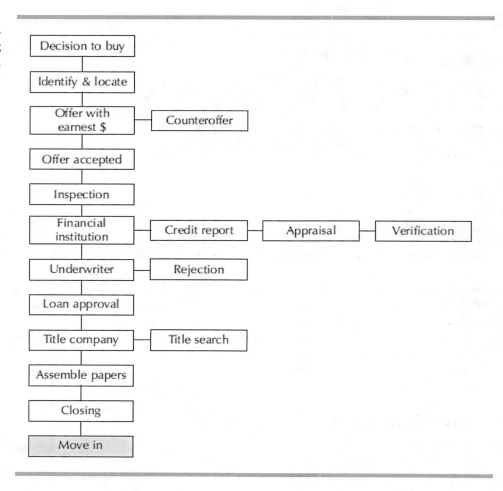

2. Source of the verified income (salary, commissions, overtime, bonuses, dividends interest, alimony, child support payments, income from rental property, social security and disability income)

3. Monthly payments on long term debts (car payments, credit cards, school loans, alimony, child support, child care)

4. Credit score (Score is based on payment history, amount owed, length of credit history, new credit and types of credit in use)

5. Amount of cash available for down payment and closing costs

QUALIFYING FOR A LOAN

The bank will allow a percentage of the buyer's gross monthly income to be spent for principal, interest, taxes, and insurance (**PITI**), otherwise known as housing expenses. The ratio of the housing expenses to the gross monthly income is called the **housing ratio** or front end ratio. The ratio of the housing expenses plus debts to the gross monthly income is called the **debt ratio** or back end ratio. The type of loan will determine an acceptable housing and debt ratio.

To estimate the monthly principal, interest, taxes, and insurance:

1. Multiply income by housing ratio.
2. Multiply income by debt ratio minus long-term debts.
3. Compare the two amounts and use the smaller amount.

Example: John Smith's gross monthly income is $5,000. Long-term debts equal $450 per month and he has $20,000 for a down payment. Use 33% and 38% for the housing and debt ratio.

    1. $5,000 × .33 = $1,650

    2 $5,000 × .38 = $1,900 − 450 = $1,450

    3. The smaller amount is $1,450 = PITI (principal, interest, taxes, insurance)

Subtracting the taxes and insurance from the PITI will give the monthly principal and interest: $1,450 − 300 = $1,150. Using an amortization chart or calculator you can easily estimate what the total loan will be. (Select an interest rate and a term. Example: 7% and 30 years.)

In the example, John Smith qualifies for a $187,884 mortgage. To this, add the $20,000 down payment, and the result is the maximum purchase price of $207,884. (See Figure 11.2)

If the buyer is putting down less than 20 percent as a down payment, you would have to include the private mortgage insurance premium with the PITI, which would have the effect of lowering the mortgage amount.

Buyers should be made aware of closing costs associated with the purchase of real estate. An estimate based on a hypothetical sale should be part of the financial picture presented to them.

Credit Scores

Besides the ratios, lending institutions use credit scores to determine how good a credit risk the buyer is. The credit score is based on a model derived from analysis of past credit history. It tries to determine the buyer's future behavior in respect to repayment and making timely payments. Lenders use this information to determine whether a buyer qualifies for a loan and if so, at what interest rate and what terms. The score is represented as a three digit number ranging from 300–900. Some of the factors that affect the score are outstanding debt, length of credit history, types of credit and number of inquiries on your credit report.

PURCHASE AND SALE AGREEMENT OFFER

At the end of the initial interview, the agent has ascertained what the buyer can afford and what he wants and needs in a home. Using this information the agent will begin to locate appropriate properties to view until the "right" home has been found.

John Smith

$207,884	Sales price
1,150	Principal & interest
200	Taxes (estimated)
100	Insurance (estimated)
$ 1,450	Total PITI each month
$20,000	Down payment
3,500	Closing costs
$23,500	

Figure 11.2
Monthly and closing costs.

At this point, the buyer is ready to make an offer. It is strongly recommended that a written explanation of the mechanics of submitting an offer for the seller's consideration and the seller's and buyer's alternatives be provided to the buyer. At the time that the offer is being written, the possibility of competing offers should be discussed so that the buyer is aware that her initial offer may be the only opportunity she has to buy the property. There is no obligation for the seller to reveal to buyers that they are in a multiple offer situation. The buyer should also be aware that the seller may accept an offer on terms other than price, such as closing date, inspections, a house to sell, etc. The buyer should also have a closing cost sheet, which will provide an estimate of what money will be needed at closing. By Maine law, the buyer should have a copy of the seller's property disclosure before signing the purchase and sale agreement. If the property disclosure is not available, the licensee should present a written statement to the buyer that the disclosure is not available. The buyer may make a decision to proceed and write an offer contingent upon receiving the disclosure or decide to wait until the disclosure is available.

The offer to purchase is signed by the buyer and a copy is given to him immediately. The offer is then delivered to the listing agent, who will analyze and study it before presenting it to the seller. This is necessary in order to advise the seller on every aspect of the offer. All offers whether written or verbal must be presented to the seller for her consideration. Some of the terms to note are:

- the amount of deposit
- the purchase price
- the date of closing
- closing costs charged to seller
- rental fees
- financial contingencies
- personal property to remain
- a house-to-sell contingency

If all terms are agreed upon, the seller will sign the offer and keep a copy. The agent notifies the buyer that the offer was accepted and gives the buyer a copy of the signed contract. An offer may be rescinded at any time prior to the acceptance of the offer being communicated to the offeror or her agent. The offer to purchase becomes a contract to purchase when the contract is signed and communicated to all parties.

Counteroffers

If the seller does not agree to all terms of the offer, she may reject it outright or make changes in the terms. This is called a **counteroffer**. The buyer's offer terminates if the offer has been countered.

A counteroffer is actually a new offer wherein the seller becomes the offeror and the prospective purchaser the offeree. The counteroffer then must be presented by the agent to the buyer for acceptance or rejection. In some real estate transactions, there are several offers and counteroffers before both the buyer and seller reach an acceptable agreement. Counteroffers should have an expiration date to avoid the possibility of more than one offer becoming a contract.

An offer can be countered by crossing out the term(s) not agreed to and writing the change(s) above, initialing and dating the change(s). The counteroffer can also be in the form of an addendum to the contract, with the parties signing and dating the addendum. When the buyer or seller signs the original purchase and sale agreement or initials any changes, he should receive a copy of the document signed. Once the negotiation is over and there is a completed purchase and sale agreement, a copy of that completed agreement must be delivered to both the buyer and seller within a reasonable amount of time.

It should be noted that when an offer is countered, the property is available for an offer by another party. If the seller counters an offer and meanwhile another offer from a second party is presented to the seller, she may accept the second-party offer by revoking the counteroffer to the first party as long as it has not been accepted by the first party.

Back-Up Offers

The agent's duty to the seller is not discharged until the final sale and conveyance of the title has been consummated. Therefore, the licensee's fiduciary duty shall include, but not be limited to, disclosing to the seller any interest in the property occurring subsequent to the property being placed under contract. Suppose a seller has accepted an offer for the purchase of a property and there is a legally binding contract on that property. He receives information from the agent that another buyer is interested in paying more for the property than the first buyer. How does the agent handle the situation?

The second offer can be written up as being subject to the first contract and if accepted by the seller becomes a back-up contract on the property. If the buyer refuses to become a back-up buyer, that buyer is free to negotiate with the first buyer to buy out her pending contract if the contract can be assigned or to buy the property from the first buyer as soon as she becomes the owner. In either event, the first buyer becomes the beneficiary of the increased value rather than the seller.

Monitoring the Transaction

When the property is under contract, a major part of the licensee's job as a selling agent still remains. The licensee needs to oversee the financing, inspections, appraisal and any other contingencies written in the purchase and sale agreement. Once all contingencies are met, the licensee will work with the title company until the property closes. At this phase, there may be title problems, last minute demands from the lender or changes in the buyer's job status that may affect the closing.

IMPORTANT POINTS

1. A licensee may be a seller agent, buyer agent, disclosed dual agent, or transaction broker depending on the office policy.
2. The real estate agent has to disclose her role in a real estate transaction before property is shown.
3. The qualifying process includes determining the financial capability as well as the wants and needs of buyers.
4. Buyers should be made aware of both the initial cost of buying a home and the monthly costs.
5. The seller has three choices upon receiving an offer: to accept, reject, or counter the offer.
6. Both buyers and sellers must be given a copy of the offer when it is either signed or initialed by them.

REVIEW QUESTIONS

Answers to these questions are found in the Answer Key section at the back of the book.

1. When an offer is made that is much less than the listed price, the licensee:
   a. may refuse to present the offer to the seller
   b. must present any and all offers to the seller
   c. may bind the seller to the offer
   d. none of the above

2. An offer from a buyer becomes a contract when it is:
   a. for the full price
   b. a cash offer
   c. signed by the seller and communicated to the buyer
   d. all of the above

3. When a seller of a piece of land changes the terms of an offer, it is called:
   a. a land contract
   b. a counteroffer
   c. breach of contract
   d. none of the above

4. A buyer agent has learned that a buyer for whom he received an offer has just lost his job. He should:
   a. not do anything. The information is confidential
   b. inform the listing agent
   c. wait and see if the buyer can get another job
   d. ask to have the offer withdrawn since the buyer is not able to get financing

5. When a seller receives an offer, she may:
   a. accept it
   b. reject it
   c. counter it
   d. any of the above

6. A seller has received an offer and the only thing he changes is the possession date. This is:
   a. a partially accepted offer
   b. a new offer that will obligate the buyer
   c. a new offer that will bind the seller if the buyer initials the changes
   d. a fully accepted offer

7. Jane Smith earns $22,000 annually and her husband John earns $23,000 plus a yearly bonus, which is 3 per-cent of his annual salary. What is their gross monthly income?
   a. $2,650
   b. $3,807
   c. $28,075
   d. $45,690

8. Calculate the maximum PITI for the following problem: The annual income is $35,000 and the long-term debts include $180 for a car loan and $35 for charge cards. The housing ratio is 25 percent and the debt ratio is 33 percent.
   a. $729.17
   b. $747.50
   c. $756.14
   d. none of the above

CHAPTER 12

IMPORTANT TERMINOLOGY

abstract of title
acknowledgment
actual notice
adverse possession
alienation
base lines
beneficiary
bequest
chain of title
constructive notice
deeds
description by reference
devise
execution
executor
executrix
grantee
grantor
habendum clause

limited warranty deed
metes and bounds
notice
plat
principal meridians
quiet title
quitclaim deed
quitclaim with covenant
race notice
ranges
rectangular survey system
testate
testator
testatrix
title examination
title insurance
title opinion
warranty deed
will

TRANSFER OF TITLE TO REAL PROPERTY

IN THIS CHAPTER

The transfer of real property between buyer and seller is the goal of the real estate transaction. When all contingencies within the contracts have been met and the loan has been approved, the title work will begin. Assuring the transfer of good title involves surveys, deeds, abstracts of title, title insurance, and the recording system.

METHODS OF TRANSFERRING PROPERTY

The transfer of a title to real property is described in law as **alienation**. The property owner is alienated or separated from the title by transfer of the title to another. The alienation may be voluntary or involuntary and may occur during life or after death.

Involuntary Alienation During Life

During life, title to real property may be transferred by involuntary alienation as a result of a lien foreclosure sale, adverse possession, or condemnation under the power of eminent domain.

Lien Foreclosure Sale

In Chapter 9 we discussed the fact that real property may be sold at public auction to satisfy a specific or general lien against the property. These foreclosure sales are without the consent of the property owner who incurred the debt resulting in a lien. Foreclosure sales are ordered by a court and title is conveyed to a purchaser at the sale by judicial deed. A judicial deed is executed by the official authorized by the court to conduct the sale and transfer the title. In these cases, titles are typically conveyed without the participation of the property owner who lost the title as the result of the foreclosure.

Adverse Possession

Title to real property can be claimed by a person other than the owner, called **adverse possession**, if the other person takes use of the land under the following conditions:

1. The possession or occupation must be open and well known to others (notorious).
2. The possession of the property must be under color of title or claim of title. That is, the occupant of the property must have some reasonable

basis to believe that he is entitled to possession of the property. This basis is typically in the form of a defective deed or a quitclaim deed.

3. The possession must be without the permission of the true owner and must be exclusive. The requirement of an exclusive possession means that only the adverse possessor may possess the property over the period.

4. The possession must be continuous and uninterrupted for a period specified by statute, 20 years.

The adverse possessor *does not automatically* acquire title to the property by merely meeting the four requirements just listed. To perfect the claim and obtain a title to the property, the claimant must satisfy the court that she has fulfilled the requirements of the adverse possession statute in the particular state by suit to **quiet title**. If the court is satisfied that the statutory requirements have been met, then the court will award the title to the claimant under adverse possession. An exception to the adverse possession rule even if the four conditions are met is in the case of a mistaken boundary. If someone builds a fence on a neighbor's land, that is a mistaken entry, and it does not ripen into title in Maine.

Condemnation Under Eminent Domain

The federal government, states, and their agencies, counties, cities, towns, and boroughs have the power of eminent domain. This power provides the right to take private property for public use. The taking of the property under the power of eminent domain is called condemnation. The property is condemned under eminent domain. The property that is condemned must be for the use and benefit of the general public. The property owner must be justly compensated for the property lost through condemnation. The condemning authority must use due process of law (that is, adequately notify the property owner of the condemnation) and the property owner must have the right to appeal the value of the property as established by the condemning authority through the court system. However, the property owner cannot prevent the condemnation and, therefore, the loss of title is involuntary.

Involuntary Alienation After Death

If a person dies and leaves a valid **will**, the individual's property will be distributed to heirs according to the terms of the will. In the absence of a will, property is distributed to heirs by descent according to the state statute enacted for this purpose. These statutes are called intestate succession statutes because a person who has died without leaving a valid will has died intestate. Escheat occurs when there is no one eligible to receive the property of the intestate as provided by statute. If a diligent search fails to reveal qualified heirs as specified by the statute, the property escheats to the state. This means that in the absence of heirs the state takes title to the property of the deceased. Since the deceased has no control over the transfer of title to the state, this results in an involuntary alienation after death. This is the only form of involuntary alienation after death.

Voluntary Alienation After Death

Voluntary alienation after death occurs as a result of a valid will or in the absence of a valid will with qualified heirs existing to receive title to the property.

If a person dies and leaves a valid will, he is said to have died **testate**. The deceased is called a **testator** if a man and **testatrix** if a woman. A person appointed in a will to carry out the provisions of the will is called an **executor** or **executrix**. Probate is the judicial determination of the validity of a will by a court of compe-

-tent jurisdiction. A gift of real property by will is a **devise** and the recipient is a devisee. A gift of personal property by will is a **bequest** and the recipient is the **beneficiary**.

Voluntary Alienation During Life

This is the type of alienation that is of primary importance to the real estate business. Voluntary alienation, or transfer of title during life, is accomplished by the delivery of a valid deed by the **grantor** to the **grantee** during the life of both of them. The contract of sale for real property is consummated by the delivery of a valid deed by the grantor to the grantee as required in the contract. In most real estate purchase and sale agreements there is a clause stating that the contract is binding on the heirs and assigns. In the event that the seller should die prior to the transfer of title, a personal representative of the estate would have to deliver the deed to complete the sale.

ELEMENTS OF A DEED

The essential elements of a deed are the following: names of the grantor and grantee, consideration, words of conveyance, property description, and signature of the grantor. The following is an explanation of the different components of the **warranty** deed (see Figure 12.1).

1. *Grantor*. The grantor (one conveying the title) must be legally competent, that is, the individual must have the capacity to contract. This is the same requirement that exists for all parties to a valid contract. The grantor must have reached the age of majority and must be mentally competent at the time of deed execution. Also, the grantor must be named with a certainty. It must be possible to positively identify the grantor.

   A corporation may receive, hold, and convey title to real property in the corporate name. Therefore, a corporation may be a grantor. If the conveyance of title by the corporation is in the ordinary course of business of the corporation, the deed may be executed on behalf of the corporation by the corporate president or vice president and countersigned by the secretary or assistant secretary. If the transfer of title is not in the ordinary course of business of the corporation, there must be an authorization for the conveyance by resolution by the board of directors of the corporation authorizing the transfer of title. When the resolution has been made, the signatures of the individuals discussed previously are sufficient. A partnership may receive, hold, and convey title to real property in the partnership name, in the name of an individual general partner, or in the name of a trustee acting for the partnership for this purpose.

   From the foregoing it can be seen that title to real property may be held in an assumed name, and it can be transferred under that name. Examples are titles in the name of a corporation or partnership. Although title may be held and transferred in an assumed name, title may not be held or transferred in the name of a fictitious person or organization. The person or organization must actually exist.

2. *Consideration*. The deed must provide evidence that consideration was given. Contract law does not require that the consideration be adequate to be valid. It is common to see the phrase "for one dollar and other good and valuable consideration" or the phrase "for valuable consideration." If the conveyance is a gift, the phrase "for love and affection" or "for the continued use of the (charity)" may be used, provided there is no fraud intended.

Figure 12.1
Warranty deed.

WARRANTY DEED

THE STATE OF
COUNTY OF

1 ⌈ That

2 ⌈ of the County of   State of   for and
in consideration of the sum or Ten and no/100 Dollars, and other good and
valuable consideration, to the undersigned cash in hand paid by the
grantee(s) herein named, the receipt of which is hereby acknowledged,

3 ⌈ have GRANTED, SOLD AND CONVEYED, and by these presents do GRANT, SELL AND
CONVEY unto

4 ⌈

5 ⌈ of the County of   State of   , all of
the following described real property in   County,
                State, to-wit:

6 ⌈   TO HAVE AND TO HOLD the above described premises, together with all
and singular the rights and appurtenances thereto in anywise belonging
unto the said grantee(s)   heirs and assigns

7 ⌈ forever; and   do hereby bind   heirs, executors and
administrators to WARRANT AND FOREVER DEFEND all and singular the said
premises unto the said grantee(s)   heirs and assigns,
against every person whomsoever lawfully claiming or to claim the same or
any part thereof.

8 ⌈ EXECUTED this   day of   , A.D. 20

_____   _____

THE STATE OF
COUNTY OF

    Before me, the undersigned authority, on this day personally
appeared   known to me to be the person(s)
whose name   subscribed to the foregoing instrument,
and acknowledged to me that   he   executed the same for the purpose
and consideration therein expressed.

    Given under my hand and seal of office on this the
day of   , A.D. 20

_____

9 ⌈ PREPARED IN THE LAW OFFICE OF: Notary Public in and for County, State
                                        RETURN TO:

3. *Words of conveyance.* The deed must contain words demonstrating that it is the grantor's intention to transfer the title to the named grantee. These words of conveyance are contained in the granting clause. Typical wording is "as granted, sold, and conveyed" in the case of warranty deeds.

4. *Grantees.* It is not necessary that grantees (persons receiving title) have legal capacity. Therefore, a minor or mental incompetent can receive and hold title to real property. However, these people cannot convey title on their own since they are not qualified to be grantors. Therefore, to effect

a conveyance of title held in the name of an incompetent there must be a guardian's deed executed by the incompetent's guardian as grantor. The conveyance by the guardian may only be accomplished with the approval of the court.

Grantees must be named with a certainty. It must be possible to identify the grantee. The grantee must actually exist and be either a natural person or an artificial person, such as a corporation or partnership. The grantee must be alive at the time of the delivery of the deed. A dead person cannot be a grantee.

5. *Property description.* The deed must contain an adequate legal description of the property including the mailing address. The three methods of providing such a description are discussed later in this chapter. (In Maine the most common means is by metes and bounds.)

6. *The habendum clause.* The **habendum clause** describes the estate granted and must always be in agreement with the granting clause. The habendum clause begins with the words "to have and to hold." A typical habendum clause appearing in a deed conveying a fee simple title will read "to have and to hold the above described premises, with all the appurtenances thereunto belonging, or in anywise appertaining, unto the grantee, his heirs, and or successors and assigns forever." By contrast, the habendum clause in a deed conveying a life estate will read "to have and to hold the premises herein granted unto the grantee for and during the term of the remainder of the natural life of the herein named grantee."

If the property is being sold subject to specific encumbrances of record, such as easements or a mortgage lien, the habendum clause will recite these encumbrances. Please note two items in regard to encumbrances: (1) transfer of a fee simple absolute title does not mean that there are no encumbrances, and (2) the warranty against encumbrances in a deed is only a warranty against encumbrances that have not been disclosed, that is, those not on record.

7. *Covenants.* The covenants of the deed are set forth in this portion of the deed. (Example: The covenant against encumbrances.)

8. *Execution.* The deed must be signed by each grantor conveying an interest in the property. This is called **execution**. Notice, only the grantors execute the deed. The grantee does not sign. Although seals are still sometimes included, they are no longer required and neither are witnesses.

9. *Acknowledgment.* For a deed to be eligible for recording, it must be acknowledged. The grantor must appear before a public officer who is eli- gible to take an **acknowledgment**, such as a notary public, and state that the signing of the deed was done by her and was a voluntary act. A deed will be perfectly valid between the grantor and grantee without an acknowledgment. However, without the acknowledgment the deed cannot be recorded by the grantee and thereby provide the grantee protection of title against subsequent creditors or purchasers of the same property from the same grantor who recorded their deed. Therefore, the grantee should always insist upon receiving a deed that has been acknowledged.

DELIVERY AND ACCEPTANCE OF A DEED

To effect a transfer of title by deed there must be a delivery of a valid deed by the grantor to the grantee, and the deed must be accepted by the grantee. Delivery may be made directly to the grantee or to an agent of the grantee. The agent for this purpose will typically be the grantee's attorney, his real estate broker, or the lending institution providing the mortgage loan to finance the purchase of the property. In almost every case there is a presumption of acceptance by the grantee. This presumption is especially strong if the deed has been recorded and the conveyance is beneficial to the grantee.

In Maine all of the activities necessary to prepare for a closing of a real estate transaction are usually performed by title companies or individual private attorneys. These companies also are in charge of the final settlement. In these situations the grantor deposits the deed with the title company to be delivered to the grantee when the grantee has fulfilled the obligations in the sales contract. The title passes from the grantor to the grantee when the deed is delivered to the grantee.

RECORDING OF A DEED

As previously discussed, a deed is eligible for recording on the public record when the grantor has acknowledged the execution of the deed and this acknowledgment appears in the deed. The purpose and benefit of recording the deed are to protect the grantee's title.

Essentially, recording statutes protect innocent purchasers by providing that deeds that are unrecorded are not effective against persons not having actual notice (knowledge) of the conveyance. There are three types of recording statutes:

1. *Notice.* A person who buys property without **notice** of an earlier conveyance of it prevails over the prior grantee who failed to record her deed. This is the case even if the earlier grantee records her deed first. Example: Jones conveys Lot 5 to Smith. Smith does not record her deed in the Registry of Deeds. Later, Jones grants Lot 5 to Wilson. Wilson prevails over Smith even if Wilson does not record and Smith later records.
2. *Race.* Under a race statute, whoever records first prevails. It makes no difference whether the second purchaser has notice of the first conveyance or not. Example: Jones conveys Lot 5 to Smith. Smith does not record his deed. Jones then conveys the property to Wilson. Whoever records first will prevail.
3. *Race notice.* The state of Maine has a **race notice** statute. The priority of a subsequent purchaser depends upon lack of notice and priority of record. Example: Jones conveys Lot 5 to Smith who does not record. Jones then conveys Lot 5 to Wilson who is unaware of the earlier conveyance. Wilson will prevail over Smith, only if she records before Smith. If Smith records first she will prevail.

Constructive notice is contrasted with **actual notice**. Constructive notice is binding on everyone though they have not actually read the deed as recorded, since it gives notice to the world. The result of the constructive notice provided by recording is to protect the title in the grantee. This protection is against everyone including other purchasers of the same property from the same grantor.

A valid conveyance of title can exist between grantor and grantee without the deed being recorded. However, the deed must be recorded to protect grantee's title from third parties, such as purchasers from the grantor, subsequent creditors, or other lien holders of the grantor.

TYPES OF DEEDS

There are variations in types of **deeds** resulting from the different forms of warranty of title contained in the deed and variations based on a special purpose for which the deeds is drawn. The following is a discussion of the various types of deeds both by type of warranty and special purpose.

Warranty Deed

The warranty deed contains the strongest and broadest form of guarantee of title of any type of deed, and therefore provides the greatest protection to the grantee. The warranty deed usually contains six covenants:

1. *Covenant of seisin.* Typical wording of this covenant is, "grantor covenants that he is seised of said premises in fee." This covenant, like the others in the general warranty deed, is a specific covenant and provides an assurance to the grantee that the grantor holds the title, which he specifies in the deed that he is conveying to the grantee. In the example cited, the grantor promises the grantee that he has fee simple title to the property.

2. *Covenant of right to convey.* This covenant usually follows the covenant of seisin in the general warranty deed and typically reads, "and has the right to convey the same in fee simple." By this covenant the grantor provides an assurance to the grantee that the grantor has legal capacity to convey the title and also has the title to convey.

3. *Covenant against encumbrances.* This covenant will typically state, "that said premises are free from encumbrances (with the exceptions above stated, if any)." The grantor is assuring the grantee that there are no encumbrances against the title except those of record. Typical encumbrances that are acceptable to grantees are the encumbrances of a lien of a mortgage when grantee is assuming grantor's existing mortgage, recorded easements, and restrictive covenants.

4. *Covenant of quiet enjoyment.* This covenant may typically read, "the grantee, his or her heirs and assigns, shall quietly and peaceably have, hold, use, possess, and enjoy the premises." This covenant is an assurance by the grantor to the grantee that the grantee shall have a quiet possession and enjoyment of the property being conveyed, and that the grantee will not be disturbed in the use and enjoyment of the property because of a defect in the title being conveyed by the grantor. In warranty deeds not containing a specific covenant of quiet enjoyment, the covenant of warranty itself ensures the grantee of quiet enjoyment of the property.

5. *Covenant for further assurances.* This covenant may typically read, "that he or she (grantor) will execute such further assurances as may be reasonable or necessary to perfect the title in the grantee." This covenant requires the grantor to perform any acts necessary to correct a defect that may exist in the title that is being conveyed and to correct any errors or any deficiencies that may exist in the deed itself.

6. *Covenant of warranty.* The warranty of title in the general warranty deed will provide that the grantor "will warrant and defend the title to the grantee against the lawful claims of all persons whomsoever." This is the best form of warranty for protection of the grantee and contains no limitations as to possible claimants protected against, since the grantor specifies that he or she will defend the title against "the lawful claims of all persons whomsoever." The covenant of warranty is the most important of all the covenants.

Should any of these covenants be broken, the purchaser may bring legal action not only against the seller, but also against any past grantors (or their heirs) who conveyed by warranty deed. If a court finds that a covenant was broken, it will award monetary damages to the purchaser compensating for any loss suffered.

Quitclaim Deed

The **quitclaim deed** contains no warranties whatsoever. It is simply a deed of release. It will release or convey to the grantee any interest, including title, that the grantor may have. However, the grantor does not state in the deed that she has any title or interest in the property. Execution of the quitclaim deed by the grantor prevents the grantor from asserting any claim against the title at any time in the future.

Quitclaim deeds may be used to clear a *cloud on a title*. This terminology is used to describe the situation that exists when someone has a possible claim against a title. As long as this possibility exists, the title is cloudy and therefore not a good and marketable title. To remove this cloud and create a good and marketable title, the possible claimant executes a quitclaim deed as grantor to the true title holder as grantee. The granting clause in a quitclaim deed will contain the words "remise, release, and quit claim" instead of "grant, bargain, sell, and convey," as used in warranty deeds.

Quitclaim with Covenant

In a **quitclaim with covenant**, known also as a **limited warranty deed**, a grantor covenants to "warrant and forever defend" the title against the claims of persons "claiming by, through or under" him. In effect, the grantor guarantees the title only against problems arising since he acquired the property, unlike the warranty covenants that guarantee against defects arising since the origin of the property.

PROPERTY DESCRIPTIONS

For effective and accurate title transfers, title insurers, abstractors, and attorneys rely on an accurate legal description of the land. The type of legal description for title transfer must be a formal description. Informal descriptions, such as street addresses or assessor/tax numbers, are not acceptable for transferring or encumbering title. Property descriptions are of three acceptable types: metes and bounds, description by reference, and the government rectangular survey system.

Metes and Bounds

The property description used in the 13 states that were the original 13 colonies is the **metes and bounds** description. The metes and bounds description is also used in those states in which the primary description is the government rectangular survey system. In those states, the metes and bounds type of description is used to describe small, irregular land areas.

In the metes and bounds description, the metes are the distances from point to point in the description, and the bounds are the directions from one point to another in the description.

A metes and bounds description is made from a survey performed by a licensed, registered land surveyor. One of the most important aspects of the metes and bounds description is the selection of the point of beginning. This point should be one that is reasonably easy to locate and that is well established. The surveyor, after starting at the point of beginning, sights the direction to the next point or monument. A monument may be a tree, or a rock, or an artificial boundary such as a road or a concrete marker. The directions in the metes and bounds description might read "north 45 east." There may be a further refinement of the direction. Degrees are divided into minutes, with 1 degree containing 60 minutes, and each minute divided into 60 seconds.

A description, then, might read: "north 45°, 30', 10 sec. east." These bearings are illustrated in Figure 12.2.

Description by Reference

A **description by reference** is a valid legal description. Sometimes an attorney will incorporate into the deed a description by reference in addition to a metes and bounds description. Sometimes the description by reference will be the only description in the deed. A description by reference may be one in which a reference is made to a **plat** and lot number that has been *recorded*. The description would state the plat book number and page number in which the plat, or map, is recorded. The reader can refer to the plat and determine the exact location and dimensions of the property. An example of a subdivision plat is shown in Figure 12.3.

Figure 12.2 Metes and bounds description in conjunction with a description by reference.

An example of a typical metes and bounds description and the plat resulting from that description follow.

*Being all of Lot No. 20 of the subdivision of a portion of the property of Mortgage Heights Land Company, Inc., Centre County, as shown by plat thereof prepared by Worley and Gray, Consulting Engineers, dated October 1, 1995, and recorded in Book 5, page 40, Records of Plats for Centre County, and more particularly bounded and described as follows:

**BEGINNING on a stake in the northeast margin of Amortization Drive, south corner of Lot No. 20 of the subdivision or a portion of the property of Mortgage Heights Land Company, Inc., and running thence North 6° 18' East 215.2 feet to a stake; thence North 8° 49' West 241.0 feet to a stake, common corner of Lot Nos. 20 and 19 of said subdivision; thence with the dividing line between said Lot Nos. 19 and 20, South 87° 50' West 138.5 feet to a stake in the east margin of a cul-de-sac; thence with the east margin of said cul-de-sac in a southwesterly direction along a curve with the radius of 50.0 feet, 61.2 feet to a stake in said margin; thence with the east margin of a drive leading to Amortization Drive, South 5° 19' West 132.8 feet to a stake in the point of intersection of said margin of said drive with Amortization Drive; thence with the northeast margin of said Amortization Drive, South 51° 17' East 84.7 feet to a stake in said margin; thence still with said margin of said drive, South 42° 27' East 47.2 feet to a stake in said margin; thence still said margin of said drive, South 29° 36' East 199.9 feet to the BEGINNING.

N 45º 30' 10 sec. EAST

PLAT OF LOT 20
OF

MORTGAGE HEIGHTS LAND CO.
PROPERTY OF
SAMUEL S. SELLER
Located in Centre County
Scale 1" = 100'

DRAWN BY W. LEONARD, R. L. S.

*Description by reference
**Description by metes and bounds

Figure 12.3
A sample
subdivision plat.

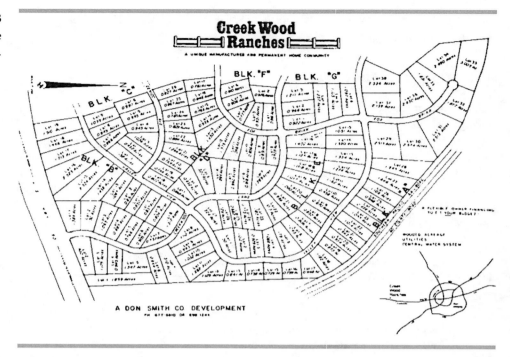

Sometimes a property will be described by reference to a previous deed that conveyed the same property. This reference incorporates the description in the previous deed by reference into the deed being prepared. If the description in the previous deed is accurate, all is well and good. However, if the description in the previous deed was faulty, the subsequent deed is still bound by that description.

Often a description will also contain a statement as to the number of acres or quan tity of land being conveyed. In the event that this quantity is inconsistent with the description by metes and bounds, the quantity of land yields to the number of acres as actually established by the metes and bounds description.

Government Rectangular Survey System

In the government **rectangular survey system** (used in townships in northern Maine), the country is divided by north-south lines called **principal meridians**, and by east-west lines called **base lines**. The areas between the base lines and north-south meridians are called **ranges**. Within the ranges, there are townships. Each township is a square, 6 miles by 6 miles, and is, therefore, 36 square miles in area. Each township is divided into 36 sections. Each section is one mile square, or one square mile. Figure 12.4 illustrates a township. As can be seen, the township is divided into 36 sections. Notice the manner in which the sections are numbered.

A section is divided into quarter sections and may be subdivided into areas less than a quarter-section. Notice in Figure 12.5 that each section contains 640 acres and, therefore, a quarter-section is 160 acres.

Examination of these sections as a measurement of land area can provide an intro-duction to the simple arithmetic of real estate. You can calculate the number of acres in a section by recalling the one familiar number of 5,280 feet per mile, and learning the new number of 43,560 square feet per acre. The number of acres in a square mile is therefore figured by calculating the total square feet, and dividing by the number of square feet per acre.

Further, you can divide a section into quarter-sections by dividing by 4, that is, 160 acres per quarter-section, and so forth.

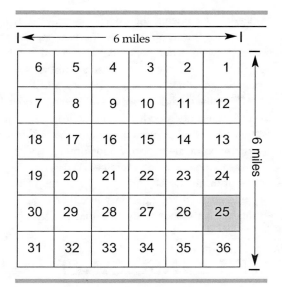

Figure 12.4
A township divided into sections.

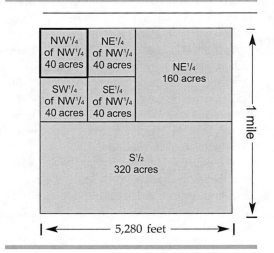

Figure 12.5
One section subdivided.

TITLE EXAMINATION AND TITLE OPINION

Regardless of the warranties in a deed, the grantee should always retain the services of an attorney or title company to conduct an examination of the public record to verify if in fact the grantee is receiving a good and marketable title free from encumbrances except those she has agreed to accept. The purpose of a **title examination** is to determine the quality of a title. It must be performed by an attorney because only an attorney can give a legal opinion as to the quality of a title.

The title search consists of an examination of all the public records possibly affecting a title to real estate. The examiner searches the grantor–grantee index at the registry for owners of the subject property. The search begins with the current deed and goes back typically 40 to 60 years to a warranty deed. This list of historical owners is called the **chain of title**. The chain must be unbroken for the title to be good. Any missing links in the chain of title create uncertainty as to the path of ownership and proof thereof. These missing links could be the result of oversight (failing to record a deed), fraud, or a dispute between parties. Any of these uncertainties is of sufficient concern to a buyer to threaten the marketability of title. If these missing links can be bridged by obtaining proper title-

-clearing documents, the transaction may safely occur. If not, the sale should not close. On completing the chain of title, the examiner searches all other public records during the period each owner held title to determine whether any mortgages or liens have been discharged. Restrictive covenants, easements, and any other recordings or documents possibly affecting the title are also researched.

Upon the completion of the title examination, the examiner provides an **abstract of title**, which is a condensed history of the title setting forth a summary of all links in the chain of title and any other matters of public record affecting the title. The abstract contains a legal description of the property and summarizes every instrument in chronological order that relates to the title being examined. When the abstract is completed, the attorney will issue a **title opinion**, which indicates the status of the title based upon his examination of the public records. The opinion will either indicate that it is a good and merchantable title or that there are clouds on the title, that is, liens or undischarged mortgages.

TITLE INSURANCE

A title examination is only concerned with recorded documents appearing on the public record. Circumstances affecting the property that are not a part of the public record are not covered. Therefore, even though a title examination indicates that a title is good and marketable, this may not actually be the case.

To protect against a financial loss, the grantee should take advantage of the protection afforded by a **title insurance** policy. The policy requires the title insurance company to compensate the insured for financial loss, up to the face amount of the policy, resulting from a title defect such as a forged deed. The policy also requires the insurance company to defend against claims, including taking any action necessary to protect the title. The policy protects the insured against any title defect existing at the time that the insured received the title.

The policy will be issued only as the result of an acceptable abstract or title opinion. A title that is acceptable to the title insurance company is called an insurable title. The premium paid for a title insurance policy is a one-time premium paid at the time that the policy is placed in effect. The two forms of title insurance policies are described in the following sections.

Owner's Policy

The owner's policy is for the protection of the owner and is written for the amount that the owner paid for the property. Additionally an owner who was insured for $150,000 five years ago may have an automatic increase in their policy amount. (Example: 10% per year for the first five years, up to a maximum 150%). This provides the owner of the policy with automatic inflation protection as well as increased value due to improvements. The policy only insures the owner against actual loss, including any costs, attorneys' fees and expenses provided under the policy resulting from the covered risks set forth in the policy. The policy remains in effect for the duration of the insured's ownership of the property, and continues in effect after the death of the owner to benefit heirs receiving an interest in the property.

Mortgagee's Policy

This policy only protects the mortgagee. Under the terms of the policy, the mortgagee is insured against defects in the title pledged as security in the mortgage. The mortgagee's insurable interest is only to the extent of the outstanding loan balance at any given time. Therefore, the mortgagee's policy decreases in face amount as the loan principal decreases, but always provides coverage equivalent to the amount of the loan balance.

Title Transfer Taxes

Approximately 37 states impose a tax on the conveyance of title to real property. The state of Maine levies a transfer tax of $1.10 for $500.00 of consideration (or fraction thereof) upon both the seller and the buyer. The tax must be paid at the county Registry of Deeds when the deed is recorded. It accompanies the declaration of value (see Figure 12.6), which states names and addresses of the grantors and grantees, description of property, date of transfer, and the consideration paid. Consideration includes the total price paid or value in money.

IMPORTANT POINTS

1. Transfer of title is alienation. Involuntary alienation occurring during life comes as a result of adverse possession, lien foreclosure sale, and condemnation under the power of eminent domain. Involuntary alienation after death is escheat. Voluntary alienation after death is by will or descent. Voluntary alienation during life can occur only by delivery of a valid deed.

2. A deed includes the following elements: (1) the deed must be written, (2) the grantor must be competent, (3) the competency of the grantee is not required, (4) the grantor and grantee must be named with a certainty, (5) the property must be adequately described, (6) a deed must contain words of conveyance, (7) it must be signed by the grantor, and (8) delivery and acceptance must occur to convey title.

3. To be eligible for recording on the public record, a deed must be acknowledged. Recording protects the grantee's title against creditors of the grantor and subsequent conveyances by the grantor.

4. A warranty deed is the strongest and broadest form of title guarantee. The warranty deed typically contains six covenants: seisin, right to convey, against encumbrances, quiet enjoyment, for further assurances, and warranty.

5. A quitclaim deed is a deed of release and contains no warranties. It will convey any interest the grantor may have. The primary use of the quitclaim deed is to remove a cloud from a title.

6. Quitclaim with covenant is a limited warranty guaranteeing the title against problems arising during the grantor's ownership.

7. The purpose of a title examination is to determine the quality of a title. The examination must be made by an attorney or title company. Only an attorney can legally give an opinion as to the quality of a title.

8. A title insurance policy protects the insured against a financial loss caused by a title defect. The types of policies are owner's and mortgagee's.

9. The three methods of property description in use in the United States are metes and bounds, reference, and rectangular survey. The most common in Maine is metes and bounds.

Figure 12.6 Declaration of value.

H.

BUREAU OF TAXATION

Property Tax Division
State House Station #24
Augusta, Maine 04333

FILE WITH COUNTY
REGISTRY OF DEEDS

STATE OF MAINE

PLACE STAMP ABOVE

REAL ESTATE TRANSFER TAX   DECLARATION   TITLE 36, M.R.S.A., SECTIONS 4641 through 4641-N

1. MUNICIPALITY OR TOWNSHIP	COUNTY	BOOK	PAGE

GRANTEE (BUYER)

2. IDENTITY: NAME(S) (LAST, FIRST, INITIAL) AND SOCIAL SECURITY NUMBER(S) OR CORPORATE NAME(S) AND FEDERAL IDENTIFICATION NUMBER(S)

3. NUMBER AND STREET	CITY OR TOWN	STATE AND ZIP CODE

GRANTOR (SELLER)

4. IDENTITY: NAME(S) (LAST, FIRST, INITIAL) AND SOCIAL SECURITY NUMBER(S) OR CORPORATE NAME(S) AND FEDERAL IDENTIFICATION NUMBER(S)

5. NUMBER AND STREET	CITY OR TOWN	STATE AND ZIP CODE

PROPERTY

6. BRIEF DESCRIPTION (Such as: Map and Lot numbers, Located at 17 Elm Street, Augusta; or 10 Acres, farmhouse and barn known as Smith Farm, Mill Road, Houlton).

On date of transfer, this property was classified under Title 36 MRSA Chapter 105 as (check only one):

☐ Tree Growth   ☐ Farmland
☐ Open Space   ☐ Not Applicable

7. DATE OF TRANSFER   MO.   DAY   YR.
(Use numerals)

CONSIDERATION

8. Consideration meaning total amount or price paid, or required to be paid, for real property valued in money, whether received in money or otherwise and shall include the amount of any mortgage, liens or encumbrances thereon. (Tax will be collected at the registry when the deed is recorded. The tax rate is $2.20 per $500 of consideration, or fractional part thereof. The tax incidence is equally divided between the buyer and seller.)
If exempt, complete line 9

▶ $ .00

EXEMPTION

9. EXPLAIN BASIS FOR EXEMPTION (Complete only if transfer is claimed to be exempt).

SPECIAL CIRCUMSTANCES

10. Were there special circumstances in the transfer which suggest that the sale price of the property was either more or less than its fair market value (Such as the fact that transfer was a forced sale, interfamily sale, intercorporate sale, gift, exchange, etc.).

▶ ☐ YES
☐ NO

OATH

11. Aware of penalties as set forth by Title 36, Section 4641-K, we hereby swear or affirm that we have each examined this return and to the best of our knowledge and belief, it is true, correct, and complete.

GRANTEE(S) or AUTHORIZED AGENT	DATE	GRANTOR(S) or AUTHORIZED AGENT	DATE

PREPARER

12. Name and address of person or firm preparing this form

PTS520
50/M (REV 7/88)

THIS DOCUMENT IS CONFIDENTIAL WHEN COMPLETED.
THE CONTENTS SHOULD BE PROTECTED—TITLE 36, M.R.S.A., SECTION 191.
THIS DECLARATION SHALL ACCOMPANY THE DEED AT THE TIME
OF RECORDING AT THE REGISTRY OF DEEDS.

REVIEW QUESTIONS

Answers to these questions are found in the Answer Key section at the back of the book.

1. Voluntary alienation may occur by which of the following?
   a.   condemnation
   b.   will
   c.   escheat
   d.   adverse possession

2. Voluntary alienation during life may only occur in which of the following ways?
   a.   will
   b.   foreclosure sale
   c.   deed delivery
   d.   devise

3. Essential elements of a valid deed include all of the following except:
   a.   acknowledgment
   b.   writing
   c.   competent grantor
   d.   execution by grantor

4. The purpose of a deed being acknowledged is to:
   a.   make the deed valid
   b.   make the deed eligible for delivery
   c.   make the deed eligible for recording
   d.   identify the grantee

5. Which of the following covenants ensures the grantee that the grantor has the legal capacity to transfer title?
   a.   covenant of quiet enjoyment
   b.   covenant of right to convey
   c.   covenant of seisin
   d.   covenant for further assurances

6. The area of a township is:
   a.   160 acres
   b.   640 acres
   c.   1 mile square
   d.   36 square miles

7. A title insurance policy may be written to protect all of the following except:
   a.   owner
   b.   licensee
   c.   lessee
   d.   mortgagee

8. With reference to the rectangular survey system, which of the following is correct?
   a. It is a description by distances and directions
   b. It is the primary method of description jused in the original thirteen states
   c. It is used in townships in Maine
   d. It refers to a plat and a lot number

9. A claim of title by adverse possession may be defeated by the property owner by which of the following?
   a. permission
   b. confirmation
   c. will
   d. condemnation

10. The successive conveyances of a title are called:
   a. releases
   b. remises
   c. links in the chain of title
   d. abstracts of title

IMPORTANT TERMINOLOGY

closing
closing disclosure
credit report
debit
discount points
down payment
escrow account
hazard insurance
HUD Form No. 1

loan origination points (fee)
mortgage discharge fee
prepaid mortgage interest
recording fees
survey
tax proration
title insurance
title search
transfer tax

CLOSING REAL ESTATE TRANSACTIONS

IN THIS CHAPTER

Closing is the consummation of the sales effort that began when the licensee obtained a listing. At the closing the buyer receives a deed and the seller receives payment for the property. Necessary functions for closing a real estate transaction are performed by an attorney, a real estate licensee and (when a loan is involved) a lending institution. A listing of the documents that may be involved in closing a real estate transaction follows. Certainly not all of these will be involved in any particular transaction, but all are possibilities.

- Bill of Sale for personal property
- Certificate of Occupancy
- Closing Disclosure
- Contract for Deed or Land Contract
- Deed
- Mortgage and Note
- Disclosure Statement
- Hazard Insurance Policy
- HUD Form No. 1 as required by the Real Estate Settlement Procedures Act
- Lease
- Lien Waivers
- Mortgage Insurance Primium-Private Mortgage Insurance
- Option and Exercise of Option
- Sales Contract
- Survey
- Title Insurance Policy
- Title Opinion

Prior to closing there are a number of things that must be accomplished. The listing and selling agent should check the purchase and sale agreement to see if all contingencies have been met. The buyer should be reminded to bring the homeowner's insurance policy or binder, a paid receipt for one year's insurance, and a photo I.D. To protect both the buyer and the seller, it is good practice for a buyer to complete a walk-through of the property. This is a final inspection of the property just prior to the closing date to determine whether the property is in the same condition as it was prior to signing the purchase and sale agreement. All parties should be notified as to the date, time, and location of the closing and whether all parties will be present.

PREPARATION OF CLOSING DISCLOSURES

In essence, a **closing disclosure** is simply an accounting of the funds involved in a particular real estate transaction. There are actually two statements, one for the buyer and one for the seller. Each closing disclosure must also contain the date of closing, the name of seller and buyer, the location of the property, and the signature of the person who prepared the statement. The licensee is responsible for seeing that each party to the transaction receives copies. These parties include the buyer and the seller. The licensee must retain a copy of each statement in his file.

A closing disclosure is a historical document prepared in advance. That is, the statement is prepared in advance of the closing, but it records what must happen at closing. The statement sets forth the distribution of monies involved in the transaction; that is, who is to pay a specific amount for each expense and who is to receive that amount.

The first step in preparing statements is to list all items in the transaction. Some of these items involve both the buyer and the seller, other items are only of concern to the buyer, while a third category includes items only of concern to the seller. The allocation of these items between the statements as well as the determination of whether an entry is a debit or credit and to whom is mainly a matter of logic. Debit or cost means that the item is to be paid for by the person in whose statement that item appears as a debit. In other words, it is an expense for that party. A debit can also mean a reduction in credits because of monies received to be applied toward the payment of a credit. Credit means that the money is received by the person in whose statement it appears as a credit. A credit is also given for monies paid against an expense obligation in the transaction. We will discuss these in the explanations of the illustrations that follow.

In the closing disclosure illustrations, each entry is based on the facts given for the particular statement. These are based, in most cases, on the typical allocations of the expense in a real estate transaction. You must realize, of course, that any of these typical or traditional allocations of expense items can be changed by the sales contract. In any given real estate transaction, either buyer or seller could agree in the sales contract to pay for various items normally paid by the other party. All prorated expenses are prorated as of the day of closing. Who is responsible for the expenses on the day of closing is settled by language in the purchase and sale agreement, such as the closing day belongs to seller (buyer). There are examples in this chapter of both situations.

Buyers' Closing Costs and Credits

Buyers' Costs

1. *Purchase price or down payment.* If it is a cash transaction, the purchase price will be due at closing. If financed, the down payment will be part of the amount due by the buyer at closing.
2. *Transfer tax.* This is a tax imposed by the state on the conveyance of real estate and the rate is $2.20 for each $500 of the sale price of the property. Buyer and seller each pay half of the tax. Therefore a buyer's portion of the tax will be $1.10 per $500 of value or any part thereof. *Example: $94,000 ÷ 500 = 188 × 1.10 = $206.80 for the buyer.*
3. *Tax proration.* If the taxes have been paid at the time of closing, the buyer will reimburse the seller for the period of time from the closing to the end of the tax year.
4. *Boundary Survey.* With a boundary survey, the surveyor determines the actual boundaries of the property.
5. *Mortgage Loan Inspection.* This is a surveyor's profession opinion based only on preliminary information, of the relative location of the apparent boundary lines of the property and determines whether visible improvements are located with the apparent boundaries. The purpose is to detect boundary problems that would affect the security of the loan.

6. *Title search.* This is an examination of the public records to determine what, if any, defects there are in the chain of title, and whether the title is marketable.

7. *Title insurance.* This is an insurance policy protecting the lender and/or purchaser from a financial loss caused by a defect in a title to real property. To provide this coverage to the lender is an underwriting requirement of the secondary mortgage market. Each is a one-time payment.

8. *Credit report fee.* The fee covers the lender's cost of obtaining a **credit report** from a credit reporting company. It provides information regarding the applicant's credit history (how he or she pays obligations). Lending institutions rely heavily on this information when making their decision to approve a loan request.

9. *Loan origination fee.* The fee or points, usually the responsibility of the buyer, are used to cover the lender's expenses in originating the loan and to offset any losses when the mortgage is sold in the secondary market. Point charges are always based upon loan amount. One point represents 1 percent of the mortgage amount.

10. *Recording fees.* The county Registry of Deeds assesses this fee for the recording of the warranty deed and mortgage.

11. *Appraisal fee.* In order to confirm that the market value of the property is sufficient to repay the loan in the event of a default, an appraisal is required.

12. *Prepaid mortgage interest.* Lenders require borrowers to pay at the closing interest that accrues on the mortgage from the date of the closing to the first of the next month.

13. *Hazard insurance.* One year's insurance premium and the policy must be brought to the closing for protection against a total or partial destruction of the property.

14. *Attorney's fees.* This would include preparation of mortgage and note instruments, closing the loan, examining the title binder, contract, and related documents.

Other fees not included in the case study:

15. *Escrow account.* These are funds paid by the borrower and held in an account by the lender to ensure future payment of such expenses as hazard insurance and property taxes.

16. *Loan discount fees.* These fees, often referred to as points, are a one-time charge to adjust the yield on the loan to what the secondary mortgage

1. Down payment
2. Transfer tax
3. Proration of taxes
4. Survey (Class D)
5. Title search
6. Title insurance
7. Credit report
8. Loan origination fee
9. Recording of mortgage documents
10. Appraisal
11. Mortgage interest
12. Hazard insurance
13. Attorney's fees for preparation of mortgage and note
14. Escrows
15. Discount points
16. Tax proration

Figure 13.1
Buyers' closing costs.

market conditions demand if the loan is to be sold. Each one point is equal to one percent of the mortgage amount.

Credit to the Buyer

1. *Earnest money.* This is the good faith deposit the buyer puts down at the time the purchase and sales agreement is signed. The money is placed in the agency's trust account until closing. The listing agency trust account usually holds the earnest money deposit.
2. *Rent Proration.* The rent amount per month is divided by the number of days in the month of closing. The closing day may belong to either the buyer or seller depending on what is stated in the Purchase and Sale Agreement. The rent day is multiplied by the number of days remaining in the month from the day of closing. In the following example the closing day belongs to the seller. *Example: Closing is July 18 and the rent is $500 per month. $500 divided by 31 = $16.13. $16.13 x 14 = $225.82*

Sellers' Closing Costs and Credits

Sellers' Costs

1. *Commission.* In the listing contract, the seller has hired the broker to market the property. In this agreement, the seller has agreed to pay the broker a fee or commission of 7 percent of the final sales price of the property.
2. *Transfer tax.* At closing, the seller pays half the transfer tax of $2.20 per $500. Therefore the tax for the seller is $1.10 per $500 of value (sales price) or any part thereof.
3. *Seller's existing mortgage.* When the seller has a mortgage on the property, she would have to pay this off to convey a clear title to the buyer, who in this example has obtained a new mortgage.
4. *Mortgage discharge fee.* The mortgage discharge fee covers the recording of this discharge in the Registry of Deeds.
5. *Deed preparation.* In the sales contract, the seller has agreed to convey a marketable title to the buyer. To accomplish the conveyance, the seller must deliver a valid deed to the buyer. Therefore, the seller retains an attorney to prepare this deed.
6. *Proration of taxes.* If taxes have not been paid at the time of closing, the seller will reimburse the buyer for the period of time from the beginning of the tax year to closing.

Figure 13.2
Items credited to buyer.

1. Earnest money deposit

Figure 13.3
Sellers' closing costs.

1. Commission
2. Transfer tax
3. Existing mortgage
4. Preparation and recording of mortgage discharge
5. Preparation of warranty deed
6. Tax proration
7. Seller points

7. *Sellers' points.* Through the involvement of the Maine State Housing Authority (MSHA), sellers may agree to pay points if they agree to accept a contract with this type of financing.

Credit to the Seller

1. *Purchase Price (sale price).* In a cash transaction, the buyer brings a check in the amount of the full purchase price. If the property is mortgaged, the buyer brings a check in the amount of the down payment, and the lender will provide the difference between the down payment and full purchase price.
2. *Sale of personal property.* At the closing, the licensee should review all parts of the closing disclosure with the buyer and seller, check the computations, make sure the buyer and seller get a copy of the statement and obtain a copy of the closing disclosure for his or her file.

CLOSING DISCLOSURE CASE STUDY

This is a transaction in which the purchaser is obtaining a loan from a lending institution. The security for this loan is a mortgage given by the buyer to the lending institution. Closing day belongs to the buyer. See Figure 13.8 for application of this data.

Closing Date: August 20, 20XX
Tax year January 1 to December 31
Taxes paid April 15: $1,128 per year
Sales Price: $94,000
Earnest Money Deposit: $2,500

Mortgage: 80% of Sales Price ($75,200), 10% for 30 years
Seller's Existing Mortgage: $46,000
Discharge of Existing Mortgage: $10
Hazard Insurance: $240
Warranty Deed Preparation: $60
Title Insurance: ($1.75 per thousand of loan amount)
Credit Report: $35

---

1. Purchase price

Figure 13.4
Items credited to seller.

---

1. Interest is from the date of closing until the first of next month.
2. Closing is July 15 and first payment is September 1. First payment will cover interest back to August 1 thus leaving the period July 15 to July 31 not paid.

Example: Mortgage $75,000
           Interest 9%

$75,000 × 9%	=	$6,750 interest for one year
$6,750 ÷ 365	=	$18.49 per day
$18.49 × 17 days	=	$314.33 interest paid at closing
		(closing day belongs to buyer)

Figure 13.5
Interest paid by buyer.

Figure 13.6

Rules for
prorating taxes.

1. Identify the tax period January 1–December 31. If sellers have paid the tax, then the buyer reimburses them for their share from date of closing to end of tax year.
2. If taxes have not been paid, the buyer will expect to pay them when due. Seller will pay to buyer at closing his or her share of the taxes.
3. Reduce the pro rata period to an interval rate, e.g., divide the annual rate by the number of days in the year to get the daily rate.

   Example: Taxes of $1,005 per year are $\frac{$1,005}{365}$ = $2.75 per day

4. Determine who will be reimbursed
   a. Taxes due

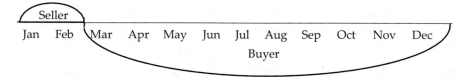

   b. Closing February 23
   c. Buyer will be in possession of the house when taxes are due and will be responsible for 12 months' worth of taxes.
   d. Therefore, at closing, seller will reimburse buyer for the portion of taxes from January 1 to February 22.
5. Determine the number of days of the pro rata period that have been used
   Example: a. date of closing belongs to the buyer
              b. days in settlement   January 31
                            February <u>22</u>
           Total days before closing   53
6. Multiply the daily rate times the days used
   Example: 53 days × $2.75 per day = $145.75
             $145.75 will be reimbursed by the seller to the buyer

Figure 13.7

Tax escrow
computation.

1. Purpose of the escrow is to have one year's taxes (12 monthly) payments in the account before the taxes are due to be paid.
2. If the number of payments between the first payment and the date taxes are due is less than 12, then those payments have to be paid at closing.
   Example: a. Assume taxes are paid September 18
              b. Taxes: $1,200 or $100 monthly
              c. Closing: February 21 and first payment April 1. The buyer will have made 5 monthly payments (April to September) into the escrow account. In order to have 12 payments in the account by September 18, 7 more payments must be paid at closing for a total of $700.

Survey: $125
Loan Origination Fee: 2 points
Attorney's Fee: Preparation of Mortgage Deed and Note and Facilitating Closing, $250
Title Search: $360
Cost of Recording Deed: $6 (Usually $6 for first page and $2 for each additional page)

Figure 13.8   New first mortgage closing disclosure.

Buyer's Statement	Costs	Credits	Seller's Statement	Costs	Credits
1. Down payment	$18,800.00		1. Commission	$ 6,580.00	
2. Transfer tax	206.80		2. Transfer tax	206.80	
3. Tax proration	414.06		3. Existing mortgage	46,000.00	
4. Survey	125.00		4. Discharge existing		
5. Title search	360.00		mortgage	10.00	
6. Title insurance	131.60		5. Deed preparation	60.00	
7. Credit report*	35.00		6. Tax proration		414.06
8. Loan origination	1,504.00		7. Sales price		94,000.00
9. Recording fees	16.50				
10. Appraisal*	200.00				
11. Prepaid interest	247.20				
12. Hazard insurance*	240.00				
13. Attorney's fees	250.00				
14. Earnest money		2,500.00			—
Total	$22,530.16	$2,500.00		$52,856.80	$94,414.06
	$22,530.16				
	−2,500.00				
Total amount needed	$20,030.16			$94,414.06	
at closing				−52,856.80	
			Seller's Net Closing	$41,557.26	

* Credit report and appraisal fee are paid for at the time of the application for the loan. The hazard insurance premium must be paid to the insurance carrier before closing.

Cost of Recording Mortgage: $10.50

Broker's Fee: 7% of sales price

Appraisal: $200

REAL ESTATE SETTLEMENT PROCEDURES ACT (RESPA)

The Real Estate Settlement Procedures Act (RESPA) was enacted by Congress in 1974. It regulates lending activities of lending institutions in making mortgage loans for housing.

Purpose of the Act

RESPA was enacted by Congress for the following purposes:

1. To effect specific changes in the settlement process resulting in more effective advance disclosure of settlement costs to home buyers and sellers.
2. To protect borrowers from unnecessarily expensive settlement charges resulting from abusive practices.
3. To ensure that borrowers are provided with greater and more timely information on the nature and cost of the settlement process.
4. To eliminate referral fees or kickbacks that increase the cost of settlement services. In this regard, lenders are only permitted to charge for services

that are actually provided to home buyers and sellers, and in an amount that the service actually costs the lender.

TILA RESPA INTEGRATED DISCLOSURES

Beginning October 3, 2015 the requirements relating to the application documents and closing documents changed. Prior to the change, consumers received overlapping federal disclosure forms with the terms and costs of mortgage loans. Two different federal agencies developed these forms separately under the two federal statutes: The Truth In Lending Act (TILA) and The Real Estate Settlement Procedures Act of 1974 (RESPA). Because these forms were confusing to consumers, Congress directed the Consumer Finance Protection Bureau (CFPB) to create new forms.

The Good Faith Estimate and the initial Truth in Lending Disclosure have been combined into a three page form called the **Loan Estimate**. The information on this form includes the monthly payment, estimated cash to close, a breakdown of the closing costs, total payments after 5 years and the total interest payment over the life of the loan. The loan estimate must be delivered or placed in the mail no later than the third business day after receiving the consumer's application. (See Appendix F)

HUD-l and the final TIL Disclosure have been combined into a 5 page form called the **Closing Disclosure**. The information on the first page of this form is virtually the same information as on the Loan Estimate. Consumers can compare what they were given initially with the final accounting. Other information on this form includes the breakdown of the closing costs, summary of the real estate transaction and contact information for the participants in the transaction. The form must be given 3 business days before closing. (See Appendix G)

The TILA RESPA rule covers most closed end consumer credit transactions secured by real property, vacant land loans and construction-only loans. It does not apply to reverse mortgages, home equity lines of credit and personal property loans.

Congress also required the CFPB to revise an existing booklet called the Settlement Costs Booklet. The new booklet is called Your Home Loan Toolkit. It was reduced from 71 to 25 pages and is designed to be used with the Loan Estimate and Closing disclosure. Lenders are required to give the booklet within 3 business days after the consumer has applied for a loan. With this booklet the consumer is provided with information critical to their understanding of the entire buying process.

igure 13.9
Disclosure

Closing Disclosure

This form is a statement of final loan terms and closing costs. Compare this document with your Loan Estimate.

Closing Information		Transaction Information		Loan Information	
Date Issued	4/15/2013	Borrower	Michael Jones and Mary Stone	Loan Term	30 years
Closing Date	4/15/2013		123 Anywhere Street	Purpose	Purchase
Disbursement Date	4/15/2013		Anytown, ST 12345	Product	Fixed Rate
Settlement Agent	Epsilon Title Co.	Seller	Steve Cole and Amy Doe		
File #	12-3456		321 Somewhere Drive	Loan Type	☒ Conventional ☐FHA
Property	456 Somewhere Ave		Anytown, ST 12345		☐VA ☐_____
	Anytown, ST 12345	Lender	Ficus Bank	Loan ID #	123456789
Sale Price	$180,000			MIC #	000654321

Loan Terms

		Can this amount increase after closing?
Loan Amount	$162,000	**NO**
Interest Rate	3.875%	**NO**
Monthly Principal & Interest *See Projected Payments below for your Estimated Total Monthly Payment*	$761.78	**NO**
		Does the loan have these features?
Prepayment Penalty		**YES** • As high as $3,240 if you pay off the loan during the first 2 years
Balloon Payment		**NO**

Projected Payments

Payment Calculation	Years 1-7		Years 8-30	
Principal & Interest		$761.78		$761.78
Mortgage Insurance	+	82.35	+	—
Estimated Escrow *Amount can increase over time*	+	206.13	+	206.13
Estimated Total Monthly Payment		**$1,050.26**		**$967.91**

Estimated Taxes, Insurance & Assessments *Amount can increase over time* See page 4 for details	$356.13 a month	This estimate includes ☒ Property Taxes ☒ Homeowner's Insurance ☒ Other: Homeowner's Association Dues *See Escrow Account on page 4 for details. You must pay for other property costs separately.*	In escrow? YES YES NO

Costs at Closing

Closing Costs	$9,712.10	Includes $4,694.05 in Loan Costs + $5,018.05 in Other Costs – $0 in Lender Credits. *See page 2 for details.*
Cash to Close	$14,147.26	Includes Closing Costs. *See Calculating Cash to Close on page 3 for details.*

PRACTICE PROBLEM

Using the following information, determine the buyer's closing costs and the seller's net proceeds. (Solution at the end of chapter.)

Sale Price: $80,000
Existing Mortgage Balance: $45,000
New Mortgage: 80% financed
Real Estate Taxes: $1,200
Tax Year: January 1–December 31
Closing: August 1
Taxes Paid: July 1
Loan Origination Fee: 2 points
Discharge of Existing Mortgage: $8
Recording Fees: $14
Appraisal: $200
Credit Check: $35
Attorney's Fees: $500
Commission: 7%
Title Insurance: ($1.75 per thousand of the mortgage) Deed Preparation: $60
Earnest Money: $2,000

IMPORTANT POINTS

1. At the closing, the buyer receives a deed and the seller receives payment for the property.
2. The closing disclosure is prepared by an attorney, a lending institution, or a title company.
3. There are closing costs that involve both the buyer and the seller, while other costs are exclusive to either buyer or seller.
4. Prior to the closing, the licensee should review all parts of the closing disclosure with the buyer and seller and keep a copy of the statement for his file.
5. If there is mortgage through a lending institution, the lender is required to use a standard settlement form known as the Closing Disclosure.

REVIEW QUESTIONS

Answers to these questions are found in the Answer Key section at the back of the book.

1. The amount of the earnest money deposit appears as a:
   a. Credit to the buyer
   b. Cost to the seller
   c. Cost to the buyer
   d. Credit to the seller

2. If property was listed for sale at $30,000 and sold for $28,500, the 6 percent broker's fee would appear in the seller's statement as:
   a. a debit of $1,710
   b. a credit of $1,710
   c. a debit of $1,800
   d. a credit of $1,800

3. The cost of preparing a deed appears as:
   a. a debit in the buyer's statement
   b. a credit in the seller's statement
   c. a credit in the buyer's statement
   d. a debit in the seller's statement

4. All of the following items are usually prorated at closing except:
   a. Real Estate Taxes
   b. Appraisal fees
   c. Prepaid interest
   d. rents

5. In a real estate transaction, a buyer obtained a loan in the amount of $60,000. The lending institution charged 6 discount points. The cost of these points appears as:
   a. a debit to the seller of $3,600
   b. a credit to the seller of $3,600
   c. a debit to the buyer of $3,600
   d. a credit to the buyer of $3,600

6. A buyer purchased a rental property and closed the transaction on July 20. The tenant had paid rent for the month of July in the amount of $210 on July 1. The rent should be shown as:
   a. a debit to the buyer of $81.29
   b. a credit to the buyer of $81.29
   c. a debit to the seller of $128.70
   d. a credit to the seller of $128.70

7. All of the following are required by RESPA except:
   a. Closing Disclosure
   b. Loan Estimate
   c. Home Loan Toolkit
   d. Title insurance

8. A two percent loan origination fee on a $160,000 loan with a sales price of $170,000 would be:
   a. $1600
   b. $1700
   c. $3200
   d. $3400

9. All of the following would be charged to the buyer's closing disclosure except:
   a. purchase price
   b. recording deed
   c. proration of taxes paid in advance by sellers
   d. commission

10. Expenses shown on the seller's statement will include all of the following except:
    a. commission
    b. transfer tax
    c. mortgage discharge
    d. mortgage interest

9. All of the following would be charged to the buyer's closing disclosure except:
   a. purchase price
   b. recording deed
   c. proration of taxes paid in advance by sellers
   d. commission

10. Expenses shown on the seller's statement will include all of the following except:
   a. commission
   b. transfer tax
   c. mortgage discharge
   d. mortgage interest

SOLUTION TO PRACTICE PROBLEM

Buyer's Statement	Costs	Credits
1. Down payment	$16,000.00	
2. Transfer tax	176.00	
3. Tax proration	503.01	
4. Attorney's fees	500.00	
5. Title insurance	112.00	
6. Credit report	35.00	
7. Loan orig. fee	1,280.00	
8. Recording fees	14.00	
9. Appraisal	200.00	
10. Earnest money		2,000.00
Total	$18,820.01	$2,000.00

$18,820.01
−2,000.00

Buyer's closing costs $16,820.01

Seller's Statement	Costs	Credits
1. Commission	$ 5,600.00	
2. Transfer tax	176.00	
3. Tax proration		503.01
4. Existing mortgage	45,000.00	
5. Discharge	8.00	
6. Deed preparation	60.00	
7. Sale price		80,000.00
	$50,844.00	$80,503.01

$80,503.01
−50,844.00

Seller's net proceeds $29,659.01

IMPORTANT TERMINOLOGY

Americans with Disabilities Act
blockbusting
Civil Rights Act of 1866
Civil Rights Act of 1968
Department of Housing and Urban Development
  (HUD)
disability

discriminatory advertising
Fair Housing Act of 1968
Fair Housing Amendments Act of 1988
Maine Fair Housing Law
redlining
steering

FAIR HOUSING

IN THIS CHAPTER

This chapter provides a discussion of the two federal laws prohibiting discrimination in housing. Of major importance is the federal **Fair Housing Act of 1968** and the 1974 and 1988 amendments. The other significant law is the **Civil Rights Act of 1866**. The 1968 act applies specifically to housing, whereas the 1866 law prohibits discrimination only because of race in both real and personal property. In civil rights, fair housing, and equal opportunity, it is important to view the laws with an understanding of protected classes.

CIVIL RIGHTS ACT OF 1866

A significant statute that affects equal housing opportunity is the federal Civil Rights Act of 1866. Far from being an obsolete law, this statute has had a major impact on fair housing concepts. Although the 1968 statute has a number of exemptions described in this chapter, the 1866 law has no exemptions, and contains the blanket statement that all citizens have an equal right to inherit, buy, sell, or lease all real and personal property. The basic interpretation of this statute is that of prohibiting all racial discrimination.

In the case of *Jones v. Alfred H. Mayer Company*, the United States Supreme Court applied the Civil Rights Act of 1866 to prohibit any racially based discrimination in housing, notwithstanding the exemptions being written into the Fair Housing Act of 1968. The exemptions provided for in the 1968 law cannot be used to enforce any racial discrimination.

FAIR HOUSING ACT OF 1968

Originally enacted by Congress as Title VIII of the **Civil Rights Act of 1968**, this law prohibited discrimination in housing on the basis of race, color, religion, or national origin. An amendment in the Housing and Community Development Act of 1974 added the prohibition against discrimination on the basis of sex. The **Fair Housing Amendments Act of 1988** added provisions to prevent discrimination based on mental and physical handicap or familial status. It is illegal to discriminate on the basis of race, color, religion, sex, national origin, mental and physical handicap, and familial status in (1) the sale or rental of housing or residential lots, (2) the advertising of the sale or rental of housing, (3) the financing of housing, and (4) the provision of real estate brokerage services. The act also makes blockbusting and steering illegal. Following is a discussion of the various specific acts prohibited in each of these categories.

Sale or Rental of Housing: Prohibited Acts

In this category there are a limited number of special exemptions available to owners in renting or selling their property. These exemptions are examined subsequently in the chapter. In the absence of an exemption, the following specific acts are prohibited:

1. Refusing to sell housing or rent, or negotiate the sale or rental of residential lots on the basis of discrimination because of race, color, religion, sex, or national origin. This includes representing to any person on discriminatory grounds "that any dwelling is not available for inspection, sale, or rental when such dwelling is in fact available." Also, it is illegal "to refuse to sell or rent after the making of a bona fide offer, or to refuse to negotiate for the sale or rental of, or otherwise make unavailable or deny, a dwelling to a person" because of race, color, religion, sex, or national origin.

   Examples of violations of these prohibited acts are (a) advising a prospective buyer that a house has been sold when it has not because of the prospect's national origin, (b) refusal to accept an offer to purchase because the offeror is a member of a particular religious faith, and (c) telling a rental applicant that an apartment is not available for inspection because the applicant is a female (or male), when the apartment is actually vacant and available for inspection.

2. The act makes it illegal "to discriminate against any person in the terms, conditions, or privileges of sale or rental of a dwelling, or in the provision of services or facilities in connection therewith, because of race, color, religion, sex, or national origin."

Figure 14.1

History of equal housing opportunity.

1865	The 13th amendment to the Constitution abolished slavery.
1866	Civil Rights Act provided all citizens the same rights to real property.
1866	The 14th Amendment guaranteed all citizens equal protection under the law.
1896	The Supreme Court established the "separate but equal" doctrine in the case of Plessy v. Ferguson.
1917	Supreme Court decision of Buchanan v. Warley prohibited zoning as a means of segregation.
1924	Article 24 of REALTORS® code prohibited members from introducing members of a race thought to be detrimental to a
1939	FHA manual instructed valuators to determine incompatible racial and social groups in a neighborhood.
1948	Supreme Court prohibited racially restrictive covenants in Shelley v. Kramer and Hurd v. Hodge.
1950	REALTORS® Article 24 deleted.
1954	Brown v. Board of Education decision outlawed "separate but equal" doctrine.
1968	Fair Housing Act passed.
1972	Recording of deeds with racially restrictive covenants prohibited.
1974	REALTORS® code prohibits all discrimination in services. Amendment to Housing and Community Development Act prohibited against discrimination on the basis of sex.
1975	NAR adopts Affirmative Marketing Agreement plan.
1988	Amendment to Fair Housing Act of 1968 prohibited discrimination in housing based on handicap or familial status.
1992	Americans with Disabilities Act.

Examples of prohibited acts in this category are (a) the manager of an apartment complex routinely requires tenants to have a security deposit in an amount equivalent to one month's rent unless the rental applicant is a black person, in which case a deposit equivalent to two months' rent is required; (b) the manager of an apartment complex restricts use of the complex swimming pool to white tenants only; and (c) the owner of a condominium will include in the purchase of a condominium apartment a share of stock and membership in a nearby country club provided the purchaser is not from Israel.

Discriminatory Advertising

The Fair Housing Act specifies that it is illegal "to make, print, or publish, or cause to be made, printed, or published any notice, statement, or advertisement, with respect to the sale or rental of a dwelling that indicates any preference, limitation, or discrimination based on race, color, religion, sex, or national origin, or an intention to make any such preference, limitation, or discrimination." This is called **discriminatory advertising**. Examples of violations are:

1. an advertisement for the sale of condominium units or rental apartments that contains pictures showing owners or tenants on the property that are invariably of only one race,
2. an advertisement that states that the owner prefers tenants that are male college students,
3. a "For Sale" sign that specifies "no Puerto Ricans,"
4. a statement to prospective white tenants by a real estate agent that black tenants are not permitted, and
5. an apartment advertisement stating "adults only."

Illegal Practices

Redlining describes violations of the Fair Housing Act by lending institutions. The term is based on the theory that some lending institutions, prior to the enactment of the act, may have circled certain local areas with a red line on the map and refused to make loans within the areas circled. The act prohibits lending institutions to refuse to make loans to purchase, construct, or repair a dwelling by discriminating on the basis of race, color, religion, sex, or national origin.

In the past, areas were redlined because they were highly integrated or populated by minorities. Today, however, the Fair Housing Act does not limit the prohibition against financial discrimination to the refusal to make loans because of the character of the neighborhood in which the property is located. The prohibition against discrimination applies to individuals by making it illegal "to deny a loan or other financial assistance to a person applying therefore for the purpose of purchasing, constructing, improving, repairing, or maintaining a dwelling," or "to discriminate against him in fixing the amount, interest rate, duration, or other terms or conditions of such loan or other financial assistance."

Discrimination in Providing
Real Estate Brokerage Services

The act prohibits discrimination in the provision of brokerage services and states "it shall be unlawful to deny any person access to or membership or participation in any multiple listing service, real estate brokers' organization, or other service, organization, or facility relating to the business of selling or renting dwellings, or to discriminate against him in the terms or conditions of such access, membership or participation on account of race, color, religion, sex, national origin., mental and physical handicap or familial status."

This provision of the Fair Housing Law makes the denial of membership or the imposition of special terms or conditions of membership in any real estate organization on discriminatory grounds illegal. Additionally, the refusal of a multiple listing service to accept a property for inclusion in the service or the refusal of a member broker to place a listing in the service on discriminatory grounds is illegal. The act requires real estate organizations and real estate agents to provide their services without discrimination.

Blockbusting

The act specifically makes **blockbusting** illegal and defines the practice as "for profit, to induce or attempt to induce any person to sell or rent any dwelling by representations regarding the entry or prospective entry into the neighborhood of a person or persons of a particular race, color, religion, sex, or national origin." Blockbusting describes the practice of real estate agents to induce owners to list property for sale or rent by telling them that persons of a particular protected class are moving into the area.

Steering

Steering, another possible violation of the Fair Housing Act by real estate agents, may be defined as the practice of real estate agents to direct prospective purchasers, especially minority purchasers, toward or away from specific neighborhoods to avoid changing the ethnic and/or racial makeup of neighborhoods. The prohibition against steering falls under the general prohibition of refusing to sell, rent, or negotiate the sale or rental of housing or residential lots. Examples of steering include (1) a real estate agent showing a white prospect only properties located in areas populated only by white people, (2) showing African-American prospects only properties in integrated areas or areas only populated by African-American persons, and (3) showing Polish prospects properties only in areas populated by Poles.

Exemptions

The Fair Housing Law provides exemptions to property owners under certain conditions:

1. An owner who does not own more than three single-family dwellings at any one time is exempt. Unless the owner was living in, or was the most recent occupant of the house sold, she is limited to only one exemption in any 24-month period.
2. An owner of an apartment building containing not more than four apartments is exempt in the rental of the apartments provided the owner occupies one of the apartments as a personal residence.
3. Religious organizations are exempt as to properties owned and operated for the benefit of their members only and not for commercial purposes, provided membership in the organization is not restricted on account of race, color, religion, sex, or national origin.
4. A private club not open to the public is exempt as to properties owned by the club to provide lodging for the benefit of the membership and not for commercial purposes.

None of these exemptions is available if either of the following has occurred:

1. Discriminatory advertising has been used.
2. The services of a real estate broker, agent, or salesperson, or any person in the business of selling or renting dwellings is used if (a) the individual has, within the preceding twelve months, participated as principal in three or more transactions involving the sale or rental of any dwelling or any interest therein, or (b) the person has, within the preceding twelve months, participated as agent, other than in the sale of personal residence in providing sales or rental facilities or sales or rental services in two or more transactions involving the sale or rental of any dwelling or any interest therein, or (c) the individual is the owner of any dwelling designed or intended for occupancy by, or occupied by five or more families.

1988 AMENDMENTS TO THE FAIR HOUSING ACT

The 1988 Amendments Act amends Title VIII of the Civil Rights Act of 1968 in two significant respects. First, it makes it illegal to discriminate against physically and mentally disabled people (including hearing mobility and visual impairments, chronic alcoholism, chronic mental illness, AIDS, and mental retardation) and familial status (including children under the age of 18 living with parents or legal custodians, pregnant women, and people securing custody of children under 18). Second, it changes the way Title VIII is enforced and the penalties that can be imposed for violations. The amendment became effective March 13, 1989.

1. Protected classes now include persons with mental or physical handicaps that impair any of their life functions. Landlords must now allow disabled persons to make reasonable modifications to an apartment, at the tenant's expense, to accommodate their special needs. For example, a tenant must be allowed to install a ramp or widen doors to accommodate a wheelchair, or install grab bars in a bathroom. At the end of the tenancy, the tenant must return the premises to their original condition at his own expense.

   In addition, new multifamily dwellings of four or more units that are available for occupancy March 13, 1991, must meet certain accessibility standards for the disabled; for example, switches and thermostats must be at a level that can be operated from a wheelchair, walls must be reinforced to accommodate possible grab-bar installation, and kitchen and bathroom space must permit maneuverability in a wheelchair.
2. Landlords may not discriminate on the basis of familial status. Thus, adults with children under 18, pregnant women, and anyone who has legal custody of a child or is in the process of obtaining custody, cannot be denied housing. Landlords are prohibited from recruiting for "Adults Only" in most circumstances. However, provision has been made for housing for the elderly provided that (a) all units are occupied by a person 62 or older, or (b) 80 percent of the units have at least one person age 55 or older.
3. Major enforcement provisions were added by the 1988 amendment. For the first time, the **Department of Housing and Urban Development (HUD)** can now file a formal charge and refer it to an administrative law judge, unless the aggrieved party or the respondent elect a jury trial in a civil court. The administrative law judge can impose substantial fines—that is, $10,000 for a first violation and up to $50,000 for two or more violations within a seven-year period. Additionally, the attorney general will take the role of the aggrieved party in such a case, thus freeing the party from the legal expense of pursuing the case.

The prior statute of limitations under Title VIII has also been changed. It has been extended to one year if the aggrieved party files a charge with HUD, and to two years if a direct action in federal court is filed.

Real estate offices should be aware of an amendment to the 1968 law that requires all offices to prominently display the Fair Housing Poster shown in Figure 14.2. Failure to display the poster could be considered failure to comply with fair housing requirements. With some exceptions, the fair housing symbol should be used in advertising listings.

AMERICANS WITH DISABILITIES ACT

The **Americans with Disabilities Act**, which took effect on January 26, 1992, specifically protects the rights of individuals with disabilities. **Disability** is defined in USC 42, Sec. 12101, as a physical or mental impairment that substantially limits one or more of the major life activities of a person.

Under this law, individuals with disabilities cannot be denied access to public transportation, any commercial facility, or public accommodation. This Act applies to all owners and operators of public accommodations and commercial facilities, regardless of the size or number of employees. It also applies to all local and state governments.

Public accommodations are defined as private businesses that affect commerce and trade, such as inns, hotels, restaurants, theaters, convention centers, bakeries, laundromats, banks, barber shops, attorneys' offices, museums, zoos, places of education, day-

Figure 14.2
Poster for equal housing opportunity.

U.S. Department of Housing and Urban Development

EQUALHOUSING
OPPORTUNITY

We Do Business in Accordance With the Federal Fair Housing Law

(The Fair Housing Amendments Act of 1988)

| It is Illegal to Discriminate Against Any Person Because of Race, Color, Religion, Sex, Handicap, Familial Status, or National Origin |

- In the sale or rental of housing or residential lots
- In the provision of real estate brokerage services
- In advertising the sale or rental of housing
- In the appraisal of housing
- In the financing of housing
- Blockbusting is also illegal

Anyone who feels he or she has been discriminated against may file a complaint of housing discrimination:
1-800-669-9777 (Toll Free)
1-800-927-9275 (TDD)

U.S. Department of Housing and Urban Development
Assistant Secretary for Fair Housing and Equal Opportunity
Washington, D.C. 20410

Previous editions are obsolete

form HUD-928.1A(8-93)

care centers, and health clubs. *Commercial facilities* are those intended for nonresidential use and affect commerce, such as factories.

To comply with this law, public accommodations and commercial facilities are to be designed, constructed, and altered to meet the accessibility standards of the new law if readily achievable. "Readily achievable" means easily accomplishable and able to be carried out without much difficulty or expense. Considerations in determining if the commercial facility or public accommodation can be made accessible are:

1. Nature and cost of the needed alteration.
2. Overall financial resources of the facility involved and number of persons employed.
3. Type of operation of the entity.

Public accommodations must remove structural, architectural, and communication barriers in existing facilities if the removal is readily achievable. Examples of barriers to be removed or alterations to be made include placing ramps, lowering telephones, making curb cuts in sidewalks and entrances, widening doors, installing grab bars in toilet stalls, and adding raised letters on elevator controls. Commercial facilities are not required to remove the barriers in existing facilities.

In the construction of new public accommodations and commercial facilities, all areas must be readily accessible and usable by individuals with disabilities as of January 26, 1993. The Americans with Disabilities Act is enforced by the U. S. Attorney General. Punishment for violating this law includes injunctions against operation of a business, a fine up to $50,000 for the first offense, and a fine of $100,000 for subsequent offenses.

Be aware that individuals with AIDS, alcoholism, or mental illness are included in the category of people with a mental or physical disability that impairs any of their life functions.

MAINE FAIR HOUSING LAW

The **Maine Fair Housing Law** also prohibits discrimination in housing based upon race, color, sex, physical or mental handicap, religion, ancestry, national origin, or sexual orientation. Note that the law adds physical or mental handicap and ancestry, as well as sexual orientation, as grounds for a violation, in addition to the more traditional basis specified in federal law. The law prohibits the following acts, if they discriminate, or seek to discriminate on the basis of any of the previous classifications.

- To fail or refuse to show an applicant for housing accommodations listed for sale, lease, or rental.
- To misrepresent to an applicant or potential occupant the availability or asking price of housing accommodations, listed for sale, lease, or rental.
- To fail to communicate to the person having the right to sell or lease such housing accommodations any offer.
- To discriminate in any manner against an applicant for housing.
- To discriminate against Seeing Eye dogs and hearing aid animals.
- To accept for listing any housing accommodation when the person having the right to sell or lease directly or indirectly indicated an intention to discriminate against prospective tenants or purchasers, or when the broker knows or has reason to know that the person having the right to sell or lease has made a practice of discriminating since July 1, 1972.

As an example, a broker cannot manage a rental property where the owner requires higher security deposits from single males than single females, or where the owner advertises that the units are to be rented to women only.

EQUAL HOUSING OPPORTUNITY TODAY

When the concept of fair housing is discussed, many persons have the idea that the issue has long been resolved, through actions such as the civil rights movement of the 1960s. Despite the intention of the 1866 amendment, the 1968 Civil Rights Acts, and the 1988 amendment to provide equal housing opportunity for all citizens, this goal has not been achieved in practice. A recent study by HUD found that minorities are still confronted with a 48 percent chance of encountering discrimination in the purchase of a home, or a 72 percent chance in leasing a rental unit.

Many proposals have been developed to correct this situation. Presidential administrations have proposed increasing the force of the law with severe legal penalties. One means of enforcing the law is through an organized program of testing by civil rights groups. In 1986, the administration supported a Fair Housing Initiatives Program (FHIP) to provide funding of testers. The National Association of REALTORS® (NAR) negotiated an agreement with HUD to ensure that funded testing will be objective, reliable, and controlled, and then provided its endorsement to the program.

In order to address attitudes against discrimination, NAR has developed a Voluntary Affirmative Marketing Program. The association has encouraged its affiliates and members to adopt the program by signing an Affirmative Marketing Agreement. Provisions of the agreement pledge signatories to adopt affirmative advertising, recruitment, and educational programs.

As each April is celebrated with observances of the passage of the Fair Housing Act of 1968, it is hoped that the spirit and intention of the law will be accomplished.

Definitions

The Federal Housing Act offers definitions of certain terms used in the act, as follows:

1. *Dwelling.* Any building, structure, or portion thereof which is occupied as, or designed or intended for occupancy as, a residence by one or more families, and any vacant land which is offered for sale or lease for the construction or location thereon of any such building, structure, or portion thereof.
2. *Elderly housing.* (1) A community in which all of the units are occupied by a person 62 years or older or (2) housing in which 80 percent of the units are occupied by at least one person age 55 or older.
3. *Familial status.* Includes children under age 18, pregnant persons, or persons with, or in the process of obtaining, custody of children.
4. *Handicap.* Any physical or mental impairment that limits one or more of the functions of life, but does not include any person who currently abuses a controlled substance or presents a threat to the health, safety, or property of others.
5. *Person.* Includes one or more individuals, corporations, partnerships, associations, labor organizations, legal representations, mutual companies, joint stock companies, trusts, unincorporated organizations, trustees, trustees in bankruptcy, receivers, and fiduciaries.
6. *To rent.* Includes to lease, to sublease, to let, and otherwise to grant for a consideration the right to occupy premises not owned by the occupant.

IMPORTANT POINTS

1. The Civil Rights Act of 1866 prohibits discrimination only on the basis of race. The prohibition is not limited to housing, but includes all real estate transactions. The act may be enforced by civil suit in federal court.

2. The Fair Housing Act of 1968, as amended, prohibits discrimination in housing because of race, color, religion, sex, national origin, handicap, or familial status.

3. Discrimination is prohibited in (1) the sale or rental of housing, (2) advertising the sale or rental of housing, (3) financing of housing, and (4) the provision of real estate brokerage services. The act also makes blockbusting and steering illegal.

4. There are four exemptions provided to owners in selling or renting housing, namely, (1) owners who do not own more than three houses, (2) owners of apartment buildings in which there are not more than four apartments and the owner occupies one of the apartments, (3) religious organizations with properties used for the benefit of members only, and (4) private clubs with lodging used for the benefit of members only.

5. The owners' exemptions are not available if the owner used discriminatory advertising or the services of a real estate broker. Additionally, real estate licensees are prohibited from any discriminatory practices in their own personal affairs.

6. Enforcement of Title VIII of the 1968 Fair Housing Act was amended significantly in 1988. Enforcement procedures now include (1) administrative procedure through the Office of Equal Opportunity of HUD, which first attempts voluntary conciliation and then can refer the case to an administrative law judge who can impose financial penalties of $10,000 to $50,000; (2) civil suit in federal court, and (3) the U.S. attorney general filing a suit in federal court and imposing penalties of up to $50,000 on the first offense in a "pattern of discrimination."

7. Maine has a fair housing act that is very similar to the federal act in its prohibitions of discrimination.

8. The Americans with Disabilities Act provides that individuals with disabilities cannot be denied access to public transportation, any commercial facility, or public accommodation. Barriers in existing buildings must be removed if readily achievable. New buildings must be readily accessible and usable by individuals with disabilities.

REVIEW QUESTIONS

Answers to these questions are found in the Answer Key section at the back of the book.

1. The practice of attempting to induce any person to sell any dwelling by representations regarding the entry into the neighborhood of a person of a protected class is called:
   a. Redlining
   b. Blockbusting
   c. Steering
   d. Directing

2. Which of the following is not a basis of discrimination prohibited by the Fair Housing Act of 1968?
   a. race
   b. color
   c. age
   d. religion

3. The Fair Housing Act is administered by the:
   a. Office of Equal Opportunity
   b. Justice Department
   c. Department of Housing and Urban Development
   d. Federal Trade Commission

4. Seller's Town Multiple Listing Service refuses to accept a listing for inclusion in the service because the owner is Russian. Which of the following is correct?
   a. a multiple listing service does not come under the act because it is a private, nonprofit organization
   b. the act does not prohibit discrimination against Russians
   c. the listing broker's membership in the MLS may be terminated for taking the listing
   d. the MLS is in violation of the 1968 act for denying access to the service because of the owner's national origin

5. A property manager refuses to rent an office because the rental applicant is black. The applicant has legal recourse under the:
   a. Fair Housing Act of 1968
   b. Civil Rights Act of 1866
   c. Fair Housing Amendments of 1988
   d. 13th Amendment to the constitution

6. In an advertisement offering her only house for sale, the owner states that she will give preference to cash buyers who are female and members of the Catholic religion. The owner subsequently refused a cash offer because the offeror was a male Presbyterian. Which of the following is (are) correct?
   a. since the seller only owned one house, she is exempt from the 1968 act
   b. since the advertisement only stated a preference, it is not discriminatory
   c. since the seller's main purpose was to obtain cash, the refusal is not discriminatory
   d. since the advertisement was in fact discriminatory, the seller's exemption is lost and she has violated the 1968 act in two ways

7. A real estate agent only showed white prospects homes in all-white areas. This discriminatory practice is called:
   a. redlining
   b. blockbusting
   c. steering
   d. directing

8. Which of the following is exempt from the provisions of the 1968 act?
   a. an owner of four houses
   b. an owner occupying one of four apartments in his building
   c. a religious organization renting one of 16 apartments it owns and operates for commercial purposes
   d. an owner who has listed a residential lot for sale with a real estate broker

9. The following ad appears in a local paper: "Home for rent; limited to mature persons; 2 bedrooms; 1 bath." Which of the following is correct?

   a. the ad is in compliance with the Fair Housing Act of 1968 as amended in 1988

   b. the ad violates the Civil Rights Act of 1866

   c. the ad is in compliance with the Civil Rights Act of 1974

   d. the ad violates the Fair Housing Amendments of 1988

10. A person confined to a wheelchair requests that an apartment be modified to meet his physical needs. Which of the following is correct?

   a. the owner must make appropriate modifications at the owner's expense

   b. at the end of the tenancy, the renter must pay for returning the premises to their original condition

   c. the owner may refuse to rent to the disabled tenant because of the needed modifications

   d. the owner may charge increased rent because of the disability and the needed modifications

CHAPTER 15

IMPORTANT TERMINOLOGY

adjusted basis
Over 55 exclusion
boot
capital improvements
depreciation
economic depreciation
inheritance basis
installment sales
like-kind property

multiple exchange
rollover rule
Starker exchange
tax basis
tax deductible expenses
tax-deferred exchanges
tax depreciation
Tax Reform Act of 1986 (TRA)
tax shelter

TAX IMPLICATIONS OF REAL ESTATE OWNERSHIP AND TRANSACTIONS

IN THIS CHAPTER

It is very important that real estate agents have a basic knowledge and understanding of the federal income tax laws affecting real property. However, real estate agents may not give tax advice to buyers and sellers. Each taxpayer's situation is different. Therefore, advice should only be given by competent professional tax counsel familiar with the taxpayer's position. Real estate agents should recommend that buyers and sellers seek such counsel when appropriate.

This chapter presents the fundamentals of tax implications in the ownership and sale of a principal residence and business and investment property. The special tax benefits provided to owners and sellers of real property are illustrated and explained to enable you to achieve a good understanding of these advantages.

TAX REFORM ACT OF 1986 AND SUBSEQUENT LEGISLATION

The Tax Reform Act of 1986 (TRA) brought a number of sweeping changes to the tax laws, a number of them particularly less generous to the real estate industry. Although the top individual income tax rate was reduced from 50 percent to 28 percent over a two-year period, the elimination of other favorable aspects of the new code meant that certain real estate investors actually saw their taxes increase significantly. Some of the other provisions of the Tax Reform Act were:

- Amending the rules for qualifying as a real estate investment
- Altering the method of calculating depreciation
- Repealing the investment tax credit for property placed in service after 1985

Capital Gain

Almost everything you own and use for personal purposes, pleasure or investment is a capital asset such as property, household furnishings, cars, and jewelry. When you sell a capital asset such as property, the profit realized on the sale is a capital gain. If there is a loss on the sale it is a capital loss. Capital gains and losses are classified as long-term or short-term, depending on how long the property is held before being sold. Long term capital gains are usually taxed at a lower rate than ordinary income. If it is held for one year or less, the capital gain or loss is short term and the gain will be taxed as ordinary income. Capital losses may be deducted only on investment property, not property held for personal use.

Depreciation

Depreciation is an income tax deduction that allows the taxpayer to spread the cost of an asset over a period of time and take an annual allowance for the wear and tear, deterioration or obsolescence of the property. Only the cost of the structure is allowed as a depreciation deduction; the value of the land cannot be depreciated. Under the Tax Act of 1981, a straight line depreciation of 15 years was established and later modified to 18 years and then to 19 years. One of the provisions of the Tax Reform Act of 1986 was to reset the schedule for 27.5 years for residential property and 31.5 years for most non-residential property. Under TRA 1993, if the non-residential property was placed in service on or after May 13, 1993, the depreciable life increased from 31.5 years to 39 years.

Example: The residential rental property was purchased for $300,000. The value of the land was assessed at $100,000 and the building at $200,000. The recovery period for residential rental property is 27.5 years. If the $200,000 is divided by 27.5, it results in a yearly depreciation of $7272.73.

Depreciation recapture is the IRS procedure for collecting income tax on a gain realized by a taxpayer when the taxpayer disposes of an asset that had previously provided an offset to ordinary income for the taxpayer through depreciation. It is completely taxable in the year of the sale which is currently 25%. Depreciation recapture can cause a significant tax impact for people who are selling residential rental properties.

Passive Loss

The Internal Revenue Service views the income from rental properties and any business in which the taxpayer does not materially participate in as passive income. A taxpayer will be considered as materially participating if she meets one of seven possible tests. (Test Example: Does taxpayer work more than 500 hours a year in the business?). Passive losses are allowed against passive activity income, but cannot be used to shelter active income such as wages, dividends or interest. Generally, losses from passive activities that exceed the income from passive activities are disallowed for the current year. Disallowed passive losses are carried forward to the next taxable year. Any unrealized losses from a passive activity are allowed in full upon taxable disposition of the activity.

There are two exceptions to the passive loss rule. The first exception exists for individuals who actively manage their own rental property, have at least a 10% ownership and are not a limited partner in the property. If they have modified adjusted gross incomes of $100,000 or less, the maximum rental real estate loss they may claim is $25,000 per year. This allowance is phased out for taxpayers whose adjusted gross income exceeds $100,000 and eliminated entirely when the income exceeds $150,000. The other exception is a complete exemption of the rule. It occurs when landlords who materially participate in real estate activities "qualify" as real estate professionals by IRS standards. This qualification does not mean that they have a real estate license, but that they have spent a certain amount of time and are involved on a regular, continuous and substantial basis in the real estate activities.

Mortgage Interest and Property Taxes

While the most valuable tax deduction may be for mortgage interest for both a principal residence and a second home, a taxpayer can also claim a property tax deduction for their principal residence and second home.

TAXPAYERS RELIEF ACT OF 1997

This legislation, effective May 7, 1997, made some important changes to the way the gain on the sale of a principal residence is taxed or not taxed. The law repeals the **rollover rule** and the Over 55 exclusion. Under the rollover rule, as long as the homeowner bought a replacement residence more expensive than the one that was sold, the gain on the sale was deferred. If the homeowner sold at a profit, the gain was rolled over into the new purchase, but if he bought a new home where the cost was less than the amount realized on the previous sale or did not buy a home at all, this would affect the deferment of the tax. Under the **Over 55 exclusion**, the homeowner would have to wait until the "magic" age of 55 to enjoy any exclusion. At age 55, he could exempt from any tax up to $125,000 of gain in the sale of a property that was used as a principal residence three out of the last five years preceding the date of the sale.

Married Couples

Under TRA97, married couples filing a joint return can exclude up to $500,000 of gain on the sale of a principal residence. The exclusion applies where:

1. either spouse has owned the home as a personal residence for two out of the last five years,
2. both spouses occupy the home for two out of the last five years, and
3. neither spouse has had a sale in the preceding two years subject to this exclusion

The exclusion will be $250,000 if one spouse has not occupied the property for the full two years or if one spouse has claimed exclusion in the past two years. Married couples filing a joint return who do not share a principal residence are each entitled to an exclusion of $250,000.

Single Taxpayers

Single return filers can exclude up to $250,000 of the gain on the sale of a principal residence, if the taxpayer:

1. owned and occupied the home as a personal residence for two out of the last five years and
2. has not claimed an exclusion in the past two years

Changes in Marital Status

A divorced taxpayer may tack on the ownership and use of the residence by his or her former spouse. Example: If the divorce decree specifies that the wife will reside in the house until it sells and the husband moves out, he may tack on his ex-wife's continued use of the residence to meet the two-year use test. Each one is entitled to exclude $250,000 of gain from the sale. If the wife is awarded the house in the divorce decree, and sells the house two years after the divorce, she can only claim $250,000 exclusion because of her single status.

A widowed spouse can file jointly within 2 years of the spouse's death and claim a $500,000 exclusion. If the sale takes place the year after the 2 years, the spouse is a single taxpayer and only allowed the $250,000 exclusion.

A new marriage may also double the tax break. Example: A single woman sells her principal residence on September 21, 20XX, realizing $500,000 in gain. She and her fiancée have been living in the house for three years prior to the sale. They marry on December 7 of the same year as the sale. They can file a joint return for that year and exclude the entire $500,000 of profit.

Other Effects of TRA97

The gain exclusion rules apply every two years. For example, a taxpayer can sell her residence on December 31, 2009, and claim the gain exclusion. The taxpayer can then sell another residence on January 1, 2012 (assuming the taxpayer owned and occupied it on January 1, 2010) and again claim the gain exclusion.

Before January 1, 2009, a second home owner could convert the property to a primary residence by living in it for two years and thus exclude $250,000 or $500,000of taxable gain upon sale. A provision of the 2008 Housing and Economic Recovery Act made the sale of a primary residence used as a second home for any time after January 1, 2009 subject to capital gain tax regardless of how long the owner lives in the home. There are some exceptions to this rule. Example: The home was owned for 5 years and it was used as a vacation home for 3 years or 60% of the time and the gain when sold was $155,000. $155,000 x 60% = $93,000 which is taxable gain. If the home was rented out in order to claim deductions for depreciation, the sale would also be subject to cost recovery recapture taxed at 25%.

There is a formula provided to give partial exclusion to those who cannot satisfy the two-year requirement. If the taxpayer sells his residence due to an employee relocation, health problem, or other "unforeseen circumstances" (to be determined) the maximum $250,000/$500,000 excluded gain is prorated based on the number of days within the two-year period of occupancy.

Tax Reform ACT of 2003

This Act reduced taxes on capital gains. As a result of this Act, the capital gains tax rate for most people is 15 percent for an elapsed time between purchase and sale of more than one year, and the gain is taxed as regular income for an elapsed time of one year or less. For taxpayers in the 10 percent and 15 percent tax brackets, long-term capital gains are taxed at 5 percent. In 2008 the rate for these lower income taxpayers is reduced to zero.

Gift Taxes

The annual gift tax exclusion amount is currently $13,000 per donee. This means that any individual can give up to $13,000 each year ($26,000 with a spouse) to anyone without the transfer being treated as a taxable gift. If a couple had four children, the total that the couple could give to their four children tax free would be $104,000 ($26,000 × 4 = $104,000). Rental property can be conveyed by gifts giving a fractionalized interest to a donee each year.

TAX IMPLICATIONS OF HOMEOWNERSHIP
Tax Deductible Expenses

The tax deductible expenses involved in homeownership are mortgage interest (not principal) and real property taxes paid to local taxing authorities. Additionally, the fact that the taxpayer has mortgage interest as a deductible item will usually make it advantageous to itemize and take advantage of other tax deductible expenses not associated with home

-ownership. The combination of mortgage interest and other itemized expenses provides greater tax relief than available in taking the allowable standard deduction.

To put this in the form of a realistic example, let's assume a home buyer purchases a residence for $100,000 with a $10,000 down payment and the balance financed for 30 years at 8 percent interest. The monthly payment of principal and interest necessary to fully amortize the remaining $90,000 over a period of 30 years is $660.39. During the first 12 months of loan payments, the borrower will pay a total of $7,172.83 in interest. A proportionate amount of this interest is available as a tax deduction for the year in which the loan was created. For instance, if 6 payments are made during the tax year, approximately half of the interest will be deductible for that particular tax year. In subsequent years the full amount of interest paid is available as a tax deduction. It is not until the 25th year of the loan that the monthly payment is allocated approximately one-half to interest and one-half to the reduction of principal.

Another way to look at this is to relate the taxpayer's income tax bracket to the mortgage interest rate. For instance, if our taxpayer is in a 28 percent bracket, take 28 percent of the 8 percent interest rate, which is 2.24 percent, and deduct that amount from the mortgage interest rate. The result is an after-tax interest rate to our 28 percent bracket taxpayer of 5.76 percent.

Computing Taxable Gain

In computing the gain or loss in the sale of a principal residence, the first step is to establish the owner's **tax basis** in the property. The tax basis consists of the price paid for the property, less any gain realized in the sale of the previous residence on which the payment of tax was deferred under the rollover rule, plus expenses incurred in acquiring the property (other than those incurred in arranging financing), plus the cost of any capital improvements (not repairs) made during ownership.

The **adjusted basis** is the original cost (purchase price and closing costs) of the property plus **capital improvements** minus **depreciation** if any. Improvements that materially add to the value and prolong the useful life of a residence, such as a fireplace or new roof, are considered capital improvements. By referring to Figure 15.1, we can see that it is to the advantage of the homeowner to have as large a basis as possible, so as to minimize the tax gain realized when the property is eventually sold. Alternately,

Purchase price	
+ Closing cost	} original cost
+ Capital improvements	Amount realized from sale
− Depreciation	− Adjusted basis
Adjusted basis	Gain

Figure 15.1
Computation of gain.

Basis of home (purchase price)	$35,000
Plus: Closing costs	+ 1,000
Improvements	+ 2,000
Adjusted basis of home	$38,000
Selling price of home	$85,000
Less: Selling expenses	− 7,000
Amount realized	$78,000
Amount realized	$78,000
Minus: Adjusted basis	−38,000
Gain realized	$40,000

Figure 15.2
Calculation of gain.

the gain is minimized by being able to deduct certain items from the sale price. Since the gain of $40,000 is less than $250,000/$500,000 exclusion allowed, there is no tax due.

Inheritance Basis

The tax basis for all real property received by heirs, the inheritance basis, is the market value of the property on the date of the death of the decedent and not the market value at the time the decedent acquired the property. This provides a substantial benefit to heirs when they sell the property.

Effect of Purchase and Sale

There are certain expenses for both buyer and seller in the purchase and sale of a personal residence. The following are examples of these expenses and their application by buyer or seller in calculating taxable gain.

1. The premium paid for a title insurance policy may be subtracted from the selling price if paid by the seller. It may be added to his basis if paid by the buyer.
2. Transfer taxes paid by the seller may be deducted by the seller from the selling price. The tax paid by the buyer is added to the buyer's basis.
3. Attorney's fees paid by the seller are deductible from the selling price. Attorney's fees paid by the buyer are added to the buyer's basis. However, attorney's fees incurred by the buyer to obtain financing may not be added to the buyer's basis.
4. The fee for preparation of the deed may be deducted by the seller if paid by the seller.
5. Buyer's closing costs that are allocable to purchasing the property may be added to the buyer's basis. However, expenses of borrowing the purchase price may not be added to the buyer's basis. Examples of expenses involved with obtaining the loan include such things as appraisal fees, mortgage insurance premiums, charges by the lender's attorney, and credit report cost.
6. Discount points charged by lending institutions may be deducted from the selling price if paid by the seller to enable the buyer to obtain a loan. These discount points may not be deductible as interest by the seller because the seller has not borrowed the money and therefore has no obligation to repay. Since the points are treated as a selling expense, they will reduce the gain on the sale.

   Discount points paid by the buyer are deductible as interest by the buyer *for the year in which the points are paid*. In 1986 the IRS ruled that discount points paid by the buyer for the purchase of a second home, investment property, or to refinance an existing loan would have to be spread out over the *term of the loan*. The essential difference is that if the buyer paid $2,000 in points for a new home, she could deduct all $2,000 in the year paid. However, if the buyer refinanced her present loan for 20 years, she could only deduct $100 per year. If the mortgage loan was not obtained to purchase or improve a principal residence, deduction of the discount points as interest must be spread out over the life of the loan. For example, if a borrower paid $2,000 in discount points to obtain a 20-year conventional loan to purchase an apartment building, the discount points are deductible at the rate of $100 per year for 20 years.
7. If the loan origination fee is expressed as a percent, the loan amount is

considered pre-paid interest. Also, the borrower may not add the cost of a loan origination or processing fee to the basis of the property because this is an expense of borrowing the purchase price rather than a cost for obtaining the property. Loan origination fees paid by the seller are a selling expense and may be deducted from the sales price in arriving at the amount realized.

8. Other expense items such as surveys, escrow fees, title abstracts, recording fees, and advertising costs may be added to the buyer's basis if paid by the buyer or subtracted from the selling price if paid by the seller.

9. The real estate commission paid by the seller may be deducted from the selling price. The commission paid is not deductible from ordinary income by the seller.

10. Fix-up expenses are costs incurred by the seller in preparing a residence for sale. To qualify as deductions from the amount realized to establish the adjusted sale price, these costs must have been incurred within 90 days prior to signing the contract of sale that results in the completed sale of the home and must be paid for within at least 30 days after the sale.

11. Moving expenses connected with starting work at a new job location at least 50 miles farther from a former residence than the old job location are tax deductible expenses. A deduction is available for both employees and self-employed taxpayers. (If your old main job was 5 miles from your former home, your new main job must be at least 55 miles from that former home.)

The tax deductible costs of moving household goods and personal effects and the tax deductible expenses incurred for travel and lodging in moving from the old residence to the new residence are not limited in dollar amount. Pre-move house-hunting trips, meals, and temporary living quarters are no longer deductible, pursuant to the TRA of 1993.

Vacation Homes

Under the TRA of 1986, homeowners are allowed to deduct mortgage interest on both a principal residence as well as a second home such as a vacation property, but the combined mortgage amounts cannot be more than $1 million. . Special rules apply in the classification of this second property. The vacation property is considered a second home if it is occupied for personal use more than 14 days per year or 10 percent of its useful rental period. In this case, the mortgage interest and property taxes on both the principal residence and second home can be deducted, to the extent the mortgages do not exceed the original purchase price of the properties, plus improvements, unless the home is refinanced for medical or educational purposes.

If, however, the personal use of the second property is limited to less than 14 days or 10 percent of the useful rental period, the home will be treated as a business property. If the property value exceeds $150,000, all gain must be reported in the year of the sale, no matter how little cash the seller actually received at that time. In this case, it will be eligible for the 27.5-year depreciation schedule, repairs and maintenance deductions, as well as full deduction of the mortgage interest and property taxes, subject to passive loss rules discussed previously.

INSTALLMENT SALES

An **installment sale** is a sale of property where at least one payment is received after the tax year in which the sale occurs. An owner may sell his principal residence on an installment sale basis and avoid the substantial impact of tax in one year.

Installment sales may be used to spread the impact of federal income taxes on profits over a period of several years or to postpone taxes to a future year or years. This enables the taxpayer to avoid the impact of tax on profit in the sale of property in a single year. In installment sales, the tax laws apply to the sale of real property, businesses, securities, and personal property.

The TRA of 1986 made the installment sales method much less attractive than the previous laws. The installment sale benefit is limited to investors. Sellers of noninvestment properties should seek tax advice before agreeing to carry a mortgage. Installment sales of investment property will provide the assumption that the seller received a minimum cash payment each year, meaning that such payment is recognized for tax purposes, regardless of whether any cash is in fact actually received during that year.

TAX IMPLICATIONS OF THE OWNERSHIP AND SALE OF BUSINESS AND INVESTMENT PROPERTY

As we have seen, there are special tax benefits in the ownership and sale of a principal residence. There are also special tax benefits in the ownership and sale of real property held as an investment or for use in a trade or business. These tax benefits include depreciation, deductible expenses, and tax-free exchanges of like-kind property.

Depreciation

There are actually two types of depreciation: tax depreciation and economic depreciation. **Economic depreciation** results from physical deterioration of property caused by normal use of the property, damage caused by natural and other hazards, and failure to adequately maintain the property. **Tax depreciation** is a provision of the tax law, applicable to certain types of assets, that permits a property owner to take an ordinary business deduction for the amount of annual depreciation. This permits the owner to recover the cost or other basis of an asset over the period of the useful life of the asset. Tax depreciation is a deduction from net income in calculating taxable income.

The Tax Reform Act of 1986 established two depreciation schedules for real property, that is, 27.5 years for residential property and 39 years for nonresidential property. Additionally, the TRA of 1986 limited the amount of losses to the income of similar passive activities. Passive investors who do not actively manage their own property cannot apply excess losses to other active income. There is a limited exce tion to this rule for owners with adjusted gross income less than $100,000 who actively manage their own property. Such owners may shelter up to $25,000 of other wages or active income.

Depreciable property includes such assets as buildings, equipment, machinery, and other assets that are used in business to produce income (other than inventories) or that are held as an investment. Assets held for personal use, including a personal residence, are not depreciable assets. Also, land is not a depreciable asset. Therefore, the value of the land and the value of structures on the land must be separated to arrive at a basis for determining depreciation. This basis is normally the cost of acquiring the property reduced by the estimated salvage value of the property at the end of the useful life.

When a depreciable asset is sold, the basis of the asset used to compute the taxable gain realized in the sale is the depreciated value. For example, if a depreciable asset was purchased for $100,000, and $40,000 of tax depreciation had been taken by the purchaser at the time the property was sold for $130,000, the taxable gain would be $70,000 ($130,000 sales price minus $60,000 depreciated value = $70,000 taxable gain).

Tax Shelter

Depreciation is a deductible allowance from net income of the property when arriving at taxable income. Examples of expenses deductible from gross income include operating expenses, real estate taxes, and mortgage interest. Mortgage principal payments are not deductible in arriving at taxable income.

To see the benefit of this concept, let's consider the operating statement for an apartment building. We assume the subject property was purchased for $6,200,000. Since land does not depreciate, we have to make an allocation between the land and the improvement of the building. If we assume that 15 percent of the price is allocated to the land, the depreciable property becomes 85% × $6,200,000, or

$5,270,000. Since the property can be depreciated over a 27.5-year period, one year's depreciation is $1/27$, or $191,636, which may be used to offset income from the property itself (called a **tax shelter**). Additionally, interest on the debt service is deductible. The final figures are illustrated in Figure 15.3.

Viewed another way, we can see that if the property owner is in a 28 percent tax bracket, the exclusion (sheltering) of the depreciation allowance of $191,636 means that the property owner saved 28 percent of this figure or $53,658 in federal income taxes.

Deductible Operating Expenses

Unlike the expenses of operating property held for personal use, such as a personal residence, the expenses of operating property held for use in business or as an investment may be deducted from gross income in arriving at net income. Before deducting operating expenses, losses from vacancies and credit losses are deducted from gross scheduled rental income to arrive at gross operating income. Operating expenses are deducted from gross operating income. Examples of operating expenses include the following:

> Accounting and legal fees
> Advertising
> Property taxes
> Property management fees
> Property insurance
> Licenses and permits
> Wages and salaries
> Services
> Maintenance and repairs
> Supplies
> Utilities

Net operating income	$745,600
Less: Interest	−463,836
Depreciation	−191,636
Net taxable income	$ 90,128

Figure 15.3
Net taxable income.

The result obtained by deducting operating expenses is net operating income. To arrive at net taxable income, deductions for mortgage interest and real property taxes are made from net operating income. This otherwise taxable income may be completely or partially sheltered from tax liability as a result of the depreciation allowance. As a result, the building may have no taxable income.

TAX-DEFERRED EXCHANGES

The Internal Revenue Code provides that when a qualified exchange of properties is made, some or all of the gain on an economic basis may not have to be recognized for tax purposes. The property exchanged must be investment property or business property. If a qualified exchange occurs, the tax on the gain is postponed and the deduction of a loss must also be postponed. These requirements are not discretionary with the taxpayer or the government. If a transaction qualifies as an exchange, no gain or loss may be recognized in the year of the exchange. The property received by each exchangor is treated as if it were the same property each owned prior to the exchange.

Like-Kind Property

To qualify as an exchange, **like-kind properties** (within the U.S.) must be exchanged. Essentially, like-kind properties include an exchange of personal property for other personal property or the exchange of real property for other real property. Exchanges of like-kind real property include the following examples: the exchange of an office building for a shopping mall, apartment house for a tract of land, an office building for an apartment building. Examples of exchanges of personal property include a truck for a machine, an automobile for a truck. Personal residences and foreign property do not qualify for an exchange.

Business or Investment Property

The property exchanged must be held for use in business or as an investment. Property held for personal use will not qualify. Therefore, an exchange of residences by homeowners will not qualify as a tax-free exchange, but will be treated as a sale and a purchase.

Property Not Held for Sale

The property exchanged must not be property held for sale to customers, such as inventories of merchandise or inventories of lots held for sale by a developer.

Boot

If an exchangor receives cash or some other type of nonqualifying property in addition to like-kind property in exchange, the transaction will still qualify as a tax-deferred exchange. However, the recipient of the cash (**boot**) or other nonqualifying property incurs tax liability on the boot or other unlike-kind property (property not similar in nature and character to the property exchanged) in the calendar year of the exchange.

Basis

The basis of the property received by an exchangor is the basis of the property given up in exchange. Therefore, an exchangor does not change the basis of an asset as a result of the exchange. For example, Exchangor #1 trades a property with a market value of $100,000 and a basis of $20,000 for another property also worth $100,000. The property received by Exchangor #1 will also have a basis of $20,000 regardless of what the basis was to the other exchangor.

Multiple Exchange

A **multiple exchange** is one in which more than two properties are exchanged in one transaction. Usually, multiple exchanges are three-way exchanges. For example, A, B, and C each own like-kind real property held for investment or business purposes. In the exchange, A acquires the property owned by C, B acquires the property owned by A, and C acquires the property owned by B. Multiple exchanges qualify as tax deferred exchanges in the same manner that two-way exchanges qualify. It is not necessary for an exchangor to receive property in exchange from the same person to whom she is transferring her property in exchange.

Starker Exchange

The **Starker exchange** was held to qualify for tax deferment by a United States Circuit Court of Appeals in 1979. In this case, Starker sold land to a corporation. However, the purchaser withheld the purchase price until Starker subsequently found a suitable property to be purchased with the proceeds of the sale. The court held that this procedure qualified for treatment as a tax-deferred exchange because the sale proceeds were held beyond the control of the taxpayer seeking the tax-deferred exchange. The court viewed the exchange as one continuous transaction. Therefore, if the proceeds of a sale of property are held beyond the control of the seller until the seller can locate a like-kind property in which to invest the proceeds, the transaction may constitute a tax-free exchange.

IMPORTANT POINTS

1. Real estate agents must refrain from giving tax advice.
2. The Tax Reform Act of 1986 eliminated capital gains benefits and lengthened depreciation schedules for investment property.
3. Homeowner's real estate property taxes and mortgage interest are deductible expenses in calculating federal income tax liability.
4. Losses incurred in the sale of a home are not tax deductible.
5. The maximum capital gains tax rate is 15 percent for long-term capital gains.
6. There is a $250,000 exclusion of gain on a principal residence for a single taxpayer who owns and occupies his or her home for two out of the last five years.
7. There is a $500,000 exclusion of gain on a principal residence for married couples who own and occupy their home for two out of the last five years.
8. The installment sale tax laws apply to a principal residence as well as to business and investment property.
9. Depreciation enables the owner of business or investment property to recover the cost or other basis of the asset.
10. Land is not depreciable. Only structures on the land are depreciable real property.

11.   Depreciation for real property is now calculated at 27.5 years for residential property, and 39 years for all other property.

12.   When a depreciable asset is sold, the basis of the asset used to compute taxable gain is the depreciated value and not the price paid for the property by the seller.

13.   Depreciation is a deductible allowance from net income in arriving at taxable income. Thereby, it provides a tax shelter for the property owner.

14.   Expenses of operating business or investment property are deductible expenses in arriving at taxable income.

15.   To qualify as a tax-deferred exchange, like-kind property must be exchanged. An exchangor receiving cash (boot) or other unlike-kind property in addition to like-kind property is taxed on the value of the boot or other unlike-kind property received.

16.   To qualify as a tax-deferred exchange, the property exchanged must have been held for use in business (other than inventory) or as an investment. Property held for personal use does not qualify.

REVIEW QUESTIONS

Answers to these questions are found in the Answer Key section at the back of the book.

1. Which of the following is a tax deductible expense resulting from homeownership?
   a.   operating expenses
   b.   depreciation
   c.   mortgage interest
   d.   energy usage

2. The waiting period before the full $250,000/$500,000 exclusion may be reused is:
   a.   12 months
   b.   2 years
   c.   18 months
   d.   5 years

3. A widowed spouse can claim a:
   a. $500,000exclusion only in the year of the spouses death
   b. $500,000 forever if they bought the property jointly
   c. $250,000 only because she is a single taxpayer
   d. $500,000 exclusion within 2 years of the death of spouse

4. Discount points paid by the borrower to obtain a conventional mortgage loan to purchase a principal residence:
   a.   Do not increase the yield on the mortgage
   b.   Are not deductible by the borrower as interest
   c.   Are deductible by the borrower as interest
   d.   Have to be spread out over the term of loan

5. A mortgage prepayment penalty paid by a borrower as a requirement for early loan pay-off:
   a.   may be deducted as interest in the year paid
   b.   may be deducted as interest over a five-year period
   c.   may only be deducted from selling price as a selling expense
   d.   may not be taken as a deduction for any purpose

6. Under the Taxpayers Relief Act of 1997:
   a. The gain must be rolled over into a new purchase
   b. The homeowner must wait until he reaches the age of 55 to use exclusions
   c. Single taxpayers may exclude up to $250,000 of gain on principal residence
   d. May only exclude up to $125,000 of gain

7. Tom Taylor and Sarah Smith traded an office building for an apartment building. In the trade, Tom received $20,000 in cash in addition to Sarah's office building. With regard to this transaction, which of the following is correct?
   a. The transaction is not a tax-free exchange but just a sale and purchase
   b. The cash received disqualifies this as tax deferred exchange
   c. The cash received is called boot and is taxable for the year of the exchange
   d. The office building and apartment are not like-kind properties

8. Deductible expenses for a business property, but not a personal residence, include all of the following except:
   a. advertising
   b. utilities
   c. mortgage principal
   d. insurance

9. Charles and Carole own a vacation chalet that they use three weeks of the year and rent out the rest. What item can't they deduct?
   a. Mortgage Interest
   b. Property Taxes
   c. Rents
   d. Depreciation

10. In 2010 Ed and Margaret took advantage of the low interest rates to refinance their existing 30 year 8.5% mortgage with a 15 year 5% mortgage on their present home. They paid $1500 in discount point to refinance the loan. How will the cost of these points be treated in their income tax?
    a. The cost is added to the basis of their home
    b. The $1500 from their 2010 income
    c. They may deduct only $100 per year
    d. There is no deduction benefit at all.

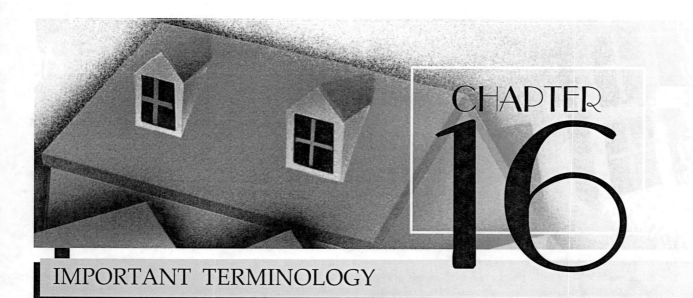

IMPORTANT TERMINOLOGY

REAL ESTATE MATH

IN THIS CHAPTER

The math normally involved in real estate transactions consists of nothing more than simple math. All that is required is the ability to add, subtract, multiply, and divide. These calculations are made with whole numbers, fractions, and decimal numbers.

The difficulty that some people encounter in solving real estate math problems is the conversion of word problems into the math symbols illustrating the calculations to be performed. For example, the word "of" is always translated into a multiplication sign. If something is one-half of something else, this means that the solution requires the multiplication of the fraction one-half times the other unit.

Some people entering the field of real estate brokerage have not dealt with math problems since their school days. Consequently, they are often a little rusty on math. For this reason we will begin our discussion of real estate math with a review of the basics.

PERCENTAGES

In the real estate brokerage business, many math calculations involve the use of percentages. For example, a real estate broker's commission is a percentage of the sales price.

A percentage is simply a number that has been divided by 100. To use a percentage in a math calculation, the percentage must be changed to its decimal equivalent. The rule for changing a percentage to a decimal is to remove the percent sign and move the decimal point two places to the left. The decimal point, in the percentage, is always between the last whole number in the percentage and the percent sign. Examples of converting a percentage to a decimal follow.

98%	= .98		$1^1/2\%$ =	1.5%	= .0150
1.42%	= .0142		$1^1/4\%$ =	1.25%	= .0125
.092%	= .00092		$^3/4\%$ =	.75%	= .0075

To change a decimal or a fraction to a percentage, simply reverse the procedure. This is done by moving the decimal point two places to the right and adding the percent sign. The following are some examples of this operation.

$$1.00 = 100\% \qquad\qquad \frac{1}{2} = \frac{.5}{2\,)\,1.0} = 50\%$$

$$.90 = 90\% \qquad\qquad \frac{3}{8} = \frac{.375}{8\,)\,3.000} = 37.5\%$$

$$.0075 = .75\% \qquad\qquad \frac{2}{3} = \frac{.666}{3\,)\,2.000} = 66.6\%$$

AREA PROBLEMS

Problems involving the determination of the size of an area in square feet, cubic feet, number of acres, and so forth are quite frequent in the real estate brokerage business. In taking a listing, the broker should determine the number of square feet of heated area in the house. In establishing the lot size, the number of square feet should be determined so that it may be translated into acreage, if desired. For measures and formulas to use in solving area problems, see Table 16.1.

Determining the Surface Area of a Rectangle or Square

The surface area of a rectangle or square is determined by simply multiplying the width by the length. In a square, the width and length are the same. In terms of a simple formula,

$$AREA = LENGTH \times WIDTH$$

or

$$A = L \times W \text{ (for a rectangle)}$$

or

$$A = S \times S \text{ (for a square)}$$

Table 16.1
Measures and formulas.

Linear Measure

12 inches = 1 foot

3 feet = 1 yard

$16^1/_2$ feet = 1 rod, 1 perch or 1 pole

66 feet = 1 chain

5,280 feet = 1 mile

Square Measure

144 sq. inches = 1 sq. foot

sq. feet = 1 sq. yard

$30^1/_4$ sq. yards = 1 sq. rod

160 sq. rods = 1 acre

43,560 sq. ft. = 1 acre

640 acres = 1 sq. mile

1 sq. mile = 1 section

36 sections = 1 township

Formulas

1 side × 1 side = area of a square

width × depth = area of a rectangle

$^1/_2$ base × height = area of a triangle

$^1/_2$ height × (base$_1$ + base$_2$) = area of a trapezoid

$^1/_2$ × sum of the bases = distance between the other two sides
at the mid-point of the height of a trapezoid

length × width × depth = volume (cubic measure)
of a cube or a rectangular solid

Cubic Measure

1,728 cubic inches = 1 cubic foot

27 cubic feet = 1 cubic yard

144 cubic inches = 1 board foot
(12" × 12" × 1")

Circular Measure

360 degrees = circle

60 minutes = 1 degree

60 seconds = 1 minute 9

Tax Valuation

Per $100 of Assessed Value: Divide the
AV by 100, then multiply by tax rate.

$$\frac{\text{Assessed Value}}{100} \times \text{Tax Rate}$$

Per Mill: Divide the AV by 1000,
then multiply by tax rate.

$$\frac{\text{Assessed Value}}{1000} \times \text{Tax Rate}$$

1. A rectangular lot measures 90 feet by 185 feet. How many square feet does this lot contain?

   Solution: $A = L \times W$
   $\quad\quad\quad\quad = 185 \times 90$
   $\quad\quad\quad\quad = 16{,}650$ square feet (SF)

   Answer: 16,650 SF

2. An acre of land has a width of 330 feet. If this acre of land were rectangular in shape, what would be its depth?

   Solution: Since $A = L \times W$,

   we can transpose this formula to solve for the length by applying the arithmetic operation of dividing both sides of the equation by WIDTH, or:

   $\dfrac{A}{W} = L$

   A number to learn at this time is that there are *43,560 square feet per acre.* Therefore, since we know the area in square feet and the width, we can solve for length.

   $43{,}560 = 330 \times L$

   or $\dfrac{43{,}560}{330} = 132$

   Answer: The lot is 132 feet deep.

3. If a parcel of land contained 32,670 square feet, what percent of an acre would it be?

   Solution: $\dfrac{32{,}670}{43{,}560} = 0.75$

   $.75 = 75\%$

   Answer: 75%

4. A room measures 15 feet by 21 feet. We want to install wall-to-wall carpet and need to calculate the exact amount of carpet required.

   Solution: Since carpet is sold by the square yard, we need to convert square feet to square yards.

   The number of square feet per square yard is $3 \times 3 = 9$ sq. ft. per square yard. Therefore, to convert size in square feet to size in square yards, we need to divide by 9.

   Area = $15 \times 21 = 315$ sq. ft.

   Answer: $\dfrac{315}{9} = 35$ square yards of carpet

5. A property owner's lot is 80 feet wide and 120 feet deep. The lot is rectangular. The property owner plans to have a fence constructed along both sides and across the rear boundary of the lot. The fence is to be 5 feet high. The property owner has determined that the labor cost in constructing the fence will be $1.25 per linear foot. The material cost will be $3.00 per square yard. What is the total cost of constructing the fence?

   Solution:
   Step 1: First determine the linear footage to establish the labor cost.
   $\quad\quad\quad 2 \times 120$ feet + 80 feet = 320 linear feet
   $\quad\quad\quad 320$ feet $\times$ $1.25 per linear foot = $400 labor cost

Step 2: Establish the number of square yards in the fence to determine material cost.

5 feet × 320 feet = 1600 square feet

1600 sq. ft./9 (9 sq. ft. in 1 sq. yd.) = 177.78 square yards

177.78 × $3.00 per sq. yd. = $533.34 material cost Step 3:

Total cost

$533.34 + $400 = $933.34

Answer: $933.34 total cost

6. The property owner in the previous problem plans to put a fence post every 10 linear feet for the total length of the fence. How many fence posts will be required?

Solution: $\dfrac{320 \text{ linear feet}}{10} = 32$

32 + 1 = 33

Answer: 33 posts

7. The property owner in the preceding two problems decides to enclose the property with a fence across the fourth side. How many fence posts will be required to enclose the entire property if the fence post interval is maintained at 10 feet?

Solution: (2 × 80 feet) + (2 × 120 feet) = 400 feet

$\dfrac{400}{10} = 40$

Answer: Total fence posts required for 400 linear feet is 40.

8. If a rectangular map measures 10 inches × 16 inches and 1 square inch of map surface represents an area of 20 square miles, how many square miles is represented by the map in total?

Solution: 10 inches × 16 inches = 160 square inches

160 × 20 sq. mi. = 3200 sq. mi.

Answer: 3200 square miles

9. A triangular lot measures 200 feet along the street and 500 feet in depth on the side that is perpendicular to the front lot line. If the lot sold for 10 cents per square foot, what is the selling price?

Solution: Try to visualize a triangle as half a rectangle.

Instead of measuring a triangle in length and width, we label the dimensions as base and height. Therefore, we can visualize the formula for a triangle as half of the product of height times base or:

$A = \dfrac{h \times b}{2}$

$= \dfrac{500 \times 200}{2}$

= 50,000 square feet

50,000 square feet × $0.10 = $5,000

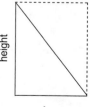

height

base

Answer: $5,000.00 sales price

10. The plan shown is to be changed so that the garage doors are located at the east end of the garage. There is to be a new driveway installed that will be parallel to and the same width as the driveway shown and is to extend from the north end

of the garage to the street. The paving cost is $.35 per square foot. What will be the minimum cost to pave the new driveway?

Solution:

Step 1:   Area = length × width

A = (90 + 25) × 20

A = 115 × 20

A = 2300 square feet

Step 2:   Cost = 2300 × $.35

Cost = $805.00

Answer: $805.00 cost

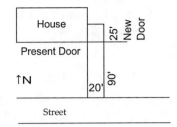

11. What percentage of the lot is occupied by the house shown in the diagram?

Solution:

Step 1:   Divide lot into one triangle and one rectangle

Area of triangle = 1/2 base × height

A = 1/2 × 250 feet × 150 feet

A = 18,750 square feet

Area of rectangle = length × width

A = 400 feet × 150 feet

A = 60,000 square feet

Total lot area = 18,750 sq. ft. + 60,000 sq. ft. Lot area = 78,750 square feet

Step 2:   Divide house into two rectangles Area of small rectangle = L × W

A = 30 feet × 30 feet

A = 900 square feet

Area of large rectangle = L × W

A = 150 feet × 30 feet

A = 4500 square feet

Total house area = 900 sq. ft. + 4500 sq. ft.

A = 5400 square feet

Step 3:   Percentage of lot occupied by house = house footage/lot footage

$$\frac{5,400}{78,750} = 0.0685$$

0.685 = 6.85%

Answer: 6.85% of lot occupied by house

12. How many square feet are in the following lot?

Solution: Divide the figure into common shapes that you can work with, such as a rectangle and two triangles. By drawing two parallel lines, we carve the figure into a rectangle that measures 80 × 240 feet, and two triangles that have a height of 240 feet. We can figure the base of each by subtracting the 80 feet of the rectangle from the total of 160 feet, which is a total of 80 feet for the two triangles, or 40 feet each.

Step 1:   Area of the rectangle is

A = 80 × 240 = 19,200 square feet

Step 2:   Calculate the area of each triangle. Since there are two triangles,

2 × 4,800 = 9,600 square feet

Answer: Total area is, therefore, 19,200 sq. ft. + 9,600 sq. ft. = 28,800 square feet

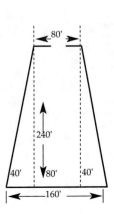

13. A house measures 28 feet wide by 52 feet long and sells for $64,000. What is its price per square foot?

Solution:

Step 1: Calculate the area

A = 28 × 52 = 1456 square feet

Step 2: Divide the price by the area

Answer: $\frac{\$64,000}{1456}$ = $43.96 square feet

Caution: Since there is always a possibility of getting mixed up and dividing the wrong way, always check your answer before looking at the answer key.

For example: $43.96 per square foot × 1456 = $64,000

If you were to look at the answer key before doing this check, you may well find your answer even though it is wrong, because the test is specifically designed to include all of the likely wrong answers as distracter items to fool the unwary.

14. A rectangular lot that measures 250 feet by 350 feet sells for $10,000. What is the price per square foot?

Solution:

Step 1: A = 250 × 350 = 87,500 square feet

Step 2: Divide the price by the size $\frac{\$10,000}{87,500}$ = $0.114

Answer: $0.114

Caution: As discussed in the previous problem, check your answer before looking at the answer key. It is easy to come up with an answer of $8.75 which is, of course, wrong but also guaranteed to be a choice in the answer key.

15. The perimeter of a rectangular lot (see below) is 1800 yards. The length is twice the width plus 6 yards. What is the length in feet?

Solution: Perimeter of a rectangle = (2 × width) + (2 × length)

Length = 2W + 6 yards

Width = W

Therefore:

6 × width + 12 yards = perimeter (1800 yards)

6 × width = 1800 − 12

6W = 1788 yards

W = $\frac{1788}{6}$

W = 298 yards

2 × 298 + 6 = length

596 + 6 = 602 yards

602 × 3 = 1806 (length in feet)

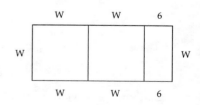

Answer: 1806 feet

16. The house with an area as shown on page 259 originally cost $15 per square foot to build. If it were built today, it would cost $56,000. How much has the cost per square foot increased (in dollars)?

Solution: Divide the house into 3 triangles and 1 square

Area of a triangle = ½ bh

A = ½(40 × 20)

A = 400 sq. ft.

3 × 400 = 1200 sq. ft

Area of a square = 1 side × 1 side
A = 20 × 20
A = 400

Total area = 1200 + 400

Total area = 1600 square feet
$56,000/1600 = $35 cost per square foot today
$35 − $15 = $20 per square foot cost increase

Answer: $20 per square foot

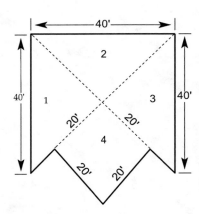

Cubic Area (Volume)

The next type of area problem that is to be considered involves cubic area. Cubic area is three dimensional. To determine the amount of cubic area or volume in a given space, multiply length × width × depth.

17. A house under construction contains a rectangular basement that is 20 feet wide and 30 feet long. If the basement is excavated to a uniform depth of 12 feet, how many cubic yards of dirt must be removed?

   Solution: Volume = Length × Width × Depth
   Cubic feet per cubic yard is therefore
   V = L × W × D or
   Cubic feet per cubic yard = 3 × 3 × 3 = 27
   Therefore:
   a. There are 27 cubic feet per cubic yard.
   b. To change from cubic feet to cubic yards, you have to divide by 27.
      20 ft. × 30 ft. × 12 ft. = 7200 cu. ft.
      7200/27 (cu. ft. in 1 cu. yd.) = 266.67 cu. yds.

   Answer: 266.67 cubic yards of dirt must be removed.

18. A home contains a triangular attic that is 15 feet wide, 30 feet long, and 6 feet high at the ridge beam of the roof. How many cubic feet of space are there in the attic?

   Solution: $\dfrac{15 \times 30 \times 6}{2} = 1350$

   Answer: 1350 cubic feet

19. A homeowner obtains a quotation to have his driveway paved. The driveway is to be 9 feet wide, 30 yards long, and 4 inches thick. The quotation specifies that the labor cost will be $3.00 per square yard. The material cost is quoted at $4.00 per cubic foot. What will be the total cost of the driveway?

   Solution: Labor cost
   3 yds. × 30 yds. = 90 sq. yds.
   90 sq. yds. × $3.00 = $270.00 labor cost

   Material cost
   9 ft. × 90 ft. × 1/3 ft. = 270 cu. ft.
   270 cu. ft. × $4.00 per cu. ft. = $1,080 material cost

   Total cost
   $270 labor cost + $1,080 material cost = $1,350

   Answer: $1,350 total cost of driveway construction

In the previous problems the information was given in a mixture of feet, yards, and inches. In this type of problem, care must be taken to convert the dimensions to the same basis to arrive at a correct answer. In calculating the labor cost, the dimensions to obtain the surface area were all converted to yards because the labor cost was quoted at $3.00 per square yard. In calculating the material cost, the dimensions were converted to feet because the material cost was quoted at $4.00 per cubic foot. The 4 inches is 1/3 of a foot.

PRORATION PROBLEMS

Proration is involved in the real estate brokerage business in dividing between seller and buyer the annual real property taxes and rents and in establishing the cost to the buyer of an insurance policy that is being purchased from the seller. Prorating is the process of dividing something into appropriate shares.

In prorating calculations, the best method to follow is to first determine the used portion. In calculating prorations for closing disclosures, the amount is figured to the day of closing. An example of this would be in prorating the real property tax for a closing to take place on June 1, where the annual real property tax is $240. In the example, the monthly tax rate would be $20. Five months have transpired in the tax year from January 1 through the end of May. Therefore, five months × $20 per month = $100 for the seller's share of the real property taxes. This amount then appears in the closing disclosure as a debit to the seller and a credit to the buyer.

In problems that require the calculation on a daily rate, divide the total taxes by 365 to arrive at a daily tax rate. Multiply the daily tax rate by the number of days to be reimbursed to either buyer or seller.

1. If in this example, the closing date were May 13 instead of May 30, and the seller wants to reimburse the buyer from January 1 to May 13, the number of days would be

   January 31
   February 28
   March 31
   April 30
   May 12
   132 days

   $$\frac{\$240}{365} \times 132 = \$86.79$$

   One other rule to remember in prorating various costs for the closing disclosure is that the day of closing is charged to the buyer.

2. In preparing a closing disclosure for a closing to be held on August 14, a real estate broker determined that the annual real property taxes in the amount of $365 had not been paid. What will the broker put in the buyer's statement as her entry for real property taxes?

   Solution: $365 ÷ 365 = $1 per day
   Jan. 31, Feb. 28, March 31, April 30, May 31, June 30, July 31, Aug. 13 =
   225 days × $1 = $225

   Answer: Credit to buyer in the amount of $225. This is the seller's share of the real property taxes to cover the 225 days of the tax year during which he owned the property.

3. A sale is closed on September 16. The buyer is assuming the seller's mortgage, which has an outstanding balance of $32,000 as of the date of closing. The annual interest rate is 8% and the interest is paid in arrears. What would be the interest proration on the closing disclosures prepared by the broker?

Solution: $32,000 × .08 = 2,560 annual interest

$2,560 ÷ 12 = $213.33 interest for September

$\frac{1}{2}$ × $213.33 = $106.67 interest for ½ monrh

or

$2,560 ÷ 24 = $106.67 interest for ½ month

Answer: Credit buyer $106.67
Debit seller $106.67

THE $\dfrac{I}{R \times V}$ FORMULA

Problems involving commissions are readily solved by a simple formula illustrated as follows:

$$\frac{I}{R \times V}$$

In this formula, I represents income, R represents rate, and V represents value. In these problems, one of the three elements will be the unknown quantity that will be the answer to the problem. The other two will be provided. In using the formula, simply cover the letter representing the unknown quantity and perform the calculation indicated. For example, if the unknown quantity or answer sought is income, covering the I in the formula reveals that rate is to be multiplied by value (R × V). The result of this multiplication will be the income. If the known quantities are income and rate and the unknown quantity is value, covering the V results in an indicated calculation of dividing rate into income. The result of this division will be the value.

To clarify the formula and its application in solving for any one of three possible unknowns, the following material is presented to demonstrate its use.

The formula may be written in three different ways to solve for different unknowns, as follows:

Income = Rate × Value

Rate = $\dfrac{\text{Income}}{\text{Value}}$

Value = $\dfrac{\text{Income}}{\text{Rate}}$

Or, as previously discussed, the formula may be written and applied as follows: The horizontal line separating income from R × V indicates that, in solving for rate, value is to be divided into income. When value is the unknown, rate is to be divided into income. The multiplication sign between R and V shows that rate is to be multiplied by value to solve for income, when income is the unknown quantity. Simply cover up the unknown item and perform the indicated calculations.

Commission Problems

1. A real estate broker sold a property for $80,000. Her rate of commission is 6%. What was the amount of commission in dollars?

   Solution: Commission value = $80,000, rate = 0.06, income is unknown
   $80,000 × 0.06 = $4,800

   Answer: $4,800 commission

2. A real estate broker earns a commission of $3,000 in the sale of a residential property. His rate of commission is 6%. What was the selling price of the property?

   Solution: Income = $3,000, rate = 0.06, value is unknown

   $$\frac{\$3,000}{0.06} = \$50,000$$

   Answer: $50,000 sales price

3. A real estate broker earns a commission of $1,500 in the sale of a property for $25,000. What was her rate of commission?

   Solution: Value = $25,000, income = $1,500, rate is unknown

   $$\frac{\$1,500}{\$25,000} = 0.06$$

   Answer: 6% commission rate

4. A real estate salesperson sells a property for $70,000. The commission on this sale to the real estate firm with whom the salesperson is associated is 6%. The salesperson receives 60% of the commission paid to the real estate firm. What is the firm's share of the commission in dollars?

   Solution: Value = $70,000, rate = 0.06, income is unknown
   $70,000 × 0.06 = $4,200
   100% − 60% = 40% (firm's percentage of commission)
   $4,200 × 0.40 = $1,680

   Answer: $1,680 firm's share of the commission

5. A broker's commission was 10% of the first $50,000 of the sales price of a property and 8% on the amount of sales price over $50,000. The broker received a total commission of $7,000. What was the total selling price of the property?

   Solution:

   Step 1:   Rate = 0.10, value = $50,000, income is unknown
   $50,000 × 0.10 = $5,000 commission on first $50,000 of sales price

   Step 2:   Total commission minus commission on first $50,000 = commission on amount over $50,000
   $7,000 − $5,000 = $2,000 commission on selling price over $50,000

   Step 3: $2,000 = income, 0.08 = rate, value is unknown

   $$\frac{Income}{Rate} = Value$$

   $$\frac{\$2,000}{0.08} = \$25,000$$

   Step 4: $50,000 + $25,000 = $75,000

   Answer: $75,000 total selling price

6. A seller advises a broker that he expects to net $50,000 from the sale of his property after the broker's commission of 6% is deducted from the proceeds of the sale. For what price must the property be sold to provide a $50,000 net return to the seller after paying the broker a 6% commission on the total sales price?

Solution: 100% = gross sales price

100% − 6% = 94%

94% = net to owner

$50,000 = 94% × sales price

Solving for the sales price

$\frac{50,000}{94\%}$ = minimum sales price = $53,191.48

Answer: $53,191.48 gross selling price

Capitalization Problems

Capitalization problems revolve around rate, income, and value, in which one of these is unknown. The solution to these problems is based on the use of the formula in the same manner that the commission problems are solved.

1. An apartment building produces a net income of $4,320 per annum. The investor paid $36,000 for the apartment building. What is the owner's rate of return on investment?

   Solution: Income = $4,320, value = $36,000, rate is unknown

   $\frac{\$4,320}{\$36,000}$ = 0.12 or 12%

   Answer: 12% is annual rate of return on the investment

2. An investor is considering the purchase of an office building for $75,000. The investor insists upon a 14% return on investment. What must be the amount of the annual net income from this investment to return a profit to the owner at a rate of 14%?

   Solution: Value = $75,000, rate = 14%, income is unknown

   $75,000 × 14% = $10,500

   Answer: $10,500 annual net income

3. In appraising a shopping center, the appraiser has established that the center produces a net income of $97,500. The appraiser has developed the capitalization rate to be 13%. What should be the appraiser's estimate of market value for this shopping center?

   Solution: Income = $97,500, rate = 13%, value is unknown

   $\frac{\$97,500}{13\%}$ = $750,000

   Answer: $750,000 value estimate

Interest Problems

Interest problems also use the income, rate, value formula.

The amount of interest is the income, the percent return on the money owed or invested is the rate, and the amount of money invested or borrowed is the value.

1. On October 1, a mortgagor made a $300 payment on her mortgage, which is at the rate of 10%. Of the $300 total payment for principal and interest, the mortgagee allocated $200 to the payment of interest. What is the principal balance due on the mortgage on the date of payment?

   Solution: $200 × 12 months = $2,400 annual interest income

   $$\frac{Income}{Value} = Rate$$

   $$\frac{\$2,400}{10\%} = \$24,000$$

   Answer: $24,000 mortgage balance due

2. If an outstanding mortgage balance is $16,363.64 on the payment due date and the amount of the payment applied to interest is $150, what is the rate of interest charged on the loan?

   Solution: $150 × 12 months = $1,800 annual interest

   $$\frac{Income}{Value} = Rate$$

   $$\frac{\$1,800.00}{\$16,363.64} = 0.11$$

   Answer: 11% interest rate

3. If $27,000 is invested at 8.25%, what will be the annual income resulting from the investment?

   Solution: Rate is 8.25%, value is $27,000, income is unknown
   Income = Rate × Value
   $27,000 × 8.25% = $2,227.50

   Answer: $2,227.50 annual income

4. A mortgage loan of $50,000 at 11% interest requires monthly payments of principal and interest in the amount of $516.10 to fully amortize the loan for a term of 20 years. If the loan is paid over the 20-year term, how much interest does the borrower pay?

   Solution: 20 years × 12 months per year = 240 payments
   240 × $516.10 = $123,864 total amount paid

   Total amount paid – principal borrowed = interest paid
   $123,864 – $50,000 = $73,864

   Answer: $73,864 interest paid

5. When making the second monthly payment of $548.85 on a $60,000 mortgage loan at 10.5% for 30 years, how much interest does the borrower pay?

   Solution: $60,000 × 0.105 = $6,300 annual interest
   $6,300 ÷ 12 months = $525 interest first month
   $548.85 – $525.00 = $23.85 principal first month
   $60,000 – $23.85 = $59,976.15 principal balance after first payment
   $59,976.15 × 0.105 = $6,297.495 annual interest
   $6,297.495 ÷ 12 months = $524.79 interest second month

   Answer: Borrower pays $524.79 in the second month. This same procedure can be followed to calculate interest or principal paid in third, fourth, or fifth month.

PERCENT CHANGE PROBLEMS

Depreciation and Appreciation Problems

Depreciation is a loss in value from any cause. The two examples of depreciation problems that follow are representative of the types of depreciation problems that a real estate student or practitioner may encounter.

In problem one, the present value of a building is given and the requirement is to calculate the original value. Problem two provides the original value to be used in arriving at the present depreciated value. Problem three is an example of a typical appreciation problem, but it also illustrates the method of calculating the percentage of appreciation. Notice that in this problem, the house and lot appreciate at different rates and as usual have different original values. Therefore the appreciation must be calculated separately and then combined into a total appreciated or current value.

1. The value of a six-year-old building is estimated to be $45,900. What was the value when new if the building had depreciated 12%?

   Solution: 6 yrs. × 2% = 12% depreciation
   100% (new value) − 12% = 88%
   88% = $45,900 (present value)
   $45,900 ÷ 0.88 = $52,159.09

   Answer: $52,159.09 was value when new

2. A 14-year-old building has a total economic life of 40 years. If the original value of the building was $75,000, what is the present undepreciated value?

   Solution: 100% ÷ 40 yrs. = yearly depreciation rate
   1.00 ÷ 40 = 0.025 or 2.5% yearly depreciation
   14 yrs. × 2.5% = 35% depreciation to date
   100% − 35% = 65% remaining value

   Original cost × % of remaining value = remaining dollar value
   $75,000 × 0.65 = $48,750

   Answer: Present undepreciated value is $48,750

Percent change problems can also be analyzed by simply comparing the amount of change in any value to the starting amount of that same item, i.e., dividing the change by the original value:

$$\frac{\text{Amount of change}}{\text{Original value}} \times 100 = \% \text{ Change}$$

3. A 10-year-old house was constructed at a cost of $20,000. The land cost was $2,000. The house has appreciated 40% and the land has appreciated 80%. What is the total percentage of appreciation for the house and the land together?

   Solution: Current value = Original value × Appreciation
   House CV = $20,000 × 1.40
   House CV = $28,000

   Lot CV = $2,000 × 1.80

   Lot CV = $3,600

   Total current value = $28,000 + $3,600

   TCV = $31,600

Value increase = Current value less original value

VI = $31,600 − $22,000

VI = $9,600

Percentage appreciation = Value increase ÷ Original value

PA = $9,600 ÷ $22,000

Answer: 43.63%

Change in Equity Problems

1. An owner bought a home for $50,000 with an 80% loan. A few years later the home was worth $60,000 and the loan was paid down to $35,000. What was the percentage change in equity?

    Solution:

    Step 1:   Calculate the original equity.
                   $50,000 value × 80% = $40,000
                   $50,000 value − $40,000 loan = $10,000 equity
    Step 2:   Calculate the new equity.
                   $60,000 − $35,000 = 25,000 equity
    Step 3:   Calculate the change in equity.
                   $25,000 − $10,000 = $15,000 change in equity
    Step 4:   Divide the amount of change by the original value.

                   $\dfrac{\$15,000}{\$10,000} \times 100 = 150\%$ increase in equity

    Answer: 150% increase in equity

TAXATION PROBLEMS

Certain terms must be understood to solve problems involving real property taxes. "Assessed value" is the value established by a tax assessor. The tax value or assessed value is usually a percentage of the estimated market value of the property and may be up to 100 percent of market value. The amount of tax is calculated by multiplying the assessed value by the tax rate, which is expressed in mills (one mill is one-tenth of a cent) per $1,000 of assessed value.

1. If the assessed value of a property is $40,000 and the mill rate is 40 mills, what is the annual tax?

    Solution: Assessment $40,000
                       Mill rate 40 mills (40 × 0.001) = 0.040
                       Taxes $1,600 (40,000 × 0.040)

    Answer: $1,600 annual taxes

2. A property is sold at the assessed value. The annual real property tax is $294.40 at a tax rate of 80 mills. What is the selling price?

    Solution: Taxes $294.40
                       Mill rate 80 mills (80 × 0.001) = 0.080
                       $294.40 ÷ 0.080 = $3,680

    Answer: $3,680 selling price

3. If the assessed value of a property is $68,000, and the annual tax paid is $850, what is the mill rate?

Solution: 850 ÷ 68,000 = 0.0125
0.0125 × 1,000 = 12.5

Answer: Mill rate 12.5 mills

4. If the market value is $70,000, the tax rate is 120 mills, and the assessment is 80%, what is the semiannual tax bill?

Solution: Assessed value = 0.80 × $70,000
Assessed value = $56,000
Annual tax bill = $56,000 × 0.120
Annual tax bill = $6,720
Semiannual tax bill = $6,720 ÷ 2
Semiannual tax bill = $3,360

Answer: $3,360

PERCENTAGE LEASE PROBLEMS

1. The rental clause in a commercial lease specified a minimum monthly rental of $400 plus 2.5% of the gross yearly income of the tenant over $160,000. The lessee did a gross business of $240,000 during the first year of the lease. What was the annual rent paid by the lessee?

Solution: 12 × $400 = $4,800 basic rent
$240,000 − $160,000 = $80,000 (excess income over $160,000)
$80,000 × 0.025 = $2,000 (rent on excess over $160,000)
$4,800 + $2,000 = $6,800

Answer: $6,800 total rent first year

2. A percentage lease specifies a rent of $600 per month and 3% of the gross sales of the lessee over $130,000. The total rent paid at the end of the year was $8,300. What was the lessee's gross business income?

Solution: 12 × $600 = $7,200 (minimum rent for one year)
$8,300 − $7,200 = $1,100 (rent exceeding minimum)

Income ÷ Rate = Value
$1,100 ÷ 0.03 = $36,666.67 (gross over $130,000)
$130,000 + $36,666.67 = $166,666.67

Answer: $166,666.67 gross income

3. If a lease specifies the rent to be 2% of gross sales per annum, with a minimum annual rent of $8,000, what is the annual rent if gross sales were $1,200,000?

Solution: $1,200,000 × 0.02 = $24,000

Answer: $24,000 annual rent

MISCELLANEOUS PROBLEMS

1. If 18 pumps produce 4,000 gallons of water in 6 hours, how many pumps would be required to pump 6,000 gallons of water in 3 hours?

Solution: $\frac{18}{?} \times \frac{6000}{4000} \times \frac{6}{3} = \frac{648}{12} = 54$

Answer: 54 pumps

As previously illustrated, a simple method for solving this problem is to merely restate the problem and invert the gallon quantities in the restatement. The zeros in the gallon quantities can be cancelled out to reduce the size of the numbers generated. After the problem has been restated, multiply the numbers in the numerators by each other. The result of this multiplication is 648. Multiply the two numbers in the denominators by each other. The result of this multiplication is 12. Divide the denominator into the numerator to arrive at the answer: $648 \div 12 = 54$.

2. A subdivision contained 400 lots. If a broker sold 25% of the lots and his sales force sold one-half of the remaining lots, how many lots are still unsold?

    Solution: $0.25 \times 400 = 100$
    $400 - 100 = 300$
    $300 \times \dfrac{1}{2} = 150$

    Answer: 150 lots still unsold

3. In planning the development of a tract of land, the developer allocated one-half of the total area to single-family dwellings, one-third of the area to multifamily dwellings, and 60 acres to be used for roads and recreation areas. What is the total number of acres in the tract?

    Solution: Single-family one-half $= \dfrac{3}{6}$

    Multifamily one-third $= \dfrac{2}{6}$

    $\dfrac{3}{6} + \dfrac{2}{6} = \dfrac{5}{6}$

    $\dfrac{6}{6} =$ entire tract

    $\dfrac{6}{6} - \dfrac{5}{6} = \dfrac{1}{6}$

    $\dfrac{1}{6} = 60$ acres

    $6 \times 60 = 360$ acres

    Answer: 360 acres total

4. A developer paid $1,200 per acre for a 100-acre tract. If the developer constructs 18 houses at a cost of $30,000 each and the cost for the other improvements to the land is $36,000, what would be the average sales price of the houses to ensure a profit of 16% to the developer?

    Solution: 100 acres × $1,200 = $120,000
    18 houses × $30,000 = $540,000
    Improvements = $36,000
    $120,000 + $540,000 + $36,000 = $696,000 total investment
    116% of $696,000 = total sales price of 18 houses
    1.16 × $696,000 = $807,360.00
    $807,360.00 ÷ 18 = $44,853.33

    Answer: $44,853.33 average sales price per house

5. The market value of a property was estimated to be $70,000 in 1975. During 1977, the owner put it on the market for 15% above the 1975 market value. She accepted an offer for 10% less than the asking price. What was the amount of the offer?

Solution: $70,000 × 115% = asking price
$70,000 × 1.15 = $80,500
Asking price × 90% = offer
$80,500 × 0.90 = $72,450 offer

Answer: $72,450 amount of offer

6. An owner purchased his home at 8% below market value. He then sold the property for the original market value. What was the rate of profit?

Solution: Market value = 100%
100% ÷ 8% = 92% of market value (purchase price)
8% ÷ 92% = rate of profit
0.08 ÷ 0.92 = 0.0869 or 8.69%

Answer: 8.69% rate of profit

REVIEW QUESTIONS

Answers to these questions are found in the Answer Key section at the back of the book.

1. A sale is closed on February 12. The buyer is assuming the seller's mortgage, which has an outstanding balance of $28,000 as of the date of closing. The annual interest rate is 7.75 percent and is paid in arrears. What would be the interest proration appearing in the buyer's closing statement?
   a. $65.45 credit
   b. $77.52 credit
   c. $180.83 debit
   d. $253.19 credit

2. A real estate broker earns a commission of $2,400 at a rate of 6 percent. What was the selling price of the property?
   a. $14,400
   b. $24,000
   c. $25,000
   d. $40,000

3. A property is sold at market value. The market value and the tax value are the same. If the tax value is 100 percent of assessed value, the tax rate is 20 mills, and the annual tax is $720.00, what was the selling price of the property?
   a. $24,000
   b. $27,770
   c. $36,000
   d. $81,000

4. If 36 pumps produce 9,000 gallons of water in 4 hours, how many pumps would be required to pump 12,000 gallons of water in 12 hours?
   a. 8
   b. 9
   c. 12
   d. 16

5. What is the annual rent if a lease specifies the rent to be 2.5 percent of gross sales per annum, with a minimum annual rent of $4,800.00, if the lessee's gross sales were $192,000?
   a. $4,800
   b. $7,680
   c. $12,000
   d. $16,000

6. The scale of a map is 1 inch equals 2.5 miles. What would be the distance represented by 4.5 inches on the map?
   a. 7 miles
   b. 11.25 miles
   c. 18 miles
   d. 180 miles

7. A rectangular lot measured 40 yards in depth and had a frontage of 80 feet. How many acres did the lot contain?
   a. .07
   b. .21
   c. .22
   d. .70

8. A real estate salesperson earns $18,000 per year. If she receives 60 percent of the 6 percent commissions paid to her firm on her sales, what is her monthly dollar volume of sales?
   a. $25,000.00
   b. $33,333.33
   c. $41,666.67
   d. $90,000.00

9. How many fence posts would be required in the construction of a three-sided fence if each side were 30 feet long and 5 feet high and the posts were placed at 10-foot intervals starting at one corner?
   a. 8
   b. 10
   c. 12
   d. 15

10. A parking lot containing two acres nets $12,000 per year. The owner wishes to retire and sell his parking lot for an amount that will net him $12,000 per year by investing the proceeds of the sale at 8.5 percent per annum. What must the selling price be to accomplish the owner's objective?
    a. $96,000
    b. $102,000
    c. $120,000
    d. $141,176

11. A group of investors purchased two tracts of land. They paid $48,000 for the first tract. The first tract cost 80 percent of the cost of the second tract. What was the cost of the second tract?
    a. $9,600
    b. $28,800
    c. $60,000
    d. $125,000

12. A buyer obtains a commitment for an FHA loan in the amount of $27,000. If the current FHA interest rate is 7.75 percent and the lender requires sufficient discount points to increase the effective interest rate to 8 percent, what dollar amount will be paid for the necessary discount points?
    a. $270
    b. $540
    c. $675
    d. $1,080

13. A property owner constructed a 6-foot high fence around her rectangular lot, which measured 140 feet by 265 feet. The fence cost $3 per square yard. What was the total cost of the fence?
    a. $540
    b. $1,215
    c. $1,458
    d. $1,620

14. An office building produces a gross income of $12,600 per year. The vacancy factor is 5 percent and the annual expenses are $3,600. What is the market value if the capitalization rate is 12 percent?
    a. $15,120
    b. $69,750
    c. $99,750
    d. $105,000

15. If the monthly interest payment due on a mortgage on December 1 is $570 and the annual interest rate is 9 percent, what is the outstanding mortgage balance?
    a. $52,000
    b. $61,560
    c. $76,000
    d. $108,000

16. A building has a total economic life of 50 years. The building is now 5 years old and has a depreciated value of $810,000. What was the value of the building when new?
    a. $891,000
    b. $900,000
    c. $972,000
    d. $1,234,568

17. If the tax value is 100 percent of the assessed value and the assessed value is $63,000, what are the annual taxes if the rate is 30 mills?
    a. $1,328
    b. $1,890
    c. $3,011
    d. $3,320

18. If the perimeter of a rectangle is 1,800 yards and the yards length is 6 more than twice the width, how long is the length in feet?
    a. 298 feet
    b. 596 feet
    c. 602 feet
    d. 1,806 feet

19. If Jackson buys three parcels of land for $4,000 each and sells them as four separate parcels for $4,500 each, what percent profit does he make?
    a. 33%
    b. 50%
    c. 60%
    d. 150%

20. The current value of a 12-year-old house is $26,000. If this house has an economic life of 40 years, what was its value when new?
    a. $31,951.22
    b. $32,527.85
    c. $37,014.29
    d. $37,142.86

21. What would be the answer as a decimal of this problem?

    $$\frac{3}{5} \times \frac{5}{8} \div \frac{5}{6} =$$

    a. 0.313
    b. 0.45
    c. 0.78
    d. 1.25

22. The outside dimensions of a rectangular house are 35 feet by 26.5 feet; if the walls are all 9 inches thick, what is the square footage of the interior?
    a. 827.5 sq. ft.
    b. 837.5 sq. ft.
    c. 927.5 sq. ft.
    d. 947.7 sq. ft.

23. A buyer is to assume a seller's existing loan with an outstanding balance of $20,000 as of the date of closing. The interest rate is 9 percent and payments are made in arrears. Closing is set for October 10. What will be the entry in the seller's closing disclosure?
    a. $44.37 credit
    b. $44.37 debit
    c. $150 credit
    d. $150 debit

24. A house is listed for $40,000. An offer was made and accepted for $38,500, if the seller agreed to pay 5.5 percent discount points on a VA loan of $33,000. The broker's fee was at a rate of 6 percent. How much will the seller net from the sale?
    a. $34,375
    b. $35,875
    c. $36,382.50
    d. $38,500

25. A house and lot were assessed for 60 percent of market value and taxed at a rate of $3.75 per $100 of assessed value. Five years later the same tax rate and assessment rate still exist, but annual taxes have increased by $750. How much has the dollar value of the property increased?

    a. $8,752.75
    b. $20,000
    c. $33,333.33
    d. $38,385.82

26. What would be the sales price of an apartment complex having an annual rental of $80,000 with expenses of $8,000 annually if the purchaser receives an 8 percent return?
    a. $800,000
    b. $864,000
    c. $900,000
    d. $1,000,000

27. A city with rent-control guidelines says that a landlord may increase the rent on apartments by 2.25 percent of the cost of improvements made to the property. The landlord spent $1,200 per unit for improvements, and then raised the rent from $180 to $215. By how much has the owner exceeded the guidelines?
    a. $8
    b. $15
    c. $27
    d. $35

28. A lease specifies that there is to be a minimum monthly rental of $500 plus 3 percent of all business over $185,000. If the lessee did a gross business of $220,000, how much rent was paid that year?
    a. $6,000
    b. $7,050
    c. $11,550
    d. $12,600

29. A tract of land was divided up as one-half the total area for single-family dwellings, one-fourth the area for a shopping area, and one-eighth of the area for streets and parking areas. The remaining 7 acres are used for parks. What would be the total acreage of the entire tract?
    a. 28 acres
    b. 49 acres
    c. 56 acres
    d. 70 acres

30. An apartment building contains 20 units. Each unit rents for $180 per month. The vacancy rate is 5 percent. Annual expenses are $3,500 for maintenance, $1,200 insurance, $1,500 taxes, $900 utilities, $15,000 interest, and 10 percent of the gross effective income for management fee. What was the investor's net rate of return for the first year if she paid $195,000 for the property?
    a. 7.61 percent
    b. 8.62 percent
    c. 13.43 percent
    d. 22.05 percent

31. A house had an assessed value of $35,000 and the lot had an assessed value of $7,000. The property was taxed at 80 percent of assessed value at a rate of 21.2 mills. If the assessed valuation is to be increased by 18 percent, what will be the amount of taxes to be paid on the property?
    a. $712.32
    b. $840.54
    c. $890.40
    d. $1,050.67

32. A building was valued at $110,000 four years ago. Each year since that time, it has depreciated 3 percent of each preceding year's value. What is the value today?

    a. $77,000
    b. $96,800
    c. $97,382
    d. $106,700

33. An owner listed a property for sale with a broker. At what price must the property be sold to net the owner $7,000 after paying a 7 percent commission and satisfying the existing $18,000 mortgage?

    a. $19,354
    b. $26,750
    c. $26,882
    d. $27,750

34. A 12-year-old house was constructed at a cost of $32,000 on a lot costing $4,000. The house has appreciated 42 percent and the lot has appreciated 36 percent. What is the total percent appreciation for the house and lot combined?

    a. 29.24 percent
    b. 41.33 percent
    c. 70.75 percent
    d. 78.89 percent

35. The value of a 7-year-old building is estimated to be $63,000. What was the value when new if the building had depreciated 17.5 percent over 7 years?

    a. $67,725
    b. $74,025
    c. $76,363
    d. $114,975

36. An investor built an office building at a cost of $320,000 on land costing $40,000. Other site improvements totaled $20,000. What must be the amount of the annual net income from the property to return a profit to the owner at an annual rate of 12 percent?

    a. $31,666
    b. $38,400
    c. $43,200
    d. $45,600

37. A real estate sale was closed on February 20. The real property taxes have not been paid. The assessed value of the property is $67,500 and the tax value is 80 percent of the assessed value. Tax rate is 15 mills. What is the proper entry on the seller's settlement statement regarding the real property taxes?

    a. $111.00 credit
    b. $111.00 debit
    c. $697.50 credit
    d. $697.50 debit

38. A triangular lot measures 350 feet along the street and 425 feet in depth on the side that is perpendicular to the street. If the lot was sold by a broker for 75 cents per square foot and his commission rate was 9 percent, what was the amount of commission earned?

    a. $5,020.31
    b. $6,693.75
    c. $10,040.63
    d. $14,875.00

39. A property owner is having a concrete patio poured at the rear of the house. The patio is to be rectangular in shape and will be 12 feet by 8 yards. The patio is to be six inches thick. The labor cost for the project is $3.50 per square yard and the material cost is $1.50 per cubic foot. What will be the total cost of the patio?

    a. $112
    b. $198
    c. $328
    d. $552

40. A broker's commission was 8 percent of the first $75,000 of the sales price of a house and 6 percent on the amount over $75,000. What was the total selling price of the property if the broker received a total commission of $9,000?

    a. $79,500
    b. $93,000
    c. $105,000
    d. $125,000

41. A buyer paid $45,000 for a home. Five years later she put it on the market for 20 percent more than she originally paid. The house eventually sold for 10 percent less than the asking price. At what price was the house sold?

    a. $44,100
    b. $48,600
    c. $49,500
    d. $54,000

42. The owner of a rectangular unimproved parcel of land measuring 600 feet in width × 145.2 feet in depth was offered $15 per front foot or $4,000 per acre. What is the amount of the higher offer?

    a. $2,187
    b. $7,680
    c. $8,000
    d. $9,000

43. The present value of an office building is $280,000. This value represents an appreciation of 35 percent during the 8 years since the building was purchased by the present owner. What did he pay for the building?
    a. $182,000
    b. $198,000
    c. $207,407
    d. $430,769

44. $150 is 2.5 percent of what amount?
    a. $375
    b. $600
    c. $1,666
    d. $6,000

45. After purchasing a home containing 2,300 square feet on a rectangular lot 150 feet × 210 feet, the owner added a two-car garage with interior dimensions of 23 feet by 22 feet. The house is valued at $26 per square foot, the lot at 25 cents per square foot, and the garage at $12 per square foot. What was the percentage of increase in value of the property resulting from the addition of the garage?
    a.   8.23 percent
    b.   8.97 percent
    c.   10.15 percent
    d.   11.15 percent

46. A broker negotiated the sale of the NE ¼ of the NE ¼ of the NE ¼; section 25, township 2, south; range 1 east for $700 per acre. The listing agreement with the owner specified a 12 percent commission. How much did the broker earn?
    a. $480
    b. $840
    c. $3,360
    d. $8,400

47. A tract of land containing 560 square rods was sold for 12 cents per square foot. What was the total selling price?
    a. $6,720
    b. $11,088
    c. $18,295
    d. $20,160

48. A property owner plans to fence her land, which is rectangular in shape and measures 300 feet × 150 feet. How many fence posts will be required if there is to be a post every 15 feet?
    a.   45
    b.   60
    c.   61
    d.   450

49. A triangular tract is 4,000 feet deep and has 900 feet of highway frontage that is perpendicular to the 4,000-foot boundary. How many square yards does the tract contain?
    a.   200,000
    b.   300,000
    c.   400,000
    d.   1,800,000

50. The owner of an apartment building earns a net income of $10,200 per year. The annual operating cost is $3,400. The owner is realizing a gross return of 14 percent on investment. What was the price paid for the building?
    a. $48,572
    b. $72,857
    c. $97,143
    d. $142,800

51. A percentage lease stipulates a minimum rent of $1,200 per month and 3 percent of the annual gross sales of the lessee over $260,000. The total rent paid by the end of the year was $16,600. What was the lessee's gross business income for the year?
    a. $73,333.33
    b. $260,000
    c. $333,333.33
    d. $553,333.33

52. A building now 14 years old has a total economic life of 40 years. If the original value of the building was $150,000, what is the present depreciated value?
    a. $52,500
    b. $60,000
    c. $97,500
    d. $202,500

53. On February 1, a mortgagor makes a $638 payment on his mortgage, which is at the rate of 10 percent. The mortgagee allocates $500 to the payment of interest. What is the principal balance due on the mortgage on February 1?
    a. $38,400
    b. $60,000
    c. $79,750
    d. $95,700

54. A house under construction contains a rectangular basement that is 30 feet wide, 90 feet long, and is to be excavated to a uniform depth of 14 feet. A subcontractor received 25 cents per cubic yard for the excavating work. How much did the subcontractor receive?
    a. $315
    b. $350
    c. $1,050
    d. $1,400

55. A house valued at $60,000 was insured for 85 percent of value. The annual premium was 60 cents per $100 of the face amount of the policy. The homeowner paid a three-year premium on February 28. On April 30 the following year she closed the sale of the home. The buyer is having this policy endorsed to him. What will be the cost to the buyer?
   a. $306
   b. $357
   c. $510
   d. $561

56. The perimeter of a rectangular lot is 120 yards. The length is twice the width plus 8 yards. What is the length in feet?
   a. 52
   b. 76
   c. 128
   d. 188

57. In planning the development of a tract of land, the developer allocated one-half of the total area to single-family dwellings, one-third to multifamily dwellings, and 20 acres for roads and recreation areas. What is the total number of acres in the tract?
   a. 36.67
   b. 56.67
   c. 120
   d. 320

58. A developer paid $450 per acre for a 125-acre tract. His costs for grading, paving, and surveying totaled $125,000. He constructed 200 houses at an average cost of $45,000 each. What was the average sales price per house if the developer realized a net return of 14 percent on his total investment?
   a. $45,906.25
   b. $52,333.13
   c. $54,062.50
   d. $64,267

59. A tract of land one and one-quarter miles square was sold by Action Realty Company for $200 per acre. Action Realty received a commission of 9 percent on the sale. They paid 45 percent of the commission to the selling associate. How much did Action Realty net?
   a. $4,950
   b. $8,100
   c. $9,900
   d. $18,000

60. A farm earns $3,600 net after allowing $24 a month for all expenses. A buyer wants 6 percent return on investments. What should she have to pay for the farm so as to gross 6 percent?
   a. $59,800
   b. $60,000
   c. $60,600
   d. $64,800

61. If a shopping center had an annual rental of $50,000 and total annual expenses of $5,000, and if you desired a net profit of 9 percent per annum, what would be the purchase price?
   a. $490,500
   b. $494,505
   c. $500,000
   d. $555,000

62. A broker sold a lot 125 feet wide and 160 feet deep for 17 cents per square foot, but the purchaser assumed a paving lien of $2.25 per front foot. What total amount would the purchaser have to ask for the property if he expected to make a profit of $295 and give a clear title to the property?
   a. $3,976.25
   b. $4,869.50
   c. $44,212
   d. $48,695

63. An office building has a total income of $53,200 per year. The yearly expenses are: taxes—$8,925.25, insurance—$1,510.60, heating and air-conditioning—$4,920.05, miscellaneous expense—$3,644.10. If a buyer pays $360,000 for the building, what will be the net return?
   a. $5,420
   b. $19,000
   c. $34,200
   d. $53,200

64. An enterprise earns $14,000 per year net after allowing $500 per month for all expenses. Assuming that these figures will hold constant, what price could a buyer afford to pay for the enterprise in order to gross 25 percent annually on the investment?
   a. $5,000
   b. $6,000
   c. $80,000
   d. $320,000

65. On the following diagram: It cost $15 per square foot to build this house. If it had to be built today, it would cost $56,000. How much has the cost per square foot increased?

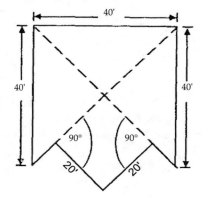

   a. $13
   b. $15
   c. $20
   d. $35

66. If a woman has a $325 weekly gross income from her property and a monthly expense of $845, what is the net annual percentage of interest return on her investment of $84,500?

   a. 2.75 percent
   b. 6.0 percent
   c. 8.0 percent
   d. 67.5 percent

67. A broker has a problem of subdividing a ten-acre tract into 50 × 100 foot lots; after allowing 85,600 square feet for the necessary streets, how many lots will the broker realize from this subdivision?

   a. 70
   b. 87
   c. 92
   d. 116

68. The tax valuation of a property being sold at $50,000 is 75 percent of the sales price. If the tax rate is 45 mills, what is the semiannual payment for taxes?

   a. $750.25
   b. $843.75
   c. $1,500.50
   d. $1,687.50

69. A lot has 50 feet of frontage by 180 feet deep. The buyer had only $5,000 cash. The lot cost $63 per front foot, and the house cost was $9,216. He secured a mortgage for the balance. If his interest was 5.5 percent per annum, payable semiannually, what was the amount of his first semiannual interest payment?

   a. $101.26
   b. $202.57
   c. $405.13
   d. $7,366.00

70. A broker brought a three-story office building. Each story is 80 feet by 75 feet. She paid $300 per front foot for the lot, which is 100 feet of frontage by 200 feet.
   She estimated the building cost at $25 per square foot and paving the lot exclusive of the building would be $3 per square foot. What would the total cost of the lot and construction be?

   a. $480,000
   b. $492,000
   c. $522,000
   d. $552,000

71. See the following diagram. If the house costs $21 per square foot to build and the lot costs $4,000 per acre, what would the selling price be if you wanted to make 10 percent gross profit on the finished house and lot?

   a. $44,180
   b. $48,000
   c. $53,460
   d. $54,000

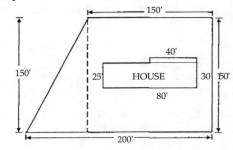

72. An investor wishes to build a flat-roofed building 130 feet long, 30 feet wide, and 24 feet high. Champion Construction Company offers to build such a structure for $18.90 per square foot. Action Construction Company offers to build the building for 80 cents per cubic foot. How much will the investor save by giving the building contract to Champion?

   a. $1,170
   b. $1,769
   c. $3,900
   d. $9,360

73. The house below occupies what percentage of the lot?

   a. 9 percent
   b. 10 percent
   c. 15 percent
   d. 18 percent

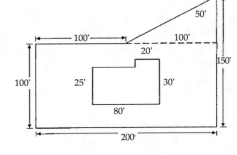

74. A new house and lot cost $64,000. Of the total price, it was estimated that the lot was worth $9,500. The owner had the property for six years. Assuming depreciation of 15 percent on the house and an increase in value of 48 percent on the lot, what was the total value of the property at the end of six years?
    a. $50,200
    b. $54,500
    c. $60,385
    d. $68,560

75. The commission schedule for negotiating a 20-year ground lease was 6 percent for the first year, 5.5 percent for each of the next 2 years, 5 percent for each of the next 3 years, 4.5 percent for each of the next 4 years, and 2 percent for each year thereafter. What was the total commission earned if the annual rental was $8,500?
    a. $4,415
    b. $5,950
    c. $8,500
    d. $10,000

76. The diagrammed tract of land was sold for $25,380. What was the price per acre?
    a. $982.58
    b. $1,042
    c. $1,200
    d. $1,333

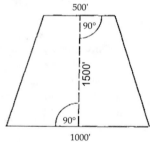

77. A rectangular acre of land has a width of 165 feet. What is the depth of the property?
    a. 264 feet
    b. 275 feet
    c. 379 feet
    d. 718.74 feet

78. If the assessed value of a property is $136,000 and the annual tax paid is $1,700, what is the mill rate?
    a. 8
    b. 12.5
    c. 23.1
    d. 1,250

79. If a lease specifies the rent to be 2 percent of gross sales per annum with a minimum annual rent of $12,000, what is the annual rent if gross sales are $400,000?
    a. $8,000
    b. $8,240
    c. $12,000
    d. $14,000

80. Ms. Jones paid fair market value of $60,000 for a new home. The property is assessed at 80 percent of market value. If the semiannual tax bill is $900, what is the mill rate?
    a. 18.8
    b. 24
    c. 30
    d. 37.5

81. A tract 300 feet square was sold by a broker for $2,750 per acre. If the commission rate was 9 percent, how much did the broker earn?
    a. $511.34
    b. $568.15
    c. $1,893.93
    d. $2,066.00

82. What is the area of the shaded portion?
    a. 14,750 sq. ft.
    b. 15,000 sq. ft.
    c. 16,400 sq. ft.
    d. 18,500 sq. ft.

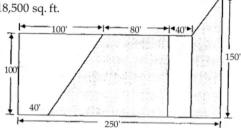

83. A broker's average sale during one year was $41,500. His commission schedule is 7 percent. If he averaged one sale for every 16.5 showings of properties, how many showings did he accomplish to earn $46,480 in this year?
    a. 176
    b. 237
    c. 247
    d. 264

84. An investor purchased a building at 15 percent below market value. Ten days later she sold it at the originally quoted market value price. What was her rate of profit?
    a. 5.67 percent
    b. 12.75 percent
    c. 15.00 percent
    d. 17.65 percent

85. A tract of land contained 14,520 square yards. If the tract was valued at $27,000, what would be the value of a rectangular lot 150 feet by 300 feet?
    a. $3,099
    b. $9,000
    c. $9,297
    d. $9,680

86. The value of a building now 26 years old is $54,000. What was the value when new, if the building had an economic life of 50 years?
    a. $79,920
    b. $82,080
    c. $103,846
    d. $112,500

87. If a property sold at tax value and the annual tax was $588.80 at a tax rate of 23 mills, what was the selling price?
    a. $13,542
    b. $17,664
    c. $25,600
    d. $51,200

88. If a real estate broker earned a commission of $5,600 at a commission rate of 7 percent, at what price was the property sold?
    a. $39,200
    b. $68,000
    c. $80,000
    d. $125,000

89. A purchaser negotiates a loan for 80 percent of the purchase price of her new home. If the interest rate is 9 percent and the first monthly payment on the loan includes $337.50 for interest, what did the woman pay for the home?
    a. $37,500
    b. $46,875
    c. $50,625
    d. $56,250

90. A broker was paid a commission of 9 percent for negotiating the sale of the tract illustrated. If the sale price was $1,200 per acre, what was the amount of the broker's commission?
    a. $1,673.55
    b. $1,928.88
    c. $2,008.26
    d. $2,333.33

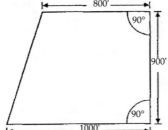

91. An owner sold three houses for an average price of $32,000. He made a profit of 12 percent on his original investment. What amount did he have invested in all three houses?
    a. $28,571.43
    b. $84,480
    c. $85,714.29
    d. $96,000

92. What is the cost, at $12 per square yard, to put a 3-foot wide concrete walk around the garden?
    a. $425.97
    b. $567.96
    c. $1,133.28
    d. $5,112

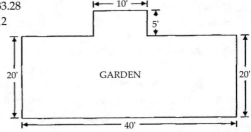

93. If a building sold for $200,000, which represented a profit of 25 percent, what was the seller's original cost?
    a. $150,000
    b. $160,000
    c. $184,000
    d. $187,500

94. An investor had a net return of $12,500 in the first year of operation of an office building. If her expenses totaled $7,000 and the investment in the building is capitalized at 12 percent, what did she pay for the property?
    a. $45,833
    b. $58,333
    c. $104,167
    d. $150,000

95. A broker received a commission of $64,000 at a rate of 10 percent in the sale of a tract of land one mile square. What was the price per acre at which the property sold?
    a. $640
    b. $1,000
    c. $6,400
    d. $10,000

96. A broker sold one-quarter of the SW 1/4 of the SW 1/4, and half of the NW 1/4 of Section 20, Township 3, Range 2, East. How many acres are included in the sale?
    a. 80
    b. 90
    c. 160
    d. 340

97. An owner sold a building for $98,000. Later he sold a second building. The first building sold for 70 percent of the amount received for the second building. What was the sale price of the second building?
    a. $68,600
    b. $140,000
    c. $166,600
    d. $169,428

98. If one month's interest paid on a mortgage is $200 and the principal balance is $30,000, what is the rate of interest?
    a. 6%
    b. 6.67%
    c. 7.25%
    d. 8%

99. A house valued at $80,000 was insured for 85 percent of value. The cost of the insurance was 70 cents per $100 of face amount of the policy. The owner paid an annual premium on March 15. On September 30 of the same year, the sale of the home was closed. The unused value of the policy was purchased by the buyer. What was the buyer's cost?

    a. $218.14
    b. $257.86
    c. $260.81
    d. $476.00

100. An apple orchard nets the owners $28,000 per year. If they decide to sell the orchard for $400,000 and retire, at what rate of interest must they invest the sale proceeds to receive $24,000 per year?
    a. 6%
    b. 8%
    c. 9.6%
    d. 11.2%

The purpose of this appendix is to provide an elementary understanding of the principles, terminology, and the methods of residential construction. The material is confined to wood-frame construction, which is the most typical construction method for houses.

GENERAL CONSIDERATIONS

Location on Site

The location of the house on the building site is an item that must be given serious consideration by the builder. The proper location can have a significant effect on value. Such factors as the required setback from the street and side, and rear property lines are of definite importance. Also, a location that makes the most of available views, privacy, and ease of ingress and egress adds to the value as well as the enjoyment of the home.

Footings

Once the site is definitely established and the batter boards have been erected to lay out the perimeter of the foundation and the height of the foundation walls, the trenches are dug for the footings. The footings are normally made of poured concrete. The concrete must be poured on soil that has not been disturbed and is below the frost line. The width of the footing has to be at least twice the width of the foundation wall that will be erected upon it. The depth of the footing should be at least 6 inches and it should be as deep as the foundation wall is thick. The purpose of the footings is to support the foundation wall and the load that will be placed upon the foundation wall. The footings should provide an adequate base for the structure so as to avoid excessive settling of the house.

Foundation Walls

Foundation walls are usually constructed of concrete blocks. Sometimes these blocks are faced with brick from the footing to the top of the foundation wall. The best protection against termite infestation is the use of a chemical compound by a licensed exterminator in the area within the foundation walls as well as in the ground immediately adjoining the exterior of the foundation walls. This chemical treatment of the soil within the foundation and without establishes a barrier through which termites are not able to penetrate.

Sometimes the foundation consists of a concrete slab instead of a foundation wall. In such cases the concrete slab is poured directly on the ground and there is no excavation, that is, no crawl space at all. The slab provides the floor of the dwelling and the support for the exterior and interior walls. The concrete slab method is less expensive than the foundation wall construction.

The foundation walls should contain adequate ventilation. The house must be ventilated under the floor to avoid dry rot and decay. This ventilation is provided by vents in the upper part of the foundation wall all around the perimeter of the house.

Flooring and Framing

The top of the foundation wall is finished off with a course of solid concrete block. On top of this course of solid block rests the foundation sill or subsill. This wooden subsill is anchored to the foundation wall by anchor bolts and is used as a bearing and nailing surface.

The box sill rests on the subsill and is usually 2" X 8" lumber, whereas the subsill would more likely be 2" X 6" lumber. The box sill runs around the top of the foundation wall attached to the subsill.

Across the span of the foundation are the floor joists. These joists should be made from 2" X 8" or 2" X 10" lumber and should be 12" or 16" on center depending on the bearing load. Depending on the area to be spanned, the joists are put in double or even triple to support the load. Additionally, there are columns within the foundation area on concrete footings and made from concrete blocks for the floor joists to rest upon where there would otherwise be a span of too great a length to be supported.

On top of the floor joists is the subflooring. This is made of plywood sheets or boards. Around the perimeter of the house 2" X 4" strips are nailed to the subflooring. These are called bottom plates or sole plates. The wall studs, which are 2" X 4" usually on 16" centers, stand upright on the bottom plate. On top of these studs around the perimeter of the dwelling are the top plates, which are 2" X 4" on top of each other.

The ceiling joists span the structure between the outer walls. The ceiling joists rest upon the top plates and are therefore supported by the exterior walls and the interior wall framing.

The interior wall framing consists of two 2" X 4" on 16" centers placed on bottom plates affixed to the subflooring.

Above the subflooring is the finished floor. This might be a highly finished wood surface or material placed on the subfloor to support wall-to-wall carpeting.

Roof Construction

The roof construction consists of roof rafters, in older homes, normally 2" X 8" or 2" X 10", which rest upon the top plates of the exterior walls of the house. The rafters are joined at the peak of the roof and are fastened to the ridge board. Modern construction usually employs truss roof systems. The roof rafters are covered by boards or exterior plywood sheets. On top of this material, building paper or felt is nailed. The shingles are then put on top of the felt or building paper. To provide satisfactory roof drainage and to avoid the shingles being blown up by the wind, the pitch of the roof, that is the degree of slant of the roof, should not be less than 4 inches in every 12 feet.

The roof should extend at least 12 inches beyond the exterior walls of the structure. The larger this extension, or overhang, the more protection there is from sun and rain for the exterior walls as well as the windows. The area under the roof extension is called the soffit. The area of material facing the outer edge of the roof extension is called the fascia.

Exterior Finishes

The exterior of the dwelling may be covered with a great variety of materials. Some of the many choices are brick, board and batten, ship lap siding, or stone.

Insulation

The house should be properly insulated to control heat, cold, sound, and moisture. There should be sufficient insulation in the side walls as well as overhead to make the home comfortable in summer and in winter. If the dwelling has an electric heating system there should also be insulation under the subflooring. Electric heat requires more insulation than other types of heat to minimize the heating cost. A variety of insulation materials are used, such as fiberglass, mineral wool, and vermiculite.

Interior Finishes

We should next turn our attention to the interior finish of the dwelling. In most homes constructed today the interior walls are finished by using a dry wall construction. This construction consists of panels of sheetrock board material. These sheetrock panels, when properly finished, look as good or better than plaster and the age old problem of plaster cracks is eliminated. Wood paneling, either in sheets or individual boards, makes a very attractive interior finish. Often a home will contain a combination of sheetrock and wood paneling.

The most durable and satisfactory finish in bathrooms has been ceramic tile. This tile is used on the floors as well as a wainscot up to waist high or so around the bathroom wall and head high around the tub and shower area. The use of fiberglass tubs, showers, or tub and shower combinations has gained in popularity in recent years. The installation of these fiberglass units eliminates the necessity for ceramic tile around the tub or shower area.

A good deal of attention should be given to the finished carpentry on the interior of the house. The quality of the materials and/or the workmanship in the construction of window frames, baseboards, door casings, doors, and hardware are strong indications of the overall quality of construction of the dwelling.

Floor Plans

The layout and design of the floor plan that provides functional utility are of prime importance. Good floor planning greatly increases the amenities of family living. This includes adequate closets and storage space, an entrance hall to protect the living room from the immediate front door area, the proper placing of windows as well as the size of the windows to provide sufficient light and ventilation for all the rooms. Additionally, the grouping of the bedroom and bathroom areas to provide privacy is important. These rooms should be grouped in one area or wing of the house. The kitchen should be designed to provide an efficient as well as attractive work area. The kitchen should be located near a rear entrance for access to the outside. Rooms should be a reasonably good size and should be sized proportionately to each other. Hallways should be at least 3 feet wide.

Electrical Systems

Care should be taken to ascertain whether the electrical system is adequate. In modern homes the great number of electrically operated appliances makes adequate wiring of extreme importance. Modern construction requires a 110/220 volt wiring system that has a capacity of 150–200 amps. The system is fitted with circuit breakers. There should be sufficient electrical wall receptacles for the use of the household. They should be spaced at regular intervals in every room.

Plumbing

The adequacy and quality of the plumbing system are also important factors to be investigated in establishing the quality of construction. Copper piping or PVC is quite superior to galvanized piping. Each bathroom should be vented to the exterior by the use of a metal pipe through the roof's surface. The venting of the trap in the kitchen sink is also necessary. All water fixtures should have separate cutoffs so that a repair could be effected without shutting down the entire system.

Heating and Air Conditioning

The heating and air conditioning should be a central system with warm or cool air circulating through ducts to each room in the house. Additionally, each room should have a duct for air return to the furnace.

Summary

In summary every real estate broker and real estate salesperson should learn to distinguish those features in a dwelling that show quality construction as well as those things that indicate construction of inferior quality. As a suggestion, salespersons not familiar with construction techniques might well spend some time looking at homes in various stages of construction in their areas. In doing so, a knowledge of the construction process and various qualities of workmanship and materials can be gained.

The drawing appearing on the next page illustrates a typical wall section of a single-family dwelling. Notice that on this drawing the various components of the wall section are identified and the dimensions of the materials are shown.

Terminology

Bridging Short wooden pieces placed between timbers to help hold them in place.

Column A vertical shaft used to support the frame not supported by a foundation wall.

Concrete slab A foundation of poured concrete.

Fascia The wood covering attached to the end of the roof rafters at the outer end.

Floating slab A slab and footings poured in separate forms.

Footing A concrete base used to support a foundation wall.

Foundation wall Bearing wall, set on footing, that supports the structure of a house.

Gable roof One consisting of two inclined planes joined over the center line of a house and resting on the two opposite roof plates on top of the studs. The triangular end walls are called gables.

Gambrel roof Similar to a gable roof except each of two sides consists of two inclined planes. The upper planes are relatively flat and the lower planes are quite steep.

Header Timber used to support the free ends of joists, studs, or rafters over openings in the frame.

Hip roof One consisting of four inclined planes joined to form a rectangle.

Joists Horizontal timbers to support a floor or ceiling.

Mansard roof One like a gambrel roof except there are two planes on each of four sides.

Monolithic slab A concrete slab poured in one piece to form an entire foundation.

Pilasters Rectangular concrete or concrete block columns attached to a foundation wall to provide additional support to the frame.

Plates Timbers placed horizontally on top of studs in a wall framework.

Sill Wood member of the frame attached to the foundation wall.

Soffit The covering, usually plywood, on the under side of a roof overhang.

Stud A vertical 2" X 4" or 2" X 6" timber used in the framework of a wall.

Subflooring Material on which the finished flooring is laid.

Truss A triangular framework to provide support over a long span as in roof constructi

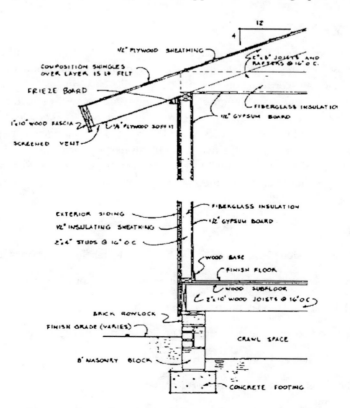

WALL   SECTION

CONSTRUCTION TECHNIQUES*

There are several factors that need to be considered in the attempt to name or define a particular house. Fundamental to the identification of any house is the technique with which it was constructed—what materials were used, and how they were put together. The five most common techniques are described below. In addition, since one of the most easily identifiable features of a building is its roof, a special section illustrating various roof shapes is also included.

Masonry: Brick, Stone, or Concrete

Exterior walls constructed of one of the above heavy materials support the upper floors and the roof. Brick was used frequently in the 19th century; stone was also used locally, but rarely. Concrete blocks, while not common, were sometimes used by the early 20th century.

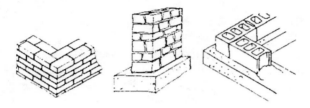

Braced Frame (or Post-and-Beam)

Framework is constructed of heavy timbers mortised and pegged together, often with corner posts protruding into the rooms. This technique was used from earliest times through the mid-19th century, though frames were somewhat lighter in later years. Post-and-beam construction is currently enjoying a revival in this area.

Factory-Built

Usually constructed in panels or sections. Some, like mobile homes, are completely assembled at the factory, while others are made of large sections taken to the site and then erected.

---

*The remainder of this Appendix is reprinted from "What Do We Call It? A Guide to Maine Houses," by Joyce K. Bibber, Portland, ME: Center for Real Estate Education, 1986. Reprinted with permission from Center for Real Estate Education, University of Southern Maine, 96 Falmouth Street, Portland, ME 04103.

Balloon Frame

A lighter framework than the post-and-beam, the balloon frame is composed of smaller (2 X 4, 2 X 6, 2 X 10) sawn timbers that are nailed together. Invented in the 1830s, this technique was not widely used in Maine until the second half of the 19th century. It is currently used in a modified form—levels are now framed separately and stud spacing has been altered to conform to sizes of plywood and chipboard, when used.

Log

Entire or hewn logs are placed on top of one another to form solid walls. The corners are usually lapped. This technique, too, has been enjoying a revival in recent years.

Note: All may not be as it appears—by the early 19th century, beams were often cut out so as not to protrude into rooms, so that a braced frame is well hidden, whereas 20th century houses may be of frame construction, but with a facing of brick or stone or even half logs!

ROOFS

Characteristics to look for in roof identification include roof shape (or type), construction technique, style, and specialized forms. The roof is one of the most easily identifiable components of a house and can often serve as a general description of the entire building. Some of the most common forms are illustrated below and on page 287.

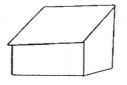

Shed roof
(lean-to or single-pitch roof)

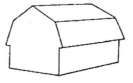

Gambrel roof

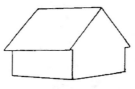

Gable roof
(pitched roof)

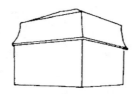

Mansard roof

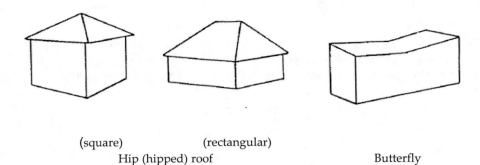

(square)   (rectangular)
Hip (hipped) roof   Butterfly

Variations

Clipped Gable—or Jerkinhead—Roof

Like a hip roof at the top, a gable roof below.

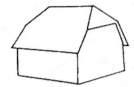

Dormers

May pierce almost any steeply pitched roof. The dormers will usually have shed, gable, or hip roofs, though a few may be arched. Wall dormers have their own roofs, but are continuations of the house wall on their facades.

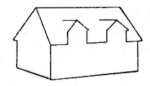

EARLY HOUSE TYPES

It is important to differentiate between what may be called a "type" and what is known as a "style." The term style, when applied to houses, refers to what might be called the "essence" of all the characteristics of a given period (sometimes "revived" from the near or distant past). These characteristics include roof shape, floor plan, location of windows and doors and decorative details, as well as materials used. Most "high-style" structures had characteristic shapes or "types," and never did ALL houses get built in the same shape; thus there are numerous house "types" that appear in a variety of "styles." Some of the more common house types presented here have spanned centuries.

Hall-and-Parlor House

One room deep, with a single chimney to serve the two rooms on the main floor as well as those, if any, above. The entry is usually in front of the chimney. This type of structure was common through the early 1800s.

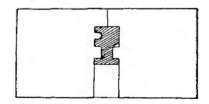

Center-Chimney House

Two rooms deep, usually with three fireplaces in the central chimney—one for each of the three large rooms on the main floor. The entry is in front of the central chimney.

It is often found in two stories, but one is not uncommon. In the latter—often called a "Cape Cod"—it was possible to finish off one or two rooms under the roof. The center chimney house was most often built from the early 18th century through the mid 19th century.

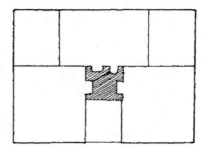

Center-Hall House

Also two rooms deep. Usually the four rooms of the first floor are located with two on either side of an entry/stairhall that extends front to back, with upper floors similarly arranged. Earlier, more conservative versions had two chimneys, one between each set of end rooms. Later homes had a chimney in each room, which was located on the outer wall. This design is found most commonly in houses built from the late 18th century to the mid- 19th century.

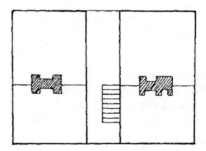

One Room Deep, Two End or Rear Chimneys

Similar to hall-and-parlor shapes, but, in this area, the chimney locations indicate a later date—1800 or after. Unlike the earlier forms, most of these houses were built with an ell or a wing for the kitchen, which might have its own chimney or share one of the others (especially one on a rear wall).

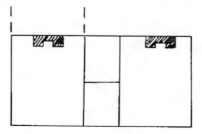

Side-Hall Houses

More likely to be built with kitchen ells or wings. They differed from earlier houses in that the entry was in the narrow end of the house. Usually 1 1/2 stories or higher, they had stairs along the side, in the entry hall. Two large rooms filled the other side or the main section.

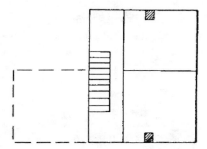

SPECIALIZED TYPES: MULTIPLE UNIT CONSTRUCTION

Row Houses

Also called *town houses*, these can be found in most of the 19th-century styles. Fewer were constructed in the 20th century until recently, when they began to be constructed outside towns in suburban and rural locations. Styles and materials still vary, but what is consistent is that these dwellings are constructed in rows, with common walls between adjacent homes.

Duplexes

Smaller versions of the row house, duplexes are single houses built with two living units. Traditionally, the units are side-by-side, though in this area many turn-of-the-century houses were built with one flat above another. *Note*: The term *duplex* may also refer to an apartment that has two floors and its own staircase between. A flat is an apartment on a single floor.

Triple-Deckers

Built in or on the outskirts of many New England cities around the turn of the century, triple-deckers tend to reflect the styles of that period. Local versions were built in the Colonial Revival or Craftsman Styles. As their name suggests, they have three flats each. The front staircases are inside the front door; the rear ones are on rear porches or in enclosed areas adjacent to these. Most triple-deckers are of frame construction but a few are brick.

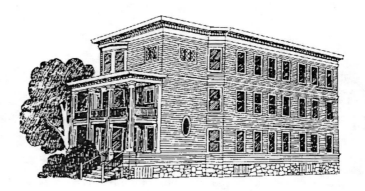

Apartment House

A general term referring to any structure with numerous living units.

Condominium

Refers to the terms of sale and ownership, rather than the type of structure. Presumably, any of the previous multiple unit arrangements could be condominiums.

EARLY HOUSES: THE CLASSICAL PERIOD
Colonial Period/Georgian Style

Colonial is probably the most abused term in real estate today. Properly, it belongs only to houses built in the Colonial period—i.e., before 1776. The style built during most of the 18th century (few Maine houses predate 1700) was Georgian, a style characterized by symmetry and balance with heavy, decorative (often, dentilled) eaves and a fairly elaborate doorway. Inside walls were panelled—particularly fireplace walls— and there was usually a sweeping staircase. Most remaining today are two-story frame constructions, either of the hall-and-parlor or center-chimney types, though brick was not unknown and smaller or otherwise different forms can be found.

Cape Cod (1750–1850 and after 1930)

Cape Cod is a runner-up for most-abused term in real estate. It originated to describe a certain single-story house type built over a period of about a century, beginning in the mid-18th century. First noticed on Cape Cod, they were termed "Cape Cod cottages," though they were built regularly in Maine and other northern states as well. Exterior walls were low, while the roof pitch was fairly steep. This usually was a gable roof, though a few had gambrels (and, on Cape Cod anyway, some roofs were bowed). There were originally no *dormers*. Built over a long period, the Cape Cod appears in a number of styles—some are truly "Colonial," but most have Federal characteristics, while a very few were given a Greek Revival doorway and some Greek trim. As simple structures, the Cape Cods usually lacked external ornamentation, so there was very little roof overhang on the *gable ends* and the *eaves* were very plain.

Federal Style (1780s–1820s)

Federal period housing appeared less heavy than had earlier structures. The "lightness" came, as a rule, from the larger windows and from the *sidelights* added to the upper portions of the areas on either side of the doors. With an elliptical fanlight—or a wooden fan—above both door and *sidelights*, a distinctive period doorway was created. House shapes showed change, too. While three-story mansions appeared in urban areas, many two-story versions, with a now-stylish low-pitched hip roof, were built in town and country alike. Chimneys and fireplaces were properly built on the outside walls, so that end chimneys or chimneys on the rear wall of a house were common. Many homes were but one room deep in the main section, but planned to include an ell (the normal kitchen location) from the first. This held true with both two-story houses and the smaller single-story ones, though many of the latter would more properly be considered story-and-a-half, as they were sufficiently high-posted to make space for sleeping rooms on the upper level. Conservative builders, however, still utilized the old center-chimney house type or the Georgian center-hall with two chimneys plan. Interior trim featured more delicate moldings, with little or no panelling even on the fireplace walls.

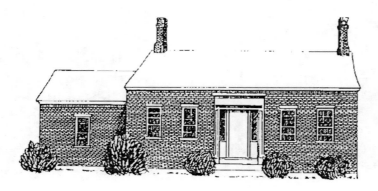

Greek Revival Style (1830s–1860s)

Unlike those in the Federal style, houses from the Greek Revival period tended to look rather heavy. Influenced by the marble temples of Greece, they might have *columns* across the front, but more likely settled for cornerboards widened to be *pilasters*, heavy boxy eaves with a broad *entablature*, and a *post-and-lintel* form doorway with *sidelights* often to the floor. Because the gable end of the temple was seen as the front, Greek-style houses were often oriented with the *gable* end toward the street— an innovation for Maine— though, at the same time, the "front door" was more likely to be found on the side. Conservatives continued to build in the old ways, and there are many two-story houses with hip or gable roofs and single-story or story-and-a- half versions that show their Greek influence only in that their doorways are in the later style, their windows sport wider surrounds, and they have the stylish combination of wide pilasters and heavy

entablatures. A variant doorway of the period had corner blocks and often a panel in the center of the *lintel*; similar corner blocks were used for window trim, inside and out. Chimneys tended to be much smaller than earlier. By the end of the period, stoves often made fireplaces unnecessary. Plaster walls often lacked even a chair rail. Porches became more common.

The Victorian Era (c. 1803–1900)

Victorian is a term that can be useful, though it covers a wide range of buildings. Center-hall, side-hall, and one-room-with-end-chimney houses were still built; but ells, wings, and other projections were so frequent and so varied that many Victorian houses were quite complex in shape. In addition, woodworking machinery had been so improved as to make highly carved architectural ornaments widely available, and houses of the period were often quite ornate—and builders did not hesitate to mix details from different styles. Thus, the general term *Victorian* is handy in instances where a home has features from a variety of the styles of the period.

Note that not all the styles of this era deserve the title, however. Victoria was the English queen from 1837–1901. Therefore, house styles like Shingle and Colonial Revival—whose roots are primarily on this side of the Atlantic—are not truly "Victorian," despite their dates.

Gothic Revival Style (1830s–1850s; some later)

Most Maine versions of this style were built in the later years of the period given. A few showed the inspiration of medieval castles, but the majority took the form of the "cottage ornée," with a steeply pitched gable roof set into the front of a gable or hip roof and ornamented with decorative *bargeboards* and *pinnacles*, both of which may since have deteriorated and been removed. Siding was often of flush boards or of *board-and-batten,* to further emphasize the vertical. In line with the Romanticism of the period, many Gothic cottages boasted *bay windows*, numerous porches, and even towers. A pointed-arch doorway or window was typical; even the rectangular windows were given characteristic *drip moldings*. These were also used inside at times, where the pointed arch might be seen on door panels or at fireplace openings.

Italianate Style (1850s–1870s)

Italianate is a general term that includes the revivals of both Italian villas and of Renaissance palazzos, as well as their various local adaptations. The villa featured an asymmetrical appearance, a rectangular tower, and a variety of window shapes. The palazzo was balanced and regular—and in Maine many houses seem to combine features of both. Features that both the villa and the palazzo shared include a low-pitched roof with wide overhangs and *brackets* under the *eaves*, arched openings, *bay windows*, and heavy trim or hoods at the tops of the windows and doors. Either might have *quoins* on the corners. Many Italianate homes were crowned with a *cupola*—a feature not unknown in earlier periods, but more common now. Doorways seldom had *sidelights*, as glass panels (often arched, sometimes etched) were set into the doors themselves. On the interior, arched openings were found between rooms or at the fireplace—where an imported marble (or marbleized slate) mantel was normal. Woodwork around windows and doors was of heavy molding, often mitered. Conservatives continued to build in earlier forms, with the two-story center-hall house and the side-hall plan being very common. Corner *pilasters*—being easier to construct than quoins—were still occasionally used as well.

Mansard or Second Empire Style (1860s–1880s)

This is one style that is difficult to mistake. Except for a few instances in which a mansard roof has obviously been added to a much earlier building or a modern house has been built with this old type of French roof, a house with a mansard roof is in the Mansard style! The style shares many characteristics—*bay windows*, towers or *cupolas*, heavy window trim and *brackets*—with the Italianate houses. In practice, the Mansard houses were probably more formal and their trim was more standardized and machine-made; but the main clue is in the roof. Both single-story with mansard and double-story with mansard versions were common as residences; higher structures were built for commercial reasons.

Romanesque Style (1880s–1890s)

Always of masonry (and, in some parts of the country, of stone).
Look for wide arches at the doorway—accented with rough-cut
stone or with designs in *terracotta*—some round towers, and
wall *dormers*.

Stick Style (1860s–1880s)

Essentially, the Stick style was built in wood, with board trim on the exterior forming
panels of clapboarding. Accompanying this were stick-shaped *brackets* at the *eaves*, and
arrangement of sticks in the *gables*, and porches whose supports were of rectangular
pieces, which were often *chamfered*. Porch *balusters* were also rectangular: the term *Stick
style* is definitely descriptive! Many houses have the *gable* or the porch trim, but they lack
the proper surface treatment to be "good" examples of the style.

Queen Anne Style (1880s–1900s)

The most elaborate of the common house styles, the Queen Anne's keynote was variety.
With a number of *ells, gables, dormers, bays,* towers, and porches, the shape was seldom dull.
Surface treatment was usually different on the first story than on the second—and a third
or attic story might not match either of the others. Expect to find clapboards, shaped
shingles, panels, imitation half-timbering, and three-dimensional designs in carved wood,
terracotta, or a sort of plaster, and even vertical boarding in places. On a brick house,
ornamental bricklaying and *terracotta* sections provided surface variety. *Gables* might have
heavy *cornices*, or a carved (but seldom lacy) *bargeboard*. There might be an overhang
between stories, perhaps with *brackets* strategically located. Windows were often of three
or four shapes or sizes on the same wall, having varying arrangements of glass panes in
each window as well. Porches were frequent, being supported by turned (often bulbous)
posts and with turned *balusters* in the railing, often with decorative rows of *spindles*
added near the roofline. Chimneys were also used as additional decorative features on
houses.

Here a problem presents itself: if such a house has been denatured by having its decorative elements stripped off or covered with vinyl siding—or whatever—should it still be called a "Queen Anne"? Probably not—where much of the charm comes from the detail, what is left without it might be virtually indistinguishable from other "Victorians."

Shingle Style (1880s–1890s)

In many ways the antithesis of the Queen Anne style, the Shingle style house featured natural-colored or stained shingles on broad surfaces of walls and roof, relieved only by occasional areas of native stone or rough brick. *Dormers, bay windows*, and even towers (usually appearing shorter than on a Queen Anne house) were covered with the same shingled skin—which sometimes rounded the corners where two elements joined without a break. Roofs swept down to shelter porches. The roofs might be gambrel, the first use of that roof shape since the Colonial period. Although the windows themselves were like those on Queen Anne houses, the decorative trim was lacking. In general, the emphasis was on informality—suitable for the large "cottages" that appeared on the East coast in the 1880s.

Colonial Revival

About a century after the end of the Colonial period, Americans developed a certain nostalgic feeling toward their past and began incorporating what they believed to be Colonial details into their homes. Sometimes this meant just adding a few "old" motifs to a "modern" house; at other times (1890s and later) it came closer to producing near copies of the older houses, though few were exact. For example, the wealthier preferred larger houses than had colonial merchants, and adaptations had to be made. Moreover, it was generally accepted that the Federal doorway, with its *fanlights* and *sidelights*, was both handsomer and more practical in providing light for an entry; thus one frequently sees a "Georgian Revival" house with a Federal doorway. Colonial Revival (or Neo-Colonial) homes were, of course, constructed to accommodate changes in technology—for heating, lighting, and plumbing—and usually had larger windows than had the real Colonial houses. Also, the frame construction tended toward the lighter "balloon" type.

EARLY 20TH CENTURY

Though increasing numbers of architects began designing houses in the average price ranges, the proliferation of details from which they could still choose allows many turn-of-the-century homes to defy categorization. Most, however, can be classified generally as "Traditional" or "Revival" styles or "Craftsman" styles. (*Note:* Though popular in other parts of the country at this time, neither the midwestern "Prairie Style" of Frank Lloyd Wright nor the boxlike "International Style" made many in-roads in Maine.)

Craftsman Style (1900–1920s)

Because it represents a rejection of emphasis on the machine and a return to hand crafting, the Craftsman movement is not completely nontraditional. At the same time, the houses inspired by the movement did represent something essentially new in architecture, though with inspiration from the Shingle and Stick styles. The stress was on simplicity and honesty, so exterior materials were shingle or stone, with some brick, concrete, and stucco; decoration came only from the materials themselves, or from flat boards that formed panels by the windows or on large flat surfaces. Roofs usually featured wide overhangs, and extensions of the *rafters or purlins*—sometimes with stick-like *brackets* added—accented the overhang. Craftsman houses came in a variety of shapes, but among the most common forms were the Foursquare and the Bungalow, either of which might also be traditional in detailing.

Foursquare Type (1890s–1930s)

Whether square or rectangular in plan, the Foursquare presents a boxlike facade to the street, usually with a porch across the front and one or two hipped or shed *dormers* in the hip roof. Some have *bay windows*, some have grouped windows; most have glass set into the front door. Probably the majority have shingles on one or both levels; some are of clapboard, but stucco, brick, or even concrete blocks were also used. Many feature light oak interior woodwork, with a two-run staircase. A few were given Colonial Revival details.

Bungalow (1890s–1930s)

Especially popular in the 1910s and 1920s, the bungalow was named for a single-story, porch-surrounded house in British India. The term came to refer to most one-story houses of the period. Many were deliberately informal, with extensions of *rafters* and *purlins* shaped at the ends to lend decoration to porch and roof overhangs. Porches with heavy supports, *bay windows*, and large exterior fireplace chimneys of stone or rough brick added to the informality, as did the exterior wall, which was often shingled. The Bungalow may be found in many shapes, with perhaps the most common in Maine being a low, narrow-end-to-front, hip-roofed structure with a front (and perhaps a rear) porch under the one low roof, and *dormers* to make the upper-level bedrooms usable. This type usually does *not* have exposed *rafters* and *purlins*, but has enclosed *eaves*. Gable-roofed forms more frequently have the less formal treatment. Though some consider this a *style*, because larger homes were considered "Bungalow Style" or "Bungaloid," it should be noted that literature of the period spoke of "Spanish Bungalows," "Japanese Bungalows," or even "Colonial Revival Bungalows."

Traditional (Revival) Styles

Colonial Revival styles continued, with a few very large and more average-sized houses being built. Among the latter were the specific styles and forms described in the following sections.

Dutch Colonial Style (1900s–1930s)

The most common form of this style had a single full-sized story, with a large gambrel roof and *dormers* making the second level almost a full story. Others were pseudo-gambrel, with the structure actually being built as a two-story house with a low-pitched gable roof, then with trim being applied to make false *eaves* and give the appearance of a gambrel roof with large shed *dormers*. These were meant to resemble houses built in Dutch-settled areas of New York and New Jersey. Another form of Dutch Colonial (more like the actual Colonial houses of that area) had a steep gable roof, often with flared *eaves*. All forms often had attached sunrooms—as did many Colonial Revival homes.

Spanish Colonial Revival (1920s–1930s)

Less frequent in the East and in Maine, the Spanish Colonial home usually had a tiled roof, smooth stucco walls, and arched openings.

Saltbox (1920s–present)

An old New England shape (though seldom found in Maine in the Colonial period), the Saltbox has two stories at the front and one story at the rear, with a long rear roof. The Saltbox was first created when a shed-roofed addition was made to a hall-and- parlor house.

Garrison (1920s–present)

The Garrison is named for fortified structures found in early colonies. The jetty or second-floor overhang was a common feature. Usually of frame construction, many modern versions have lower facades of brick or stone.

Cape Cod Revival (1930s–present)

Around 1930, some architects "rediscovered" the Cape Cod cottage and recognized its practicality as a comfortable small home. Many have tried to copy its lines and to retain its special characteristics—including the large central chimney—even while reworking the interior to suit modern living. Others have ignored the real thing, but tried to apply the term to anything with a gable roof! Only if used carefully can the term have meaning.

English Cottage Styles (1920s–1930s)

At times sold as "Tudor" or "Cotswold," these cottages were a variety of small homes that may be considered generally as "English Cottages." Often of stucco or rough brick exteriors, they sometimes had imitation half-timbering and frequently featured an outside chimney near the front. Most had a small, steeply *gabled* entry. Roofs were often fairly steep in pitch and sometimes asphalt shingles were wrapped around the *eaves* to resemble thatch. Casement windows often had small panes, and doorways might have a round or pointed arch at the top. Interiors often had rough plaster walls and imitation "beamed" ceilings in at least one room. (*Note*: A few larger English-type houses were built—more like English manor houses than cottages!)

CONTEMPORARY (SINCE 1940)

Like the term *Victorian*, *Contemporary* refers more to a time period than to a particular architectural style. It has become a kind of catch-all definition that generally refers to any "modern" house that does not fit into any other category. As such, it is a useful term, but it is also one that could mean something entirely different in a few years. Again, beware of assigning this definition simply on the basis of date, as many traditional forms continue to be built—particularly the two-story Colonial Revival, the Saltbox, the Garrison, and the modernized Cape Cod. In addition to these, however, many new designs have become popular.

Ranch

In this design the house is basically long and low, and everything is on one level. The roof, which may be gable or hip, often extends to cover an attached garage as well.

A-Frame

The ultimate gable-roofed house: basically it is all in the roof! Popular as a cabin in snowy mountain areas, but sometimes needing side projections to be functional as a home.

Split Level

One common form has a garage at ground level, with bedroom above; living area is at mid-level, with basement below that. However, there are many variations possible (see also Split-Level Entry).

Split-Level Entry

In this variation, the living and sleeping areas are on the upper floor and the lower level is only partially below ground, thus making it more usable than a normal cellar. The entry is at ground level, making it necessary to go up half a flight to the main floor or down half a flight to the lower level.

ILLUSTRATED GLOSSARY

baluster—one of the posts or supports of a stairwell, or porch railing, often elaborately carved. (End posts are newels.)

bargeboard—vertical faceboard at roof edge on a gable. Prominent in Gothic Revival, where it is often sawn or carved to a lacy pattern; and on Queen Anne, where it is usually more solid in appearance.

bay window—angular windows projecting from a wall—from the ground up. (When curved, it is called a bow window; when not reaching the ground, it is an oriel window.)

board-and-batten—siding of vertical boards, in which the seams of the wide boards are covered by narrow boards (battens), which are sometimes molded.

bracket—member supporting a projecting roof on Italianate, Mansard, and some Queen Anne homes; or, if stick-like, on Stick and Craftsman styles. Also found under overhanging second or third stories.

chair rail—strip of wood or molding set horizontally in plaster walls to protect from chair backs. Sometimes located above a panelled wainscotting.

chamfered—with corner (of beam or post) cut away, leaving a bevelled edge.

column—round pillar or supporting post—classical forms may be fluted, and will have decorative capital at top.

cornice—see entablature

cupola—terminal structure like a small room rising above the roof—originally domed, but not always. Found on all styles from Georgian through late Victorian era, but most frequent on Italianate and Mansard houses locally.

dentil—one of a series of block (or toothlike) projections under overhang, as at eaves, door and window lintels. On classically influenced buildings, especially Georgian and some Greek Revival.

dormer—window set vertically in a projection from a roof.

drip molding—molding set to protect Gothic windows from dripping water.

eave—edge of a roof that projects over the wall.

ell—addition to a house at right angles to the main block.

entablature—three-part area (includes frieze) above columns in a classical temple; thus, wide board or boards above pilasters on Greek Revival house.

fanlight—semicircular or semielliptical window above a door. Mostly on Federal houses locally.

gable—upper part of end wall under pitched roof. Also on dormers.

lintel—see post-and-lintel

pier—rectangular counterpart of a column.

pilaster—rectangular vertical projection on a wall, often with details from classical columns. Frequently as part of doorway framing or as wide cornerboards on Greek Revival houses.

pinnacle—vertical pointed detail, often found on roof of Gothic Revival house.

post-and-lintel—in construction, upright supports (posts) bearing beams (lintels); often the finish of openings—especially doorways.

purlin—horizontal beam supported by rafters and supporting roof boards.

quoins—rectangular stones at corners of buildings—or wooden or brick formations built to resemble these, found mostly on Georgian and Italianate houses.

rafter—usually sloping beams to support roof (sometimes used with purlins).

sidelight—one of a pair of flanking narrow windows beside a door (upper portion only in Federal period, often full-length on Greek Revival doorways).

spindle—small decorative pieces of woodwork sometimes placed under the roofline of a Queen Anne style porch.

terracotta—"cooked earth"—bricklike material, usually elaborately molded—found mostly on Queen Anne and Romanesque buildings.

wing—secondary portion of a building, sometimes an addition.

A GUIDE TO COMMON REAL ESTATE ENVIRONMENTAL HAZARDS*

INTRODUCTION

Does this home fit my needs and those of my family? Is this a safe, secure home, free from potential hazards? Is this home a good investment and will it retain and increase its value in the years ahead?

These are among the hundreds of questions that home buyers ask themselves as part of the home-buying thought process. It is a good policy, this questioning, a means of gathering hard facts that can be used to balance the emotional feelings that are so much a part of buying a home.

In ever-increasing numbers, home buyers today find it necessary to add new kinds of questions to their quest for information. Environmental concerns are becoming an element of the home-buying thought process.

Although it is unrealistic to expect that any home will be free of all forms of environmental influences, most homes (and the areas surrounding most homes) in the United States generally do not contain materials and substances that pose a health threat. However, in recent years, new concerns have been raised as our understanding of the natural environment has increased. Substances, such as radon gas and asbestos, have provoked new questions about how and where we build homes and manage their upkeep.

HOME-BUYING CONSIDERATIONS

For the majority of Americans, the purchase of a home is the single greatest investment of a lifetime. Will the presence of an undetected environmental hazard have a long-term negative impact on that investment? Does the pres-

ence of a hazard have the potential to affect the health of the occupants? If hazards can be safely removed or miti-gated, will the process alter the homeowner's lifestyle? These questions—and others like them—are, and should be, part of the home buyer's thought process today.

As our knowledge of the natural environment evolves, the body of law governing potentially harmful environmental hazards and their effect on real estate transactions also is evolving. The rights and responsibilities of buyers and sellers are determined by state and local laws or terms negotiated into the sales contract between the buyer and seller.

Thus, before buying a home, prudent home buyers may want to obtain information about the potential impact of environmental hazards. Local, county, or state health or environmental departments are sources of such information. And while builders, real estate appraisers, real estate sales licensees, and lenders are not experts about the environment, these individuals may be of assistance in locating additional sources of information regarding environmental matters. Private home inspectors also may be useful in detecting the existence of potentially hazardous conditions if the sales contract provides for such an inspection.

The pages that follow provide general information about some of the environmental hazards that have the potential to affect the home environment. While this information is believed to be accurate, it is not meant to be comprehensive or authoritative. This publication provides introductory information to help home buyers understand the possible risk of exposure to potentially harmful environmental hazards in and around the home.

The agencies and individuals contributing to or assisting in the preparation of this booklet—or any individual acting on behalf of any of these parties—do not make any warranty, guarantee, or representation (express or implied) with

*Compiled by: National Council of Savings Institutions; Office of Thrift Supervision; Society of Real Estate Appraisers; The Appraisal Foundation; U.S. Environmental Protection Agency; U.S. League of Savings Institutions. This document is in the public domain.

respect to the usefulness or effectiveness of any information, method, or process disclosed in this material or assume any liability for the use of (or for damages arising from the use of) any information, method, or process disclosed in this material.

RADON

What is radon and where is it found?

Radon is a colorless, odorless, tasteless gas that occurs worldwide in the environment as a byproduct of the natural decay of uranium present in the earth. Radon is present in varying quantities in the atmosphere and in soils around the world.

How does radon enter a home?

Radon that is present in surrounding soil or in well water can be a source of radon in a home. Radon from surrounding soil enters a home through small spaces and openings, such as cracks in concrete, floor drains, sump pump openings, wall/floor joints in basements, and the pores in hollow block walls. It also can seep into ground water and remain entrapped there. Therefore, if a home is supplied with water taken from a ground water source (such as a well), there is greater potential for a radon problem. The likelihood of radon in the water supply is greatly reduced for homes supplied with water from a municipal water supply.

Is radon found throughout a home, or just in certain rooms or areas?

Radon generally concentrates most efficiently in the areas of a home closest to the ground. Radon levels generally decrease as one moves higher up in the structure.

How can I tell if a home has a radon problem?

The only way to know whether a home has a radon problem is to test it. Radon levels vary from house to house depending on the construction of the house and the soil surrounding it. There are several ways to make a preliminary screening test for radon. Preliminary screening test kits can be bought over the counter in many hardware, grocery, and convenience stores. Tests that measure the amount of radon in water normally require you to send a sample of tap water to a laboratory for analysis. State agencies should be consulted if the home water supply is suspected as a source of radon.

When purchasing a radon detection kit, you should examine the package for indications that the kit has been approved by federal or state health, environmental protection, or consumer protection agencies. Directions should be followed carefully when using a radon detection kit to assure that proper measurements are obtained. Short-term testing (ranging from a few days to several months) is one way to determine if a potential problem exists. Long-term testing (lasting for up to one year) is a more accurate way to determine if radon is present. Both short and long-term testing devices are easy to use and relatively inexpensive.

Why is radon harmful?

Radon gas breaks down into radioactive particles (called decay products) that remain in the air. As you breathe these particles, they can become trapped in your lungs. As these particles continue to break down, they release bursts of energy (radiation) that can damage lung tissue. This damage can cause lung cancer. When radon gas and its decay products enter your home, they remain in circulation in the enclosed air. Out of doors, radon is not a problem for human beings because the surrounding air allows the gas to diffuse in the atmosphere.

What health risks are associated with radon?

The health risk associated with prolonged inhalation of radon decay products is an increased risk of developing lung cancer. There are indications that risk increases as the level of radon concentration and duration of exposure increase. The U.S. Environmental Protection Agency (EPA) has determined that short-term exposure to a high concentration of radon is not as severe a risk as long-term exposure to a lower level of the gas.

What is an acceptable level of indoor radon?

The concentration of radon in air is measured in units of picocuries per liter of air (pCi/L). Estimates suggest that most homes will contain from one to two picocuries of radon per liter of air. If preliminary tests indicate radon levels greater than four picocuries per liter of air in livable areas of the home, the EPA recommends that a follow-up test be conducted. No level of radon is considered safe; there are risks even at very low levels. To put this into perspective, the EPA estimates that the risk of dying from lung cancer as the result of an annual radon level of four picocuries is equivalent to the risk from smoking 10 cigarettes a day or having 200 chest x-rays a year. A picocurie level of 40 equates to smoking two packs of cigarettes a day, while a level of 100 equates to 2000 chest x-rays a year.

How are radon risk levels calculated?

The EPA's risk assessments assume an individual is exposed to a given concentration of radon over a lifetime of roughly 70 years, and spends 75 percent of his or her time in the home.

Can the level of radon in a home be reduced?

Yes, there are many effective and relatively inexpensive methods of reducing radon levels in a home. The method used will vary from house to house and from region to region. The techniques used will depend on the source of the gas, the ways in which it enters the home, and the kind of construction used in the home. If radon is present in water supplies, it can be removed altogether or reduced by the installation of special filter systems.

What will it cost to reduce the level of radon in a home?

The costs for radon reduction will depend on the number of sources, the amount of radon in the surrounding land or in the water supply, and the kind of construction used in the home. Normally, the costs of installing radon reduction equipment range from several hundred dollars to several thousand dollars. If the system chosen involves fans, pumps, or other appliances, operating costs for these devices may cause increases in monthly utility bills.

Is radon removal a "do-it-yourself project"?

Not usually. In some cases, homeowners should be able to treat the problem themselves; however, it is not always possible for homeowners to diagnose the source of radon or to install systems that will reduce the level. Radon source diagnosis and mitigation normally require skills, experience, and tools not available to the average homeowner; therefore, it is always prudent to consider the use of trained personnel. When seeking a contractor to assist with a radon problem, you should first consult local, county, or state government agencies for recommendations of qualified radon-reduction contractors.

What is the government doing about radon?

The federal government has undertaken an extensive public outreach effort to encourage individuals to test their homes. This effort includes a national hotline, 1-800-SOS-RADON, for obtaining further information on radon testing. EPA also is working closely with state and local governments and the private sector to research and demonstrate cost-effective methods for reducing indoor radon levels and with builders to develop radon-resistant new construction techniques.

You also may contact Maine's radon office at (207) 289-3826.

The following resources and publications can provide additional information about radon.

Brochures

- *A Citizen's Guide to Radon*
- *Radon Reduction Methods (A Homeowner's Guide)*
- *Removal of Radon from Household Water*
- *The Inside Story—A Guide to Indoor Air Quality*

The above are available from:

U.S. Environmental Protection Agency
Public Information Center
401 M Street, SW
Washington, DC 20460
(202) 475-7751

ASBESTOS

What is asbestos and where is it found?

Asbestos is a fibrous mineral found in rocks and soil throughout the world. Asbestos has been used in architectural and construction applications because it is strong, durable, fire retardant, and an efficient insulator. Alone or in combination with other materials, asbestos can be fashioned into a variety of products that have numerous applications within the building industry—such as flooring, walls, ceiling tiles, exterior housing shingles, insulation or fire retardant for heating and electrical systems, etc.

Is asbestos dangerous?

Asbestos has been identified as a carcinogen. Once ingested, asbestos fibers lodge in the lungs. Because the material is durable, it persists in tissue and concentrates as repeated exposures occur over time. It can cause cancer of the lungs and stomach among workers and others who have experienced prolonged work-related exposure to it. The health effects of lower exposures in the home are less certain; however, experts are unable to provide assurance that any level of exposure to asbestos fibers is completely safe.

Under what circumstances do asbestos-containing products in the home become a health risk?

Home health risks arise when age, accidental damage, or normal cleaning, construction, or remodeling activities cause the asbestos-containing materials to crumble, flake, or deteriorate. When this happens, minute asbestos fibers are released into the air and can be inhaled through the nose and mouth. The fibers can cling to clothing, tools, and exposed flesh; cleanup operations can then dislodge the fibers and free them to circulate in the air.

Can I expect to find asbestos in newer homes, and where in the home should I look for asbestos?

According to the EPA, many homes constructed in the United States during the past 20 years probably do not contain asbestos products. Places where asbestos sometimes can be found in the home include: around pipes and furnaces in older homes as insulating jackets and sheathing; in some vinyl flooring materials; in ceiling tiles; in exterior roofing, shingles, and siding; in some wallboards; mixed with other materials and troweled or sprayed around pipes, ducts, and beams; in patching compounds or textured paints; and in door gaskets on stoves, furnaces, and ovens.

How can I identify asbestos in the home?

You may hire a qualified professional who is trained and experienced in working with asbestos to survey the home. A professional knows where to look for asbestos, how to take samples properly, and what corrective actions will be the most effective. EPA regional asbestos coordinators can provide information on qualified asbestos contractors and laboratories. In addition, the manufacturer of a product may be able to tell you, based on the model number and age of the product, whether or not the product contains asbestos.

What should I do if I think there is asbestos in a home I have purchased?

Generally, if the material is in good condition and is in an area where it is not likely to be disturbed, leave the asbestos-containing material in place. Extreme care should be exercised in handling, cleaning, or working with material suspected of containing asbestos. If the material is likely to be banged, rubbed, handled, or taken apart—especially during remodeling—you should hire a trained contractor and reduce your exposure as much as possible. Common construction and remodeling operations can release varying amounts of asbestos fibers if the material being worked on contains asbestos. These operations include hammering, drilling, sawing, sanding, cutting, and otherwise shaping or molding the material. Routine cleaning operations (such as brushing, dusting, vacuum cleaning, scraping, and scrubbing) can also release hazardous fibers from asbestos-containing materials. Vinyl flooring products that contain asbestos can be cleaned in a conventional manner, but these products can release some asbestos fibers if they are vigorously sanded, ground, drilled, filed, or scraped.

The repair or removal of asbestos-containing products from a home is generally a complicated process. It depends on the amount of these products present, the percentage of asbestos they contain, and the manner in which asbestos is incorporated into the product. Total removal of even small amounts of asbestos-containing material is usually the last alternative. You should contact local, state, or federal health or consumer product agencies before deciding on a course of action. To assure safety and elimination of health hazards, asbestos repair or removal should be performed only by properly trained contractors.

Many home repair or remodeling contractors do not yet have the requisite tools, training, experience, or equipment to work safely with asbestos or to remove it from a home. Furthermore, asbestos removal workers are protected under federal regulations that specify special training, protective clothing, and special respirators for these workers.

Are exterior asbestos shingles a health risk?

When properly installed on the exterior of a home, asbestos-containing products present little risk to human health. However, if siding is worn or damaged, spray painting it will help seal in the fibers.

What is being done about the potential problem of exposure to asbestos in the home?

Over the years, the U.S. Environmental Protection Agency (EPA) and the Consumer Product Safety Commission (CPSC) have taken several steps to reduce the consumer's exposure to asbestos.

Most recently these steps include requiring labeling of products containing asbestos and announcing a phased in ban of most asbestos products by 1996.

The following sources and publications can provide additional information about asbestos in the home.

Brochures

* *Asbestos (Environmental Backgrounder)*
* *The Inside Story—A Guide to Indoor Air Quality*

The above are available from:

U.S. Environmental Protection Agency
Public Information Center
401 M Street, SW
Washington, DC 20460
(202) 475-7751

* *Asbestos in the Home*

Available from:

U.S. Environmental Protection Agency
TSCA Assistance Information Service 401
M Street, SW
Washington, DC 20460

Hotline

* *The Toxic Substances Control Act (TSCA) Assistance Information Service Hotline*

  This Hotline provides both general and technical information and publications about toxic substances (including asbestos) and offers services to help businesses comply with TSCA laws (including regulatory advice and aid, publications, and audiovisual materials). The Hotline operates Monday through Friday from 8:30 A.M. to 5:00 P.M., Eastern Time. (202) 554-1404

LEAD

What is lead, and why is it hazardous to our health?

Lead is a metallic element found worldwide in rocks and soils. The toxic effects of lead have been known since ancient times. Recent research has shown that lead represents a greater hazard at lower levels of concentration than had been thought. Airborne lead enters the body when an individual breathes lead particles or swallows lead dust. Until recently, the most important source of airborne dust was automobile exhaust.

When ingested, lead accumulates in the blood, bones, and soft tissue of the body. High concentrations of lead in the body can cause death or permanent damage to the central nervous system, the brain, the kidneys, and red blood cells.

Even low levels of lead may increase high blood pressure in adults.

Infants, children, pregnant women, and fetuses are more vulnerable to lead exposure than others because the lead is more easily absorbed into growing bodies and their tissues are more sensitive to the damaging effects of the lead. Because of a child's smaller body weight, an equal concentration of lead is more damaging to a child than it would be to an adult.

What are the sources of lead in and around the home?

Lead can be present in drinking water, in paint used to decorate the interior or exterior of a home, in the dust within a home, and in soil around the home.

Lead in Drinking Water

Are there acceptable levels of lead in drinking water?

The EPA Office of Drinking Water has proposed regulations under the Safe Drinking Water Act (SDWA) that establish a maximum contaminant level for lead in drinking water of five micrograms per liter and a maximum contaminant level goal of zero. [Note: One microgram per liter is equal to one part per billion (ppb).] These levels or goals are set by the EPA to control contamination that may have an adverse effect on human health. Nonenforceable health-based goals are intended to protect against known or anticipated adverse health effects with an adequate margin of safety. Both the current maximum contamination level and goal are 50 micrograms per liter. Although the Public Health Service first set these levels in the 1960s before much of the current knowledge about the harmful effects of lead at low levels was gained, the EPA included them unchanged in the Safe Drinking Water Act of 1985. EPA, however, is now revising these standards to reflect its increased concern.

I have heard that materials containing lead have been banned from use in public water supplies. If this is true, how does lead enter drinking water in the home?

In 1986, amendments to the Safe Drinking Water Act banned any further use of materials containing lead in public water supplies and in residences connected to public water supplies. In 1988, the U.S. Congress banned the use of lead-based solder in plumbing applications within homes and buildings. However, many homes built prior to 1988 contain plumbing systems that use lead-based solder in pipe connections. In such systems, lead can enter drinking water as a corrosion byproduct when plumbing fixtures, pipes, and solder are corroded by drinking water. In these instances, lead levels in water at the kitchen tap can be far higher than those found in water at treatment plants.

The combination of copper pipes connected with lead-based solder is found in many homes and can result in high levels of lead in water. In these circumstances, galvanic corrosion between the two metals releases relatively large amounts of lead into the water. The amount of lead in this kind of home water system will be higher when water has been at rest in the pipes for a period of time.

The EPA has determined that newly installed solder is most easily dissolved. As the home ages, mineral deposits build up on the inner walls of water pipes and act as an insulating barrier between the water and the solder. Data compiled by the EPA indicates that during the first five years following home construction, water in the home may have high levels of lead, with the highest levels recorded during the first 24 months.

Can I tell by looking at pipes and plumbing fixtures whether or not water in the home will contain harmful levels of lead?

No. Visual inspection of pipe joints and solder lines is not an accurate means of determining whether or not decaying solder is a source of lead.

A simple chemical test can determine whether the solder used in a home is lead-containing or not. Many jurisdictions make use of this test as a regular procedure in plumbing inspections. And while many newer homes rely on non-metallic plumbing lines, the majority of faucets and plumbing fixtures used today can contribute some lead to home water supplies. However, these contributions can be eliminated effectively by running the faucet for 15 seconds before drawing drinking water.

How can I tell if a home has a problem with lead in the water?

The only way to determine lead levels in water is to test a sample of the water. Should you suspect that lead is present in drinking water, or if you wish to have water tested, contact local, county, or state health or environmental departments for information about qualified testing laboratories.

Is lead in water a concern in newly renovated older homes?

If the renovation included replacement of aging water pipes with copper or other metal piping, you should check with the renovating contractor to ensure that lead solder was not used in pipe joints. Further, some old homes contain water systems made of pipes that can contain high levels of lead. If the original water lines remain in the house, you should question the renovating contractor regarding his or her knowledge of pipe composition.

Lead-Based Paint

How prevalent is lead-based paint?

According to the EPA, it is estimated that lead-based paint was applied to approximately two-thirds of the houses built in the United States before 1940; one-third of the houses built from 1940 to 1960; and an indeterminate (but smaller) portion of U.S. houses since 1960. The federal government banned lead-based paint from housing in 1978. Federal and Maine law requires that individuals receive a disclosure on lead-based paint before renting or buying pre-1978 housing. All leases and purchase and sale contracts must include this disclosure about lead-based paint.

How can I tell whether the paint in a home contains lead?

The only accurate way to determine if paint in a home contains lead is to remove a sample of the paint and have it tested in a qualified laboratory. Should you suspect that lead is present in paint, or if you wish to have paint tested, contact local, county, or state health or environmental departments for information about qualified testing laboratories.

I have heard about problems when children eat chips of lead-based paint, but are there any other ways that lead-based paint can be harmful?

While the health hazards to children from eating lead-based paint chips have been known for some time, other sources of exposure to lead in household air and dust have been documented only recently.

Lead can enter the air within a home when surfaces covered with lead-based paint are scraped, sanded, or heated with an open flame in paint-stripping procedures. Once released into the home atmosphere, lead particles circulate in the air and can be inhaled or ingested through the mouth and nose. Lead particles freed in fine dust or vapors settle into carpet fibers and fabric and can be recirculated in the air by normal household cleaning (such as sweeping and dusting) and through the normal hand-to-mouth behavior of young children, which results in the ingestion of potentially harmful amounts of any lead present in household dust. Fine lead particles penetrate the filter systems of home vacuum cleaners and are recirculated in the exhaust air streams of such appliances. Lead also can enter household air from outdoor sources (such as contaminated soil) and from recreational activities that require the use of solder or materials containing lead.

How can I get rid of lead-based paint safely?

It is best to leave lead-based paint undisturbed if it is in good condition and there is little possibility that it will be eaten by children. Other procedures include covering the paint with wallpaper or some other building material, or completely replacing the painted surface. Pregnant women and women who plan to become pregnant should not do this work. Professional paint removal is costly, time-consuming, and requires everyone not involved in the procedure to leave the premises during removal and subsequent clean-up operations. In addition, if the house was built prior to 1950, there is a good chance that lead from exterior surface paint has accumulated in surrounding soils.

Keep the yard well vegetated to minimize the likelihood of children being exposed to contaminated dust. Clean the floors, window-sills, and other surfaces regularly, preferably with wet rags and mops. Practice good hygiene with your children, especially frequent hand washing.

The following publications provide additional information about lead in the home.

Brochures

- *Protect Your Family from Lead in Your Home*
- *Reducing Lead Hazards*

The above are available from:

The National Lead Information Center 1-800-424-5323
www.epa.gov/leed

Hotline

For additional information about lead in drinking water, contact EPA's Safe Drinking Water Hotline: (800) 426-4791; (202) 382-5533 (in the Washington, DC, area)

HAZARDOUS WASTES

What are hazardous wastes?

Hazardous wastes are those waste products that could pose short or long-term danger to personal health or the environment if they are not properly disposed of or managed. These wastes can be produced by large business and industries (such as chemical and manufacturing plants), by some small businesses (such as dry cleaners and printing plants), and by individuals who improperly apply, store, or dispose of compounds that contain potentially toxic ingredients (which can be found in chemical fertilizers, pesticides, and household products).

Concentrations of hazardous wastes occur in the environment when these wastes are handled, managed, or disposed of in a careless or unregulated manner. For many decades, hazardous industrial wastes were improperly disposed of on land, and their toxic components remained in the earth or seeped into ground water and drinking water supplies. The widespread use of pesticides and other agricultural chemicals also has resulted in the seepage and run-off of toxic compounds into land and water supplies. In addition, EPA estimates that as many as two million of the more than five million underground storage tanks in the United States may be leaking—discharging gasoline, petroleum products, and other hazardous liquids into the soil and, potentially, into ground water sources.

What is being done to locate and clean up hazardous waste sites?

During the past 20 years, the U.S. Congress has enacted a body of interlocking laws and regulatory procedures aimed at the abatement of environmental hazards. The Superfund Act was enacted in 1980 (and amended in 1986) to provide more than $10 billion for the detection and cleanup of sites where hazardous waste is a problem.

The revenue for Superfund is raised through taxes on petrochemical companies and other manufacturers. Under the law, the EPA, other federal agencies, and individual states may draw the necessary funds to allow them to react in hazardous waste emergency situations and to conduct long-term, permanent cleanups of hazardous waste sites.

How can I determine if a home is affected by a hazardous waste site?

Generally, testing for hazardous waste involves skills and technology not available to the average homeowner or home remodeling contractor.

The EPA has identified more than 30,000 potentially contaminated waste sites nationwide and has completed a preliminary assessment of more than 27,000 of these sites. The Agency publishes a National Priorities List of sites that will require action through the Superfund. Sites suspected of containing hazardous wastes are mapped at the time of the EPA preliminary assessment and communities likely to be affected by the site are notified. Thus, the nearest regional office of the EPA should have information on the location and status of local hazardous waste sites. The addresses and telephone numbers of these regional offices are listed in the back of this publication.

Furthermore, local and state governments maintain offices and agencies for locating and managing hazardous waste sites. These offices often are good sources for current information about the location and possible effects of these sites.

What are the primary health hazards associated with hazardous wastes?

The specific health hazards in homes contaminated by hazardous wastes are determined by the kinds and amounts of toxic substances present. Some hazardous wastes can cause death even when ingested in small amounts. Other hazardous wastes have been linked to elevated risks of cancer, permanent damage to internal body organs, respiratory difficulties, skin rashes, birth defects, and diseases that attack the central nervous system.

Can hazardous waste concentrations be removed from my property or reduced to non-hazardous levels?

The ability to remove or mitigate hazardous wastes will depend on the kinds, amounts, and sources of the wastes that are present. Generally, the removal of hazardous wastes from a property is beyond the capability of an individual homeowner.

The following sources and publications provide additional information about hazardous wastes.

Brochures

- *A Consumer's Guide to Safer Pesticide Use*
- *Citizen's Guide to Pesticides*
- *Hazardous Wastes (Environmental Backgrounder)*

The above are available from:

U.S. Environmental Protection Agency Public
Information Center
401 M Street, SW Washington,
DC 20460
(202) 475-7751

Hotlines

- *National Poison Control Center Hotline*

  This Hotline provides information on accidental ingestion of chemicals, poisons, or drugs. The Hotline is operated by Georgetown University Hospital in Washington, DC. (800) 222-1222

- *RCRA (Superfund) Hotline*

  This Hotline responds to questions from the public and regulated community on the Resource Conservation and Recovery Act and the Comprehensive Environmental Response, Compensation and Liability Act (Superfund). The Hotline operates Monday through Friday from 8:30 A.M. to 7:30 P.M., Eastern Time. (800) 424-9346; (202) 382-3000 (in the Washington, DC, area)

- *Emergency Planning and Community Right-to-Know Information Hotline*

  This Hotline complements the RCRA (Superfund) Hotline and provides communities and individuals with help in preparing for accidental releases of toxic chemicals. The Hotline operates Monday through Friday from 8:30 A.M. to 7:30 P.M., Eastern Time. (800) 535-0202; (202) 479-2449 (in the Washington, DC, area)

GROUND WATER CONTAMINATION

What causes ground water contamination?

Ground water contamination occurs when hazardous chemical wastes, pesticides, or other agricultural chemicals (such as fertilizer) seep down through the soil into underground water supplies. Faulty private septic systems, improperly managed municipal sewer systems, and leaking industrial injection wells can also contribute to ground water contamination. In recent years, leaking underground storage tanks also have posed a threat to ground water. Half of all Americans and 95 percent of rural Americans use ground water for drinking water.

Is ground water contamination harmful?

The U.S. Center for Disease Control reports an average of approximately 7,500 cases of illness linked to drinking water in the United States each year. This estimate generally is thought to be considerably lower than the actual figures because drinking water contaminants are not always considered in the diagnoses of illnesses.

How can I tell if the water in a home is contaminated?

The only way to know whether or not the water in a home is contaminated is to test it. Since 1977, federal law has required water suppliers to periodically sample and test the water supplied to homes. If tests reveal that a national drinking water standard has been violated, the supplier must move to correct the situation and must also notify the appropriate state agency of the violation. Customers must be notified also, usually by a notice in a newspaper, an announcement on radio or television, or a letter from the health department that supervises the water supplier. If the home is supplied with water from its own private well, laboratory testing of a water sample is the only way to determine if the water supply is contaminated. Should you suspect that water is contaminated, or if you wish to have water tested, contact local, county, or state health or environmental departments for information about qualified testing laboratories.

What can be done to decontaminate a home water supply?

If the home is supplied by an outside water supply source, federal law requires the provider to correct any contamination problems. When homes are supplied by private wells, analysis and treatment of the contaminated water may solve the problem.

What will it cost to decontaminate a home water supply?

Normally, consumers bear no direct financial responsibility for eliminating contamination from water supplied by an outside source (if the water was contaminated when it was delivered); the supplier bears the primary responsibility for correcting contamination problems. In the case of contaminated water supplied from a private well (or water from an outside source that becomes contaminated after it is received from the supplier), the cost of decontamination will depend on the kinds and amounts of contaminants present.

In the majority of cases, decontamination of a private water source involves technology and knowledge beyond the scope of the average homeowner. State and local environmental and water quality officials may be able to provide additional information and assistance for decontamination of private water sources.

What is being done about ground water contamination?

The U.S. Environmental Protection Agency has the lead responsibility for assuring the quality and safety of the nation's ground water supply. The EPA's approach is focused in two areas: minimizing the contamination of ground water and surface waters needed for human consumption and monitoring and treating drinking water before it is consumed.

In 1986, the U.S. Congress passed a set of amendments that expanded the protection provided by the Safe Drinking Water Act of 1974. These amendments streamlined the EPA's regulation of contaminants, banned all future use of lead pipe and lead solder in public drinking water systems, mandated greater protection of ground water sources, and authorized the EPA to file civil suits or issue administrative orders against public water systems that are in violation of the Act.

Working with the states, the EPA has set national standards for minimum levels of a number of contaminants and is mandated to set such standards for additional contaminants by 1991. In addition, the EPA and the states are working to devise a national strategy for the monitoring and management of ground water supplies.

The following sources and publications provide additional information on ground water contamination.

Brochure

•   *Is Your Drinking Water Safe?*

Available from:

U.S. Environmental Protection Agency
Public Information Center
401 M Street, SW
Washington, DC 20460
(202) 475-7751

Hotline

•   *Safe Drinking Water Hotline*

This Hotline provides information and publications to help the public and the regulated community understand the EPA's drinking water regulations and programs. The Hotline operates Monday through Friday, 8:30 A.M. to 4:30 P.M., Eastern Time. (800) 426-4791; (202) 382-5533 (in the Washington, DC, area)

FORMALDEHYDE

What is formaldehyde?

Formaldehyde is a colorless, gaseous chemical compound that is generally present at low, variable concentrations in both indoor and outdoor air. It is emitted by many construction materials and consumer products that contain formaldehyde-based glues, resins, preservatives, and bonding agents. Formaldehyde also is an ingredient in foam that was used for home insulating until the early 1980s.

Where is formaldehyde found in the home?

Sources of formaldehyde in the home include smoke, household products, and unvented fuel-burning appliances (like gas stoves or kerosene space heaters). Formaldehyde, by itself or in combination with other chemicals, serves a number of purposes in manufactured products. For example, it is used to add permanent press qualities to clothing and draperies, as a component of glues and adhesives, and as a preservative in some paints and coating products.

In homes, the most significant sources of formaldehyde are likely to be in the adhesives used to bond pressed wood building materials and in plywood used for interior or exterior construction. Urea-formaldehyde (UF) resins are found in wood products that are intended for indoor use. Phenol-formaldehyde (PF) resins are used in products intended for exterior uses. UF resins emit significantly more formaldehyde gas than PF resins.

Certain foam insulating materials once widely used in housing construction (urea-formaldehyde foam or UFFI) also contain large amounts of formaldehyde. While contractors have voluntarily stopped using UFFI foam insulation, the material is present in many homes that were originally insulated with UFFI.

What health risks are associated with formaldehyde?

Formaldehyde has been shown to cause cancer in animals, but there is no definitive evidence linking the chemical to cancer in humans. Higher-than-normal levels of formaldehyde in the home atmosphere can trigger asthma attacks in individuals who have this condition. Other health hazards attributed to formaldehyde include skin rashes; watery eyes, burning sensations in the eyes, throat, and nasal passages; and breathing difficulties. Most persons will first react to formaldehyde when the levels are in the range of 0.1 to 1.1 parts per million. Some individuals acquire a reduced tolerance to formaldehyde following their initial exposure to the gas. In these instances, subsequent exposures to even small amounts of formaldehyde will cause reactions.

Do some kinds of homes carry a greater formaldehyde health risk than others?

Yes, materials containing formaldehyde were used extensively in the construction of certain prefabricated and manufactured homes. Since 1985, the federal government, through the U.S. Department of Housing and Urban Development, has enforced regulations that sharply curtail the use of materials containing formaldehyde in these types of housing to the lower-emitting products. However, use of formaldehyde compounds is still widespread in the manufacture of furniture, cabinets, and other building materials.

What can be done to reduce formaldehyde levels in a home?

Reducing formaldehyde levels in the home can be a simple or complex task depending on the source of the gas. Initial procedures often include steps to increase ventilation and improve circulation of outside air through the home. If new furniture, drapery, or other sources are contributing to higher-than-normal levels of formaldehyde, removal of these items (or limiting the number of new items introduced into the home) may be all that is needed.

In some instances, home subflooring or walls may be the source of formaldehyde, or foam insulation between inner and outer walls may be emitting the gas. If increased ventilation does not produce acceptable results in these instances, homeowners may be required to remove the formaldehyde-bearing material. Such procedures will be costly, time-consuming, and temporarily disruptive of life in the home.

How can I tell if the home I wish to buy contains formaldehyde-bearing materials?

In the case of a new home, you should consult with the builder before you purchase the house if you suspect the presence of materials that emit high levels of formaldehyde. Most builders will be able to tell you if construction materials contain urea-formaldehyde or they may direct you to manufacturers who can provide information about specific products. In the case of an older home, formaldehyde-emitting materials may not be visually evident and the current owners may not have specific product information. Because formaldehyde emissions from building materials decrease as the materials age (particularly over the first two or three years), older urea-formaldehyde building materials most probably will not be a significant source of formaldehyde emissions.

If you suspect the presence of formaldehyde, you may wish to hire a qualified building inspector to examine the home for the presence of formaldehyde-emitting materials. In addition, home monitoring kits are currently avai able for testing formaldehyde levels in the home. Be sure that the testing device will monitor for a minimum of 24 hours to assure that the sampling period is truly representative.

The following sources and publications provide additional information about formaldehyde in the home.

Brochures

- *The Inside Story — A Guide to Indoor Air Quality*

Available from:

U.S. Environmental Protection Agency Public
Information Center
401 M Street, SW Washington,
DC 20460
(202) 475-7751

- *Air Pollution in Your Home*
- *Home Indoor Air Quality Checklist*

Available from:

Local chapters of the American Lung Association.

- *Formaldehyde: Everything You Wanted to Know But Were Afraid to Ask*

Send a self-addressed, stamped envelope to: Consumer

Federation of America
1424 Sixteenth Street, NW
Washington, DC 20036

ARSENIC

What is arsenic and where is it found?

Arsenic is a naturally occurring chemical found in soil and rocks. Some rocks have higher levels of arsenic, and this may explain why some drilled wells have high arsenic water. In some areas, past use of arsenic-containing pesticides on blueberry, apple and potato crops may add to the arsenic water problem. Some homes also have arsenic treated wood. This wood is treated with arsenic to protect against rot and insects.

How dangerous is arsenic?

Too much arsenic can cause cancer. Drinking water very high in arsenic can also cause stomach pain, nausea, vomiting and diarrhea, numbness or tingling in the hands and feet as well as effects on blood and the heart. How likely you are to get cancer or other health effects from arsenic in water depends on how much arsenic is in the water, how much tap water you drink and how long you have been drinking the water. Children touching unsealed treated wood (CCA wood), and then putting their hands in their mouths is the biggest concern.

What is CCA wood and what can be done about it?

CCA wood is made by dipping the wood in a mixture of chemicals. These chemicals include chromium, copper and arsenic. The amount of arsenic on the surface of the wood can be lowered by applying a coating on the wood every

1-2 years. Oil-based sealants, varnishes or polyurethane work best for sealing the arsenic in the wood. After December 31, 2003 no more CCA wood was made for use around homes. Maine CDC has information on testing the wood to see if it has arsenic.

How much is too much arsenic in well water?

Test results for arsenic in water are often reported as the number of milligrams of arsenic in a litter of water (mg/L). The Bureau of Health guideline for arsenic in domestic well water is 0.01 milligrams of arsenic per liter of water.

How likely is it that well water has high arsenic?

Based on current information we have, it looks like about 1 out of every 10 Maine homes with a private well have arsenic levels of concern. Drilled bedrock wells are more likely to have high arsenic levels than dug wells, wellpoints or wells that are drilled into sand and gravel.

Can I use water for cooking and/or bathing if it has high arsenic?

Studies have shown that little arsenic gets into adults from bathing. There is no present study on young children. In cooking, it depends on how much water is absorbed or used when cooking a food and how often the food is eaten. Pasta, rice, and oatmeal are examples of foods that absorb a lot of water when cooked. Soup and jello are examples of foods that use water by recipe. If the water has more than 0.05 mg/L arsenic, the Maine Bureau of Health should be contacted.

Is there a way to remove arsenic from well water?

There are arsenic removal systems and the choice of a treatment system depends on what else is in your water and how much water to treat. The system should be certified for arsenic removal by NSF International (www.nsf.org) and tested once a year after any system is installed to make sure it is working.

The following sources can provide more information on arsenic:

Arsenic Treated Wood
Eric Frohmberg
Environmental and Occupational Health Program Maine CDC
Toll free in Maine – 866-292-3474
www.maine.gov/dhhs/eohp

Health Effects of Arsenic
Andrew E. Smith, SM, ScD State
Toxicology Program Bureau of Health
11 State House Station
Augusta, ME 04333
Toll Free 866-292-3474

Treatment Systems for Removing Arsenic
David Braley, Geologist
Drinking Water Program
Bureau of Health
11 State House Station
Augusta, ME 04333
(297) 287- 3194

SOURCES OF ADDITIONAL INFORMATION

The EPA operates a variety of telephone hotlines to provide the public with easy access to the EPA's programs, capabilities, and services. In addition to the hotlines, the EPA has a variety of clearinghouses, libraries, and dockets that may provide information about a broad range of environmental issues. Information related to all of these sources is published in the *Guide to EPA Hotlines, Clearinghouses, Libraries, and Dockets*, which is available from the EPA's Public Information Center (401 M Street, SW, Washington, DC 20460).

The regional offices of the U.S. Environmental Protection Agency are perhaps the best sources of additional information about environmental hazards in specific states and local areas. Each EPA regional office has information on states and areas within a single geographic area.

EPA Region 1

One Congress St. Boston,
MA 02114-2023
1(888) 372-7341

Areas served: Connecticut, Maine, Massachusetts, New Hampshire, Rhode Island, and Vermont

Figure B.1 Arsenic

Arsenic in Well Water: The Problem You Can't See, Smell, or Taste

It's hard to believe that water that looks, smells, and tastes fine may not be safe to drink. But the truth is that many private wells in Maine yield water that is high in arsenic.

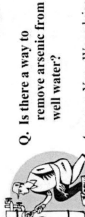

Arsenic is a naturally occurring chemical found in soil and rocks. Some rocks have higher levels of arsenic, and this may explain why some drilled wells have high arsenic water. And in some areas, past use of arsenic-containing pesticides on blueberry, apple and potato crops may add to the arsenic water problem.

The Harm Caused by Arsenic

People who drink water high in arsenic for many years are more likely to get cancer. Drinking water very high in arsenic can also cause stomach pain, nausea, vomiting and diarrhea, numbness or tingling in the hands and feet, as well as effects on blood and the heart.

How likely you are to get cancer or any other health effects from arsenic in water depends on three major factors:

- How much arsenic is in your water;
- How much tap water you drink;
- How long you have been drinking the water.

If you are concerned about health problems possibly due to arsenic in your well water, you should discuss them with your doctor. The Bureau of Health recommends that all household wells be tested for arsenic.

Answers to Some Commonly Asked Questions

Q. How much is too much arsenic in well water?

Answer: Test results for arsenic in water are often reported as the number of *milligrams* of arsenic in a *liter* of water (mg/L for short). A liter is about a quart. The Bureau of Health guideline for arsenic in domestic well water is 0.01 milligrams of arsenic per liter of water. The current federal government standard for regulated water supplies is 0.05 mg/L, but this will be lowered to 0.01 mg/L.

Q. I just found out I have high arsenic water. What should I do?

Answer: If your water has more than 0.01 mg/L arsenic, we recommend you begin taking steps to reduce how much of this water you drink. Switching to bottled water will greatly reduce how much arsenic gets into your body. It will also allow you to safely take your time in deciding what, if any, treatment you want to have installed to remove arsenic from your well water. Sometimes, simply switching to bottled water is all that is needed.

Q. Is there a way to remove arsenic from well water?

Answer: Yes. We advise consulting one or more water treatment companies to help in choosing an arsenic removal system. This is because the choice of a treatment system depends on what else is in your water and how much water you need to treat. While we do not recommend any specific treatment system, we do advise selection of treatment systems that have been certified for arsenic removal by NSF International (www.nsf.org). Also, be sure to test at least once a year after any system is installed to make sure it is working.

Figure B.1 Arsenic (continued)

HAVE YOU TESTED YOUR WELL WATER FOR ARSENIC?

Health Information for Private Well Users

Arsenic in Well Water

Maine Bureau of Health

How do I get more information about arsenic in private well water?

♦ For more information on the health effects of arsenic, contact:

Andrew E. Smith, SM, ScD.
State Toxicologist
Environmental Toxicology Program
Bureau of Health
11 State House Station
Augusta, ME 04333
Toll Free: 866-292-3474
Email: andy.e.smith@state.me.us

Website:
janus.state.me.us/dhs/bohetp/index.html

♦ For more information on treatment systems for removing arsenic from well water, contact:

David Braley, Geologist
Drinking Water Program
Bureau of Health
11 State House Station
Augusta, ME 04333
Tel: (297) 287-3194
Email: david.braley@state.me.us

Website:
janus.state.me.us/dhs/eng/water/index.htm

Kevin W. Concannon, Comissioner
May 13, 2002

Q. Can I use my water for bathing if it has high arsenic?

Answer: Studies have shown that little arsenic gets into adults from bathing. But we do not have studies on young kids. Kids might get more arsenic in them while bathing because of their bathing habits. We have a study underway to check this. For now, if you are concerned, call us toll-free to discuss exposure from bathing.

Q. Can I use my water for cooking if it has arsenic in it?

Answer: The answer depends on how much arsenic is in your water, how much water is either absorbed or used when cooking a food, and how often you eat such foods. Pasta, rice, oatmeal and dried beans are examples of foods that absorb a lot of water when cooked. Soup and jello are examples of foods that use water by recipe. If your water has more than 0.05 mg/L arsenic, contact us for information about use in cooking.

Q. How likely is it that my well water has high arsenic?

Answer: Based on the current information we have, it looks like about 1 out of every 10 Maine homes with a private well have arsenic levels of concern. Drilled bedrock wells are more likely to have high arsenic levels than dug wells, wellpoints, or wells that are drilled into sand and gravel.

4

EXAMINATION TERMINOLOGY

The Maine Real Estate Commission has adopted a state examination as part of the requirements to obtain a sales agent license. There is the independent testing company that developed and administers the test. The examination is divided into two parts: Part One covers general topics and Part Two covers state laws.

The practice of real estate from state to state may be slightly or vastly different. The terminology accompanies the practice. Because this is a Maine specific book, we did not want to put practice or terminology in the main part of the text, but we did want to accommodate those potential agents who were using this book to study for the course test and the state test. What follows are terms that could be found on that part of the state test that is general.

AGENCY

Agency by Ratification—Agency created after the fact by the principal approving an unauthorized act of the agent

Agency by Estoppel—An agency created when the principal's words or actions lead a third party to believe the broker to be the owner's agent

Attorney-in-fact—A person operating as an agent under a power of attorney

Designated Agency—Appointed agency

Facilitator/Intermediary—Transaction broker in Maine

Ostensible Agency—An agency relationship that arises out of the actions of the parties rather than by express agreement

General Agent—An agent having all necessary authority to conduct a business or trade

Principal Broker—Designated broker

LAND USE CONTROLS

Accretion—The gradual addition of land by natural action of rivers or streams. The added land becomes the property of the owner of the land.

Avulsion—A loss of land by action of water such as a change in a stream's course. The owner retains title to the land washed away by sudden avulsion.

Dereliction/reliction—The dry land that forms after the gradual receding of water. The rules of accretion apply to this land.

Government Lot—A parcel of land less than a quarter section (less than 160 acres) because of some physical features such as a lake that limits the size of the lot

Laches—Losing a right due to the failure to assert it in a timely manner

Littoral Rights—An owner's right to reasonable use of water from a lake, ocean, or pond bordering the property

Severance Damage—When only part of the owner's land is taken by eminent domain causing a reduced value for the remaining land

Upzoning—A rezoning to a higher or more productive use

ESTATES IN REAL PROPERTY

Community Property—Property acquired during marriage is considered to be equally owned by both spouses. Upon the death of one spouse, one-half of the community property is retained by the surviving spouse and the other half passes to the heirs.

Curtesy—A husband's right to a life estate in the wife's property upon her death

Dower—A wife's right to a life estate or an ownership interest in her husband's home upon his death

Law of Testate Distribution—How a decedent's real estate and personal property is to be passed on by the terms of a will

Tenancy by the Entirety—A form of joint ownership reserved for married couples with a right of survivorship upon the death of one spouse. Neither spouse can separately convey an interest during the other's lifetime. Divorce would change the ownership to a tenancy in common.

Tenancy in Severalty—Sole ownership by one individual or entity such as a corporation or partnership

Special Warranty Deed—Quitclaim with Covenant

General Warranty Deed—Warranty Deed

Tenement for Years—Estate for Years

Tenement from year to year or Periodic Estate—Estate from year to year

FINANCING/CLOSINGS

Administrator—A man appointed by the court to act as a representative of the deceased. A woman is called an administratrix.

Bargain and Sale Deed—A deed for consideration that used the terms bargain and sale. It contains no warranties other than an implied interest by the grantor.

Escrow Closings—A process of transferring title where the buyer and seller select a neutral party who acts as the escrow agent. There is a conditional delivery of funds and documents to the escrow agent together with the escrow instructions. The instructions can be either bilateral (presented by both the buyer and seller together) or unilateral (prepared by each party separately). Once the terms have been satisfied, delivery and transfer of the funds and documents takes place.

Hypothecation—When a borrower keeps control of the loan collateral but gives the lender a lien

Mortgage Warehousing—The practice of mortgage companies of accumulating a stock of mortgages and borrowing on them until sold

Non-disturbance Clause—A lease clause in which a mortgagee agrees to honor a lease should the mortgagee foreclose

Take-out loan—A permanent loan that replaces a construction loan

Title Commitment—A report of title company on examination of public records to issue a title insurance policy

Torren's system—System to register titles. An application is made with the clerk of the court in the county where the real estate is located. If the court is satisfied that the applicant is the owner of the property, court enters an order to register the real estate and the registrar of titles if further directed to issue a Torrens certificate of title.

Trust Deed—The transfer of title from the borrower to a third party (trustee) as security for a note to the lender (beneficiary)

MAINE REAL ESTATE COMMISSION

CONTENTS

MINIMUM STANDARDS OF PRACTICE

This appendix clarifies and establishes standards for practicing real estate brokerage.

1. Advertising

1. Definition

   As used in this Section, the terms "advertise," "advertising" and "advertisement" include all forms of representation, promotion and solicitation disseminated in any manner and by any means of communication for any purpose related to real estate brokerage activity, including, at a minimum, advertising the sale or purchase of real estate or promotion of real estate brokerage services conducted by mail, telephone, the Internet, the World Wide Web, E-mail, electronic bulletin board or other similar electronic common carrier systems, business cards, signs, television, radio, magazines, newspapers, and telephonic greetings or answering machine messages.

2. Trade Name

   Advertising must be done in the real estate brokerage agency's trade name as licensed with the Commission and the trade name must be prominently displayed.

3. Prominent means standing out so as to be seen easily; conspicuous; particularly noticeable.

4. Advertising by Affiliated Licensees

   Advertising by affiliated licensees must be under the supervision of the designated broker. Such advertising may include an affiliated licensee's name and phone number or other contact information, provided the real estate brokerage agency's trade name is also included as required.

5. Written Permission of Owner Required to Advertise

   A real estate brokerage agency or its affiliated licensees shall not advertise any real estate for sale without first obtaining the written permission of the owner or the owner's authorized representative.

6. Advertising of Exclusive Listing Held by Another Agency

   A real estate brokerage agency or its affiliated licensees shall not publish or cause to be published an advertisement that makes reference to the availability of real estate which is exclusively listed for sale by another real estate brokerage agency unless the licensee obtains the prior written consent of the designated broker who has been authorized by the owner to provide consent.

7. Deception and Misrepresentation Prohibited

   Advertising must be free from deception and shall not misrepresent the condition of the real estate, terms of the sale or purchase, real estate brokerage agency policies, or real estate brokerage services.

2. Acting in Self-Interest

A licensee holding an active real estate license shall disclose, in the offer to purchase, that the licensee is a real estate licensee:

1. When buying real estate not listed with a real estate brokerage agency;

2. When buying real estate listed with the licensee's real estate brokerage agency; or

3. When buying real estate and sharing in the brokerage fee resulting from the sale of such real estate.

3. Market Value

1. When Opinion Permitted
A licensee may provide a free opinion of value to a buyer or seller when the licensee is soliciting the buyer or seller to provide brokerage services and before an agreement to provide any services has been reached or executed.

2. When Advice Prohibited
At any time after the solicitation to provide brokerage services, as described in Section 3(1) of this chapter, a transaction broker may not provide advice to either party regarding market value.

3. Provision of Comparable Market Data
A licensee who provides comparable market data to a buyer or seller for the buyer or seller to determine market value or list price is performing a ministerial act as defined in 32 MRSA §13271 (9).

4. Factors or Conditions That May Impact Client's Interest
A licensee who represents a buyer or seller client shall advise the client of any factors or conditions actually known by the licensee, or if acting in a reasonable manner, should have been known by the licensee, that may materially impact the client's interest as it pertains to the market value of real estate.

4. Net Listing Prohibited

A net listing shall be prohibited. A net listing is a type of listing in which the real estate brokerage agency receives, as commission, all excess money over and above the minimum sale price set by the seller.

5. Duty to Furnish Real Estate Brokerage-Related Documents

A licensee shall furnish copies of brokerage agreements, offers, counteroffers, and all types of contracts to all parties at the time of their signatures. Upon obtaining a written acceptance of an offer or counteroffer to purchase real estate, a licensee shall, within a reasonable time, deliver true, legible copies of the purchase and sale contract, signed by the seller and buyer, to both seller and buyer.

6. Disclosure of Real Estate Brokerage Agency Compensation Policy

1. Other Agencies
Written brokerage agreements must include a statement disclosing the real estate brokerage agency's policy on cooperating with and compensating other real estate brokerage agencies in the sale or purchase of real estate.

If the real estate brokerage agency's policy is not to compensate all other real estate brokerage agencies in the same manner, this policy must be included in the statement and include a notice to the buyer or seller that this policy may limit the participation of other real estate brokerage agencies in the marketplace.

2. Affiliated Licensees

When a real estate brokerage agency's policy on paying commissions to its affiliated licensees provides for an incentive to an affiliated licensee for a greater commission for an in-house sale versus transactions involving a co-operating real estate brokerage agency, this policy must be disclosed in a written brokerage agreement with a buyer or seller.

7. Disclosed Dual Agency

A real estate brokerage agency which has a written company policy that permits disclosed dual agency shall obtain the informed written consent, as set forth in 32 MRSA §13275, of the seller or buyer to the disclosed dual agency relationship at the time of entering into a written brokerage agreement that creates an agent-client relationship.

8. Appointed Agent Procedures and Disclosure

1. Designated Broker Responsibilities—Appointed Agent

   a. A designated broker appointing an affiliated licensee(s) to act as an agent of a client shall take ordinary and necessary care to protect confidential information disclosed by the client to the appointed agent.

   b. An appointed agent may disclose to the agency's designated broker, or a designee specified by the designated broker, confidential information of a client for the purpose of seeking advice or assistance for the benefit of the client in regard to a possible transaction. Confidential information shall be treated as such by the designated broker or other specified representative of the broker and shall not be disclosed unless otherwise required by 32 MRSA Chapter 114 or related rules or requested or permitted by the client who originally disclosed the confidential information.

   c. A designated broker who is appointed to act as the agent of the client must select a designee to fulfill the responsibilities as listed in Section 8(1)(B) of this chapter.

2. Appointed Agent – Disclosure

   The appointed agent disclosure shall be provided to the client prior to entering into a written brokerage agreement and shall include, at a minimum, the following provisions:

   a. The name of the appointed agent and type of license held;

   b. A statement that the appointed agent will be the client's agent and will owe the client fiduciary duties which, among other things, include the obligation not to reveal confidential information obtained from the client to other licensees, except to the designated broker or the designated broker's designee, as listed in Section 8(1)(B) of this chapter, for the purpose of seeking advice or assistance for the benefit of the client;

c.   A statement that the real estate brokerage agency may be representing both the seller and the buyer in connection with the sale or purchase of real estate;

d.   A statement that other agents may be appointed during the term of the written brokerage agreement should the appointed agent not be able to fulfill the terms of the written brokerage agreement or as by agreement between the designated broker and client. At the appointment of new or additional agent(s), the designated broker must comply with the provisions of this Section, including but not limited to, obtaining the client's signature consenting or not consenting to the appointment. An appointment of another agent as a new or additional agent does not relieve the first appointed agent of any of the fiduciary duties owed to the client; and

e.   A section for the client to consent or not consent, in writing, to the appointment.

9.   Real Estate Brokerage Relationship Disclosure Procedures

1. Real Estate Brokerage Relationships Form
    The Commission incorporates into this chapter by reference the Real Estate Brokerage Relationships Form attached to this chapter. (Maine Real Estate Commission Form #3 revised 07/06).

2. Obligation to Furnish Real Estate Brokerage Relationships Form
    Except as provided in Section 9(3) of this chapter, a licensee shall furnish a prospective buyer or seller with a copy of the Real Estate Brokerage Relationships Form when there is substantive communication regarding a real estate transaction by either a face-to-face meeting, a written communication, or an electronic communication with the prospective buyer or seller.

3. Exceptions
    A licensee is not required to provide a copy of the form to a prospective buyer or seller in the following instances:

    a.   The real estate is land without a residential dwelling unit or is land with more than 4 residential dwelling units;

    b.   The licensee is acting solely as a principal in a real estate transaction;

    c.   The written communication from the licensee is a solicitation of business; or

    d.   The licensee has knowledge, or may reasonably assume, that another licensee has given a copy of the form to a prospective buyer or seller in that transaction.

4. Completion of Real Estate Brokerage Relationships Form
    The licensee shall complete the appropriate section of the form relating to the presentation of the form.

10.   Solicitation of Written Brokerage Agreements

A licensee shall not solicit a written brokerage agreement from a seller or buyer if the licensee knows, or acting in a reasonable manner should have known, that the buyer or seller has contracted with another real estate brokerage agency for the same real estate brokerage services on an exclusive basis. This Section does not preclude a real estate brokerage agency from entering into a written brokerage agreement with a seller or buyer, when the initial contact is initiated by the seller or buyer, provided that the written brokerage agreement does not become effective until the expiration or release of the previous written brokerage agreement.

11. Inducements

The offering of a free gift, prize, money or other valuable consideration by a real estate brokerage agency or affiliated licensee as an inducement shall be free from deception, and shall not serve to distort the true value of the real estate or the service being promoted.

12. Confidentiality of Offers and Purchase and Sale Contract Terms

During the pendency of the transaction, the real estate brokerage agency or affiliated licensee shall not disclose any terms of an offer, counteroffer or purchase and sale contract to anyone other than the buyer and seller without the prior written permission of the buyer and seller, except said documents shall be made available to the director of the Commission upon request.

13. Licensee's Duty to the Designated Broker

An affiliated licensee shall keep the designated broker fully informed of all activities conducted on behalf of the agency and shall notify the designated broker of any other activities that might impact on the responsibilities of the designated broker as required under Chapter 400, Section 1 of the Commission's rules.

An affiliated licensee must provide originals or true copies of all real estate brokerage documents and records prepared in a real estate transaction and as listed in Chapter 400, Section 3 of the Commission's rules to the designated broker within 5 calendar days after execution of the document or record.

14. Licensee's Duty to Obtain and Provide Disclosure Information on Private Water Supply, Heating, Waste Disposal System and Known Hazardous Materials

1. Listing Licensee
   A listing licensee shall be responsible for obtaining information necessary to make disclosures, as set forth in Sections 15 to 18 of this chapter, to buyers and shall make a reasonable effort to assure that the information is conveyed to a selling licensee.

2. Selling Licensee
   A selling licensee shall be responsible for obtaining from the listing licensee the information necessary for making disclosures, as set forth in Sections 15 to 18 of this chapter, and for assuring that the disclosures are made to buyers.

3. Unlisted Property

A licensee shall be responsible for obtaining from the seller in a real estate brokerage transaction where the property is not listed with a real estate brokerage agency, the information necessary for making disclosures, as set forth in Sections 15 to 18 of this chapter, and for assuring that the disclosures are made to the buyer.

15.   Private Water Supply Disclosure

A licensee listing a single-family residential property, a multifamily property, a residential lot or a commercial property with a residential component served by a private water supply, and a licensee in such transactions when the property is not listed with a real estate brokerage agency, shall ask the seller for the following information:

1. Type of system;

2. Location;

3. Malfunctions;

4. Date of installation;

5. Date of most recent water test; and

6. Whether or not the seller has experienced a problem such as an unsatisfactory water test or a water test with notations.

Such information and any other information pertinent to the private water supply shall be conveyed, in writing, to a buyer prior to or during preparation of an offer. The fact that information regarding the private water supply is not available shall also be conveyed, in writing, when such is the case.

16.   Heating Disclosure

A licensee listing a single-family residential property, a multifamily property or a commercial property with a residential component, and a licensee in such transactions when the property is not listed with a real estate brokerage agency, shall ask the seller for the following information regarding the heating system(s) and/or source(s):

1. Type(s);

2. Age of system/source(s);

3. Name of company who services system/source(s);

4. Date of most recent service call;

5. Annual consumption per system/source (i.e. gallons, kilowatt hours, cords);

6. Malfunctions per system/source within the past 2 years.

Such information and any other information pertinent to the heating system(s) and/or source(s) shall be conveyed, in writing, to a buyer prior to or during the preparation of an offer. The fact that information pertinent to the heating system(s) and/or source(s) is not available shall be conveyed, in writing, when such is the case.

17.   Waste Disposal System Disclosure

1. Private Waste Disposal System

A licensee listing a single-family residential property, a multifamily property, a residential lot or a commercial property with a residential component served by a private waste disposal system, and a licensee in such transactions when the property is not listed with a real estate brokerage agency, shall ask the seller for the following information:

   a.   Type of system;

   b.   Size of tank;

   c.   Type of tank;

   d.   Location of tank;

   e.   Malfunctions of tank;

   f.   Date of installation of tank;

   g.   Location of leach field;

   h.   Malfunctions of leach field;

   i.   Date of installation of leach field;

   j.   Date of most recent servicing of system; and

   k.   Name of the contractor who services the system.

Such information and any other information pertinent to the waste disposal system shall be conveyed, in writing, to a buyer prior to or during preparation of an offer. The fact that information regarding the waste disposal system is not available shall also be conveyed, in writing, when such is the case.

2.   Municipal or Quasi-Public Waste Disposal System
    A licensee listing a single-family residential property, a multifamily property, a residential lot or a commercial property with a residential component served by a municipal or quasi-public waste disposal system, and a licensee in such transactions when the property is not listed with a real estate brokerage agency, shall ask the seller if the seller has experienced any system or line malfunction. This information shall be conveyed, in writing, to a buyer prior to or during the preparation of an offer.

18. Known Hazardous Materials Disclosure

1.   Duty to Keep Informed
    A licensee shall keep informed of any federal, state or local laws, rules, regulations or ordinances concerning known hazardous materials that may impact negatively upon the health and well being of buyers and sellers.

2.   Duty to Disclose
    A listing licensee, and a licensee in transactions when the property is not listed with a real estate brokerage agency, shall disclose, in writing, whether the seller makes any representations regarding current or previously existing known hazardous materials on or in the real estate. In addition, the licensee shall give a written statement to the buyer encouraging the buyer to seek information from professionals regarding any specific hazardous material issue or concern. Such written representation and statement shall be conveyed to a buyer prior to or during the preparation of an offer.

3.   Request for Information From Seller
    A licensee listing a single-family residential property, a multifamily property, a commercial property with a residential component and a licensee in such transactions when the property is not listed with a real estate brokerage agency, shall ask the seller whether the seller has any knowledge of current

or previously existing asbestos, radon, lead based paint, and underground storage tanks. Such information and any other information pertinent to hazardous materials shall be conveyed, in writing, to a buyer prior to or during preparation of an offer. The fact that information regarding hazardous materials is not available shall also be conveyed, in writing, when such is the case.

19. Referral Fees

1. Certain Referral Fees Prohibited

A licensee may not receive compensation or other valuable consideration from a title company, lender or closing company or any affiliated employee for directing a buyer or seller in a real estate transaction to a company or an individual for financing, title or closing services.

2. Disclosure of Certain Referral Fees Required

A licensee who anticipates receiving compensation or other valuable consideration from a company or person for a referral of services, other than the services listed in Section 19(1) of this chapter or real estate brokerage services, to a buyer or seller during a real estate brokerage transaction may not accept such compensation or valuable consideration unless the licensee discloses in writing to the person paying for such service, and to the client if not the same person, that the licensee anticipates receiving such compensation or other valuable compensation for such referral.

STATUTORY AUTHORITY: 32 MRSA §§13065(3), 13279, 13280

Figure D.1 Multiple Offers Guidelines—Seller/Buyer Client Guidelines

DEPARTMENT OF PROFESSIONAL & FINANCIAL REGULATION
OFFICE OF PROFESSIONAL AND OCCUPATIONAL REGULATION
MAINE REAL ESTATE COMMISSION
REAL ESTATE TRANSACTIONS
OFFERS/COUNTER OFFERS – GUIDELINES
Approved June 2014

Guiding Principles – Seller/Buyer Client

• **Communicate early and often**	*When taking a listing or entering into a buyer representation agreement the agent should explain to the client how offers and counter offers are handled and the possibility of multiple offers.*
• **The agent advises – the client decides**	*The decisions about how offers will be presented, negotiated and ultimately accepted or rejected are made by the client – not the agent. All offers must be communicated and agent must keep client informed of stated interest in property.*
• **Offers and counter offers in writing**	*Offers and counter offers should be in writing to ensure that the terms, time frames and legal obligations of the parties are understood. Written counter offers should include a specific time period for acceptance. Withdrawal of a written offer or counter offer should be made in writing.*
• **Terms of offers and counter offers are confidential**	*The terms of offers and counter offers may not be disclosed by agent without the prior written consent of both the seller and buyer. Disclosing that a full price offer has been made is disclosing a term and is a violation.*
• **The existence of an offer is not confidential**	*Disclosing that an offer has been made or that an offer may be received is not confidential information.*
• **Full-price offer does not obligate the seller to accept the offer**	*Listing property for sale is an invitation from the seller for buyers to make offers. The seller is not obligated to sell the property even if a buyer makes a full price, cash offer.*
• **No priority to offers**	*The first or highest offer made does not bind or otherwise limit the seller to act upon that offer before considering any other offers.*
• **Agent communication**	*Agents should make reasonable efforts to keep cooperating brokers informed, consistent with client's instructions.*
• **Agents are not attorneys**	*Agents should advise clients to seek legal counsel from attorneys regarding any questions about the legal status of an offer or contract.*

The Seller Client – *An informed seller will be ready to make the right decision when an offer or multiple offers are received.*	
When taking the listing:	• *Discuss seller's motivation for selling.* • *Discuss impact of current market conditions, i.e., season, types of financing, length of time on market.* • *Review Guiding Principles (on page one).* • *Explain that multiple offers may be received and that the client decides whether to disclose the existence of other offers to other agents and/or buyers.* • *Confirm that decisions about how offers will be presented, negotiated and ultimately accepted or withdrawn will be made by the seller – not the agent.*

When the offer is received:	• *Discuss the terms of the offer(s) – if multiple offers, compare terms.*
	
	• *Inform seller of any other interest in the property.*
	   ✓ *Potential of other offers*
	   ✓ *Scheduled showings*
	   ✓ *Recent showings that may require follow-up.*
	
	• *Seller may instruct agent to keep the existence of offers or interest confidential.*

Seller's options – one offer:	• *Accept, reject, counter, delay during time for acceptance, seek out other offer or do nothing.* • *Explain pluses and minuses of each option – including the potential of a buyer withdrawing an offer during a delay.*
Seller's options – multiple offers:	• *Accept one offer.* • *Reject all offers and encourage "best" offers.* • *Counter one offer (may withdraw counter, in writing, prior to acceptance) – do not inform other buyers.* • *Delay during time for acceptance.* • *Alert one or more buyers that they are in a multiple offer situation.* • *Reject all offers.* • *Do nothing.* • *Consider the pluses and minuses of each option – delaying or inviting all buyers to make their "best" offer may produce better offer(s) or may discourage buyers who may withdraw.*

	***The Buyer Client** – An informed buyer will be ready to make the right decision when making an offer.*
When entering into a buyer agent agreement:	• *Discuss buyer's motivation for purchasing.* • *Discuss current market conditions, i.e. season, types of financing, average length of time for properties on the market.* • *Review Guiding Principles (on page one).* • *Explain that multiple offers may be made on one property. In those situations, only one offer may result in a sale and one (or more) buyer(s) may be disappointed.* • *Explain that buyer agent may have more than one client interested in the same property. In those situations, buyer agent will notify all clients who have expressed an interest in the property of any other interest and/or that an offer has been made.* • *Explain that seller is not obligated to acknowledge, counter or reject an offer and may inform other buyers of existence of an offer or may do nothing.* • *Confirm that decisions about how offers will be negotiated and presented or withdrawn will be made by the buyer – not the agent.*

When the offer is made – discuss with buyer the possibility of multiple offers:	• *Initial offer may be the only opportunity to buy.*
	
	• *Inform buyer of any other interest in property buyer agent is aware of, even if from other clients of buyer agent who have expressed an interest in the property. Remind buyer client that buyer agent will notify those other clients that an offer has been made (terms and conditions remain confidential).*
	
	• *There is no requirement that the buyer be informed by the seller or listing agent of the existence of other offers.*
	
	• *Seller has the right to negotiate with only one buyer at a time and not reveal this to other buyers.*
	
	• *The agent may not disclose the terms of buyer's offer but the existence of the offer may be communicated to other buyers.*
	
	• *Seller may accept an offer on terms other than the price.*
	
	• *All buyers may be notified to present their "best" offer – buyer may choose to:*
	    ✓ *make different offer*
	    ✓ *leave original offer*
	    ✓ *withdraw offer in writing if period for acceptance is current*
	    ✓ *do nothing.*

Figure D.3 Multiple Offers Guidelines—Buyer–Client Guidelines

Offers and Counter Offers – FAQ's (Customer Status)

A customer is a buyer or seller not represented by a real estate licensee in a transaction.

1. What should I expect when I make or receive an offer?
- Offers, counter offers or withdrawal of an offer should be in writing;
- Terms of offers and counter offers are confidential;
- The existence of an offer is not confidential;
- A full-price offer does not obligate seller to accept the offer;
- There is no priority to offers.

2. I'm ready to make an offer. Who can prepare the offer for me?
The listing agent (the seller's agent) or another licensee can perform ministerial acts* for a buyer such as filling in the blanks on the company's purchase and sale agreement

3. Can I ask the listing agent (seller's agent) to tell me if other offers have been submitted to the seller?
You can ask, but the listing agent is not required to answer your question. The listing agent has fiduciary duties to the seller client; the seller client may authorize the agent to inform you of the existence of other offers.

4. Can I ask a licensee for advice about offers I make or receive?
You can ask, but licensee may not provide advice to or counsel a customer.

*"Ministerial acts" means those acts that a real estate brokerage agency performs for a person who is not a client and that are informative or clerical in nature and do not rise to the level of active representation on behalf of the person.

Figure D.5 Field Experience form.

Real Estate Associate Broker Qualifying Education Documented Field Experience Form

To satisfactorily complete the Real Estate Associate Broker course, students must pass a course consisting of a minimum of 60 classroom hours of study with a grade of 75 or higher and demonstrate hands-on experience as evidenced by completion of the training tasks (Sections 1 – 6) in this form and documented by the designated broker or mentor(s)* assigned by the designated broker. It is estimated that completion of the tasks will require a minimum of 40 hours of training. To satisfactorily complete the Associate Broker course, the student will be required to return the completed and signed Field Experience Form to the course instructor for approval.

Please note: Designated Brokers may have adopted different or additional procedures, policies, brokerage forms or information than found in some or all of the sections. For example, Section 1 is intended to orient the sales agent to the real estate company's policies, office structure and procedures. The information included in this Section should not be viewed as mandatory for all real estate companies. It is expected, however, that the designated broker or mentor(s) will provide training as identified in each of the training tasks.

*A mentor is selected by the designated broker and may be another licensee within the real estate company, company manager or other person within the company with expertise in the task to be completed or a trainer engaged by the designated broker to offer in-house training exclusively to assist the sales agent of that company to complete the required tasks.

A note about forms: Except for the Real Estate Brokerage Relationships Form (Form 3), the Maine Real Estate Commission does not provide forms for the practice of real estate brokerage. Any reference to forms in this document recognizes that most Designated Brokers provide certain forms for the affiliated licensees to use in the conduct of their business. Your Designated Broker will likely provide you with various forms and will review their proper use with you during this training.

Sales Agent Name: _____

License Number: _____

Figure D.5 Field Experience form (continued).

Sales Agent Name: _____

License Number: _____

<u>*Section 1: Real Estate Office Orientation*</u>
A. Policy and Procedures Manual

Review the following with Designated Broker or Office Manager:

Brokerage Relationship Policies	Commission schedule
Cooperation and compensation	Fee schedule
Real Estate transaction forms	Referrals
Policies on confidentiality	Office hours
Insurance Issues	Anti-Trust
Errors and Omissions	Retention of documents
Auto	Advertising Preparation
Equipment owned by agent in office	"Do Not Call" list
Fair Housing	Other

*Date Completed*_____   *Certified by*_____

                                                       (Designated Broker or mentor)

B. Independent Contractor Agreement (or employment agreement if applicable)

Review the following with Designated Broker or Office Manager:

Tax implications	Reference to Policy Manual
Authority to bind the agency	Departure/Termination procedures

*Date Completed*_____   *Certified by*_____

                                                       (Designated Broker or mentor)

C. Office equipment, forms, personnel and policies

Review the following with Designated Broker or Office Manager:

Office personnel & job descriptions	Operation of office equipment
Office files and forms	Copier
How listings are processed	Phone
Checklist for complete listing files	Fax
How under contracts are processed	Designated Broker's policies on
Checklist for under contract files	communication in the office:
Answering inquiries and phone etiquette	Mail distribution
How to answer phone	Electronic mail
"Do Not Call" policies	Office opening & closing procedures
	Other

*Date Completed*_____   *Certified by*_____

                                                       (Designated Broker or mentor)

Figure D.5 Field Experience form (continued).

Sales Agent Name: _____

License Number: _____

Section 2: Taking a listing
A. Getting Property Information

1. At Registry of Deeds, learn how to perform the following tasks:
    A.   Get a Copy of the Deed
    B.   Read the Deed
    C.   Get a Copy of the Recorded Plan, if any.
    D.   Get a copy of recorded covenants/restrictions, if any.
2. At the Town Hall, learn how to perform the following tasks:
    A.   Go to tax office and get a copy of the tax map.
    B.   Get a copy of the tax card.
    C.   Check for square footage.
    D.   Check for tax exemptions.
    E.   Go to the Code Enforcement Office
    F.   Get a copy of the Code Enforcement File
            Are there any apparent discrepancies between property and code file?
    G.   Get a copy of HHE 200 (plan for septic system) if on file.
    H.   Note where private well is located, if applicable.
3. If property is part of an association (condominium, road maintenance association, etc.), know where to get copies of:
    A. Road Maintenance Agreement
    B. Declaration of Condominium
    C. Association By-Laws
    D. Rules and Regulations
4. Other sources of information – company data form
5. View the entire property, from basement to attic
6. Ask the Seller for Maine Real Estate Commission required property disclosures:
    A. Private Water Supply
    B. Private Waste Disposal System
    C. Public or Quasi-Public System
    D. Heating System
    E. Hazardous Materials
7. Ask the Seller about any material defects in the physical condition of the property.
8. Ask the Seller about the presence of lead paint or lead-based paint hazards.

Date Completed_____   Certified by_____
                                             (Designated Broker or mentor)

Figure D.5 Field Experience form (continued).

Sales Agent Name: _____

License Number: _____

B. Developing the Listing Packet for listing presentation

1. Plan your presentation and list the points to cover with the Seller.
2. Review your presentation with your Designated Broker.
3. Your listing packet for the Seller may include some or all of the following:

   Personal Information   Sample Advertising

   Company Information   Sample Marketing Plan
4. Forms:

   Real Estate Brokerage Relationship Form #3

   Lead Paint and Protect Your Family from Lead in Your Home
5. DisclosureRequirements (forms may be company specific):

   Lead Paint   Arsenic brochure   Property Disclosure Form
6. Sample Purchase and Sale Agreement
7. Estimated Sellers Net Sheet
8. Listing Agreement
9. Maine Real Estate Commission Offer and Counter Offer Guidelines
10. Appropriate brochures and marketing information

         Preparing the property for sale

         Fair Housing brochure

         Pricing for best price

Date Completed_____ Certified by_____

                                                               (Designated Broker or mentor)

C. Prepare for Meeting the Seller

1. Develop a CMA (Comparative Market Analysis) for the Seller
2. Have all Listing forms prepared, including:

        Listing Agreements   Property Disclosure Form

        Lead Paint Disclosure form if property built before 1978 (or per your company's policies.

        Any other documents you will present to Seller
3. Proofread all forms to be sure there are no mistakes.
4. Review Property Marketing Plan with Designated Broker or mentor. Some or all of the following tools will be presented to the seller:

   Multiple Listing service(if   Websites for properties   Advertising your company participates)

   Public Open Houses   Broker Open Houses and Broker Caravans

   Brochures   Mailings   Signs   Other
5. Review showing protocol with Designated Broker or mentor, which may include:

   Lock boxes   Setting up appointments

   Keys (consider security of keys)   Feedback to listing agents

   Be sure to secure the property   Feedback to Sellers
6. Review your listing presentation with Designated Broker or mentor. Be sure you can explain every line on all agreements.

Date Completed_____ Certified by_____

                                                               (Designated Broker or mentor)

Figure D.5 Field Experience form (continued).

Sales Agent Name: _____

License Number: _____

D. Meeting with the Seller

1. Present CMA (Comparative Market Analysis)
2. Present Marketing Plan (which may include any or all of the following):

Multiple Listing service	Websites for properties
Advertising	Public Open Houses
Broker Open Houses	Brochures
Broker Caravans	Signs
Mailings	Other

3. Signing of forms (which forms are necessary?)

Listing Agreement – be prepared to explain every line.

Property Disclosure Form – signature of Seller if required by Company Policy

Disclosed Dual Agency	Appointed Agency
Lead Paint Brochure	Arsenic Brochure

Showing Instructions: Lock box? Listing Agent present at all showings?

Date Completed_____   Certified by_____
(Designated Broker or mentor)

E. Office Procedures for New Listing

Process New listing
 Company submits property to multiple listing service, web site, other advertising.
 Set up company listing file and showing procedures.

Proofreading
 Licensee is responsible for accuracy of disclosures and information
 Be careful of taxes, acreage, square footage, etc.

Executing the Marketing Plan for new listing

Multiple Listing service	Websites for properties
Advertising	Public Open Houses
Broker Open Houses	Brochures
Broker Caravans	Signs
Mailings	Other

Set up schedule for communication with Seller
 Some sellers complain that the listing licensee never contacts them. Contact the Seller on an agreed-upon schedule and by a method of the seller's choosing (i.e. mail, phone, email, in person).

Date Completed_____   Certified by_____
(Designated Broker or mentor)

Figure D.5 Field Experience form (continued).

Sales Agent Name: _____

License Number: _____

Section 3: Working With a Buyer
A. Develop a Buyer Presentation

Work with your Designated Broker or mentor to develop a buyer presentation packet of informative materials. This packet is designed to give buyers confidence that they are working with a competent professional. Materials may include:

Real Estate Brokerage Relationship Form #3
Maine Real Estate Commission Offer and Counter Offer Guidelines
Pamphlet: <u>Protecting Your Family from Lead in Your Home.</u>
Sample Purchase and Sale Agreement
An explanation of how you find homes for buyers
An explanation of the importance of prequalification/preapproval for financing
Fair Housing Brochure   Arsenic Brochure   Other
The following documents may also be included:
Your Resume   Company Information   Marketing Brochures

Date Completed_____   Certified by_____
                                                (Designated Broker or mentor)

B. Buyer counseling session

You will likely take 45 minutes to an hour and a half during this first meeting with buyer to explain how the industry works, what they need to consider while looking for a home and what services you can offer. Use the Buyer Packet to guide your presentation.

Present Real Estate Brokerage Relationship Form #3
Decide whether you will be a Buyer Agent or Transaction Broker

Be prepared to discuss ordering and/or paying for the following inspections:

General building inspection	Air Quality	Arsenic-treated wood
Chimney inspection	Mold	Zoning
Environmental Scan	Lead Paint	Flood Plain
Water Quality and Quantity	Pools	Insurance
Sewage Disposal	Pests	Code Conformance

Explain how you will use the Multiple Listing Service to find their property (if applicable)
Set up a communication schedule.
Discuss Open Houses
Discuss FSBO's (For Sale By Owners).
Discuss how much buyers can afford and what their needs are.
Fill out brokerage agreement if appropriate
Make arrangements to have buyer pre-qualified/pre approved.

Date Completed_____   Certified by_____
                                                (Designated Broker or mentor)

Maine Real Estate Commission Field Experience Form #05/06   *REVISED 01/18/2008*   *Page 6 of 8*

Figure D.5 Field Experience form (continued).

Sales Agent Name: _____

License Number: _____

C. Communicate Regularly with Buyer.

At least once per week, or as agreed upon with the Buyer. Abandonment or Estrangement can defeat a claim of procuring cause. Discuss procuring cause with your Designated Broker or mentor.

Date Completed_____ Certified by_____

(Designated Broker or mentor)

Section 4: Making the Offer

A. Preparing the Purchase and Sale Agreement and Writing up Offers:

Review Purchase and Sale agreement with Designated Broker or mentor
Be able to explain the various paragraphs and terms used in the Purchase and Sale Agreement.
Be familiar with all company contract forms and addenda
Be able to explain your company policy regarding drafting contingencies.
Know agency guidelines for handling earnest money

Date Completed_____ Certified by_____

(Designated Broker or mentor)

B. Writing an Offer:

Write first offer.
Review Maine Real Estate Commission Offer and Counter Offer guidelines with buyers
Conduct negotiations and put property under contract.

C. Presentation of Offers and Counter Offers:

Understand what to do with offers received on unfamiliar forms.

Date Completed_____ Certified by_____

(Designated Broker or mentor)

Section 5: Under Contract to Closing

A. Monitor contingencies and key dates in the contract

Develop system for tracking key dates
    Inspections   Appraisal
    Finance Terms   Other
Draft a letter to client regarding time frames
    Application for Finance   Appraisal
    Finance Approval   Inspections
    Secure Insurance   Other

Date Completed_____ Certified by_____

Figure D.5 Field Experience form (continued).

(Designated Broker or mentor)

Sales Agent Name: _____

License Number: _____

B. Prepare for closing:

Communicate with Title company regarding closing
Discuss title insurance with buyer
Make sure your buyer/seller is ready for closing
Review Settlement Statement before closing
Draft a letter to client/customer a week before closing with check list

Date Completed_____ Certified by_____
(Designated Broker or mentor)

Section 6: Record Keeping

A. Possible or Suggested Company requirements for complete transaction files

For Buyers:

> Real Estate Brokerage Relationship Form #3
> Brokerage Agreement, if appropriate
> Deed
> Purchase and Sale Agreement
> Property Disclosure
> Lead Paint Disclosure
> Settlement Statement if available
> Property Brochure
> Home Warranty
> Other Documents relevant to the transaction

For Sellers:

> Real Estate Brokerage Relationship Form #3
> Brokerage Agreement, if appropriate
> Deed
> Purchase and Sale Agreement
> Property Disclosure
> Lead Paint
> Settlement Statement if available
> Property Brochure
> Home Warranty
> Unaccepted offers and fall through contracts
> Other Documents relevant to the transaction

Date Completed_____ Certified by_____
(Designated Broker or mentor)

Code of Ethics and Standards of Practice of the National Association of Realtors®

Effective January 1, 2018

Where the word Realtors® is used in this Code and Preamble, it shall be deemed to include Realtor-Associate®s.

While the Code of Ethics establishes obligations that may be higher than those mandated by law, in any instance where the Code of Ethics and the law conflict, the obligations of the law must take precedence.

Preamble

Under all is the land. Upon its wise utilization and widely allocated ownership depend the survival and growth of free institutions and of our civilization. Realtors® should recognize that the interests of the nation and its citizens require the highest and best use of the land and the widest distribution of land ownership. They require the creation of adequate housing, the building of functioning cities, the development of productive industries and farms, and the preservation of a healthful environment.

Such interests impose obligations beyond those of ordinary commerce. They impose grave social responsibility and a patriotic duty to which Realtors® should dedicate themselves, and for which they should be diligent in preparing themselves. Realtors®, therefore, are zealous to maintain and improve the standards of their calling and share with their fellow Realtors® a common responsibility for its integrity and honor.

In recognition and appreciation of their obligations to clients, customers, the public, and each other, Realtors® continuously strive to become and remain informed on issues affecting real estate and, as knowledgeable professionals, they willingly share the fruit of their experience and study with others. They identify and take steps, through enforcement of this Code of Ethics and by assisting appropriate regulatory bodies, to eliminate practices which may damage the public or which might discredit or bring dishonor to the real estate profession. Realtors® having direct personal knowledge of conduct that may violate the Code of Ethics involving misappropriation of client or customer funds or property, willful discrimination, or fraud resulting in substantial economic harm, bring such matters to the attention of the appropriate Board or Association of Realtors®. *(Amended 1/00)*

Realizing that cooperation with other real estate professionals promotes the best interests of those who utilize their services, Realtors® urge exclusive representation of clients; do not attempt to gain any unfair advantage over their competitors; and they refrain from making unsolicited comments about other practitioners. In instances where their opinion is sought, or where Realtors® believe that comment is necessary, their opinion is offered in an objective, professional manner, uninfluenced by any personal motivation or potential advantage or gain.

The term Realtor® has come to connote competency, fairness, and high integrity resulting from adherence to a lofty ideal of moral conduct in business relations. No inducement of profit and no instruction from clients ever can justify departure from this ideal.

In the interpretation of this obligation, Realtors® can take no safer guide than that which has been handed down through the centuries, embodied in the Golden Rule, "Whatsoever ye would that others should do to you, do ye even so to them."

Accepting this standard as their own, Realtors® pledge to observe its spirit in all of their activities whether conducted personally, through associates or others, or via technological means, and to conduct their business in accordance with the tenets set forth below. *(Amended 1/07)*

Duties to Clients and Customers

Article 1
When representing a buyer, seller, landlord, tenant, or other client as an agent, REALTORS® pledge themselves to protect and promote the interests of their client. This obligation to the client is primary, but it does not relieve REALTORS® of their obligation to treat all parties honestly. When serving a buyer, seller, landlord, tenant or other party in a non-agency capacity, REALTORS® remain obligated to treat all parties honestly. *(Amended 1/01)*

- **Standard of Practice 1-1**
REALTORS®, when acting as principals in a real estate transaction, remain obligated by the duties imposed by the Code of Ethics. *(Amended 1/93)*

- **Standard of Practice 1-2**
The duties imposed by the Code of Ethics encompass all real estate-related activities and transactions whether conducted in person, electronically, or through any other means.

The duties the Code of Ethics imposes are applicable whether REALTORS® are acting as agents or in legally recognized non-agency capacities except that any duty imposed exclusively on agents by law or regulation shall

not be imposed by this Code of Ethics on REALTORS® acting in non-agency capacities.

As used in this Code of Ethics, "client" means the person(s) or entity(ies) with whom a REALTOR® or a REALTOR®'s firm has an agency or legally recognized non-agency relationship; "customer" means a party to a real estate transaction who receives information, services, or benefits but has no contractual relationship with the REALTOR® or the REALTOR®'s firm; "prospect" means a purchaser, seller, tenant, or landlord who is not subject to a representation relationship with the REALTOR® or REALTOR®'s firm; "agent" means a real estate licensee (including brokers and sales associates) acting in an agency relationship as defined by state law or regulation; and "broker" means a real estate licensee (including brokers and sales associates) acting as an agent or in a legally recognized non-agency capacity. *(Adopted 1/95, Amended 1/07)*

- **Standard of Practice 1-3**
REALTORS®, in attempting to secure a listing, shall not deliberately mislead the owner as to market value.

- **Standard of Practice 1-4**
REALTORS®, when seeking to become a buyer/tenant representative, shall not mislead buyers or tenants as to savings or other benefits that might be realized through use of the REALTOR®'s services. *(Amended 1/93)*

- **Standard of Practice 1-5**
REALTORS® may represent the seller/landlord and buyer/tenant in the same transaction only after full disclosure to and with informed consent of both parties. *(Adopted 1/93)*

- **Standard of Practice 1-6**
REALTORS® shall submit offers and counter-offers objectively and as quickly as possible. *(Adopted 1/93, Amended 1/95)*

- **Standard of Practice 1-7**
When acting as listing brokers, REALTORS® shall continue to submit to the seller/landlord all offers and counter-offers until closing or execution of a lease unless the seller/landlord has waived this obligation in writing. REALTORS® shall not be obligated to continue to market the property after an offer has been accepted by the seller/landlord. REALTORS® shall recommend that sellers/landlords obtain the advice of legal counsel prior to acceptance of a subsequent offer except where the acceptance is contingent on the termination of the pre-existing purchase contract or lease. *(Amended 1/93)*

- **Standard of Practice 1-8**
REALTORS®, acting as agents or brokers of buyers/tenants, shall submit to buyers/tenants all offers and counter-

offers until acceptance but have no obligation to continue to show properties to their clients after an offer has been accepted unless otherwise agreed in writing. REALTORS®, acting as agents or brokers of buyers/tenants, shall recommend that buyers/tenants obtain the advice of legal counsel if there is a question as to whether a pre-existing contract has been terminated. (*Adopted 1/93, Amended 1/99*)

• **Standard of Practice 1-9**
The obligation of REALTORS® to preserve confidential information (as defined by state law) provided by their clients in the course of any agency relationship or non-agency relationship recognized by law continues after termination of agency relationships or any non-agency relationships recognized by law. REALTORS® shall not knowingly, during or following the termination of professional relationships with their clients:

1) reveal confidential information of clients; or
2) use confidential information of clients to the disadvantage of clients; or
3) use confidential information of clients for the REALTOR®'s advantage or the advantage of third parties unless:
   a. clients consent after full disclosure; or
   b. REALTORS® are required by court order; or
   c. it is the intention of a client to commit a crime and the information is necessary to prevent the crime; or
   d. it is necessary to defend a REALTOR® or the REALTOR®'s employees or associates against an accusation of wrongful conduct.

Information concerning latent material defects is not considered confidential information under this Code of Ethics. (*Adopted 1/93, Amended 1/01*)

• **Standard of Practice 1-10**
REALTORS® shall, consistent with the terms and conditions of their real estate licensure and their property management agreement, competently manage the property of clients with due regard for the rights, safety and health of tenants and others lawfully on the premises. (*Adopted 1/95, Amended 1/00*)

• **Standard of Practice 1-11**
REALTORS® who are employed to maintain or manage a client's property shall exercise due diligence and make reasonable efforts to protect it against reasonably foreseeable contingencies and losses. (*Adopted 1/95*)

• **Standard of Practice 1-12**
When entering into listing contracts, REALTORS® must advise sellers/landlords of:
1) the REALTOR®'s company policies regarding cooperation and the amount(s) of any compensation that will be offered to subagents, buyer/tenant agents, and/or brokers acting in legally recognized non-agency capacities;
2) the fact that buyer/tenant agents or brokers, even if compensated by listing brokers, or by sellers/landlords may represent the interests of buyers/tenants; and
3) any potential for listing brokers to act as disclosed dual agents, e.g., buyer/tenant agents. (*Adopted 1/93, Renumbered 1/98, Amended 1/03*)

• **Standard of Practice 1-13**
When entering into buyer/tenant agreements, REALTORS® must advise potential clients of:
1) the REALTOR®'s company policies regarding cooperation;
2) the amount of compensation to be paid by the client;
3) the potential for additional or offsetting compensation from other brokers, from the seller or landlord, or from other parties;
4) any potential for the buyer/tenant representative to act as a disclosed dual agent, e.g., listing broker, subagent, landlord's agent, etc., and
5) the possibility that sellers or sellers' representatives may not treat the existence, terms, or conditions of offers as confidential unless confidentiality is required by law, regulation, or by any confidentiality agreement between the parties. (*Adopted 1/93, Renumbered 1/98, Amended 1/06*)

• **Standard of Practice 1-14**
Fees for preparing appraisals or other valuations shall not be contingent upon the amount of the appraisal or valuation. (*Adopted 1/02*)

• **Standard of Practice 1-15**
REALTORS®, in response to inquiries from buyers or cooperating brokers shall, with the sellers' approval, disclose the existence of offers on the property. Where disclosure is authorized, REALTORS® shall also disclose, if asked, whether offers were obtained by the listing licensee, another licensee in the listing firm, or by a cooperating broker. (*Adopted 1/03, Amended 1/09*)

• **Standard of Practice 1-16**
REALTORS® shall not access or use, or permit or enable others to access or use, listed or managed property on terms or conditions other than those authorized by the owner or seller. (*Adopted 1/12*)

Article 2

REALTORS® shall avoid exaggeration, misrepresentation, or concealment of pertinent facts relating to the property or the transaction. REALTORS® shall not, however, be obligated to discover latent defects in the property, to advise on matters outside the scope of their real estate license, or to disclose facts which are confidential under the scope of agency or non-agency relationships as defined by state law. *(Amended 1/00)*

• Standard of Practice 2-1

REALTORS® shall only be obligated to discover and disclose adverse factors reasonably apparent to someone with expertise in those areas required by their real estate licensing authority. Article 2 does not impose upon the REALTOR® the obligation of expertise in other professional or technical disciplines. *(Amended 1/96)*

• Standard of Practice 2-2

(Renumbered as Standard of Practice 1-12 1/98)

• Standard of Practice 2-3

(Renumbered as Standard of Practice 1-13 1/98)

• Standard of Practice 2-4

REALTORS® shall not be parties to the naming of a false consideration in any document, unless it be the naming of an obviously nominal consideration.

• Standard of Practice 2-5

Factors defined as "non-material" by law or regulation or which are expressly referenced in law or regulation as not being subject to disclosure are considered not "pertinent" for purposes of Article 2. *(Adopted 1/93)*

Article 3

REALTORS® shall cooperate with other brokers except when cooperation is not in the client's best interest. The obligation to cooperate does not include the obligation to share commissions, fees, or to otherwise compensate another broker. *(Amended 1/95)*

• Standard of Practice 3-1

REALTORS®, acting as exclusive agents or brokers of sellers/landlords, establish the terms and conditions of offers to cooperate. Unless expressly indicated in offers to cooperate, cooperating brokers may not assume that the offer of cooperation includes an offer of compensation. Terms of compensation, if any, shall be ascertained by cooperating brokers before beginning efforts to accept the offer of cooperation. *(Amended 1/99)*

• Standard of Practice 3-2

Any change in compensation offered for cooperative services must be communicated to the other Realtor® prior to the time that Realtor® submits an offer to purchase/lease the property. After a Realtor® has submitted an offer to purchase or lease property, the listing broker may not attempt to unilaterally modify the offered

compensation with respect to that cooperative transaction. *(Amended 1/14)*

• Standard of Practice 3-3

Standard of Practice 3-2 does not preclude the listing broker and cooperating broker from entering into an agreement to change cooperative compensation. *(Adopted 1/94)*

• Standard of Practice 3-4

REALTORS®, acting as listing brokers, have an affirmative obligation to disclose the existence of dual or variable rate commission arrangements (i.e., listings where one amount of commission is payable if the listing broker's firm is the procuring cause of sale/lease and a different amount of commission is payable if the sale/lease results through the efforts of the seller/landlord or a cooperating broker). The listing broker shall, as soon as practical, disclose the existence of such arrangements to potential cooperating brokers and shall, in response to inquiries from cooperating brokers, disclose the differential that would result in a cooperative transaction or in a sale/lease that results through the efforts of the seller/landlord. If the cooperating broker is a buyer/tenant representative, the buyer/tenant representative must disclose such information to their client before the client makes an offer to purchase or lease. *(Amended 1/02)*

• Standard of Practice 3-5

It is the obligation of subagents to promptly disclose all pertinent facts to the principal's agent prior to as well as after a purchase or lease agreement is executed. *(Amended 1/93)*

• Standard of Practice 3-6

REALTORS® shall disclose the existence of accepted offers, including offers with unresolved contingencies, to any broker seeking cooperation. *(Adopted 5/86, Amended 1/04)*

• Standard of Practice 3-7

When seeking information from another REALTOR® concerning property under a management or listing agreement, REALTORS® shall disclose their REALTOR® status and whether their interest is personal or on behalf of a client and, if on behalf of a client, their relationship with the client. *(Amended 1/11)*

• Standard of Practice 3-8

REALTORS® shall not misrepresent the availability of access to show or inspect a listed property. *(Amended 11/87)*

• Standard of Practice 3-9

REALTORS® shall not provide access to listed property on terms other than those established by the owner or the listing broker. *(Adopted 1/10)*

- **Standard of Practice 3-10**

The duty to cooperate established in Article 3 relates to the obligation to share information on listed property, and to make property available to other brokers for showing to prospective purchasers/tenants when it is in the best interests of sellers/landlords. *(Adopted 1/11)*

Article 4

REALTORS® shall not acquire an interest in or buy or present offers from themselves, any member of their immediate families, their firms or any member thereof, or any entities in which they have any ownership interest, any real property without making their true position known to the owner or the owner's agent or broker. In selling property they own, or in which they have any interest, REALTORS® shall reveal their ownership or interest in writing to the purchaser or the purchaser's representative. *(Amended 1/00)*

- **Standard of Practice 4-1**

For the protection of all parties, the disclosures required by Article 4 shall be in writing and provided by REALTORS® prior to the signing of any contract. *(Adopted 2/86)*

Article 5

REALTORS® shall not undertake to provide professional services concerning a property or its value where they have a present or contemplated interest unless such interest is specifically disclosed to all affected parties.

Article 6

REALTORS® shall not accept any commission, rebate, or profit on expenditures made for their client, without the client's knowledge and consent.

When recommending real estate products or services (e.g., homeowner's insurance, warranty programs, mortgage financing, title insurance, etc.), REALTORS® shall disclose to the client or customer to whom the recommendation is made any financial benefits or fees, other than real estate referral fees, the REALTOR® or REALTOR®'s firm may receive as a direct result of such recommendation. *(Amended 1/99)*

- **Standard of Practice 6-1**

REALTORS® shall not recommend or suggest to a client or a customer the use of services of another organization or business entity in which they have a direct interest without disclosing such interest at the time of the recommendation or suggestion. *(Amended 5/88)*

Article 7

In a transaction, REALTORS® shall not accept compensation from more than one party, even if permitted by law, without disclosure to all parties and the informed consent of the REALTOR®'s client or clients. *(Amended 1/93)*

Article 8

REALTORS® shall keep in a special account in an appropriate financial institution, separated from their own funds, monies coming into their possession in trust for other persons, such as escrows, trust funds, clients' monies, and other like items.

Article 9

REALTORS®, for the protection of all parties, shall assure whenever possible that all agreements related to real estate transactions including, but not limited to, listing and representation agreements, purchase contracts, and leases are in writing in clear and understandable language expressing the specific terms, conditions, obligations and commitments of the parties. A copy of each agreement shall be furnished to each party to such agreements upon their signing or initialing. *(Amended 1/04)*

- **Standard of Practice 9-1**

For the protection of all parties, REALTORS® shall use reasonable care to ensure that documents pertaining to the purchase, sale, or lease of real estate are kept current through the use of written extensions or amendments. *(Amended 1/93)*

- **Standard of Practice 9-2**

When assisting or enabling a client or customer in establishing a contractual relationship (e.g., listing and representation agreements, purchase agreements, leases, etc.) electronically, REALTORS® shall make reasonable efforts to explain the nature and disclose the specific terms of the contractual relationship being established prior to it being agreed to by a contracting party. *(Adopted 1/07)*

Duties to the Public

Article 10

REALTORS® shall not deny equal professional services to any person for reasons of race, color, religion, sex, handicap, familial status, national origin, sexual orientation, or gender identity. REALTORS® shall not be parties to any plan or agreement to discriminate against a person or persons on the basis of race, color, religion, sex, handicap, familial status, national origin, sexual orientation, or gender identity. *(Amended 1/14)*

REALTORS®, in their real estate employment practices, shall not discriminate against any person or persons on the basis of race, color, religion, sex, handicap, familial status, national origin, sexual orientation, or gender identity. *(Amended 1/14)*

• **Standard of Practice 10-1**

When involved in the sale or lease of a residence, REALTORS® shall not volunteer information regarding the racial, religious or ethnic composition of any neighborhood nor shall they engage in any activity which may result in panic selling, however, REALTORS® may provide other demographic information. *(Adopted 1/94, Amended 1/06)*

• **Standard of Practice 10-2**

When not involved in the sale or lease of a residence, REALTORS® may provide demographic information related to a property, transaction or professional assignment to a party if such demographic information is (a) deemed by the REALTOR® to be needed to assist with or complete, in a manner consistent with Article 10, a real estate transaction or professional assignment and (b) is obtained or derived from a recognized, reliable, independent, and impartial source. The source of such information and any additions, deletions, modifications, interpretations, or other changes shall be disclosed in reasonable detail. *(Adopted 1/05, Renumbered 1/06)*

• **Standard of Practice 10-3**

REALTORS® shall not print, display or circulate any statement or advertisement with respect to selling or renting of a property that indicates any preference, limitations or discrimination based on race, color, religion, sex, handicap, familial status, national origin, sexual orientation, or gender identity. *(Adopted 1/94, Renumbered 1/05 and 1/06, Amended 1/14)*

• **Standard of Practice 10-4**

As used in Article 10 "real estate employment practices" relates to employees and independent contractors providing real estate-related services and the administrative and clerical staff directly supporting those individuals. *(Adopted 1/00, Renumbered 1/05 and 1/06)*

Article 11

The services which REALTORS® provide to their clients and customers shall conform to the standards of practice and competence which are reasonably expected in the specific real estate disciplines in which they engage; specifically, residential real estate brokerage, real property management, commercial and industrial real estate brokerage, land brokerage, real estate appraisal, real estate counseling, real estate syndication, real estate auction, and international real estate.

REALTORS® shall not undertake to provide specialized professional services concerning a type of property or service that is outside their field of competence unless they engage the assistance of one who is competent on such types of property or service, or unless the facts are fully disclosed to the client. Any persons engaged to provide such assistance shall be so identified to the client and their contribution to the assignment should be set forth. *(Amended 1/10)*

• **Standard of Practice 11-1**

When REALTORS® prepare opinions of real property value or price they must:

1) be knowledgeable about the type of property being valued,
2) have access to the information and resources necessary to formulate an accurate opinion, and
3) be familiar with the area where the subject property is located unless lack of any of these is disclosed to the party requesting the opinion in advance.

When an opinion of value or price is prepared other than in pursuit of a listing or to assist a potential purchaser in formulating a purchase offer, the opinion shall include the following unless the party requesting the opinion requires a specific type of report or different data set:

1) identification of the subject property
2) date prepared
3) defined value or price
4) limiting conditions, including statements of purpose(s) and intended user(s)
5) any present or contemplated interest, including the possibility of representing the seller/landlord or buyers/tenants
6) basis for the opinion, including applicable market data
7) if the opinion is not an appraisal, a statement to that effect
8) disclosure of whether and when a physical inspection of the property's exterior was conducted
9) disclosure of whether and when a physical inspection of the property's interior was conducted
10) disclosure of whether the REALTOR® has any conflicts of interest *(Amended 1/14)*

• **Standard of Practice 11-2**

The obligations of the Code of Ethics in respect of real estate disciplines other than appraisal shall be interpreted and applied in accordance with the standards of competence and practice which clients and the public reasonably require to protect their rights and interests considering the complexity of the transaction, the availability of expert assistance, and, where the REALTOR® is an agent or subagent, the obligations of a fiduciary. *(Adopted 1/95)*

- **Standard of Practice 11-3**

When REALTORS® provide consultive services to clients which involve advice or counsel for a fee (not a commission), such advice shall be rendered in an objective manner and the fee shall not be contingent on the substance of the advice or counsel given. If brokerage or transaction services are to be provided in addition to consultive services, a separate compensation may be paid with prior agreement between the client and REALTOR®. *(Adopted 1/96)*

- **Standard of Practice 11-4**

The competency required by Article 11 relates to services contracted for between REALTORS® and their clients or customers; the duties expressly imposed by the Code of Ethics; and the duties imposed by law or regulation. *(Adopted 1/02)*

Article 12

REALTORS® shall be honest and truthful in their real estate communications and shall present a true picture in their advertising, marketing, and other representations. REALTORS® shall ensure that their status as real estate professionals is readily apparent in their advertising, marketing, and other representations, and that the recipients of all real estate communications are, or have been, notified that those communications are from a real estate professional. *(Amended 1/08)*

- **Standard of Practice 12-1**

REALTORS® may use the term "free" and similar terms in their advertising and in other representations provided that all terms governing availability of the offered product or service are clearly disclosed at the same time. *(Amended 1/97)*

- **Standard of Practice 12-2**

REALTORS® may represent their services as "free" or without cost even if they expect to receive compensation from a source other than their client provided that the potential for the REALTOR® to obtain a benefit from a third party is clearly disclosed at the same time. *(Amended 1/97)*

- **Standard of Practice 12-3**

The offering of premiums, prizes, merchandise discounts or other inducements to list, sell, purchase, or lease is not, in itself, unethical even if receipt of the benefit is contingent on listing, selling, purchasing, or leasing through the REALTOR® making the offer. However, REALTORS® must exercise care and candor in any such advertising or other public or private representations so that any party interested in receiving or otherwise benefiting from the REALTOR®'s offer will have clear, thorough, advance understanding of all the terms and conditions of the offer. The offering of any inducements to do business is subject to the limitations and restrictions

of state law and the ethical obligations established by any applicable Standard of Practice. *(Amended 1/95)*

- **Standard of Practice 12-4**

REALTORS® shall not offer for sale/lease or advertise property without authority. When acting as listing brokers or as subagents, REALTORS® shall not quote a price different from that agreed upon with the seller/landlord. *(Amended 1/93)*

- **Standard of Practice 12-5**

REALTORS® shall not advertise nor permit any person employed by or affiliated with them to advertise real estate services or listed property in any medium (e.g., electronically, print, radio, television, etc.) without disclosing the name of that REALTOR®'s firm in a reasonable and readily apparent manner either in the advertisement or in electronic advertising via a link to display with all required disclosures. *(Adopted 11/86, Amended 1/16)*

- **Standard of Practice 12-6**

REALTORS®, when advertising unlisted real property for sale/lease in which they have an ownership interest, shall disclose their status as both owners/landlords and as REALTORS® or real estate licensees. *(Amended 1/93)*

- **Standard of Practice 12-7**

Only REALTORS® who participated in the transaction as the listing broker or cooperating broker (selling broker) may claim to have "sold" the property. Prior to closing, a cooperating broker may post a "sold" sign only with the consent of the listing broker. *(Amended 1/96)*

- **Standard of Practice 12-8**

The obligation to present a true picture in representations to the public includes information presented, provided, or displayed on REALTORS®' websites. REALTORS® shall use reasonable efforts to ensure that information on their websites is current. When it becomes apparent that information on a REALTOR®'s website is no longer current or accurate, REALTORS® shall promptly take corrective action. *(Adopted 1/07)*

- **Standard of Practice 12-9**

REALTOR® firm websites shall disclose the firm's name and state(s) of licensure in a reasonable and readily apparent manner.

Websites of Realtors® and non-member licensees affiliated with a Realtor® firm shall disclose the firm's name and that REALTOR®'s or non-member licensee's state(s) of licensure in a reasonable and readily apparent manner. *(Adopted 1/07)*

• **Standard of Practice 12-10**

REALTORS®' obligation to present a true picture in their advertising and representations to the public includes Internet content posted, and the URLs and domain names they use, and prohibits REALTORS® from:
1) engaging in deceptive or unauthorized framing of real estate brokerage websites;
2) manipulating (e.g., presenting content developed by others) listing and other content in any way that produces a deceptive or misleading result;
3) deceptively using metatags, keywords or other devices/methods to direct, drive, or divert Internet traffic; or
4) presenting content developed by others without either attribution or without permission, or
5) to otherwise mislead consumers, including use of misleading images. *(Adopted 1/07, Amended 1/18)*

• **Standard of Practice 12-11**

REALTORS® intending to share or sell consumer information gathered via the Internet shall disclose that possibility in a reasonable and readily apparent manner. *(Adopted 1/07)*

• **Standard of Practice 12-12**

REALTORS® shall not:
6) use URLs or domain names that present less than a true picture, or
7) register URLs or domain names which, if used, would present less than a true picture. *(Adopted 1/08)*

• **Standard of Practice 12-13**

The obligation to present a true picture in advertising, marketing, and representations allows Realtors® to use and display only professional designations, certifications, and other credentials to which they are legitimately entitled. *(Adopted 1/08)*

Article 13

REALTORS® shall not engage in activities that constitute the unauthorized practice of law and shall recommend that legal counsel be obtained when the interest of any party to the transaction requires it.

Article 14

If charged with unethical practice or asked to present evidence or to cooperate in any other way, in any professional standards proceeding or investigation, REALTORS® shall place all pertinent facts before the proper tribunals of the Member Board or affiliated institute, society, or council in which membership is held and shall take no action to disrupt or obstruct such processes. *(Amended 1/99)*

• **Standard of Practice 14-1**

REALTORS® shall not be subject to disciplinary proceedings in more than one Board of REALTORS® or affiliated institute, society, or council in which they hold membership with respect to alleged violations of the Code of Ethics relating to the same transaction or event. *(Amended 1/95)*

• **Standard of Practice 14-2**

REALTORS® shall not make any unauthorized disclosure or dissemination of the allegations, findings, or decision developed in connection with an ethics hearing or appeal or in connection with an arbitration hearing or procedural review. *(Amended 1/92)*

• **Standard of Practice 14-3**

REALTORS® shall not obstruct the Board's investigative or professional standards proceedings by instituting or threatening to institute actions for libel, slander, or defamation against any party to a professional standards proceeding or their witnesses based on the filing of an arbitration request, an ethics complaint, or testimony given before any tribunal. *(Adopted 11/87, Amended 1/99)*

• **Standard of Practice 14-4**

REALTORS® shall not intentionally impede the Board's investigative or disciplinary proceedings by filing multiple ethics complaints based on the same event or transaction. *(Adopted 11/88)*

Duties to REALTORS®

Article 15

REALTORS® shall not knowingly or recklessly make false or misleading statements about other real estate professionals, their businesses, or their business practices. *(Amended 1/12)*

• **Standard of Practice 15-1**

REALTORS® shall not knowingly or recklessly file false or unfounded ethics complaints. *(Adopted 1/00)*

• **Standard of Practice 15-2**

The obligation to refrain from making false or misleading statements about other real estate professionals, their businesses, and their business practices includes the duty to not knowingly or recklessly publish, repeat, retransmit, or republish false or misleading statements made by others. This duty applies whether false or misleading statements are repeated in person, in writing, by technological means (e.g., the Internet), or by any other means. *(Adopted 1/07, Amended 1/12)*

• **Standard of Practice 15-3**

The obligation to refrain from making false or misleading statements about other real estate professionals, their businesses, and their business practices includes the duty to publish a clarification about or to remove statements made by others on electronic media the REALTOR® controls once the REALTOR® knows the statement is false or misleading. (*Adopted 1/10, Amended 1/12*)

Article 16

REALTORS® shall not engage in any practice or take any action inconsistent with exclusive representation or exclusive brokerage relationship agreements that other REALTORS® have with clients. (*Amended 1/04*)

• **Standard of Practice 16-1**

Article 16 is not intended to prohibit aggressive or innovative business practices which are otherwise ethical and does not prohibit disagreements with other REALTORS® involving commission, fees, compensation or other forms of payment or expenses. (*Adopted 1/93, Amended 1/95*)

• **Standard of Practice 16-2**

Article 16 does not preclude REALTORS® from making general announcements to prospects describing their services and the terms of their availability even though some recipients may have entered into agency agreements or other exclusive relationships with another REALTOR®. A general telephone canvass, general mailing or distribution addressed to all prospects in a given geographical area or in a given profession, business, club, or organization, or other classification or group is deemed "general" for purposes of this standard. (*Amended 1/04*)

Article 16 is intended to recognize as unethical two basic types of solicitations:

First, telephone or personal solicitations of property owners who have been identified by a real estate sign, multiple listing compilation, or other information service as having exclusively listed their property with another REALTOR® and

Second, mail or other forms of written solicitations of prospects whose properties are exclusively listed with another REALTOR® when such solicitations are not part of a general mailing but are directed specifically to property owners identified through compilations of current listings, "for sale" or "for rent" signs, or other sources of information required by Article 3 and Multiple Listing Service rules to be made available to other REALTORS® under offers of subagency or cooperation. (*Amended 1/04*)

• **Standard of Practice 16-3**

Article 16 does not preclude REALTORS® from contacting the client of another broker for the purpose of offering to provide, or entering into a contract to provide, a different type of real estate service unrelated to the type of service currently being provided (e.g., property management as opposed to brokerage) or from offering the same type of service for property not subject to other brokers' exclusive agreements. However, information received through a Multiple Listing Service or any other offer of cooperation may not be used to target clients of other REALTORS® to whom such offers to provide services may be made. (*Amended 1/04*)

• **Standard of Practice 16-4**

REALTORS® shall not solicit a listing which is currently listed exclusively with another broker. However, if the listing broker, when asked by the REALTOR®, refuses to disclose the expiration date and nature of such listing, i.e., an exclusive right to sell, an exclusive agency, open listing, or other form of contractual agreement between the listing broker and the client, the REALTOR® may contact the owner to secure such information and may discuss the terms upon which the REALTOR® might take a future listing or, alternatively, may take a listing to become effective upon expiration of any existing exclusive listing. (*Amended 1/94*)

• **Standard of Practice 16-5**

REALTORS® shall not solicit buyer/tenant agreements from buyers/tenants who are subject to exclusive buyer/tenant agreements. However, if asked by a REALTOR®, the broker refuses to disclose the expiration date of the exclusive buyer/tenant agreement, the REALTOR® may contact the buyer/tenant to secure such information and may discuss the terms upon which the REALTOR® might enter into a future buyer/tenant agreement or, alternatively, may enter into a buyer/tenant agreement to become effective upon the expiration of any existing exclusive buyer/tenant agreement. (*Adopted 1/94, Amended 1/98*)

• **Standard of Practice 16-6**

When REALTORS® are contacted by the client of another REALTOR® regarding the creation of an exclusive relationship to provide the same type of service, and REALTORS® have not directly or indirectly initiated such discussions, they may discuss the terms upon which they might enter into a future agreement or, alternatively, may enter into an agreement which becomes effective upon expiration of any existing exclusive agreement. (*Amended 1/98*)

• **Standard of Practice 16-7**

The fact that a prospect has retained a Realtor® as an

exclusive representative or exclusive broker in one or more past transactions does not preclude other REALTORS® from seeking such prospect's future business. (*Amended 1/04*)

• **Standard of Practice 16-8**

The fact that an exclusive agreement has been entered into with a REALTOR® shall not preclude or inhibit any other REALTOR® from entering into a similar agreement after the expiration of the prior agreement. (*Amended 1/98*)

• **Standard of Practice 16-9**

REALTORS®, prior to entering into a representation agreement, have an affirmative obligation to make reasonable efforts to determine whether the prospect is subject to a current, valid exclusive agreement to provide the same type of real estate service. (*Amended 1/04*)

• **Standard of Practice 16-10**

REALTORS®, acting as buyer or tenant representatives or brokers, shall disclose that relationship to the seller/ landlord's representative or broker at first contact and shall provide written confirmation of that disclosure to the seller/ landlord's representative or broker not later than execution of a purchase agreement or lease. (*Amended 1/04*)

• **Standard of Practice 16-11**

On unlisted property, REALTORS® acting as buyer/tenant representatives or brokers shall disclose that relationship to the seller/landlord at first contact for that buyer/tenant and shall provide written confirmation of such disclosure to the seller/landlord not later than execution of any purchase or lease agreement. (*Amended 1/04*)

REALTORS® shall make any request for anticipated compensation from the seller/landlord at first contact. (*Amended 1/98*)

• **Standard of Practice 16-12**

REALTORS®, acting as representatives or brokers of sellers/ landlords or as subagents of listing brokers, shall disclose that relationship to buyers/tenants as soon as practicable and shall provide written confirmation of such disclosure to buyers/tenants not later than execution of any purchase or lease agreement. (*Amended 1/04*)

• **Standard of Practice 16-13**

All dealings concerning property exclusively listed, or with buyer/tenants who are subject to an exclusive agreement shall be carried on with the client's representative or broker, and not with the client, except with the consent of the client's representative or broker or except where such dealings are initiated by the client.

Before providing substantive services (such as writing a

purchase offer or presenting a CMA) to prospects, REALTORS® shall ask prospects whether they are a party to any exclusive representation agreement. REALTORS® shall not knowingly provide substantive services concerning a prospective transaction to prospects who are parties to exclusive representation agreements, except with the consent of the prospects' exclusive representatives or at the direction of prospects. (*Adopted 1/93, Amended 1/04*)

• **Standard of Practice 16-14**

REALTORS® are free to enter into contractual relationships or to negotiate with sellers/landlords, buyers/tenants or others who are not subject to an exclusive agreement but shall not knowingly obligate them to pay more than one commission except with their informed consent. (*Amended 1/98*)

• **Standard of Practice 16-15**

In cooperative transactions REALTORS® shall compensate cooperating REALTORS® (principal brokers) and shall not compensate nor offer to compensate, directly or indirectly, any of the sales licensees employed by or affiliated with other REALTORS® without the prior express knowledge and consent of the cooperating broker.

• **Standard of Practice 16-16**

REALTORS®, acting as subagents or buyer/tenant representatives or brokers, shall not use the terms of an offer to purchase/lease to attempt to modify the listing broker's offer of compensation to subagents or buyer/tenant representatives or brokers nor make the submission of an executed offer to purchase/lease contingent on the listing broker's agreement to modify the offer of compensation. (*Amended 1/04*)

• **Standard of Practice 16-17**

REALTORS®, acting as subagents or as buyer/tenant representatives or brokers, shall not attempt to extend a listing broker's offer of cooperation and/or compensation to other brokers without the consent of the listing broker. (*Amended 1/04*)

• **Standard of Practice 16-18**

REALTORS® shall not use information obtained from listing brokers through offers to cooperate made through multiple listing services or through other offers of cooperation to refer listing brokers' clients to other brokers or to create buyer/tenant relationships with listing brokers' clients, unless such use is authorized by listing brokers. (*Amended 1/02*)

• **Standard of Practice 16-19**

Signs giving notice of property for sale, rent, lease, or exchange shall not be placed on property without consent of the seller/landlord. (*Amended 1/93*)

• **Standard of Practice 16-20**

REALTORS®, prior to or after their relationship with their current firm is terminated, shall not induce clients of their current firm to cancel exclusive contractual agreements between the client and that firm. This does not preclude REALTORS® (principals) from establishing agreements with their associated licensees governing assignability of exclusive agreements. *(Adopted 1/98, Amended 1/10)*

Article 17

In the event of contractual disputes or specific non-contractual disputes as defined in Standard of Practice 17-4 between REALTORS® (principals) associated with different firms, arising out of their relationship as REALTORS®, the REALTORS® shall mediate the dispute if the Board requires its members to mediate. If the dispute is not resolved through mediation, or if mediation is not required, REALTORS® shall submit the dispute to arbitration in accordance with the policies of the Board rather than litigate the matter.

In the event clients of REALTORS® wish to mediate or arbitrate contractual disputes arising out of real estate transactions, REALTORS® shall mediate or arbitrate those disputes in accordance with the policies of the Board, provided the clients agree to be bound by any resulting agreement or award.
The obligation to participate in mediation and arbitration contemplated by this Article includes the obligation of REALTORS® (principals) to cause their firms to mediate and arbitrate and be bound by any resulting agreement or award. *(Amended 1/12)*

• **Standard of Practice 17-1**

The filing of litigation and refusal to withdraw from it by REALTORS® in an arbitrable matter constitutes a refusal to arbitrate. *(Adopted 2/86)*

• **Standard of Practice 17-2**

Article 17 does not require REALTORS® to mediate in those circumstances when all parties to the dispute advise the Board in writing that they choose not to mediate through the Board's facilities. The fact that all parties decline to participate in mediation does not relieve REALTORS® of the duty to arbitrate.

Article 17 does not require REALTORS® to arbitrate in those circumstances when all parties to the dispute advise the Board in writing that they choose not to arbitrate before the Board. *(Amended 1/12)*

• **Standard of Practice 17-3**

REALTORS®, when acting solely as principals in a real estate transaction, are not obligated to arbitrate disputes with other REALTORS® absent a specific written agreement to the contrary. *(Adopted 1/96)*

• **Standard of Practice 17-4**

Specific non-contractual disputes that are subject to arbitration pursuant to Article 17 are:

1) Where a listing broker has compensated a cooperating broker and another cooperating broker subsequently claims to be the procuring cause of the sale or lease. In such cases the complainant may name the first cooperating broker as respondent and arbitration may proceed without the listing broker being named as a respondent. When arbitration occurs between two (or more) cooperating brokers and where the listing broker is not a party, the amount in dispute and the amount of any potential resulting award is limited to the amount paid to the respondent by the listing broker and any amount credited or paid to a party to the transaction at the direction of the respondent. Alternatively, if the complaint is brought against the listing broker, the listing broker may name the first cooperating broker as a third-party respondent. In either instance the decision of the hearing panel as to procuring cause shall be conclusive with respect to all current or subsequent claims of the parties for compensation arising out of the underlying cooperative transaction. *(Adopted 1/97, Amended 1/07)*

2) Where a buyer or tenant representative is compensated by the seller or landlord, and not by the listing broker, and the listing broker, as a result, reduces the commission owed by the seller or landlord and, subsequent to such actions, another cooperating broker claims to be the procuring cause of sale or lease. In such cases the complainant may name the first cooperating broker as respondent and arbitration may proceed without the listing broker being named as a respondent. When arbitration occurs between two (or more) cooperating brokers and where the listing broker is not a party, the amount in dispute and the amount of any potential resulting award is limited to the amount paid to the respondent by the seller or landlord and any amount credited or paid to a party to the transaction at the direction of the respondent. Alternatively, if the complaint is brought against the listing broker, the listing broker may name the first cooperating broker as a third-party respondent. In either instance the decision of the hearing panel as to procuring cause shall be conclusive with respect to all current or subsequent claims of the parties for compensation arising out of the underlying cooperative transaction. *(Adopted 1/97, Amended 1/07)*

3) Where a buyer or tenant representative is compensated by the buyer or tenant and, as a result, the listing broker reduces the commission owed by the seller or landlord and, subsequent to such actions, another cooperating broker claims to be the procuring cause of sale or lease. In such cases the complainant may name the first cooperating broker as respondent and arbitration may proceed without the listing broker being named as a respondent. Alternatively, if the complaint is brought against the listing broker, the listing broker may name the first cooperating broker as a third-party respondent. In either instance the decision of the hearing panel as to procuring cause shall be conclusive with respect to all current or subsequent claims of the parties for compensation arising out of the underlying cooperative transaction. *(Adopted 1/97)*

4) Where two or more listing brokers claim entitlement to compensation pursuant to open listings with a seller or landlord who agrees to participate in arbitration (or who requests arbitration) and who agrees to be bound by the decision. In cases where one of the listing brokers has been compensated by the seller or landlord, the other listing broker, as complainant, may name the first listing broker as respondent and arbitration may proceed between the brokers. *(Adopted 1/97)*

5) Where a buyer or tenant representative is compensated by the seller or landlord, and not by the listing broker, and the listing broker, as a result, reduces the commission owed by the seller or landlord and, subsequent to such actions, claims to be the procuring cause of sale or lease. In such cases arbitration shall be between the listing broker and the buyer or tenant representative and the amount in dispute is limited to the amount of the reduction of commission to which the listing broker agreed. *(Adopted 1/05)*

- **Standard of Practice 17-5**
  The obligation to arbitrate established in Article 17 includes disputes between REALTORS® (principals) in different states in instances where, absent an established inter-association arbitration agreement, the REALTOR® (principal) requesting arbitration agrees to submit to the jurisdiction of, travel to, participate in, and be bound by any resulting award rendered in arbitration conducted by the respondent(s) REALTOR®'s association, in instances where the respondent(s) REALTOR®'s association determines that an arbitrable issue exists. *(Adopted 1/07)*

Explanatory Notes

The reader should be aware of the following policies which have been approved by the Board of Directors of the National Association:

In filing a charge of an alleged violation of the Code of Ethics by a REALTOR®, the charge must read as an alleged violation of one or more Articles of the Code. Standards of Practice may be cited in support of the charge.

The Standards of Practice serve to clarify the ethical obligations imposed by the various Articles and supplement, and do not substitute for, the Case Interpretations in *Interpretations of the Code of Ethics.*

Modifications to existing Standards of Practice and additional new Standards of Practice are approved from time to time. Readers are cautioned to ensure that the most recent publications are utilized.

Appendix F Loan Estimate

Save this Loan Estimate to compare with your Closing Disclosure.

Loan Estimate

DATE ISSUED
APPLICANTS

PROPERTY
SALE PRICE

LOAN TERM
PURPOSE
PRODUCT
LOAN TYPE   ☐ Conventional ☐ FHA ☐ VA ☐ _____
LOAN ID #
RATE LOCK   ☐ NO ☐ YES, until

Before closing, your interest rate, points, and lender credits can change unless you lock the interest rate. All other estimated closing costs expire on

Loan Terms	Can this amount increase after closing?
Loan Amount	
Interest Rate	
Monthly Principal & Interest *See Projected Payments below for your Estimated Total Monthly Payment*	
	Does the loan have these features?
Prepayment Penalty	
Balloon Payment	

Projected Payments	
Payment Calculation	
Principal & Interest	
Mortgage Insurance	
Estimated Escrow *Amount can increase over time*	
Estimated Total Monthly Payment	

	This estimate includes **In escrow?**
Estimated Taxes, Insurance & Assessments *Amount can increase over time*	☐ Property Taxes ☐ Homeowner's Insurance ☐ Other: *See Section G on page 2 for escrowed property costs. You must pay for other property costs separately.*

Costs at Closing	
Estimated Closing Costs	Includes ____ in Loan Costs + ____ in Other Costs − ____ in Lender Credits. *See page 2 for details.*
Estimated Cash to Close	Includes Closing Costs. *See Calculating Cash to Close on page 2 for details.*

Visit **www.consumerfinance.gov/mortgage-estimate** for general information and tools.

Closing Cost Details

Loan Costs		Other Costs	
A. Origination Charges		**E. Taxes and Other Government Fees**	
% of Loan Amount (Points)		Recording Fees and Other Taxes	
		Transfer Taxes	
		F. Prepaids	
		Homeowner's Insurance Premium (months)	
		Mortgage Insurance Premium (months)	
		Prepaid Interest (per day for days @)	
		Property Taxes (months)	
		G. Initial Escrow Payment at Closing	
		Homeowner's Insurance per month for mo.	
		Mortgage Insurance per month for mo.	
B. Services You Cannot Shop For		Property Taxes per month for mo.	
		H. Other	
		I. TOTAL OTHER COSTS (E + F + G + H)	
C. Services You Can Shop For		**J. TOTAL CLOSING COSTS**	
		D + I	
		Lender Credits	

Calculating Cash to Close
Total Closing Costs (J)
Closing Costs Financed (Paid from your Loan Amount)
Down Payment/Funds from Borrower
Deposit
Funds for Borrower
Seller Credits
Adjustments and Other Credits
Estimated Cash to Close

D. TOTAL LOAN COSTS (A + B + C)

Adjustable Payment (AP) Table	
Interest Only Payments?	
Optional Payments?	
Step Payments?	
Seasonal Payments?	
Monthly Principal and Interest Payments	
First Change/Amount	
Subsequent Changes	
Maximum Payment	

Adjustable Interest Rate (AIR) Table	
Index + Margin	
Initial Interest Rate	
Minimum/Maximum Interest Rate	
Change Frequency	
First Change	
Subsequent Changes	
Limits on Interest Rate Changes	
First Change	
Subsequent Changes	

Additional Information About This Loan

LENDER
NMLS/___ LICENSE ID
LOAN OFFICER
NMLS/___ LICENSE ID
EMAIL
PHONE

MORTGAGE BROKER
NMLS/___ LICENSE ID
LOAN OFFICER
NMLS/___ LICENSE ID
EMAIL
PHONE

Comparisons

Use these measures to compare this loan with other loans.

In 5 Years	Total you will have paid in principal, interest, mortgage insurance, and loan costs. Principal you will have paid off.
Annual Percentage Rate (APR)	Your costs over the loan term expressed as a rate. This is not your interest rate.
Total Interest Percentage (TIP)	The total amount of interest that you will pay over the loan term as a percentage of your loan amount.

Other Considerations

Appraisal	We may order an appraisal to determine the property's value and charge you for this appraisal. We will promptly give you a copy of any appraisal, even if your loan does not close. You can pay for an additional appraisal for your own use at your own cost.
Assumption	If you sell or transfer this property to another person, we ☐ will allow, under certain conditions, this person to assume this loan on the original terms. ☐ will not allow assumption of this loan on the original terms.
Homeowner's Insurance	This loan requires homeowner's insurance on the property, which you may obtain from a company of your choice that we find acceptable.
Late Payment	If your payment is more than ____ days late, we will charge a late fee of _____
Loan Acceptance	You do not have to accept this loan because you have received this form or signed a loan application.
Refinance	Refinancing this loan will depend on your future financial situation, the property value, and market conditions. You may not be able to refinance this loan.
Servicing	We intend ☐ to service your loan. If so, you will make your payments to us. ☐ to transfer servicing of your loan.

Appendix G   Closing Disclosure

Closing Disclosure

This form is a statement of final loan terms and closing costs. Compare this document with your Loan Estimate.

Closing Information

Date Issued
Closing Date
Disbursement Date
Settlement Agent
File #
Property

Sale Price

Transaction Information

Borrower

Seller

Lender

Loan Information

Loan Term
Purpose
Product

Loan Type   ☐ Conventional ☐ FHA
           ☐ VA ☐ _____
Loan ID #
MIC #

Loan Terms

	Can this amount increase after closing?
Loan Amount	
Interest Rate	
Monthly Principal & Interest *See Projected Payments below for your Estimated Total Monthly Payment*	
	Does the loan have these features?
Prepayment Penalty	
Balloon Payment	

Projected Payments

Payment Calculation	
Principal & Interest	
Mortgage Insurance	
Estimated Escrow *Amount can increase over time*	
Estimated Total Monthly Payment	

Estimated Taxes, Insurance & Assessments *Amount can increase over time* *See page 4 for details*	**This estimate includes** **In escrow?** ☐ Property Taxes ☐ Homeowner's Insurance ☐ Other: *See Escrow Account on page 4 for details. You must pay for other property costs separately.*

Costs at Closing

Closing Costs	Includes in Loan Costs + in Other Costs – in Lender Credits. *See page 2 for details.*
Cash to Close	Includes Closing Costs. *See Calculating Cash to Close on page 3 for details.*

Closing Cost Details

Loan Costs	Borrower-Paid		Seller-Paid		Paid by Others
	At Closing	Before Closing	At Closing	Before Closing	
A. Origination Charges					
01 % of Loan Amount (Points)					
02					
03					
04					
05					
06					
07					
08					
B. Services Borrower Did Not Shop For					
01					
02					
03					
04					
05					
06					
07					
08					
09					
10					
C. Services Borrower Did Shop For					
01					
02					
03					
04					
05					
06					
07					
08					
D. TOTAL LOAN COSTS (Borrower-Paid)					
Loan Costs Subtotals (A + B + C)					

Other Costs					
E. Taxes and Other Government Fees					
01 Recording Fees Deed: Mortgage:					
02					
F. Prepaids					
01 Homeowner's Insurance Premium (mo.)					
02 Mortgage Insurance Premium (mo.)					
03 Prepaid Interest (per day from to)					
04 Property Taxes (mo.)					
05					
G. Initial Escrow Payment at Closing					
01 Homeowner's Insurance per month for mo.					
02 Mortgage Insurance per month for mo.					
03 Property Taxes per month for mo.					
04					
05					
06					
07					
08 Aggregate Adjustment					
H. Other					
01					
02					
03					
04					
05					
06					
07					
08					
I. TOTAL OTHER COSTS (Borrower-Paid)					
Other Costs Subtotals (E + F + G + H)					

J. TOTAL CLOSING COSTS (Borrower-Paid)					
Closing Costs Subtotals (D + I)					
Lender Credits					

Calculating Cash to Close

Use this table to see what has changed from your Loan Estimate.

	Loan Estimate	Final	Did this change?
Total Closing Costs (J)			
Closing Costs Paid Before Closing			
Closing Costs Financed (Paid from your Loan Amount)			
Down Payment/Funds from Borrower			
Deposit			
Funds for Borrower			
Seller Credits			
Adjustments and Other Credits			
Cash to Close			

Summaries of Transactions

Use this table to see a summary of your transaction.

BORROWER'S TRANSACTION

K. Due from Borrower at Closing

01	Sale Price of Property
02	Sale Price of Any Personal Property Included in Sale
03	Closing Costs Paid at Closing (J)
04	

Adjustments

05	
06	
07	

Adjustments for Items Paid by Seller in Advance

08	City/Town Taxes	to
09	County Taxes	to
10	Assessments	to
11		
12		
13		
14		
15		

L. Paid Already by or on Behalf of Borrower at Closing

01	Deposit
02	Loan Amount
03	Existing Loan(s) Assumed or Taken Subject to
04	
05	Seller Credit

Other Credits

06	
07	

Adjustments

08	
09	
10	
11	

Adjustments for Items Unpaid by Seller

12	City/Town Taxes	to
13	County Taxes	to
14	Assessments	to
15		
16		
17		

CALCULATION

Total Due from Borrower at Closing (K)
Total Paid Already by or on Behalf of Borrower at Closing (L)

Cash to Close ☐ From ☐ To Borrower

SELLER'S TRANSACTION

M. Due to Seller at Closing

01	Sale Price of Property
02	Sale Price of Any Personal Property Included in Sale
03	
04	
05	
06	
07	
08	

Adjustments for Items Paid by Seller in Advance

09	City/Town Taxes	to
10	County Taxes	to
11	Assessments	to
12		
13		
14		
15		
16		

N. Due from Seller at Closing

01	Excess Deposit
02	Closing Costs Paid at Closing (J)
03	Existing Loan(s) Assumed or Taken Subject to
04	Payoff of First Mortgage Loan
05	Payoff of Second Mortgage Loan
06	
07	
08	Seller Credit
09	
10	
11	
12	
13	

Adjustments for Items Unpaid by Seller

14	City/Town Taxes	to
15	County Taxes	to
16	Assessments	to
17		
18		
19		

CALCULATION

Total Due to Seller at Closing (M)
Total Due from Seller at Closing (N)

Cash ☐ From ☐ To Seller

Additional Information About This Loan

Loan Disclosures

Assumption
If you sell or transfer this property to another person, your lender
☐ will allow, under certain conditions, this person to assume this loan on the original terms.
☐ will not allow assumption of this loan on the original terms.

Demand Feature
Your loan
☐ has a demand feature, which permits your lender to require early repayment of the loan. You should review your note for details.
☐ does not have a demand feature.

Late Payment
If your payment is more than ___ days late, your lender will charge a late fee of _____

Negative Amortization (Increase in Loan Amount)
Under your loan terms, you
☐ are scheduled to make monthly payments that do not pay all of the interest due that month. As a result, your loan amount will increase (negatively amortize), and your loan amount will likely become larger than your original loan amount. Increases in your loan amount lower the equity you have in this property.
☐ may have monthly payments that do not pay all of the interest due that month. If you do, your loan amount will increase (negatively amortize), and, as a result, your loan amount may become larger than your original loan amount. Increases in your loan amount lower the equity you have in this property.
☐ do not have a negative amortization feature.

Partial Payments
Your lender
☐ may accept payments that are less than the full amount due (partial payments) and apply them to your loan.
☐ may hold them in a separate account until you pay the rest of the payment, and then apply the full payment to your loan.
☐ does not accept any partial payments.
If this loan is sold, your new lender may have a different policy.

Security Interest
You are granting a security interest in _____
_____
_____

You may lose this property if you do not make your payments or satisfy other obligations for this loan.

Escrow Account
For now, your loan
☐ will have an escrow account (also called an "impound" or "trust" account) to pay the property costs listed below. Without an escrow account, you would pay them directly, possibly in one or two large payments a year. Your lender may be liable for penalties and interest for failing to make a payment.

Escrow		
Escrowed Property Costs over Year 1		Estimated total amount over year 1 for your escrowed property costs:
Non-Escrowed Property Costs over Year 1		Estimated total amount over year 1 for your non-escrowed property costs: You may have other property costs.
Initial Escrow Payment		A cushion for the escrow account you pay at closing. See Section G on page 2.
Monthly Escrow Payment		The amount included in your total monthly payment.

☐ will not have an escrow account because ☐ you declined it ☐ your lender does not offer one. You must directly pay your property costs, such as taxes and homeowner's insurance. Contact your lender to ask if your loan can have an escrow account.

No Escrow		
Estimated Property Costs over Year 1		Estimated total amount over year 1. You must pay these costs directly, possibly in one or two large payments a year.
Escrow Waiver Fee		

In the future,
Your property costs may change and, as a result, your escrow payment may change. You may be able to cancel your escrow account, but if you do, you must pay your property costs directly. If you fail to pay your property taxes, your state or local government may (1) impose fines and penalties or (2) place a tax lien on this property. If you fail to pay any of your property costs, your lender may (1) add the amounts to your loan balance, (2) add an escrow account to your loan, or (3) require you to pay for property insurance that the lender buys on your behalf, which likely would cost more and provide fewer benefits than what you could buy on your own.

Loan Calculations

Total of Payments. Total you will have paid after you make all payments of principal, interest, mortgage insurance, and loan costs, as scheduled.	
Finance Charge. The dollar amount the loan will cost you.	
Amount Financed. The loan amount available after paying your upfront finance charge.	
Annual Percentage Rate (APR). Your costs over the loan term expressed as a rate. This is not your interest rate.	
Total Interest Percentage (TIP). The total amount of interest that you will pay over the loan term as a percentage of your loan amount.	

? **Questions?** If you have questions about the loan terms or costs on this form, use the contact information below. To get more information or make a complaint, contact the Consumer Financial Protection Bureau at **www.consumerfinance.gov/mortgage-closing**

Other Disclosures

Appraisal
If the property was appraised for your loan, your lender is required to give you a copy at no additional cost at least 3 days before closing. If you have not yet received it, please contact your lender at the information listed below.

Contract Details
See your note and security instrument for information about
  • what happens if you fail to make your payments,
  • what is a default on the loan,
  • situations in which your lender can require early repayment of the loan, and
  • the rules for making payments before they are due.

Liability after Foreclosure
If your lender forecloses on this property and the foreclosure does not cover the amount of unpaid balance on this loan,
☐ state law may protect you from liability for the unpaid balance. If you refinance or take on any additional debt on this property, you may lose this protection and have to pay any debt remaining even after foreclosure. You may want to consult a lawyer for more information.
☐ state law does not protect you from liability for the unpaid balance.

Loan Acceptance
You do not have to accept this loan because you have received this form or signed a loan application.

Refinance
Refinancing this loan will depend on your future financial situation, the property value, and market conditions. You may not be able to refinance this loan.

Tax Deductions
If you borrow more than this property is worth, the interest on the loan amount above this property's fair market value is not deductible from your federal income taxes. You should consult a tax advisor for more information.

Contact Information

	Lender	Mortgage Broker	Real Estate Broker (B)	Real Estate Broker (S)	Settlement Agent
Name					
Address					
NMLS ID					
___ License ID					
Contact					
Contact NMLS ID					
Contact ___ License ID					
Email					
Phone					

PRACTICE TEST

The following sample questions for the salesperson's or broker's license examination are representative of the type of questions you might expect to find on the standard national testing service examinations. These questions have not been taken from any of the examinations but are intended to simulate such questions so as to give you additional practice in preparing to take your license exam.

National examination services such as Pearson Vue do provide sample test questions from their respective services at a minimal cost.

1. The characteristic of land that specifies that it is a unique commodity is which of the following?
   a. nonhomogeneity
   b. availability
   c. location
   d. indestructibility

2. Which of the following statements is (are) correct?
   I. A principal is responsible for acts of his agent while engaged in activities concerning the agency.
   II. An agent is in a fiduciary relationship to his principal.
   a. I only
   b. II only
   c. both I and II
   d. neither I nor II

3. If a salesperson listed and sold a property for $90,000 and received 60 percent of the 7 percent commission paid to her employing broker, how much did the salesperson receive?
   a. $2,520
   b. $2,646
   c. $3,780
   d. $5,400

4. Sara Seller was satisfied with all of the terms of an offer to purchase her property from Bill Buyer except the date of possession, which she changed from April 9 to April 10. Which of the following is (are) correct?
   I. Sara's acceptance created a valid contract.
   II. Sara did not accept Bill's offer.
   a. I only
   b. II only
   c. both I and II
   d. neither I nor II

5. At the time of listing a property, the owner specified that he wished to net $65,000 after satisfying a mortgage of $25,000 and paying a 7 percent brokerage fee. For what price should the property be listed?
   a. $90,000
   b. $94,550
   c. $96,300
   d. $96,774

6. When an option is exercised it becomes which of the following?
   a. lease
   b. offer
   c. multiple listing
   d. contract of sale

7. A real estate broker sold a tract of land for $1,600 per acre and earned a 9 percent commission. How much did the broker receive? (Answers rounded.)
   a. $661
   b. $952
   c. $992
   d. $1,983

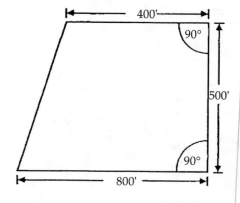

8. The characteristic of land that has the greatest effect on land value is:
   a. nonhomogeneity
   b. location
   c. indestructibility
   d. immobility

9. A real estate agent must provide:
   I. copies of listing contracts to listing sellers.
   II. copies of offers and contracts of sale to buyers and sellers.
   a. I only
   b. II only
   c. both I and II
   d. neither I nor II

10. The best type of listing contract from the standpoint of both the agent and the seller is which of the following?
    a. open
    b. exclusive agency
    c. net
    d. exclusive right to sell

11. Such things as wage and employment levels, interest rates, and real property tax rates are described as:
    a. physical factors affecting land use
    b. artificial factors affecting land use
    c. natural factors affecting land use
    d. economic factors affecting land use

12. The real estate market is:
    I. local in character.
    II. a free market.
    a. I only
    b. II only
    c. both I and II
    d. neither I nor II

13. The real estate market is:
    I. subject to recurring economic cycles.
    II. slow to react to changes in supply and demand.
    a. I only
    b. II only
    c. both I and II
    d. neither I nor II

14. Which of the following statements about license laws is (are) correct?
    I. License laws are an exercise of the police power of a state.
    II. The purpose of license laws is to protect the general public.
    a. I only
    b. II only
    c. both I and II
    d. neither I nor II

15. The acceleration clause provides for which of the following?
    a. equity of redemption
    b. prepayment penalty
    c. right of lender to require immediate payment of principal balance when borrower is in default
    d. alienation by borrower

16. Which of the following liens have priority to mortgage foreclosure sale proceeds?
    a. mortgage lien
    b. income tax lien
    c. real property tax lien
    d. commissions

17. An alienation clause makes a mortgage:
    a. defeasible
    b. unassumable
    c. incontestable
    d. adjustable

18. Which of the following is (are) ways that a veteran borrower can have eligibility fully restored?
    I. Dispose of the property and pay off the VA-guaranteed loan.
    II. Sell the property to a qualified veteran who assumes the VA-guaranteed loan.
    a. I only
    b. II only
    c. both I and II
    d. neither I nor II

19. All of the following are financing instruments EXCEPT:
    a. note
    b. junior mortgage
    c. contract for deed
    d. blanket mortgage

20. A salesperson licensee may receive commissions from which of the following?
    a. cooperating broker
    b. buyer
    c. seller
    d. employing broker

21. Which of the following regulates the advertisement of credit terms available for a house offered for sale?
    a. RESPA
    b. Fannie Mae
    c. Equal Credit Opportunity Act
    d. Regulation Z

22. Which of the following is limited to purchasing FHA-insured and VA-guaranteed mortgages?
    a. Fannie Mae
    b. Freddie Mac
    c. Maggie Mae
    d. Ginnie Mae

23. A gift of real property by will is a:
    a. remise
    b. demise
    c. devise
    d. bequest

24. Which of the following provides the grantee with the greatest assurance of title?
    a. quitclaim
    b. deed of gift
    c. warranty
    d. quitclaim with covenant

25. Which of the following is (are) a benefit of recording a deed?
    I. It protects the grantee against future conveyances by the grantor.
    II. It protects the grantee against the grantor's creditors.
    a. I only
    b. II only
    c. both I and II
    d. neither I nor II

26. Which of the following statements about the rollover rule is (are) correct?
    I. It is mandatory if the transaction qualifies.
    II. It may be used only once in a lifetime.
    a. I only
    b. II only
    c. both I and II
    d. neither I nor II

27. A real estate license may be revoked or suspended if a licensee acting as seller subagent:
    I. fails to submit all written offers to the listing seller.
    II. advises a prospective buyer that the seller will take a certain price for the property that is less than the listed price.
    a. I only
    b. II only
    c. both I and II
    d. neither I nor II

28. Which of the following statements is (are) correct?
    I. An easement provides right of possession.
    II. An estate for years is a freehold estate.
    a. I only
    b. II only
    c. both I and II
    d. neither I nor II

29. A salesperson's license:
    I. is issued to and maintained in the custody of the broker with whom the salesperson is associated.
    II. must be displayed prominently in the office of the broker with whom the salesperson is associated.
    a. I only
    b. II only
    c. both I and II
    d. neither I nor II

30. A claim, lien, charge, or liability attached to and binding upon real property is a(n):
    a. encumbrance
    b. community property
    c. license
    d. syndication

31. An estate created for the life of a person other than the life tenant is called a life estate:
    a. pur autre vie
    b. in remainder
    c. by dower
    d. in reversion

32. Freehold estates that are not inheritable are called:
    a. life estates
    b. leasehold estates
    c. defeasible estates
    d. fee simple estates

33. The Fair Housing Act of 1968 prohibits discrimination in the rental of all of the following EXCEPT:
    a. offices
    b. apartments
    c. houses
    d. residential lots

34. The Fair Housing Act of 1968 prohibits all of the following EXCEPT:
    a. discriminatory advertising
    b. use of brokerage services
    c. steering
    d. redlining

35. Inducing an owner to list property by telling the owner that persons of a particular national origin are moving into the neighborhood is called:
    a. steering
    b. redlining
    c. blockbusting
    d. profiteering

36. A trespass on the land of another as a result of an intrusion by some structure or other object is an:
    a. encroachment
    b. easement
    c. estate
    d. emblement

37. Which of the following types of listing contracts give the broker commission entitlement if the listed property is sold by anyone during the listing term?
    a. net
    b. open
    c. exclusive agency
    d. exclusive right to sell

38. The amount of commission to be paid to a cooperating broker by a listing broker is determined by agreement between:
    a. Real Estate Commission and the broker
    b. the seller and the listing broker
    c. the listing broker only
    d. the selling broker and the buyer

39. After inspecting a property, the prospective customer told the salesperson that she liked the property but would not pay the listed price of $75,000. Knowing that the owner was very anxious to sell, the salesperson suggested that the prospective buyer make an offer of $70,000. Which of the following statements about this situation is (are) correct?
    I. The salesperson violated his obligation as an agent.
    II. Since the salesperson knew the owner was anxious to sell, he acted correctly.
    a. I only
    b. II only
    c. both I and II
    d. neither I nor II

40. A salesperson received two offers for a listed property within a 10-minute period. One offer was 2 percent less than the listed price and the other was 6 percent less than the listed price. The salesperson should present to the seller:
    a. neither offer
    b. both offers
    c. highest offer
    d. lowest offer

41. A contract in which one party makes a promise and in return another party renders a service is which of the following?
    a. unilateral
    b. multilateral
    c. trilateral
    d. bilateral

42. The amount of earnest money appears on closing statements as a:
    a. credit to buyer
    b. debit to seller
    c. credit to seller
    d. debit to buyer

43. An owner listed her property with three brokerage firms. In each case she retained the right to sell the property herself without being obligated to pay a commission to any of the brokers. The type of listing contract given to each broker is called:
    a. exclusive
    b. net
    c. multiple
    d. open

44. An apartment building produces an annual net income of $10,800 after deducting $72 per month for expenses. What price for the property would provide a buyer with a gross return of 12 percent?
    a. $90,000
    b. $97,200
    c. $116,641
    d. $129,600

45. An apartment building contains 30 units. Each unit rents for $200 per month. The vacancy rate is 4 percent. Annual expenses are $3,000 for maintenance, $1,100 insurance, $1,600 taxes, $1,200 utilities, $13,000 interest, and 15 percent of the gross effective income for management fee. What was the investor's net rate of return for the first year if he paid $260,000 for the property?
    a. 6.69 percent
    b. 8.59 percent
    c. 11.64 percent
    d. 20.3 percent

46. If a rental property provides the owner with an 11 percent return on her investment of $780,000, what is the net annual income from the property?
    a. $70,512
    b. $70,909
    c. $85,800
    d. $141,025

47. A contract for deed or installment land contract is which of the following?
    I. A financing statement.
    II. A contract of sale.
    a. I only
    b. II only
    c. both I and II
    d. neither I nor II

48. Adherence to which of the following has the effect of maximizing land value?
    a. principle of contribution
    b. principle of change
    c. principle of anticipation
    d. principle of highest and best use

49. Which of the following statements about zoning is (are) correct?
    I. In exclusive-use zoning, property may use only the purposes specified for that particular zoned area.
    II. If a nonconforming structure is destroyed, then it may be replaced by another nonconforming structure.
    a. I only
    b. II only
    c. both I and II
    d. neither I nor II

50. Restrictive covenants are which of the following?
    a. conditions
    b. encumbrances
    c. public land use controls
    d. zoning classifications

51. Which of the following is (are) correct?
    I. Land does not depreciate.
    II. Structures depreciate.
    a. I only
    b. II only
    c. both I and II
    d. neither I nor II

52. The total transfer of the lessee's rights to another person is called:
    a. an assignment
    b. a sublease
    c. both a and b
    d. neither a nor b

53. Restrictive covenants are which of the following?
    a. public land use controls
    b. negative easements
    c. variances
    d. statements of record

54. Which of the following is (are) correct?
    I. A description by metes and bounds may be one in which a reference is made to a plat and lot number that have been recorded.
    II. In the rectangular survey system, the country is divided by north and south lines called baselines.
    a. I only
    b. II only
    c. both I and II
    d. neither I nor II

55. A property owner subject to a special hardship by strict compliance with a zoning standard may apply for:
    a. spot zoning
    b. variance
    c. nonconforming use
    d. cumulative zoning

56. Mary Beaver, a salesperson associated with Leisure Homes Realty, advised a seller that his property would sell for at least $150,000. Relying on this price quotation, the seller listed the property at a price of $150,000. Comparable sales and listings of competitive properties at the time were in the range of $105,000 to $110,000. The seller refused several offers between $106,000 and $112,000 during the 120-day term of the listing contract. The seller eventually sold his property for $98,000 due to depressed economic conditions existing since the expiration of the listing with Leisure Homes. Which of the following statements is (are) correct?
    I. Mary Beaver committed an act of misrepresentation and may be liable for the resulting financial loss incurred by the seller.
    II. Since Mary is an agent of Leisure Homes Realty, Leisure Homes may be held liable for the seller's damages.
    a. I only
    b. II only
    c. both I and II
    d. neither I nor II

57. While an agent was inspecting a property for listing, the property owner told the agent that the house contained 2,400 square feet of heated living area. Relying on this information, the agent listed the property and represented it to prospective buyers as containing 2,400 square feet. After purchasing the property, the buyer accurately determined that there were only 1,850 square feet and sued for damages for the difference in value between 2,400 square feet and 1,850 square feet. Which of the following is (are) correct?
   I. The agent is not liable because he relied on the seller's positive statements as to the square footage.
   II. The seller and agent are liable because the agent represented the property to the buyer as containing 2,400 square feet.
   a. I only
   b. II only
   c. both I and II
   d. neither I nor II

58. The sales associates of Executive Realty, Ltd. obtained several excellent listings in Exclusive Estates by advising homeowners that a number of Chinese families were moving into Exclusive Estates and therefore their property values would be substantially depressed. This activity is most accurately described as which of the following?
   a. steering
   b. blockbusting
   c. soliciting
   d. redlining

59. Which of the following gives the mortgagee the right to declare the entire principal balance immediately due and payable if the mortgagor is in default?
   a. acceleration clause
   b. alienation clause
   c. statutory foreclosure clause
   d. assignment clause

60. Which of the following enables the mortgagee to sell the mortgage in the secondary mortgage market?
   a. assignment clause
   b. due-on-sale clause
   c. mortgaging clause
   d. power-of-sale clause

61. A real estate broker is responsible for all of the following EXCEPT:
   a. acts of sales associates while engaged in brokerage activities
   b. maintaining a trust, or escrow, account
   c. adhering to commission schedule recommended by the local board of REALTORS®
   d. representing property honestly, fairly, and accurately to prospective buyers

62. Which of the following provides the highest loan-to-value ratio?
   a. conventional
   b. 95% insured conventional
   c. FHA 203B
   d. Guaranteed Rural Development

63. Leverage is defined as the use of borrowed money. The more borrowed funds and the less personal funds, the greater the leverage. Which of the following mortgage loan programs provides the greatest leverage?
   a. FHA 203B
   b. conventional
   c. VA
   d. 95% insured conventional

64. A broker deposited a buyer's check for earnest money in the amount of $6,000 in her escrow account. Prior to the closing and at the request of the seller, the broker paid $1,200 from the escrow account to pay for the cost of damage repairs caused by termites in the house. This expense was necessary so the seller could provide the required termite certificate to the buyer at the closing. Which of the following statements about this transaction is (are) correct?
   I. Since the $1,200 disbursement from the broker's escrow account was made at the seller's request and benefited both buyer and seller, the broker acted properly.
   II. The broker's action constituted an act of commingling and as such was improper.
   a. I only
   b. II only
   c. both I and II
   d. neither I nor II

65. Of the following types of deeds, which provides the grantee with the least assurance of title?
   a. quit claim
   b. warranty
   c. quit claim with covenant
   d. special warranty deed

66. The statement made by a grantor to a qualified public official that the signing of a deed (or other instrument) was done by him and was a voluntary act is called:
   a. an abstract
   b. a conveyance
   c. a covenant
   d. an acknowledgment

67. On June 16, 1987, a seller closed on the sale of her home. The annual taxes of $775 and the water bill of $86 for the current year had been paid in full by the seller prior to the sale. If these payments are prorated, which of the following amounts would be returned to the seller? (Answers are rounded.)
    a. $357
    b. $397
    c. $430
    d. $472

68. All of the following usually appear only in the seller's closing disclosure EXCEPT:
    a. broker's fee
    b. deed preparation
    c. earnest money
    d. discharge fee

69. RESPA requires lending institutions to provide borrowers with which of the following at the time an application is made for a mortgage loan for housing?
    a. good faith estimate
    b. HUD Form No. 1
    c. disclosure statement
    d. nonrecourse note

70. A sales contract provided that the buyer was to pay $65,000 for a seller's property by giving a purchase money mortgage for $30,000 and the balance in cash at closing. The buyer made a good faith deposit of $6,500 when she made the offer. The seller's share of the real property taxes credited to the buyer was $850. The buyer's other closing costs totaled $900. What amount must the buyer pay at closing?
    a. $27,650
    b. $27,700
    c. $28,550
    d. $35,050

71. The mutual promises in a bilateral contract supply which of the following?
    a. voidability
    b. legality
    c. consideration
    d. competency

72. All of the following statements about options are correct EXCEPT:
    a. they must be in writing to be enforceable
    b. they are binding upon optionor and optionee
    c. when exercised they become contracts of sale
    d. optionor and optionee must be competent

73. Which of the following are required to qualify for tax deferment under the rollover rule?
    a. owner must be age 55 or over
    b. owner must have occupied the house for three years
    c. owner must purchase another home within 24 months
    d. the sale must qualify as an installment sale

74. Deed restrictions that are enforced by a suit for damages or by an injunction are:
    a. conditions
    b. conveyances
    c. covenants
    d. considerations

75. Which of the following is a deductible expense for homeowners?
    a. real property taxes
    b. maintenance
    c. mortgage principal payments
    d. energy usage

76. A property owner in a recently zoned area was permitted to continue to use his property in a manner that did not comply with the zoning requirements. This use is described as which of the following?
    a. exclusive-use zoning
    b. deviation
    c. nonconforming use
    d. private control of land use

77. The covenant for further assurances may require the grantor to execute which of the following?
    a. deed of confirmation
    b. executor's deed
    c. certificate of title opinion
    d. deed of devise

78. All of the following statements about the age-55-and-over exclusion are correct EXCEPT:
    a. it may be taken only once in a lifetime
    b. it is available to co-owners
    c. it is up to $125,000
    d. it is available for commercial property

79. A deed is made eligible for recording on the public record by which of the following?
    a. abstract
    b. avoidance
    c. alienation
    d. acknowledgment

80. A real estate broker may do all of the following EXCEPT:
    a. have a buyer's deed recorded
    b. make a title examination
    c. act as agent of the grantee to accept deed delivery
    d. execute a certificate of title opinion

81. A house valued at $60,000 was insured for 85 percent of value. The annual premium was 60 cents per $100 of the face amount of the policy. The homeowner paid a three-year premium on February 28. On April 30 the following year he closed the sale of his home. The buyer is having this policy endorsed to him. What will be the cost to the buyer?
    a. $306
    b. $357
    c. $510
    d. $561

82. One co-owner of real property automatically received a deceased co-owner's share of ownership. This is called:
    a. intestate succession
    b. inheritance by devise
    c. right of survivorship
    d. inheritance by descent

83. Four brothers received title to a large tract of land from their grandfather who gave each brother a one-fourth undivided interest with equal rights to possession of the land. All four received their title on their grandfather's 70th birthday. The brothers most likely hold title in which of the following ways?
    a. in severalty
    b. joint tenants
    c. tenants by the entirety
    d. as remaindermen

84. Which of the following statements about the creation of a condominium is (are) correct?
    I. A Declaration, Articles of Association, and Association By-Laws must be recorded on the public record in the county where the property is located.
    II. A parking garage with rental spaces can be converted to condominium ownership.
    a. I only
    b. II only
    c. both I and II
    d. neither I nor II

85. An encroachment is which of the following?
    a. lien
    b. party wall
    c. trespass
    d. fixture

86. A competitive market analysis is performed when:
    a. assessing property
    b. pricing property
    c. appraising property
    d. condemning property

87. For which of the following types of property would the market data approach be the most relevant appraisal method?
    a. farm land
    b. library
    c. condominium office
    d. mobile home park

88. The principle providing that the highest value of a property has a tendency to be established by the cost of purchasing or constructing a building of equal utility and desirability is the principle of:
    a. highest-and-best use
    b. competition
    c. supply and demand
    d. substitution

89. Which of the following is (are) included in a competitive or comparative market analysis?
    I. Properties that have sold recently.
    II. Properties currently on the market.
    a. I only
    b. II only
    c. both I and II
    d. neither I nor II

90. An apartment building produces a monthly net income of $3,600. If the owner paid $440,000 for the building what is her annual rate of return?
    a. 8.18 percent
    b. 9.8 percent
    c. 10.18 percent
    d. 11.8 percent

91. The monthly payment necessary to fully amortize a 15-year mortgage loan of $50,000 at 11 percent APR is $568.50. How much interest will the mortgagor pay over the 15-year term?
    a. $17,083
    b. $52,330
    c. $69,413
    d. $102,330

92. An owner whose property is condemned is entitled to be compensated for which of the following?
    a. book value
    b. assessed value
    c. market value
    d. mortgage value

93. A lender charged a 2 percent loan origination fee and 3 discount points to make a 95 percent conventional insured mortgage loan in the amount of $47,500. What was the cost of these charges to the borrower?

    a. $922
    b. $1,188
    c. $1,425
    d. $2,375

94. Which of the following statements about promissory notes is (are) correct?

    I. They are only executed by the borrower.
    II. They provide evidence that a valid debt exists.

    a. I only
    b. II only
    c. both I and II
    d. neither I nor II

95. All of the following are ways in which a seller may finance the sale of her property for a buyer EXCEPT:

    a. wraparound mortgage
    b. contract for deed
    c. FHA-insured mortgage
    d. purchase money first mortgage

96. Regulation Z specifies that the only specific credit term that may appear in an advertisement of a house for sale without the requirement of a full disclosure is which of the following?

    a. SAM
    b. APR
    c. ECOA
    d. RESPA

97. In the sale of their home Van and Vera Vendor were required to satisfy their existing first mortgage of $40,000 so that the buyers could obtain a first mortgage to finance their purchase. The Vendors' closing disclosure contained a debit in the amount of $800 because the Vendors paid off their loan prior to the full term. From this information it can be determined that the Vendors' mortgage contained a(n):

    a. acceleration clause
    b. alienation clause
    c. prepayment clause
    d. defeasance clause

98. The age of a property based on the remaining years of useful life is described as:

    a. economic
    b. useful
    c. chronological
    d. physical

99. Which of the following statements about the secondary mortgage market is (are) correct?

    I. It provides liquidity for mortgages held by lending institutions.
    II. It benefits mortgage loan applicants.

    a. I only
    b. II only
    c. both I and II
    d. neither I nor II

100. A contract that is unenforceable is:

    a. void
    b. valid
    c. enforceable
    d. voidable

ANSWER KEY

CHAPTER-END REVIEW QUESTIONS

Chapter 1   Introduction to Real Estate Principles

1. c	6. c	11. c
2. b	7. d	12. a
3. c	8. c	13. b
4. c	9. c	14. c
5. d	10. d	15. b

Chapter 2   Licensing of Real Estate Brokers, Associate Brokers, and Sales Agents

1. c	5. b	9. b
2. b	6. c	10. d
3. c	7. c	
4. b	8. d	

Chapter 3   Property Ownership, Interests, and Restrictions

1. c	8. c	15. c
2. c	9. c	16. b
3. d	10. d	17. b
4. d	11. b	18. c
5. d	12. d	19. c
6. a	13. c	20. d
7. b	14. d	

Chapter 4   Law of Agency

1. d	4. d	7. c	10. b
2. a	5. d	8. a	
3. d	6. b	9. a	

Chapter 5   Fundamentals of Contract Law

1. c	6. d	11. c
2. c	7. b	12. c
3. d	8. b	13. b
4. c	9. c	14. a
5. a	10. d	15. b

Chapter 6   The Listing and Valuation Processes

1. d	6. b	11. c
2. d	7. b	12. a
3. b	8. b	13. b
4. d	9. d	14. c
5. c	10. a	15. b

Chapter 7   Landlord–Tenant Laws

1. a	4. c	7. d	10. a
2. b	5. a	8. a	
3. c	6. b	9. c	

Chapter 8   Land Use Controls

1. b	5. b	9. c
2. d	6. b	10. a
3. d	7. a	
4. b	8. c	

Chapter 9   Real Estate Financing

1. d	4. a	7. a	10. a
2. c	5. a	8. c	
3. b	6. d	9. b	

Chapter 10   Real Estate Financing Practices

1. c	4. a	7. c	10. d
2. b	5. d	8. b	11. d
3. b	6. a	9. a	

Chapter 11   Selling: Practices and Procedures

1. b	4. b	7. b
2. c	5. d	8. a
3. b	6. c	

Chapter 12   Transfer of Title to Real Property

1. b	5. b	9. a
2. c	6. d	10. c
3. a	7. b	
4. c	8. c	

Chapter 13   Closing Real Estate Transactions

1. a	4. b	7. d	10. d
2. a	5. c	8. c	
3. d	6. b	9. d	

Chapter 14 Fair Housing

1. b	4. d	7. c	10. b
2. c	5. b	8. b	
3. c	6. d	9. b	

Chapter 15 Tax Implications of Real Estate Ownership and Transactions

1. c	4. c	7. c	10. c
2. b	5. a	8. c	
3. d	6. c	9. c	

Chapter 16 Real Estate Math

1. $28,000 × .0775 = $2,170/yr.
   $2,170 ÷ 365 = $5.95/day
   $5.95 × 11 = $65.45 used portion
   Since payments are made in arrears, this amount will be a credit to the buyer.

2. Value = Income ÷ Rate
   V = $2,400 ÷ .06
   V = $40,000

3. 720 ÷ .020 = $36,000

4. 9,000 gal. ÷ 4 hrs. = 2,250 gal./hr. by 36 pumps
   2,250 gal./hr. ÷ 36 pumps = 62.5 gal./hr. per pump
   12,000 gal. ÷ 12 hrs = 1,000 gal./hr. by ? pumps
   1,000 gal./hr. ÷ 62.5 gal. hr./pump = 16 pumps
        or
   pumps gals. hrs.
   $\frac{36}{?} \times \frac{12,000}{9,000} \times \frac{4}{12}$ = 16 pumps

5. $4,800 minimum
   $192,000 × .025 = $4,800

6. $4\frac{1}{2} \times 2\frac{1}{2}$ miles = ?
   $\frac{9}{2} \times \frac{5}{2}$ miles = $\frac{45}{4}$ = $11\frac{1}{4}$ miles

7. 40 yds. × 3 ft. = 120 ft.
   120 ft. × 80 ft. = 9,600 sq. ft.
   9,600 sq. ft. ÷ 43,560 sq. ft. = .22 acres

8. Value = Income ÷ Rate
   R = 60% of 6% = .6 × .06 = .036
   V = $18,000 ÷ .036 = $500,000 per year
   $500,000/yr. ÷ 12 mos. = $41,666.67

9. 30 ft. × 3 sides = 90 ft.
   90 ft. ÷ 10 ft. interval = 9 posts
   9 posts + 1 (starting post) = 10 posts

10. Value = Income ÷ Rate
    V = $12,000/yr. ÷ .085
    V = $141,176 (rounded)

11. 80% of 2nd tract = 1st tract
    .8 × ? (2nd tract) = $48,000
    2nd tract = $48,000 ÷ .8
    2nd tract = $60,000

12. One point raises the effective interest rate 1/8 of 1%.
    One point costs 1% of the amount of the loan.
    8% − 7.75% = .25% = 2 pts. = 2% of loan
    $27,000 × .02 = $540

13. 140 ft. × 2 = 280 ft.
    265 ft. × 2 = 530 ft.
    280 ft. + 530 ft. = 810 ft.
    810 ft. × 6 ft. = 4,860 sq. ft.
    4,860 sq. ft. ÷ 9 sq. ft./sq. yd. = 540 sq. yds.
    540 sq. yds. × $3 = $1,620

14. $12,600 = gross income
    $12,600 × .05 = $630 (vacancy factor)
    $12,600 − $630 = $11,970 (gross effective income)
    $11,970 − $3,600 = $8,370 (net income)
    Value = Income ÷ Rate
    V = $8,370 ÷ .12
    V = $69,750

15. $570/mo. × 12 mos. = $6,840/yr.
    Value = Income ÷ Rate
    V = $6,840 ÷ .09
    V = $76,000

16. 100% ÷ 50 yrs. = 2%/yr.
    2% × 5 yrs. = 10% (depreciation to date)
    100% − 10% = 90% (remaining value)
    Original Value = Current Value ÷ % of Remaining Value
    OV = $810,000 ÷ .9
    OV = $900,000

17. $63,000 \times .030 = \$1,890$

18. Perimeter = (2 × width) + (2 × length)
    Width = W
    Length = 2W + 6 yds.
    2(2W + 6 yds.) + 2W = 1,800 yds.
    6W + 12 yds. = 1,800 yds.
    6W = 1,788 yds.
    W = 298 yds.
    2(298) + 6 = length
    602 yds. = length
    602 yds. × 3 ft./yd. = 1,806 ft.

19. $\$4,000 \times 3 = \$12,000$
    $\$4,500 \times 4 = \$18,000$
    $\$18,000 - \$12,000 = \$6,000$
    n% of $\$12,000 = \$6,000$
    n = $\$6,000 \div \$12,000$
    n = .5 or 50%

20. 100% ÷ 40 yrs. = yearly depreciation rate
    1.00 ÷ 40 = .025 or 2.5% yearly depreciation
    12 yrs. × 2.5% = 30% depreciation to date
    100% − 30% = 70% remaining value
    70% of original value = $26,000
    Original Value = $26,000 ÷ .70
    OV = $37,142.86

21. $\frac{3}{5} \times \frac{5}{8} \div \frac{5}{6} = ?$

    $\frac{3}{5} \times \frac{5}{8} \ 3 \ \frac{6}{5} = ?$

    $\frac{3}{5^1} \times \frac{5^1}{8^4} \ 3 \ \frac{6^3}{5} = \frac{9}{20}$

    9 ÷ 20 = .45

22. 9 inches thick on each of two ends = 1.5 ft.
    35 ft. − 1.5 ft. = 33.5 ft.
    26.5 ft. − 1.5 ft. = 25 ft.
    33.5 ft. × 25 ft. = 837.5 sq. ft.

23. $\$20,000 \times .09 = \$1,800$ annual interest
    $\$1,800 \div 365 = \$4.93$/day
    $\$4.93 \times 9 = \$44.37$ debit

24. $\$38,500 \times .06 = \$2,310$ brokers fee
    $\$33,000 \times .055 = \$1,815$ discount points
    $\$2,310 + \$1,815 = \$4,125$ total expenses
    $\$38,500 - \$4,125 = \$34,375$ net

25. $750 incr ÷ $3.75 = 200 ($100 units)
    200 ($100 units) × $100/unit = $20,000 tax value
    $20,000 ÷ .60 = $33,333.33

26. Gross Income − Expenses = Net Income
    $\$80,000 - \$8,000 = \$72,000$
    Income ÷ Rate = Value
    $\$72,000 \div .08 = \$900,000$

27. $\$1,200 \times .0225 = \$27$
    $\$215 - \$180 = \$35$
    $\$35 - \$27 = \$8$

28. $500/mo. × 12 mo. = $6,000/year base rent
    $\$220,000 - \$185,000 = \$35,000$ (earnings over $185,000)
    $\$35,000 \times .03 = \$1,050$
    $\$6,000 + \$1,050 = \$7,050$

29. $\frac{1}{2} + \frac{4}{4} + \frac{1}{8}$ = unknown area

    $\frac{4}{8} + \frac{2}{8} + \frac{1}{8} = \frac{7}{8}$

    $\frac{8}{8} - \frac{7}{8} = \frac{1}{8}$ remaining

    Remaining Area = 7 acres = $\frac{1}{8}$

    $\frac{1}{8}$ of Total = 7 acres

    Total = 7 acres $3 \ \frac{8}{1}$ = 56 acres

30. 20 units × $180/mo. × 12 mos. = $43,200 gross rent
    $\$43,200 - \$2,160$ (vacancy @ 5%) = $41,040 gross effective income
    $\$41,040 - \$26,204$ (expenses) = $14,836 net income
    Income ÷ Value = Rate
    $\$14,836 \div \$195,000 = .07608 = 7.61\%$

31. $\$35,000 + \$7,000 = \$42,000$ total assessed value
    $\$42,000 \times 1.18 = \$49,560$ increased valuation
    $\$49,560 \times .80 = \$39,648$ new tax basis
    $\$39,648 \times .0212 = \$840.54$

32. $\$110,000 \times .97 = \$106,700$
    $\$106,700 \times .97 = \$103,499$
    $\$103,499 \times .97 = \$100,394$
    $\$100,394 \times .97 = \$97,382$

33. $\$7,000 + \$18,000 = \$25,000$
    100% − 7% commission = 93%
    $\$25,000 \div .93 = \$26,882$ (rounded)

34. Current Value =   Original Value × Appreciation
$32,000 × 1.42 (142%) = $45,440
$4,000 × 1.36 (136%) = $5,440
$45,440 + $5,440 = $50,880 (total appreciated value)
$32,000 + $4,000 = $36,000 (total original value)
$50,880 − $36,000 = $14,880 (amount of
    appreciation)
$14,880 ÷ $36,000 = 41.33%

35. 100% − 17.5% = 82.5% remaining value
Current Value ÷ % Remaining Value = Original
    Value
$63,000 ÷ .825 = $76,363

36. $320,000 + $40,000 + $20,000 = $380,000 total
    investment
Rate × Value = Income
.12 × $380,000 = $45,600

37. $67,500 × .80 = $54,000 tax value
$54,000 ÷ $100/unit = 540 ($100 units)
540 ($100 units) × $1.50 (per $100 unit) = $810 tax
    bill
$810 ÷ 365 = 2.22 daily rate
2.22 × 50 days = $111.00 debit

38. Area of a triangle = $\frac{1}{2}$ × base × height

$\frac{1}{2}$ × 350 ft. × 425 ft. = 74,375 sq. ft.

74,375 sq. ft. × .75/sq. ft. = $55,781.25 sales price
$55,781.25 × .09 = $5,020.31

39. 4 yds. × 8 yds. = 32 sq. yds.
32 sq. yds. × $3.50/sq. yd. = $112 labor cost
$\frac{1}{2}$ ft. × 12 ft. × 24 ft. = 144 cu. ft.

144 cu. ft. × $1.50 = $216 material cost
$112 + $216 = $328

40. $75,000 × .08 = $6,000 commission on 1st $75,000
$9,000 − $6,000 = $3,000 commission on price over
    $75,000
Income ÷ Rate = Value
$3,000 ÷ .06 = $50,000
$75,000 + $50,000 = $125,000

41. $45,000 × 1.20 (120%) = $54,000 asking price
$54,000 × .90 = $48,600 sold price

42. 600 ft. × 145.2 ft. = 87,120 sq. ft.
87,120 sq. ft. ÷ 43,560 sq. ft./acre = 2 acres
2 acres × $4,000 = $8,000 acreage basis
$15 × 600 ft. = $9,000 front foot basis

43. Current Value = 100% Original Value + 35% of
    Original Value
$280,000 ÷ 1.35 = $207,407 (rounded)

44. Income ÷ Rate = Value
$150 ÷ .025 = $6,000

45. 2,300 sq. ft. × $26 = $59,800 house value
150 ft. × 210 ft. = 31,500 sq. ft. lot area
31,500 sq. ft. × $.25 = $7,875 lot value
$59,800 + $7,875 = $67,675 value house & lot
23 ft. × 22 ft. = 506 sq. ft. interior of garage
506 sq. ft. × $12 = $6,072 garage value
Value Increase ÷ Original Value = Percentage of
    Increase
$6,072 ÷ $67,675 = .0897 or 8.97%

46. $\frac{1}{4}$ × $\frac{1}{4}$ × $\frac{1}{4}$ × $\frac{640 \text{ acres}}{1 \text{ section}}$ = total acres sold
$\frac{1}{64}$ × $\frac{640 \text{ acres}}{1 \text{ section}}$ = 10 acres sold
10 acres × $700 = $7,000
Rate × Value = Income
.12 × $7,000 = $840

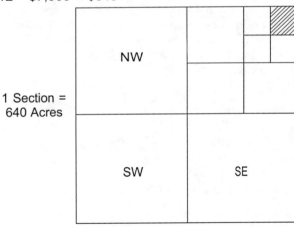

1 Section =
640 Acres

47. 160 square rods = 1 acre (43,560 sq. ft.)
560 sq. rods ÷ 160 sq. rods/acre = 3.5 acres
3.5 acres × 43,560 sq. ft./acre = 152,460 sq. ft.
152,460 sq. ft. × $.12 = $18,295

48. (2 × 300 ft.) + (2 × 150 ft.) = 900 ft.
900 ft. ÷ 15 ft./post = 60 posts

49. $\frac{1}{2}$ × base × height = Area of a Right Triangle

$\frac{1}{2}$ × 900 ft. × 4,000 ft. = 1,800,000 sq. ft.

1,800,000 sq. ft. ÷ 9 sq. ft./sq. yd. = 200,000 sq. yds.

50. $10,200 + $3,400 = $13,600 gross income
Income ÷ Rate = Value
$13,600 ÷ .14 (gross return) = $97,143 (rounded)

51. 12 mos. × $1,200 = $14,400 minimum annual rent
$16,600 − $14,400 = $2,200 rent above minimum
Income ÷ Rate = Value
$2,200 ÷ .03 = $73,333.33 sales over $260,000
$260,000.00 + $73,333.33 = $333,333.33

52. 100% ÷ 40 years = 2.5% per year depreciation
14 years × 2.5%/yr. = 35% depreciation to date
100% − 35% = 65% remaining value
Original Value × % Remaining Value = Current
Value
$150,000 × .65 = $97,500

53. $500 × 12 months = $6,000 annual interest
Income ÷ Rate = Value
$6,000 ÷ .10 = $60,000

54. Length × Width × Depth = Volume (Cubic
Measure)
90 ft. × 30 ft. × 14 ft. = 37,800 cu. ft.
37,800 cu. ft. ÷ 27 cu. ft./cu. yd. = 1,400 cu. yds.
1,400 cu. yds. × $.25 = $350

55. $60,000 × .85 = $51,000 face amount
$51,000 ÷ $100/unit = 510 ($100 units)
$.60 × 510 ($100 units) = $306 annual premium
$306 × 3 years = $918 premium for 3 years
$918 ÷ 36 months = $25.50 monthly rate
$25.50 × 14 months = $357 value used
$918 − $357 = $561

56. Perimeter = (2 × Length) + (2 × Width)
Length = (2 × Width) + 8 yds.
2(2W + 8) + 2W = 120 yds.
6 × Width + 16 yds. = 120 yds.
6W = 120 yds. − 16 yds.
6W = 104 yds.
W = 104 yds. ÷ 6
$W = 17\frac{1}{3}$ − yds.
$W = 17\frac{1}{3}$ − yds. × 3 ft./yd. = 52 ft.

Length = 2 × Width + 24 ft.
L = 2 × Width + 24 ft.
L = 2 × 52 ft. + 24 ft.
L = 128 ft.

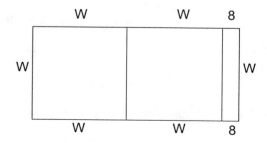

57. $\frac{1}{2} + \frac{1}{3}$ = Unknown Area

$\frac{3}{6} + \frac{2}{6} = \frac{5}{6}$

$\frac{6}{6}$ (entire area) $− \frac{5}{6} = \frac{1}{6}$

Remainder = 20 acres

$\frac{1}{6}$ of entire tract = 20 acres

Entire tract = 20 acres × 6 = 120 acres

58. 125 acres × $450 = $56,250
200 houses × $45,000 = $9,000,000
Other costs = $125,000
$56,250 + $9,000,000 + $125,000 = $9,181,250
investment
1.14 (114%) × $9,181,250 = $10,466,625 gross
sales
$10,466,625 ÷ 200 = $52,333.13

59. 5,280 ft. × 1.25 = 6,600 ft.
6,600 ft. × 6,600 ft. = 43,560,000 sq. ft.
43,560,000 sq. ft. ÷ 43,560 sq. ft./acre = 1,000 acres
1,000 acres × $200 = $200,000
Value × Rate = Income
$200,000 × .09 = $18,000 total commission
100% − 45% = 55% retained net
.55 × $18,000 = $9,900

60. $24 × 12 months = $288 annual expenses
$3,600 + $288 = $3,888 gross income
Income ÷ Rate = Value
$3,888 ÷ .06 = $64,800

61. $50,000 − $5,000 = $45,000 net income
Income ÷ Rate = Value
$45,000 ÷ .09 = $500,000

62. 125 ft. × 160 ft. = 20,000 sq. ft.
20,000 sq. ft. × .17 = $3,400 purchase price
$2.25 × 125 ft. = $281.25 paving lien
$3,400 + $281.25 = $3,681.25 total investment
$3,681.25 + $295.00 = $3,976.25

63. $8,925.25 + $1,510.60 + $4,920.05 + $3,644.10 =
$19,000
Gross Annual Income − Annual Expenses = Net
Return
$53,200 − $19,000 = $34,200

64. $500 × 12 months = $6,000 annual expenses
$14,000 + $6,000 = $20,000 gross income
Income ÷ Rate = Value
$20,000 ÷ .25 = $80,000

65. Divide house diagram into 3 triangles and 1 square.

$\frac{1}{2}$ × Base × Height = Area of Triangle

Height = 20 ft. since the two diagonal lines intersect in the center

$\frac{1}{2}$ × 40 ft. × 20 ft. = 400 sq. ft.

3 × 400 sq. ft. = 1,200 sq. ft. (area of 3 triangles)
20 ft. × 20 ft. = 400 sq. ft. (area of square)
1,200 sq. ft. + 400 sq. ft. = 1,600 sq. ft. (area of house)
$56,000 ÷ 1,600 sq. ft. = $35 present cost per sq. ft.
$35 − $15 = $20

66. $325 × 52 weeks = $16,900 annual gross income
$845 × 12 months = $10,140 annual expense
$16,900 − $10,140 = $6,760 net annual income
Income ÷ Value = Rate
$6,760 ÷ $84,500 = .08 or 8%

67. 10 × 43,560 sq. ft. (1 acre) = 435,600 sq. ft.
435,600 sq. ft. − 85,600 sq. ft. = 350,000 sq. ft. available for lots
50 ft. × 100 ft. = 5,000 sq. ft. per lot
350,000 sq. ft. ÷ 5,000 sq. ft. = 70 lots

68. $50,000 × .75 = $37,500 (tax value)
37,500 × .045 = $1,687.50 annually
$1,687.50 ÷ 2 = $843.75 semi-annual

69. 50 ft. × $63 = $3,150 lot cost
$3,150 + $9,216 = $12,366 total cost
$12,366 − $5,000 = $7,366 mortgage amount
$7,366 × .055 = $405.13 annual interest
$405.13 ÷ 2 = $202.57

70. 3 × 80 ft. × 75 ft. = 18,000 sq. ft. in building
$25 × 18,000 sq. ft. = $450,000 building cost
$300 × 100 = $30,000 cost of lot
100 × 200 = 20,000 sq. ft. lot size
20,000 sq. ft. − (80 ft. × 75 ft.) = 14,000 sq. ft. to be paved
14,000 sq. ft. × $3 = $42,000 paving cost
$450,000 + $30,000 + $42,000 = $522,000

71. Divide lot into 1 triangle and 1 square

$\frac{1}{2}$ × Base × Height = Area of Right Triangle

$\frac{1}{2}$ × 50 ft. × 150 ft. = 3,750 sq. ft. in triangle

150 ft. × 150 ft. = 22,500 sq. ft. in square
3,750 sq. ft. + 22,500 sq. ft. = 26,250 sq. ft. lot size
26,250 sq. ft. ÷ 43,560 sq. ft./acre = .60 acre
.60 acres 2 $4,000 = $2,400 lot cost

Divide house into 2 rectangles
80 ft. × 25 ft. = 2,000 sq. ft.
5 ft. × 40 ft. = 200 sq. ft.
2,000 sq. ft. + 200 sq. ft. = 2,200 sq. ft. house size
2,200 sq. ft. × $21 = $46,200 house cost
$2,400 + $46,200 = $48,600 total cost
$48,600 × 1.10 = $53,460

72. 130 ft. × 30 ft. = 3,900 sq. ft.
3,900 sq. ft. × $18.90 = $73,710 cost on square foot basis
130 ft. × 30 ft. × 24 ft. = 93,600 cu. ft.
93,600 cu. ft. × $.80 = $74,880 cost on cubic foot basis
$74,880 − $73,710 = $1,170

73. Divide house into 2 rectangles
5 ft. × 20 ft. = 100 sq. ft.
25 ft. × 80 ft. = 2,000 sq. ft.
2,000 sq. ft. + 100 sq. ft. = 2,100 sq. ft. in house
Divide lot into 1 rectangle and 1 triangle
100 ft. × 200 ft. = 20,000 sq. ft. (rectangle)
$\frac{1}{2}$ × 50 ft. × 100 ft. = 2,500 sq. ft.
20,000 sq. ft. + 2,500 sq. ft. = 22,500 sq. ft. in lot
Area of House + Area of Lot = Percentage of Lot Occupied by House
2,100 sq. ft. ÷ 22,500 sq. ft. = .0933 rounded to 9%

74. $64,000 − $9,500 = $54,500 original house value
$54,500 × 0.15 = $8,175 depreciation
$54,500 − $8,175 = $46,325 house value at end of 6 years
$9,500 × 1.48 (148%) = $14,060 lot value at end of 6 years
$46,325 + $14,060 = $60,385

75. .06 × $8,500   = $ 510
.055 × (2 yrs. 3 $8,500) =   935
.05 × (3 yrs. 3 $8,500) = 1,275
.045 × (4 yrs. 3 $8,500) = 1,530
.02 × (10 yrs. 3 $8,500) = 1,700
                           $5,950

76. Area of Trapezoid = $\frac{1}{2}$ × Height × (Base$_1$ + Base$_2$)

Area = $\frac{1}{2}$ × 1,500 ft. × (500 ft. + 1,000 ft.)

Area = 750 ft. × 1,500 ft.
Area = 1,125,000 sq. ft.
1,125,000 sq. ft. ÷ 43,560 sq. ft./acre = 25.83 acres
$25,380 ÷ 25.83 = $982.58

77. 43,560 sq. ft. (1 acre) ÷ 165 ft. = 264 ft.

78. 1,700 ÷ 136,000 = .0125
.0125 × 1,000 = 12.5 mills

79. $400,000 × .02 = $8,000
Therefore: annual rent = $12,000 minimum

80. $60,000 × .80 = $48,000 assessed value
$900 × 2 = $1,800 annual taxes
$1,800 ÷ $48,000 = .0375
.0375 × 1,000 = 37.5 mills

81. 300 ft. × 300 ft. = 90,000 sq. ft.
90,000 sq. ft. ÷ 43,560 sq. ft./acre = 2.066 acres
2.066 acres × $2,750 = $5,681.50 sales price
Value × Rate = Income
$5,681.50 × .09 = $511.34

82. $1A = \frac{1}{2} × 60$ ft. × 100 ft. = 3,000 sq. ft.

$1B = 80$ ft. × 100 ft.   = 8,000 sq. ft.

$2A = 30$ ft. × 100 ft.   = 3,000 sq. ft.

$2B = \frac{1}{2} × 30$ ft. × 50 ft. =   750 sq. ft.
 _____
14,750 sq. ft.

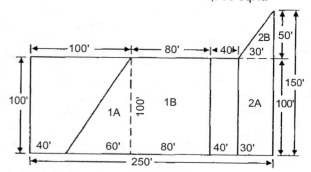

83. $41,500 × .07 = $2,905 earnings per sale
$46,480 ÷ $2,905 = 16 sales
16 sales × 16.5 = 264 showings

84. Market Value = 100%
100% − 15% = 85% of MV (purchase price)
Percentage Increase ÷ Original Value = Rate of Profit
15% ÷ 85% = Rate of Profit
.15 ÷ .85 = .1765 or 17.65%

85. 14,520 sq. yds. × 9 sq. ft./yd.^{2} = 130,680 sq. ft.
$27,000 ÷ 130,680 sq. ft. = $.2066 per sq. ft.
150 ft. × 300 ft. = 45,000 sq. ft.
45,000 sq. ft. × $.2066 = $9,297

86. 100% ÷ 50 years = 2% depreciation per year
26 years × 2% = 52% depreciation to date
100% − 52% = 48% remaining value
Current Value ÷ % remaining value = original value
$54,000 ÷ .48 = $112,500

87. $588.80 ÷ .023 = 25,600

88. Income ÷ Rate = Value
$5,600 ÷ .07 = $80,000

89. $337.50 × 12 months = $4,050 annual interest
Income ÷ Rate = Value
$4,050 ÷ .09 = $45,000 loan amount
$45,000 ÷ .80 = $56,250

90. Area of Trapezoid = $\frac{1}{2}$ × Height × (Base$_1$ + Base$_2$)

Area = $\frac{1}{2}$ × 900 ft. × (1,000 ft. + 800 ft.)

Area = 810,000 sq. ft.
810,000 sq. ft. ÷ 43,560 sq. ft./acre = 18.595 acres
18.595 acres × $1,200 = $22,314
Value × Rate = Income
$22,314 × .09 = $2,008.26

91. $32,000 × 3 = $96,000 total sale price
$96,000 ÷ 1.12 (112%) = $85,714.29

92. Step 1:
Divide garden into 2 rectangles
20 ft. × 40 ft. = 800 sq. ft.
5 ft. × 10 ft. = 50 sq. ft.
800 sq. ft. + 50 sq. ft. = 850 sq. ft. garden area
Step 2:
Calculate total area including walk
46 ft. × 26 ft. = 1,196 sq. ft.
16 ft. × 5 ft. = 80 sq. ft.
1,196 sq. ft. + 80 sq. ft. = 1,276 sq. ft. total area

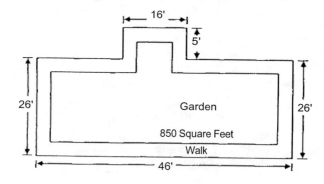

Step 3:
Determine square yards in walk and calculate cost.
1,276 sq. ft. − 850 sq. ft. = 426 sq. ft. walk area
426 sq. ft. ÷ 9 sq. ft./sq. yd. = 47.33 sq. yds.
47.33 sq. yd. × $12 = $567.96

93. Current Value = 100% Original Value + 25% of Original Value
$200,000 ÷ 1.25 = $160,000

94. Income ÷ Rate = Value
$12,500 ÷ .12 = $104,167
(Note: Net income is used with cap. rate)

95. 5,280 ft. × 5,280 ft. = 27,878,400 sq. ft.
27,878,400 sq. ft. ÷ 43,560 sq. ft./acre = 640 acres
Income ÷ Rate = Value
$64,000 ÷ .10 = $640,000 total sale price
$640,000 ÷ 640 acres = $1,000

96.

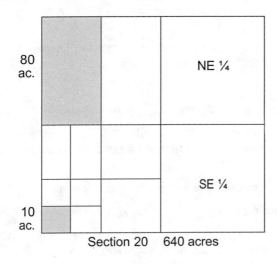

$\frac{1}{4} \times \frac{1}{4} \times \frac{1}{4} \times \frac{640 \text{ acres}}{1 \text{ section}} = 10$ acres

$\frac{1}{2} \times \frac{1}{4} \times \frac{640 \text{ acres}}{1 \text{ section}} = 80$ acres

10 acres + 80 acres = 90 acres

97. 1st building = 70% of 2nd building
$98,000 ÷ .70 = $140,000

98. $200 × 12 months = $2,400 annualized interest
Income ÷ Value = Rate
$2,400 ÷ $30,000 = .08 or 8%

99. $80,000 × .85 = $68,000 face amount
$68,000 ÷ $100/unit = 680 ($100 units)
680 ($100 units) × $.70 = $476 annual premium
$476 ÷ 12 = $39.67 premium per month
6.5 months × $39.67 = $257.86 value used
$476.00 − $257.86 = $218.14

100. Income ÷ Value = Rate
$24,000 ÷ $400,000 = .06 or 6%

PRACTICE TEST

1. a	26. a	51. c	76. c
2. c	27. c	52. a	77. a
3. c	28. d	53. b	78. d
4. b	29. a	54. d	79. d
5. d	30. a	55. b	80. d
6. d	31. a	56. c	81. d
7. c	32. a	57. b	82. c
8. b	33. a	58. b	83. b
9. c	34. b	59. a	84. c
10. d	35. c	60. a	85. c
11. d	36. a	61. c	86. b
12. c	37. d	62. d	87. a
13. c	38. c	63. c	88. d
14. c	39. a	64. d	89. c
15. c	40. b	65. a	90. b
16. c	41. a	66. d	91. b
17. b	42. a	67. d	92. c
18. c	43. d	68. c	93. d
19. a	44. a	69. a	94. c
20. d	45. d	70. c	95. c
21. d	46. c	71. c	96. b
22. d	47. c	72. b	97. c
23. c	48. d	73. c	98. a
24. c	49. a	74. c	99. c
25. c	50. b	75. a	100. a

GLOSSARY

This section presents definitions of all real estate terms appearing in the text. Also, there are definitions of some terms that are not specifically discussed in the text but may possibly be included in the license examinations.

abandonment The surrender or release of a right, claim, or interest in real property.

abstract continuation An update of an abstract of title by a memorandum of a new transfer of title.

abstract of title A history of a title and the current status of a title based on a title examination.

acceleration clause A provision in a mortgage or deed of trust that permits the lender to declare the entire principal balance of the debt immediately due and payable if the borrower is in default.

acceptance Compliance with the terms and conditions of an offer so that a contract becomes legally valid.

access The right to go onto and leave a property.

accord and satisfaction A new agreement by contracting parties that is satisfied by full performance, thereby terminating at prior contract as well.

accrued Accumulated.

accrued depreciation The amount of depreciation taken, as of a given date, for tax purposes. The loss in value in a structure measured by the cost of a new replacement.

acknowledgment A formal statement before an authorized official (e.g., notary public) by a person who executed a deed, contract, or other document that it was (is) his free act.

acquisition The act of acquiring a property.

acquisition cost The basis used by the FHA in calculating the loan amount.

acre A land area containing 43,560 square feet.

action to quiet title A lawsuit to clear a title to real property.

act of waste Violation of the right of estovers.

actual eviction The removal of a tenant by the landlord because the tenant breached a condition of a lease or other rental contract.

actual notice The knowledge that a person has of a fact.

adjoining lands Lands sharing a common boundary line.

adjustable rate mortgage (ARM) A mortgage in which the interest rate changes according to changes in a predetermined index.

adjusted basis Original cost (purchase price and closing costs) of a property plus capital improvement minus depreciation, if any.

adjusted sales price The amount realized reduced by the cost of fixing up expenses.

adjustments Additions or subtractions of dollar amounts to equalize comparables to subject property in the market data approach to the value estimate.

administrator's deed One executed by an administrator to convey title to estate property.

ad valorem Latin term meaning "according to value." Real property is taxed on an ad valorem basis.

adverse possession A method of acquiring title to real property by conforming to statutory requirement. A form of involuntary alienation of title.

affirmative easement A legal requirement that a servient owner permit a right of use in the servient land by the dominant owner.

agency The fiduciary relationship existing between a principal and agent.

agent A person authorized by another to act on her behalf.

agreement A contract. Mutual assent between two or more parties.

air rights Rights in the air space above the surface of land.

alienation Transfer of title to real property.

alienation clause A clause in a mortgage or deed of trust that entitles the lender to declare the entire principal balance of the debt immediately due and payable if the borrower sells the property during the mortgage term.

allodial system The type of landownership existing in the United States whereby title to real property may be held absolutely by individuals.

amenities Benefits resulting from the ownership of a particular property.

Americans with Disabilities Act (ADA) A federal law, effective in 1992, that is designed to eliminate discrimination against individuals with disabilities by mandating equal access to public accommodations, public transportation, jobs, communication, and government services.

amortization schedule A designation of periodic payments of principal and interest over a specific term to satisfy a mortgage loan.

amortizing mortgage One in which uniform installment payments include the payment of both principal and interest.

annexation The addition of an area into a city.

annual Yearly.

annual percentage rate (APR) The actual effective rate of interest charged on a loan expressed on a yearly basis; not the same as the simple interest rate.

anticipation The principle that property value is based on the anticipation of the future benefits of ownership.

appraisal An estimate of property value based on factual data.

appraisal process An organized and systematic program for estimating real property value.

appraisal report A report containing an estimate of property value and the data on which the estimate is based.

appreciation An increase in property value.

approaches to value Methods of estimating real property value.

appurtenance All rights or privileges that result from ownership of a particular property and move with the title.

appurtenant easement A right of use in the adjoining land of another that moves with the title to the property benefiting from the easement.

arrears Delinquent in meeting an obligation. The payment of interest for a prior period as scheduled.

artificial person A corporation or other legally recognized entity.

asking price The price specified in a listing contract.

assessed value The value to which a local tax rate is applied to calculate the amount of real property tax.

assessment A levy against property.

assessor An official of local government who has the responsibility for establishing the value of property for tax purposes.

assignee One to whom contractual rights are transferred.

assignment A transfer of legal rights and obligations by one party to another.

assignment of a lease The transfer by a lessee of the entire remaining term of a lease without any reversion of interest to the lessee.

assignor One transferring contractual rights to another.

associate broker Any person employed by or on behalf of an agency to perform real estate brokerage services and licensed by the commission as an associate broker.

assumable mortgage One that does not contain an alienation clause.

attestation Witnessing a document.

attorney-at-law A person licensed by a state to engage in the practice of law.

auction A form of property sale in which people are bidding against each other.

availability An economic characteristic of land describing that land is a commodity having a fixed supply base.

back-up contract Second contract for property on which there is already a legally binding contract. It is contingent on the failure of the prior contract.

bail bond A bond given by a defendant under criminal charges to obtain release from custody.

balloon mortgage A type of mortgage in which the scheduled payment will not fully amortize the loan over the mortgage term. Therefore, it requires a final payment called a balloon payment, larger than the uniform payments, to fully satisfy the debt.

base lines East-west lines in the rectangular method of property description.

base rent The fixed or minimum rent portion in a percentage lease.

basis The value of property for income tax purposes. It is original cost, plus capital improvements, less accrued depreciation.

beneficial title The equitable title to real property retained by a mortgagor or trustor conveying the legal title to secure a mortgage debt.

beneficiary Recipient of funds, property, or other benefits from an insurance policy, will, or other settlement.

bequest   A gift of personal property by will.

bilateral contract   An agreement based on mutual promises that provide the consideration.

bill of sale An instrument transferring ownership of personal property.

blanket mortgage One in which two or more parcels of real property are pledged to secure the payment of the note.

blockbusting For profit, to induce or attempt to induce any person to sell or rent any dwelling by representations regarding the entry or prospective entry into the neighborhood of a person or persons of a particular race, color, religion, sex, or national origin.

bona fide   Latin term meaning "in good faith."

bond for deed A contract of sale and a financing instrument in which the seller agrees to convey title when the buyer completes the purchase price installment payments.

book value The value as it appears on the books of the owner, usually for tax purposes.

boot   Cash received in a tax-free exchange.

breach of condition Failure to perform a contract contingency.

breach of contract Failure, without legal excuse, to perform any promise that forms the whole or part of a contract.

broker A person or organization acting as agent for others in negotiating the purchase and sale of real property or other commodities for a fee.

building codes Public controls regulating construction.

bundle of rights The rights of an owner of a freehold estate to possession, enjoyment, control, and disposition of real property.

buyer-agency agreement Contract between a prospective home buyer and a real estate company in which the company agrees to locate property for and negotiate in the best interest of the buyer.

bylaws Rules governing the internal affairs of an association, such as those setting forth the offices in a condominium association, how officers are elected, and the method of amending the bylaws.

capital improvement An item that adds value to the property, adapts the property to new uses, or prolongs the life of property. Maintenance is not a capital improvement.

capitalization The process of converting future income into an indication of the present value of a property by applying a capitalization rate to net annual income.

capitalization rate The rate of interest appropriate to the investment risk as a return on the investment.

carry-over clause A clause in a listing contract protecting the broker's commission entitlement for a specified period of time after expiration of the contract. Also called extender clause.

cash flow The income produced by a rental property after deducting operating expenses and debt service.

caveat emptor Latin term meaning "let the buyer beware." Applies to "sales talk" and not to statements of material facts.

certificate of eligibility A statement provided to veterans of military service setting forth the amount of loan guarantee to which they are entitled at that time.

certificate of occupancy A document issued by a local government agency, after a satisfactory inspection of a structure, authorizing the occupancy of the structure.

Certificate of Reasonable Value A document setting forth the value of a property as the basis for the loan guarantee by the Department of Veterans Affairs to the lender.

certificate of title opinion A report, based on a title examination, setting forth the examiner's opinion of the quality of a title to real property.

chain   In land measurement, a distance of 66 feet.

chain of title The successive conveyances of title to a particular parcel of land.

change The principle stating that change is continually affecting land use and therefore continually altering value.

chattel Personal property.

chattel mortgage A type of mortgage in which personal property is pledged to secure the payment of a debt.

chattel real Nonfreehold interests in real property. Also includes fixtures.

civil action   A lawsuit between private parties.

Civil Rights Act of 1866 A federal law that prohibits all discrimination on the basis of race.

Civil Rights Act of 1968   See Fair Housing Act of 1968.

client A person who has entered into a brokerage agreement creating a special agency relationship with a real estate brokerage agency.

closed-end mortgage A type of mortgage that cannot be refinanced.

closed mortgage A type of mortgage that imposes a prepayment penalty.

closing The consummation of a real estate contract. Also called settlement.

closing costs Expenses incurred in the purchase and sale of real property paid at the time of settlement or closing.

Closing Disclosure A standard settlement form required by RESPA.

closing (or settlement) statement An accounting of the funds received and disbursed in a real estate transaction.

cloud on a title A claim against a title to real property.

cluster zoning A form of zoning providing for several different types of land use within a zoned area.

Coastal Wetlands Law Law prohibiting dredging, filling, and erecting permanent structures in a coastal wetland without a permit from the Department of Environmental Protection.

code of ethics A standard of conduct required by license laws and by the National Association of REALTORS®.

collateral Property pledged as security for the payment of a debt.

color of title A defective claim to a title.

commercial facilities Those intended for nonresidential use and affecting commerce, such as factories.

commercial property Property producing rental income or used in business.

commingle To mix the money or property of others by an agent with the agent's personal or business funds or other property.

commission A fee paid for the performance of services, such as a broker's commission.

commissioner's deed A form of judicial deed executed by a commissioner.

commitment A promise, such as a promise by a lending institution to make a certain mortgage loan.

common areas Property to which title is held by co-owners as a result of ownership of a condominium unit.

common law By judicial precedent or tradition as opposed to a written statute.

community-based planning A form of land-use control originating in the grassroots of a community.

community planning A plan for the orderly growth of a city or county to result in the greatest social and economic benefits to the people.

community property A form of co-ownership limited to husband and wife. Does not include the right of survivorship.

comparable A property that is similar to a property being appraised by the market data approach.

comparable (or comparison) approach See market data approach.

compensatory damages Court-awarded compensation to an injured party for any financial loss caused by a breach of contract.

competent parties Persons and organizations legally qualified to manage their own affairs, including entering into contracts.

competition Rivalry for customers or profits.

competitive market analysis (CMA) A comparison of property that is the subject of an appraisal with other properties offering comparable utility that have sold recently.

complete performance When all terms of a contract have been fully performed by all parties; the usual manner of terminating contracts.

comprehensive plan Compilation of policy standards, goals, maps, and pertinent data relative to the past, present, and future trends of a municipality with respect to its population, land use, and public facilities.

condemnation The exercise of the power of eminent domain. The taking of private property for public use.

condemnation value Market value of property condemned.

conditional sale contract See bond for deed.

conditions Restrictions or qualifications that provide for a reversion of title if they are violated.

condominium A form of ownership of real property recognized in all states that consists of individual ownership of some aspects and co-ownership in other aspects of the property.

condominium association All unit owners form the association to provide for maintenance and management of the common areas of the condominium.

condominium declaration The document which, when recorded, creates a condominium. Also called a master deed.

conformity The homogeneous uses of land within a given area results in maximizing land value.

consideration Anything of value as recognized by law offered as an inducement to contract.

construction loan A short-term loan, secured by a mortgage, to obtain the funds to construct an improvement on land.

construction mortgage A temporary mortgage used to borrow the money to construct an improvement on land.

constructive eviction Results from some action or inaction by the landlord that renders the premises unsuitable for the use agreed to in a lease or other rental contract.

constructive notice Everyone is bound by the knowledge of a fact even though they have not been actually notified of such fact.

consumer price index (CPI) An index of the change in prices of various commodities and services that provides a measure of the rate of inflation.

consummation Fulfillment of the terms of a contract, enforced by the courts as a legal remedy.

contingency A condition in a contract relieving a party of liability if a certain event occurs.

contract An agreement between competent parties upon legal consideration to do, or abstain from doing, some legal act.

contract for deed See bond for deed.

contract rent Rent that is agreed upon in a contract between landlord and tenant.

contribution The principle that for any given part of a property, its value is the result of the contribution that part makes to the total value by being present, or the amount that it subtracts from total value as a result of its absence.

conventional life estates One created by the intentional act of the parties.

conventional mortgage loan One in which the federal government does not insure or guarantee the payment to the lender.

conversion Change in a form of ownership, such as changing rental apartments to condominium ownership.

conveyance Transfer of title to real property.

conveyance in remainder Transfer of title to real property to remaindermen. See remainderman.

cooperating broker One who participates in the sale of a property through the listing broker.

cooperative A form of ownership in which stockholders in a corporation occupy property owned by the corporation under a lease.

co-ownership Title to real property held by two or more persons at the same time. Also called concurrent ownership.

corporation A form of organization existing as an entity.

corporeal Tangible things.

cost A measure of expenditures of labor and materials made some time in the past.

cost approach An appraisal method whereby the cost of constructing a substitute structure is calculated, depreciation is deducted, and land value is added.

counteroffer A new offer made by one rejecting an offer.

covenant A promise in writing.

covenant against encumbrances A promise in a deed that there are no encumbrances against the title except those set forth in the deed.

covenant for further assurances A promise in a deed that the grantor will execute such further assurances as may be reasonable or necessary to perfect the title in the grantee.

covenant of quiet enjoyment A promise in a deed (or lease) that the grantee (or lessee) will not be disturbed in his use of the property because of a defect in the grantor's (or lessor's) title.

covenant of right to convey A promise in a deed that the grantor has the legal capacity to convey the title.

covenant of seisin A promise in a deed ensuring to the grantee that the grantor has the title being conveyed.

covenant of warranty A promise in a deed that the grantor will guarantee and defend the title against lawful claimants.

credit In a closing disclosure, money to be received or credit given for money or an obligation given.

creditor One to whom a debt is owed.

credit report Information regarding an applicant's credit history required by lending institutions.

cul-de-sac A dead-end street with a circular turnaround at the dead end.

cumulative-use zoning A type of zoning permitting a higher priority use even though different from the type of use designated for the area.

curable depreciation A condition of property that exists when correction is physically possible and the cost of correction is less than the value increase.

curtesy A husband's interest in the real property of his wife.

customer A prospective buyer or seller who does not have an agency relationship with the agent.

damages The amount of financial loss incurred as a result of the action of another.

debit In a closing disclosure, an expense or money received against a credit.

debt ratio Ratio of housing expenses plus debts to the gross monthly income.

debt service Principal and interest payments on a debt.

decedent A dead person.

declarant One who establishes a declaration of restrictions relating to a subdivision or a condominium.

declaration of restrictions The instrument used to record restrictive covenants on the public record.

decree An order of a court.

dedication An appropriation of land or an easement therein by the owner to the public.

deed A written instrument that transfers an interest in real property when delivered to the grantee.

deed in lieu of foreclosure A conveyance of title to the mortgagee by a mortgagor in default to avoid a record of foreclosure. Also called friendly foreclosure.

deed restrictions Limitations on land use appearing in deeds.

default Failure to perform an obligation.

default provision Clause in a mortgage stating that mortgage will provide the right of foreclosure to the lender if the borrower fails to make payments as scheduled or fails to fulfill other obligations as set forth in the mortgage.

defeasance clause The clause in a mortgage or deed of trust giving the borrower the right to redeem the title and have the mortgage lien released at any time prior to default by paying the debt in full.

defeasible Subject to being defeated by the occurrence of a certain event.

defeasible fee A title that is subject to being lost if certain conditions occur.

deficiency judgment A judgment obtained by a mortgagee for the amount of money a foreclosure sale proceeds were deficient in fully satisfying the mortgage debt.

demise To convey an estate for years. Synonymous with lease or let.

density The number of persons or structures per acre.

Department of Housing and Urban Development (HUD) A federal agency involved with housing.

depreciable asset Property other than land held as an investment or for use in a business.

depreciated value The original basis of a property less the amount of depreciation taken at any point in time.

depreciation Loss in value from any cause.

descent The distribution of property of one who has died intestate to legally qualified heirs.

description by reference Valid legal description in which reference is made to another document such as a plat book or a previous deed that conveyed the same property.

devise A gift of real property by will.

devisee The recipient of a gift of real property by will.

direct sales comparison See competitive market analysis.

disability A physical or mental impairment that substantially limits one or more of the major activities of a person.

disclosure statement An accounting of all financial aspects of a mortgage loan required of lenders to borrowers in residential mortgage loans by Regulation Z of the Federal Reserve Board.

discount points A percentage of the loan amount required by the lender for making a mortgage loan.

discriminatory advertising Any advertising that states or indicates a preference, limitation, or discrimination on the basis of race, color, religion, sex, or national origin in offering housing for sale or rent.

domestic corporation Corporation within the state in which it is incorporated.

dominant owner Owner of dominant tenement.

dominant tenement Land benefiting from an appurtenant easement.

dower A wife's interest in the real property of her husband.

down payment Portion of sales price that is not mortgaged.

dual agency The situation in which the real estate firm represents both the buyer and seller in the same transaction. If the agency has elected an Appointed Agency policy, dual agency will only occur when a sales agent represents both the buyer and seller in the transaction.

due-on-sale clause See alienation clause.

duress The inability of a party to exercise her free will because of fear of another party.

earnest money A deposit of money made by a buyer at the time of making an offer to demonstrate the earnest intent to purchase. Also called binder, good faith deposit, or escrow deposit.

easement A nonpossessory right of use in the land of another.

easement by necessity An easement created for the right to travel to a landlocked parcel of land.

easement in gross A personal right of use in the land of another without the requirement that the holder of the right own adjoining land.

economic depreciation Results from physical deterioration of property caused by normal use of the property.

economic life The period of time during which a property is economically beneficial to the owner.

economic obsolescence A loss in value caused by such things as changes in surrounding land-use patterns and failure to adhere to the principle of highest and best use.

economic rent The amount of rent established by the market value of a property.

economic supply Utilization of the physical supply of land.

effective age The age of a property based on the remaining economic life.

effective demand A desire for property accompanied by the financial ability to satisfy the desire by purchasing the property.

effective interest rate The actual rate of interest being paid.

ejectment   A legal action to evict a tenant from property.

emblements Personal property growing in the soil requiring planting and cultivation. Annual crops.

eminent domain The power of government to take private property for public use.

enabling acts Laws passed by state legislatures authorizing cities and counties to regulate land use within their jurisdictions.

encroachment A trespass on the land of another as a result of an intrusion by some structure or other object.

encumbrance A claim, lien, charge, or liability attached to and binding upon real property.

enforceable A contract in which the parties may legally be required to perform.

environmental impact statement A requirement of National Environmental Policy Act prior to initiating or changing a land use that may have an adverse effect on the environment.

Environmental Policy Act of 1969 Law requiring environmental impact statement to be filed with the EPA before changing or initiating a land use or development to ensure that the use will not have an adverse effect on the environment.

Environmental Protection Agency (EPA) Federal agency responsible for protecting the public against abuses of the environment resulting from the use or development of land.

Equal Credit Opportunity Act (ECOA) A federal law prohibiting discrimination in consumer loans.

equity of redemption The borrower's right to redeem the title pledged or conveyed in a mortgage or deed of trust after default and prior to a foreclosure sale by paying the debt in full, accrued interest, and lender's costs.

escalated lease One in which the rental amount changes in proportion to the lessor's costs of ownership and operation of the property.

escalation clause A clause in a lease permitting the lessor to increase the rent.

escheat The power of government to take title to property left by a person who has died without leaving a will or qualified heirs.

escrow account An account maintained by the borrower with the lender in certain mortgage loans to accumulate the funds to pay an annual insurance premium, a real property tax, and/or a homeowner's association assessment.

escrow agent A neutral third party named to carry out the provisions of an escrow agreement.

estate An interest in real property sufficient to give the owner the right to possession of the property.

estate at sufferance Describes the situation of someone continuing to occupy property after lawful authorization has expired. A form of leasehold estate.

estate at will A leasehold estate that may be terminated at the will of either party.

estate for life An interest in land that is created for the duration of a tenant's life.

estate for years   A leasehold estate of definite duration.

estate from year-to-year A leasehold estate that automatically renews itself for consecutive periods until terminated by notice given by either party. Also called estate from period-to-period or periodic tenancy.

estate in fee An estate in fee simple absolute.

estate in real property An interest sufficient to provide the right to use, possession, and control of land and establishes the degree and duration of ownership.

estate in remainder Conveyance from grantor to A for life and then to a named person or persons upon the death of A.

estates and interests in land All ownership rights in real property.

estate tax Tax upon the inheritance of real property.

estoppel The prevention of a person from making a statement contrary to a previous statement.

estoppel certificate A document executed by a mortgagor or mortgagee setting forth the principal amount. Executing parties are bound by the amount specified.

estovers The right of a life tenant or lessee to cut timber on the property for fuel or to use in making repairs.

et al Latin term for "and another."

et ux Latin term for "and wife."

eviction A landlord's action that interferes with the tenant's use or possession of the property. Eviction may be actual or constructive.

exclusive agency listing A listing given to one broker only (exclusive) who is entitled to the commission if a sale is effected by the broker or any agent of the listing broker, but imposes no commission obligation on the owner who sells the property to a person who was not interested in the property by the listing broker or an agent of the listing broker.

exclusive right to sell listing A listing given to one broker only who is entitled to the commission if the property is sold by anyone during the term of the listing contract.

exclusive-use zoning A type of zoning in which only the specified use may be made of property within the zoned district.

executed contract An agreement that has been fully performed.

execution The signing of a contract or other legal document.

executor A man appointed in a will to see that the terms of the will are carried out. Also called personal representative.

executory contract An agreement that has not been fully performed.

executrix A woman appointed in a will to see that the terms of the will are carried out. Also called personal representative.

exempt Relieved of liability.

exercise of option The purchase of optioned property by the optionee.

express contract A contract created verbally or in writing by the parties.

extender clause See carry-over clause.

Fair Housing Act of 1968 A federal prohibition on discrimination in the sale, rental, or financing of housing on the basis of race, color, religion, sex, or national origin.

Fair Housing Amendments Act of 1988 A law adding to the Fair Housing Act of 1968 provisions to prevent discrimination based on mental or physical handicap or familial status.

fair market value A price for property agreed upon between buyer and seller in a competitive market with neither party being under undue pressure.

false promise An untrue promise to a party that something will or will not occur in a real estate transaction.

Fannie Mae The shortened name for the Federal National Mortgage Association.

federal estate tax Tax imposed by the federal government on estates of deceased persons.

Federal Home Loan Bank System The federal agency that regulates federally chartered savings and loan associations.

Federal Home Loan Mortgage Corporation (FHLMC) (Freddie Mac) A corporation that is wholly owned by the Federal Home Loan Bank System that purchases FHA, VA, and conventional mortgages.

Federal Housing Administration (FHA) The federal agency that insures mortgage loans to protect lending institutions.

Federal National Mortgage Association (FNMA) (Fannie Mae) A privately owned corporation that purchases FHA, VA, and conventional mortgages.

Federal Reserve System The federal agency that regulates monetary policy and, thereby, the money supply and interest rates.

fee simple absolute An inheritable estate in land providing the greatest interest of any form of title.

fee simple determinable A defeasible fee (title).

fee simple subject to a condition subsequent A defeasible fee (title).

feudal system A type of land ownership in existence during the Middle Ages whereby only the king could hold absolute title to real property.

FHA-insured loan A mortgage loan in which the payments are insured by the Federal Housing Administration.

fiduciary A person, such as an agent, who is placed in a position of trust in relation to the person for whose benefit the relationship is created. Essentially the same as a trustee.

finance charge A charge imposed on the borrower in a mortgage loan consisting of origination fee, service charges, discount points, interest, credit report fees, and finders' fees.

financing statement Notice evidencing on the public record the existence of a security agreement.

first mortgage A mortgage that is superior to later recorded mortgages.

fixed lease A lease in which the rental amount remains the same for the entire lease term. Also called flat, straight, or gross lease.

fixed-rate mortgage A mortgage in which the interest does not change.

fixing up expenses Costs incurred by the seller of a principal residence in preparing it for sale.

fixture Personal property that has become real property by having been permanently attached to real property.

foreclosure The legal procedure of enforcing payment of a debt secured by a mortgage or any other lien.

foreign corporation A corporation doing business in another state.

forfeiture clause A clause in a contract for deed providing for forfeiture of all payments by a buyer in default.

fraud An intentional false statement of a material fact.

fraudulent representation A false statement or the concealment of a material fact with the intent to deceive or to gain unfair advantage over another.

freehold estate A right of title to land.

free market A market in which there is ample time for buyer and seller to effect a mutually beneficial purchase and sale without undue pressure or urgency.

freshwater wetlands law Law prohibiting dredging, filling, and erecting a permanent structure in an area defined as ten or more contiguous acres that are characterized predominantly by wetland soils and vegetation.

friendly foreclosure An absolute conveyance of title to the lender by the mortgagor in default to avoid a record of foreclosure. Also called a deed in lieu of foreclosure.

front foot A linear foot of property frontage on a street or highway.

fruits of industry Growing things that require planting and cultivation.

fruits of the soil Growing things that do not require planting or cultivation but grow naturally and are perennials; designated in law as real property.

fully amortizing mortgage A mortgage in which the scheduled uniform payments will pay off the loan completely over the mortgage term.

functional obsolescence A loss in value resulting from such things as faulty design, inadequacies, overadequacies, and equipment being out-of-date.

future interest An owner of an estate who will vest at some time in the future.

gain realized The excess of the amount realized over the adjusted basis.

general lien A lien that attaches to all of the property of the license within the jurisdiction of the court.

loan estimate The lender's estimate of a borrower's settlement costs that is required by RESPA to be furnished to borrowers at time of loan application.

Government National Mortgage Association (GNMA) (Ginnie Mae) A government agency that purchases FHA and VA mortgages.

government survey system A type of land description by townships and sections.

graduated lease Lease in which the rental amount changes from period to period over the lease term.

graduated payment mortgage (GPM) A mortgage in which the payments are lower in the early years but increase on a scheduled basis until they reach an amortizing level.

grant A transfer of title to real property by deed.

grantee One who receives title to real property by deed.

granting clause The clause in a deed containing words of conveyance.

grantor One who conveys title to real property by deed.

gross income Income received without the subtraction of expenses.

gross lease Lease in which the tenant pays a fixed rent and lessor pays all costs of operating and maintaining the property.

gross potential income The amount of rental income that would be received if all units were rented 100% of the time and there were no credit losses.

gross rent multiplier A method of estimating the value of income property. Also called gross income multiplier.

ground lease A lease of unimproved land only.

habendum clause The clause in a deed beginning with the words "to have and to hold" and describing the estate granted.

habitable Suitable for the type of occupancy intended.

hazard insurance Insurance that protects owner of property from partial or total destruction of property.

heirs Persons legally eligible to receive property of a decedent.

hereditaments Every kind of inheritable property, including real and personal property.

heterogeneous A variety of dissimilar uses of property. Nonhomogeneous.

highest and best use The use of land that will preserve its utility and yield a net income flow in the form of rent that forms, when capitalized at the proper rate of interest, the highest present value of the land.

holding over The act of a tenant remaining in possession of property after the termination of a lease.

holding period The length of time a property is owned.

holographic will A will handwritten by the testator.

Home Loan Toolkit A booklet explaining aspects of loan settlement required by RESPA.

homeowner's association The organization of owners having the responsibility of providing for the operation and maintenance of the common areas of a condominium or residential subdivision. Also called property owner's association.

homestead The land and dwelling of a homeowner.

homestead exemption An exemption of a specified amount of value of a homestead from the claims of creditors provided by state statute.

homogeneous Similar and compatible land uses.

Horizontal Property Act The title of condominium statutes in some states.

Housing and Urban Development (HUD) An agency of the federal government concerned with housing programs and laws.

housing ratio The ratio of housing expenses to the gross monthly income.

hypothecate Pledging property as security for the payment of a debt without giving up possession.

illusory offer An offer that does not obligate the offeror.

immobility The physical characteristic of real property describing that land cannot be moved from one location to another.

implied contract A contract created by deduction from the conduct of the parties rather than from the direct words of the parties. Opposite of an express contract.

implied warranty A warranty presumed by law to exist in a deed though not expressly stated.

improved land Land on which structures or roads exist.

improvements Structures, walls, roads, etc.

inchoate In suspension or pending, possibly occurring at some future time.

income approach The primary method of estimating the value of properties that produce rental income. Also called appraisal by capitalization.

income property Property that produces rental income.

incompetent A person who is not capable of managing his own affairs.

incorporeal Intangible things such as rights.

incurable depreciation That which is not physically correctable or not economically practical to correct.

indestructibility A physical characteristic of land describing that land is a permanent commodity and cannot be destroyed.

index lease A lease and rent is tied to an economic condition, such as inflation or profits.

ingress and egress The right to enter (ingress) and to return (egress) from a parcel of land.

inheritance basis The tax basis for all real property received by heirs, which is the market value of the property on the date of the death of the decedent and not the market value at the time the decedent acquired the property.

injunction An instruction of a court to discontinue a specified activity.

installment land contract See bond for deed.

installment sale A transaction in which the seller does not receive all of the sale price in the calendar year of the sale.

instrument A written legal document such as a contract, note, or mortgage.

insurable interest The degree of interest qualifying for insurance.

insurance value The cost of replacing a structure completely destroyed by an insured hazard.

insured conventional loan A loan in which the loan payment is insured by private mortgage insurance to protect the lender.

interest Money paid for the use of money. Also an ownership or right.

interim financing Short-term or temporary financing such as a construction loan.

Interstate Land Sales Full Disclosure Act A federal law regulating the interstate sale of land under certain conditions.

intestate A person who has died without leaving a valid will.

intestate succession Distribution of property by descent as provided by statute.

invalid Not legally enforceable.

irrevocable That which cannot be changed or canceled.

joint tenants A form of co-ownership that includes the right of survivorship.

joint venture Participation by two or more parties in a single undertaking.

judgment A court determination of the rights and obligations of parties to a lawsuit.

judgment lien A general lien resulting from a court decree.

judicial deed A deed executed by an official with court authorization.

judicial foreclosure A court proceeding to require that property be sold to satisfy a mortgage lien.

junior mortgage A mortgage that is subordinate to a prior mortgage.

jurisdiction The extent of the authority of a court.

laches The loss of legal rights because of failure to assert them on a timely basis.

land The surface of the earth, the area above and below the surface, and everything permanently attached thereto.

land capacity The degree to which land can sustain improvements created to make the land productive.

land contract See bond for deed.

land grant The conveyance of land, as a gift for the benefit of the public.

landlocked An adjective to describe property with no access to a public road.

landlord Owner or lessor of the property leased.

land trust The condition of a title to land being held by a trustee for the benefit of others.

land use controls Restrictions on the use of land. For example, public land use controls exist in the form of city planning and zoning, state and regional planning, building codes, suitability for occupancy requirements, and environmental control laws.

land use regulations Governmental controls over land use (e.g., zoning laws and building codes).

lawful Legal, not prohibited by law.

lease A contract wherein a landlord gives a tenant the right of use and possession of property for a limited period of time in return for rent.

leased fee The lessor's interest in the leased property.

leasehold estates Nonfreehold estate. One of limited duration that provides the right of possession and control but not title.

leasehold mortgage A mortgage in which a leasehold (nonfreehold) estate is pledged to secure the payment of the note.

leasehold title insurance policy A policy insuring a lessee against defects in the lessor's title.

legal capacity The ability to contract.

legal description A description of land recognized by law.

legal entity A person or organization with legal capacity.

legal life estates One created by the exercise of the right of dower, curtesy, or a statutory substitute.

legal rate of interest The maximum rate permitted by law.

lessee A tenant under a lease.

lessor A landlord under a lease.

less than freehold estate Leaseholds; estates with a length determined by agreement or statute; establishes possession of land as opposed to ownership in fee.

leverage The use of borrowed funds. The larger the percentage of borrowed money, the greater the leverage.

levy Imposition of a tax, executing a lien.

license A personal privilege to do a particular act or series of acts on the land of another.

lien A claim that one person has against the property of another for some debt or charge which entitles the lienholder to have the claim satisfied from the property of the debtor.

lienee One whose property is subject to a lien.

lienor The one holding a lien against another.

lien theory The legal theory that a mortgage creates a lien against the real property pledged in the mortgage to secure the payment of a debt.

life estate A freehold estate created for the duration of the life or lives of certain named persons. A noninheritable estate.

life estate in remainder A form of life estate in which certain persons called remaindermen are designated to receive the title upon termination of the life tenancy.

life estate in reversion A form of life estate that reverts to the creator of the estate in fee simple upon termination.

life estate pur autre vie An estate in which the duration is measured by the life of someone other than the life tenant. See also pur autre vie.

life tenant One holding a life estate.

like-kind property Real or personal property that qualifies for tax treatment as a tax-free exchange.

limited partnership An organization consisting of one or more general partners and several limited partners.

limited warranty deed A term for warranty deed with covenants.

liquidated damages An amount of money to be paid and received as compensation for a breach of contract.

liquidity The fact that an asset can be converted to cash.

lis pendens Latin term meaning "a lawsuit pending."

listing contract (listing) A contract whereby a property owner employs a real estate broker to market the property described in the contract.

litigation A lawsuit.

loan estimate The lender's estimate of a borrower's settlement costs that is required by RESPA to be furnished to borrowers at time of loan application.

loan origination points (fee) Charge to cover the lender's expenses in originating the loan and offset any losses when mortgage is sold.

loan-to-value ratio The relationship between the amount of a mortgage loan and the lender's opinion of the value of the property pledged to secure the payment of the loan.

location (situs) An economic characteristic of land having the greatest effect on value of any other characteristic.

Maine Fair Housing Law Prohibits discrimination in housing based upon race, color, sex, physical or mental handicap, religion, ancestry, national origin, or sexual orientaion.

Maine State Housing Authority (MSHA) Established in 1969 to provide housing to low- and moderate-income Maine families through the sale of tax-exempt bonds to investors.

marketable title Title that is free from reasonable doubt and that a court would require a purchaser to accept.

market data approach The primary method of estimating the value of vacant land and single-family owner-occupied dwellings. Also called comparable approach.

market value The value in terms of price agreed upon by a willing buyer and seller with neither being under any undue pressure and each being knowledgeable of market conditions at the time.

master deed The instrument that legally establishes a condominium. Also called condominium declaration.

material fact An important fact that may affect a person's judgment.

materialman A person or company that provides the materials for construction of an improvement on land.

materialman's lien A statutory lien available to persons supplying materials for the construction of an improvement on land if they are not paid.

mechanic A person who provides labor to a specific property, such as a carpenter.

mechanic's lien A statutory lien available to persons supplying labor (mechanics) to the construction of an improvement on land if they are not paid.

metes and bounds A system of land description by distances and directions.

mill One tenth of a cent.

mineral lease A nonfreehold (leasehold) estate in the area below the surface of land.

mineral rights The right of the landowner to take minerals from the earth or to sell or lease this right to others.

minor A person who has not attained the statutory age of majority.

misrepresentation A false statement of a material fact.

modification by improvement An economic characteristic of land providing that the economic supply of land is increased by improvements made to land and on land.

mortgage assumption The transfer of mortgage obligations to a purchaser of the mortgaged property.

mortgage broker One who arranges a mortgage loan between a lender and borrower for a fee.

mortgage deed A written instrument used to pledge a title to real property to secure payment of a promissory note.

mortgage discharge fee An assessment by the Registry of Deeds to record the discharge of the mortgage by the lending institution.

mortgagee The lender in a mortgage loan receiving a mortgage from the borrower mortgagor.

mortgagee's title insurance policy A policy that insures a mortgagee against defects in a title pledged by a mortgagor to secure payment of a mortgage loan.

mortgage interest Interest that accrues on the mortgage from the date of closing to the first of the next month.

mortgage lien A written instrument used to create a lien to real property to secure payment of a promissory note.

mortgage loan value The value sufficient to secure the payment of a mortgage loan.

mortgage note A promissory note between lender and borrower which establishes the amount of the debt, the terms of repayment, and the interest rate.

mortgage satisfaction Full payment of a mortgage loan.

mortgaging clause The clause in a mortgage or deed of trust that demonstrates the intention of the mortgagor to mortgage the property to the mortgagee.

mortgagor The borrower in a mortgage loan who executes and delivers a mortgage to the lender.

multiple exchange A transaction in which more than two like-kind properties are exchanged.

multiple listing service (MLS) A system that pools the listed properties of all member companies.

multiple offer guidelines Guidelines issued by the Maine Real Estate Commission to promote awareness of licensees' duty to act in the best interest of their clients and to deal fairly with customers regarding multiple offers.

mutual agreement See mutual assent.

mutual assent The voluntary agreement of all parties to a contract as evidenced by an offer and acceptance.

mutual rescission The agreement of all parties to an executory contract to release each other.

mutual savings banks Similar to savings and loan associations. These banks provide a substantial source of financing for housing.

narrative appraisal report A statement of an opinion of value containing the elements of judgment as well as the data used in arriving at the value estimate.

National Association of REALTORS® The largest and most prominent trade organization of real estate licensees.

negative covenants See restrictive covenants.

negative easement A right in the land of another prohibiting the servient owner from doing something on the servient land because it will affect the dominant land.

net income Gross income less operating expenses. Also called net operating income.

net lease Lease in which the tenant pays a base rent plus a percentage of the expenses.

net listing Not a type of listing but a method of establishing the listing broker's commission as all money above a specified net amount to the seller.

1988 Amendments Act Amends Title VIII of the Civil Rights Act of 1968 in two respects: (1) It makes it illegal to discriminate against physically and mentally disabled people and families with children (familial status); (2) It changes the way Title VIII is enforced and the penalties that can be imposed for violations.

nonconforming use A use of land that does not conform to the use permitted by a zoning ordinance for the area. It may be lawful or unlawful.

nonexclusive listing A listing given to more than one real estate agency for the purpose of procuring a buyer.

nonhomogeneity A physical characteristic of land describing that land as a unique commodity.

nonjudicial foreclosure A form of foreclosure that does not require court action to conduct a foreclosure sale. Also called foreclosure under power of sale.

nonrecourse note A note in which the borrower has no personal liability for payment.

notary public A person authorized by a state to take oaths and acknowledgments.

notice Result of recording of a deed or document so as to afford it priority over documents filed at a later date; or, information required by the terms of a contract (such as notice to terminate a rental contract).

notice of lis pendens A notice on the public record warning all persons that a title to real property is the subject of a lawsuit and any lien resulting from the suit will attach to the title held by a purchaser from the defendant.

novation The substitution of a new contract for a prior contract.

null and void Invalid, without legal force or effect.

obligee One to whom an obligation is owed.

obligor One who owes an obligation to another.

obsolescence A loss in property value caused by economic or functional factors.

occupancy Physical possession of property.

offer A promise made to another conditional upon acceptance by a promise or act made in return.

offer and acceptance Necessary elements for the creation of a contract.

offeree One to whom an offer is made.

offeror One making an offer.

open-end mortgage A mortgage that may be refinanced without rewriting the mortgage.

open listing A listing given to one or more brokers wherein the broker procuring a sale is entitled to the commission but imposes no commission obligation on the owner in the event the owner sells the property to a person who was not interested in the property by one of the listing brokers.

open mortgage A mortgage that does not impose a prepayment penalty.

operating expenses The costs of operating a property held as an investment.

operation of law The manner in which the rights and/or liabilities of parties may be changed by the application of law without the act or cooperation of the parties.

opinion of title See certificate of title opinion.

optionee One who receives an option.

optionor One who gives an option.

option to purchase A contract whereby a property owner (optionor) sells a right to purchase her property to a prospective buyer (optionee).

ordinance A law enacted by a local government.

origination fee A service charge made by a lending institution for making a mortgage loan.

Over 55 exclusion A tax exemption that was available to sellers of a principle residence who were aged 55 or over, which is no longer in effect.

ownership The right to use, control, possess, and dispose of property.

ownership in severalty Title to real property held in the name of one person only.

owner's title insurance policy A policy insuring an owner of real property against a financial loss resulting from a title defect.

package mortgage A mortgage in which personal property as well as real property is pledged to secure the payment of the note.

partially amortizing mortgage A mortgage in which the schedule of uniform payments will not completely satisfy the debt over the mortgage term and will therefore require a final payment larger than the uniform payments to completely satisfy the debt. The final payment is called a balloon payment.

participation mortgage A mortgage in which two or more lenders share in making the loan.

partition A legal proceeding dividing property of co-owners so that each holds title in severalty.

partner One of two or more owners of a partnership.

partnership A form of co-ownership for business reasons.

party wall A common wall used by two adjoining structures.

percentage lease A lease that is based on a portion of the sales.

perch A surveyor's measure $16\frac{1}{2}$ feet in length.

percolation test A test of soil to determine if it is sufficiently porous for the installation of a septic tank.

periodic tenancy A lease that automatically renews for successive periods unless terminated by either party. Also called an estate from year-to-year.

personal property All property that is not land and is not permanently attached to land. Everything that is moveable.

personal representative In the state of Maine, a person appointed by the court or by a will to oversee the probate of one's will in the intestate procedures.

physical deterioration A loss in value caused by unrepaired damage or inadequate maintenance.

PITI Letters following the amount of a mortgage payment designating that the payment includes principal, interest, taxes, and insurance.

placed in service The date when an asset is ready and available for a particular use.

plan Graphic representation of building details.

planned unit development (PUD) A form of cluster zoning providing for both residential and commercial land uses within a zoned area.

planning A program for the development of a city or county designed to provide for orderly growth.

planning board Local government organization that deals with the orderly growth and development of a town or city.

plat A property map.

plat books Books wherein plats are recorded on the public record.

pledge To provide property as security for the payment of a debt or for the performance of a promise.

plottage Combining two or more parcels of land into one tract having a value exceeding the total value of the individual parcels.

points   See discount points.

police power The power of government to regulate the use of real property for the benefit of the public interest.

population density The relationship of the number of people to a given land area.

potential income   See gross potential income.

power of attorney An instrument appointing an attorney-in-fact.

power of taxation The power of government to tax real property for the benefit of the public.

prepaid mortgage interest Interest on the mortgage that lenders require borrowers to pay at closing, from the date of the closing to the first of the next month.

prepaid items Funds paid at closing to start an escrow account required in certain mortgage loans. Also called prepaids.

prepayment penalty A financial penalty imposed on a borrower for paying a mortgage prior to the expiration of the full mortgage term.

prescription A method of acquiring an easement by continuous and uninterrupted use without permission.

prescriptive easement An easement obtained by prescription.

price   The amount of money paid for a property.

prima facie Latin term meaning "on the face of it." A fact presumed to be true unless disproved by contrary evidence.

prima facie case A case that is sufficiently strong that it can only be defeated by contrary evidence.

primary mortgage market The activity of lenders making mortgage loans to individual borrowers.

prime rate The interest rate a lender charges the most creditworthy customers.

principal In the law of agency, one who appoints an agent to represent him.

principal meridians North–south lines in the rectangular method of property description.

principal residence The home the owner or renter occupies most of the time.

private corporation Corporation not organized to perform governmental functions.

private land use control The regulations of land use by individuals or nongovernment organizations in the form of deed restrictions and restrictive covenants.

private mortgage insurance (PMI) A form of insurance coverage required in high loan-to-value ratio conventional

loans to protect the lender in case of borrower default in loan payment.

private property Property that is not owned by the government.

probate   The procedure for proving a will.

profit a prendre The right to participate in the profits of the land of another.

promissory note A written promise to pay a debt as set forth in the writing.

promulgate   To put in effect by public announcement.

proration Division of certain settlement costs between buyer and seller.

public accommodations Private businesses that affect commerce and trade, such as hotels, restaurants, theaters, convention centers, laundromats, banks, museums, places of education, and day care centers.

public corporation Governmental corporation, such as cities, towns, counties, school districts, and special bodies for public improvements.

public land use control The regulation of land use by government organizations in the form of zoning laws, building codes, subdivision ordinances, and environmental protection laws.

public offering statement Condominium documents that must be presented on the first sale of any unit.

public property   Property owned by the government.

public record Record providing constructive notice of real property conveyances and other matters.

pur autre vie Latin term meaning "for the life of another." A life estate measured by the life of someone other than the life tenant.

purchase and sale contracts Contracts in which there is an exchange of promises between buyer and seller. The buyer promises to pay an agreed-upon price and the seller promises to deliver a deed to that property.

purchase money mortgage A mortgage given by a buyer to a seller to secure the payment of all or part of the purchase price.

qualify a buyer Determination of the loan amount a buyer may obtain based on income, debts, credit history, and money available for a down payment.

quantity survey method The method most builders use to calculate a cost estimate for a construction job, involving the detailed determination of the exact quantity of each type of material to be used in the construction and the necessary material and labor costs applicable to each unit. The final estimate includes a profit to the builder.

quarter section One-fourth of a section containing 160 acres.

quiet enjoyment The use or possession of property that is undisturbed by an enforceable claim of superior title.

quiet title Use or possession of property that is undisturbed by an enforceable claim of superior title.

quiet title action A lawsuit to remove a cloud on a title.

quitclaim To relinquish or release a claim to real property.

quitclaim deed A deed of release that contains no warranty of title. It is used to remove a cloud on a title.

quitclaim with covenant See limited warranty deed.

race notice The priority of a subsequent purchaser depends upon lack of notice and priority of record.

radius The distance from the center of a circle to the perimeter. A part of a metes and bounds description.

range An area of land defined by the rectangular survey system of land description.

rate of return The percentage of the net income produced by a property or other investment.

ratify To reaffirm a previous action.

ready, willing, and able Describes a buyer who is ready to buy, willing to buy, and financially able to pay the asking price.

real estate Land and everything that is permanently attached to land. Interchangeable with the terms real property and realty.

real estate broker A person or organization who negotiates real estate sales, exchanges, or rentals for others for compensation or a promise of compensation.

Real Estate Commission A state agency charged with the obligation of enforcing real estate license laws.

Real Estate Investment Trust (REIT) A form of business trust owned by shareholders making mortgage loans.

real estate market A local activity in which real property is sold, exchanged, leased, or rented at prices set by com- peting forces.

Real Estate Settlement Procedures Act (RESPA) A federal law regulating activities of lending institutions in making mortgage loans for housing.

reality of consent Mutual agreement between the parties to the contract; meeting of the minds.

realized gain Actual profit resulting from a sale.

real property Land and everything permanently attached to land.

REALTOR® A registered trademark of the National Association of REALTORS®. Its use is limited to members only.

REALTOR ASSOCIATE® See REALTOR®.

realty Land and everything permanently attached to land.

reappraisal lease Lease in which changes in rental amount are based on changes in property value as demonstrated by periodic reappraisals of the property.

reciprocity The mutual agreement by states to extend licensing privileges to licensees in each state.

recognized gain The amount of profit that is taxable.

recordation Written registration of an owner's title in public records to protect against subsequent claimants.

recording The registration of a document on the public record.

recording fees An assessment by the Registry of Deeds for the recording of the warranty deed and mortgage.

rectangular survey system See government survey system.

redemption See equity of redemption.

redlining The refusal of lending institutions to make loans for the purchase, construction, or repair of a dwelling because the area in which the dwelling is located is integrated or populated by minorities.

reentry The right of the owner to regain possession of real property.

referral fee A percentage of a broker's commission paid to another broker for referring a buyer or seller.

refinancing Obtaining a new mortgage loan to pay and replace an existing mortgage.

Regulation Z Requirements issued by the Federal Reserve Board in implementing the Truth-in-Lending Law, which is a part of the Federal Consumer Credit Protection Act.

reject To refuse to accept an offer.

release clause A provision in a mortgage to release certain properties from the mortgage lien when the principal is reduced by a specified amount.

remainder A future interest in a life estate.

remainderman One having a future interest in a life estate.

remise To release or give up.

replacement cost The amount of money required to replace a structure with another structure of comparable utility.

repossession Regaining possession of property as a result of a breach of contract by another.

reproduction cost The amount of money required to build an exact duplicate of a structure.

rescission Cancellation of a contract when another party is in default.

residual income The income allocated to the land under the principle of highest and best use.

restrictive covenants Limitations on land use binding on all property owners. A form of private land-use control.

reversion A return of title to the holder of a future interest, such as the grantor in a life estate not in remainder.

revocation The withdrawal of an offer.

right of alienation Right of life tenant to transfer title to another person or to pledge the title as security for a debt.

right of first refusal clause A clause in a lease or condominium articles of association that provides for a lessee or an association to have the first opportunity to purchase the property before it is offered to anyone else.

right of survivorship The right of an owner to receive the title to a co-owner's share upon death of the co-owner, as in the case of joint tenancy and tenancy by the entirety.

right to emblements The right of a former owner or former tenant to reenter property to cultivate and harvest annual crops that were planted by her.

right to estovers The right to fulfill necessities, such as the right of a life tenant to cut and use a reasonable amount of timber from the land to repair buildings or to use for fuel.

riparian rights The rights of an owner of property adjoining a water course such as a river, including access to, and use of, the water.

rollover rule A provision in the tax law no longer in effect that provided that the tax on any gain realized in the sale of a principal residence would be postponed if the sale and purchase qualified.

run with the land Rights that move from grantor to grantee along with a title.

sales agent Any person employed by or on behalf of an agency to perform real estate brokerage services in a training capacity and licensed by the commission as a sales agent.

sales and leaseback A transaction whereby an owner sells her property to an investor who immediately leases the property to the seller as agreed in the sales contract.

sales contract An agreement between buyer and seller on the price and other terms and conditions of the sale of property.

salvage value The amount estimated by an owner that will be realized from the sale of an asset at the end of the useful life of the asset.

sandwich lease New lease created when lessee sublets the premises.

savings and loan associations A major source of funds for financing residential real estate.

scarcity In short supply in comparison to demand.

secondary mortgage market The market in which mortgages are sold by lenders.

second mortgage A mortgage first in priority after a first mortgage.

section An area of land described by the rectangular survey system consisting of 640 acres and being one mile square.

security agreement Instrument creating security interest in chattel until lender is paid in full.

seisin Possession of a freehold estate in land.

seizin An alternate spelling for "seisin."

separate ownership Ownership in severalty by one spouse.

servient owner Owner of servient tenement.

servient tenement Land encumbered by an easement.

setback The distance from a front or interior property line to the point where a structure can be located.

settlement The consummation of a real estate contract. Also called closing.

settlement costs Expenses paid by buyers and sellers at the time of consummation of a real estate sales contract. Also called closing costs.

shared appreciation mortgage (SAM) A mortgage in which the lender shares in the appreciation in property value in return for making the loan at a fixed rate lower than the rate in effect at the time the loan is made.

shoreland zoning Maine law requiring municipalities to zone shoreland areas within their jurisdiction within 250 feet of the normal high water mark of any pond, river, or salt water body.

single agency Relationship in which the agent is representing one client, either the seller or the buyer, in any one transaction.

situs Location of land.

sole ownership A business owned by one person.

sole proprietorship See sole ownership.

special assessment A levy by a local government against real property for part of the cost of making an improvement to the property such as street paving, installing water lines, or making sidewalks.

special warranty deed A deed containing a limited warranty of title.

specific lien A lien that attaches to one particular property only.

specific performance An instruction of a court requiring a defaulting party to a contract to buy and sell real property to specifically perform his obligations under the contract.

spot zoning Rezoning of a particular property in a zoned area to permit a different type of use than that authorized for the rest of the area. May be valid or invalid.

square foot method A method of estimating reproduction or replacement costs, calculated by multiplying the number of square feet in the structure being appraised by the cost per square foot to construct the building using the current cost per square foot.

Starker exchange A tax-free exchange in which the proceeds of a sale of property are held beyond the control of the seller until the seller can locate a like-kind property in which to invest the proceeds.

Statute of Frauds A law in effect in all states requiring certain contracts to be in writing to be valid.

statute of limitations State laws establishing the time period within which certain lawsuits may be brought.

statutory foreclosure A statutory time period after a foreclosure sale during which the borrower may still redeem the title.

steering The practice of directing prospective purchasers toward specific neighborhoods to avoid changing the ethnic and/or racial makeup of neighborhoods.

straight line depreciation A depreciation method whereby the property is depreciated in equal annual installments over the years of useful life.

subagency An agency other than the listing agency that works on behalf of the listing agency's client.

subagent A real estate brokerage agency engaged by another brokerage agency to perform brokerage tasks for a client.

subdivision In Maine, a parcel of land divided into three or more lots during a five-year period.

subdivision ordinance Public control of the development of residential subdivisions.

subletting The transfer of only part of a lease term with reversion to the lessee.

subordinate Lower in priority.

substitution The principle providing that the highest value of a property has a tendency to be established by the cost of purchasing or constructing another property of equal utility and desirability provided that the substitution can be made without unusual delay.

supply and demand The principle stating that the greater the supply of any commodity in comparison to demand the lower the value. Conversely, the smaller the supply and the greater the demand, the higher the value.

survey A marking of the property's boundaries.

survivorship The right of the surviving co-owner(s) to automatically receive the title of a deceased co-owner immediately without probate.

syndication A group of individuals or businesses that undertake an investment as a single unit.

taking title subject to a mortgage Accepting a title pledged to secure a mortgage and with no personal liability for the payment of the note.

taxable gain The amount of profit subject to tax (recognized gain).

taxation One of the four powers of government. The power of government to tax, among other things, real property.

tax basis The price paid for a property, less any gain realized in the sale of the previous residence on which the payment of tax was deferred under the rollover rule, plus any expenses incurred in acquiring the property (other than those incurred in arranging financing), plus the cost of any capital improvements (not repairs) made during ownership.

tax credit An amount of money that may be deducted from a tax bill to arrive at the net amount of tax due.

tax deductible expense An amount of money that may be deducted from gross income in arriving at net taxable income before depreciation, if any.

tax-deferred exchanges Trading of like-kind properties held as an investment or for use in business.

tax depreciation Permits a property owner to take an ordinary business deduction for the amount of annual depreciation application to certain types of assets.

tax-free exchange Trading of like-kind properties held as an investment or for use in business.

tax proration Reimbursement of tax dollars by buyer or seller at the time of closing. If taxes have been paid at the time of closing, the buyer will reimburse the seller for the period of time from the closing to the end of the tax year. If taxes have not been paid at the time of closing, seller will reimburse the buyer for the period of time from the beginning of the tax period to the closing but not to include the day of closing.

Tax Reform Act of 1986 Sweeping changes to the tax laws, a number of them particularly less generous to the real estate industry.

tax shelter A method of tax avoidance such as protecting income from taxation by allowable depreciation.

tenancy at sufferance Interest of a tenant who enters lawfully but stays on after the expiration of a lease.

tenancy at will A verbal interest created with the consent of owner and tenant.

tenancy in common A form of co-ownership that does not include the right of survivorship.

tenant One who receives a lease from a landlord.

tenant at sufferance Tenant who enters lawfully but stays on after the expiration of a lease.

Tenant Security Deposit Act Maine law which specifies the amount of security deposit that can be charged and how it must be handled by the landlord.

tenement Real property rights of a permanent nature that relate to land pass with the conveyance, such as buildings.

term mortgage A mortgage that requires the mortgagor to pay interest only during the mortgage term with the principal due at the end of the term.

testate To die leaving a valid will.

testator A man who has died and left a valid will.

testatrix A woman who has died and left a valid will.

timeshare Unit at a vacation facility which is purchased for a specified number of weeks per year.

timeshare agent One who is licensed to sell timeshares.

title Evidence of the right to possess property.

title examination A search of the public record to determine the quality of a title to real property.

title insurance An insurance policy protecting the insured from a financial loss caused by a defect in a title to real property.

title opinion Opinion attorney issues based upon her examination of the public records, indicating the status of a title.

title search An examination of the public records to determine defects in the chain of title and whether the title is marketable.

title theory The legal theory followed in some states that a mortgage conveys a title to real property to secure the payment of a debt.

title transfer tax A tax imposed on the conveyance of title to real property by deed.

torrens system A system of title recordation.

tract An area of land.

trade fixtures Items installed by a commercial tenant which are removable upon termination of the tenancy.

transferability The ability to transfer property ownership from seller to buyer.

transfer tax State tax charged to both purchaser and seller at closing in the conveyance of real estate.

trapezoid An area with two parallel sides and two non-parallel sides.

trespass Unlawful entry on the land of another.

trust account (trust) An account opened under the name of the real estate agency, used for depositing monies of clients with whom the agency is dealing.

trustee One who holds title to property for the benefit of another called a beneficiary.

trustor One who conveys title to a trustee.

Truth-in-Lending Simplification and Reform Act (TILSRA) *See Regulation Z.*

undisclosed principal A principal whose identity may not be disclosed by an agent.

undivided interest Ownership of fractional parts not physically divided.

undue influence Any improper or wrongful influence by one party over another whereby the will of a person is overpowered so that she is induced to act or prevented from acting on free will.

unencumbered property Property that is free of any lien.

Uniform Commercial Code (UCC) A standardized and comprehensive set of commercial law regulating security interests in personal property.

unilateral contract An agreement wherein there is a promise in return for a specific action which together supply the consideration.

uninsured conventional loan A loan in which the loan payment is not insured to protect the lender.

unintentional misrepresentation An innocent false statement of a material fact.

unities of title Time, title, interest, and possession.

unit-in-place method A method of estimating reproduction or replacement costs by which the cost of each component part of the structure is calculated, including material, labor, and overhead costs, plus a profit to the builder.

up-front MIP (UFMIP) Mortgage insurance premium paid at closing rather than over the life of the loan

useful life The period of time that a property is expected to be economically useful.

usury Charging a rate of interest higher than the rate allowed by law.

utility Capable of serving a useful purpose.

VA-guaranteed loan A mortgage loan in which the loan payment is guaranteed to the lender by the Department of Veterans Affairs.

valid contract An agreement that is legally binding and enforceable.

valuable consideration Anything of value agreed upon by parties to a contract.

value That which results from the anticipation of future benefits from ownership of a property.

value in exchange The amount of money a property may command for its exchange. This is the market value.

value in use The present worth of the future benefits of ownership. A subjective value that is not market value.

variance A permitted deviation from specific requirements of a zoning ordinance because of the special hardship to a particular property owner.

vendee Purchaser.

vendor Seller.

voidable contract An agreement that may be avoided by the parties without legal consequences.

void contract An agreement that has no legal force or effect.

voluntary alienation The transfer of title freely by the owner.

warranty deed Deed containing the strongest and broadest form of guarantee of title of any type of deed, thus providing the greatest protection to the grantee.

waste A violation of the right of estovers.

wetlands All lands, including submerged lands, that flow by the tide at any time except maximum storm activity.

will A legal declaration of how a person wishes his possessions to be disposed of after his death.

words of conveyance Wording in a deed demonstrating the definite intention to convey a particular title to real property to a named grantee.

wraparound mortgage A junior mortgage that is in an amount exceeding a first mortgage against the property.

yield The return on an investment.

zoning A public law regulating land use.

zoning map Map dividing a community into various designated districts.

zoning ordinance Two-part document including a zoning map, which divides a community into various designated districts, and text setting forth the type of use permitted under each zoning classification and specific requirements for compliance.

INDEX